Computer PROGRAMMING

P. KUMAR
Associate Professor
Department of IT
Rajalakshmi Engineering College
Thandalam, Chennai

WILEY

Computer PROGRAMMING

Other Wiley Editorial Offices:

John Wiley & Sons, Inc. 111 River Street, Hoboken, NJ 07030, USA

Wiley-VCH Verlag GmbH, Pappellaee 3, D-69469 Weinheim, Germany

John Wiley & Sons Australia Ltd, 42 McDougall Street, Milton, Queensland 4064, Australia

John Wiley & Sons (Asia) Pte Ltd, 1 Fusionopolis Walk #07-01 Solaris, South Tower, Singapore 138628

John Wiley & Sons Canada Ltd, 22 Worcester Road, Etobicoke, Ontario, Canada, M9W 1L1

Edition: 2014

ISBN: 978-81-265-4915-3

www.wileyindia.com

Printed at: *Radha Offset, Delhi*

Preface

Computing and programming are essential to leverage the technical skills of a student. These techniques equip the students with know-how of the latest technologies and reduce considerable time in solving problems. The course *Computer Programming* has become essential in the present age of computer and information technology, as the applications of computers can be found in all aspects of our lives.

This book is designed to meet the requirements of students having very little knowledge of computers, and journeys them from the basic fundaments of computers through application of problem-solving techniques using C programming concepts, and concludes with familiarizing students with MS Office application software. This book is useful for the "Computer Programming" course of Anna University (Affiliated Colleges) Regulation 2013, and other universities of the country offering similar courses.

Organization of the Book

The book begins with an introduction to computers and its organization, various number systems in use and operations based on them. Then the book proceeds to discuss the various generations of computer languages, and problem-solving techniques, such as algorithms, flowcharts and pseudocodes. The C programming concepts are explained next through chapters covering structure of C program, operators and expressions, input/output statements, control statements, arrays and strings, functions, structures and unions, pointers and file handling. The book then lays emphasis on the familiarizing students with the MS Office application software (MS Word, MS PowerPoint and MS Excel) with the aid of a number of screenshots.

The comprehensive and exhaustive theoretical treatment of the concepts on problem solving, C programming and MS Office helps students to perform practical applications of these concepts in the laboratory course with ease.

CHAPTERS OF THE BOOK	**LABORATORY MANUAL** (includes experiments for the following)
Introduction to Computers	MS Office
Problem-Solving through Algorithms, Flowcharts and Pseudocodes	Problem Formulation, Problem Solving (Flowcharts, Algorithms and Pseudocodes)
C Programming Basics	C Programming
Arrays and Strings	
Functions and Pointers	
Structures and Unions	
File Handling in C	
MS Office Application Software	

Salient Features

An effective pedagogy has been adopted keeping in view the scope and purpose of the book. The idea is to provide a complete coverage of topics as per syllabus in a precise yet adequate manner. References to pre-requisites for understanding the topics are made wherever essential without deviating much from the prescribed syllabus. Each chapter is divided into various subtopics and sub-subtopics in appropriate sequence for logical flow of topics within the chapter.

- **Precise content and uniform presentation** as per syllabus requirement.
- **Numerous screenshots and diagrammatic representations** spread across chapters.
- **Updated content** as per latest trends in computers and IT.
- **Ample programming codes and solved examples** to reinforce concepts.
- **Quantitative question set** with solved problems, review questions and programming assignments.
- **Previous years' university question papers solved**.

- **Useful appendices** on ASCII set, standard library functions, syntactical statements, and exercises on predicting outputs and identifying errors.
- **Model question papers** for practice based on the latest examination pattern.
- **Laboratory manual** includes experiments on MS Office tools; problem solving through flowcharts, algorithms, and pseudocodes; and C programming.

Acknowledgements

We would like to thank the following reviewers who have carefully read through our content and given valuable feedback:

- **P. Kumar**, Associate Professor, Department of IT, Rajalakshmi Engineering College, Chennai
- **K.M. Anandkumar,** Associate Professor, Department of Computer Science and Engineering, SRM Easwari Engineering College, Chennai
- **Suresh J.,** Assistant Professor, Department of Computer Science and Engineering, SSN College of Engineering, Chennai

We sincerely hope that the student community and teaching fraternity would get the maximum benefit from this endeavor. Comments and criticism are welcome from academicians and students for enrichment of the book in subsequent editions.

Executive Publisher

Syllabus Map*

Unit	Topic Covered in Section/ Chapter
UNIT I – INTRODUCTION	Chapters 1 and 2
Generation and Classification of Computers	Sections 1.2 and 1.3
Basic Organization of a Computer	Section 1.4
Number System –Binary – Decimal – Conversion – Problems	Sections 1.5–1.9
Need for logical analysis and thinking – Algorithm – Pseudocode – Flow Chart.	Sections 2.4 and 2.5
UNIT II – C PROGRAMMING BASICS	Chapter 3
Problem formulation – Problem Solving	Section 2.2 and 2.3
Introduction to ' C' programming –fundamentals	Chapter 3
Structure of a 'C' program – compilation and linking processes	Section 3.4
Constants, Variables – Data Types – Expressions using operators in 'C'	Sections 3.2 and 3.3
Managing Input and Output operations	Section 3.5
Decision Making	Section 3.6
Branching	Section 3.7
Looping statements	Section 3.7
Solving simple scientific and statistical problems	Section 3.8
UNIT III – ARRAYS AND STRINGS	Chapter 4
Arrays – Initialization – Declaration	Sections 4.1–4.3
One dimensional and Two dimensional arrays	Sections 4.2 and 4.3
String- String operations	Section 4.4
String Arrays	Section 4.4.1 and 4.4.2
Simple programs- sorting- searching – matrix operations	Solved problems and programs in Chapter 4
UNIT IV – FUNCTIONS AND POINTERS	Chapter 5
Function – definition of function	Sections 5.1
Declaration of function	Section 5.2.1
Pass by value	Section 5.2.3
Pass by reference	Section 4.10
Recursion	Section 5.3.1
Pointers – Definition – Initialization	Sections 5.1.1 and 5.1.2
Pointers arithmetic	Section 5.5.3
Pointers and arrays	Section 5.5.4
Example Problems	Solved problems and programs in Chapter 5

* [Mapped with Anna University (Affiliated Colleges) Syllabus, R2013]

UNIT V – STRUCTURES AND UNIONS	Chapter 6
Introduction – need for structure data type	Section 6.1
Structure definition – Structure declaration	Sections 6.2 and 6.3
Structure within a structure	Section 6.5
Union	Section 6.8
Programs using structures and Unions	Solved problems and programs in Chapter 6
Storage classes	Section 6.9
Pre-processor directives.	Section 6.10

COMPUTER PRACTICES LABORATORY	
1. Search, generate, manipulate data using MS office/ Open Office 2. Presentation and Visualization – graphs, charts, 2D, 3D	Exercise 1
3. Problem formulation, Problem Solving and Flowcharts	Exercise 2
4. C Programming using Simple statements and expressions 5. Scientific problem solving using decision making and looping. 6. Simple programming for one dimensional and two dimensional arrays. 7. Solving problems using String functions 8. Programs with user defined functions – Includes Parameter Passing 9. Program using Recursive Function and conversion from given program to flow chart. 10. Program using structures and unions.	Exercise 3

Fundamentals of Computing and Programming

Introduction to Computers

1

LEARNING OBJECTIVES

After completing this chapter, you will be able to understand the following:

- Major operations of the computer and its characteristics.
- Evolution of computers.
- The five computer generations.
- Classification of computers.
- Components of computer system.
- Memory and storage systems.
- Types of number systems and their interconversions.
- Signed and unsigned binary numbers.
- Arithmetic operations in binary, octal, hexadecimal and BCD systems.
- EBCDIC, ASCII and Unicode coding standards.
- Applications of computers.

1.1 Introduction

Computer is defined as an electronic machine that takes input data and instructions from the user and after processing them, it generates useful and desired output quickly. A computer performs basically the following major operations through its components (Fig. 1):

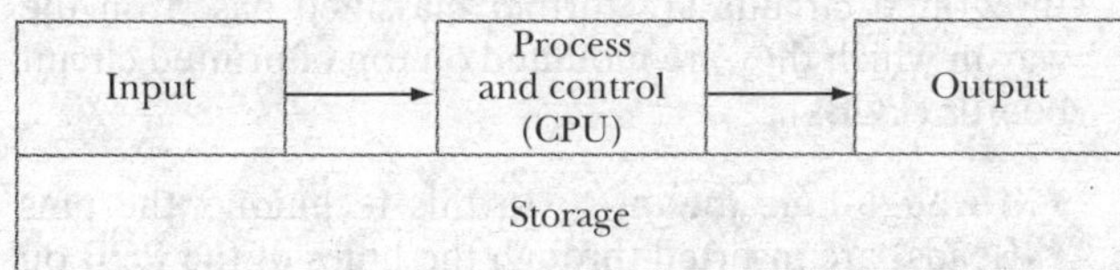

Figure 1 Major operations of the computer.

1. **Input:** It accepts data and instruction through the input devices such as keyboard, mouse, scanner, etc., from the user to process it.
2. **Process and control:** It performs the actions as per the instruction issued and processes the given input data. The processing may include arithmetic and logical operations. It also controls the overall operations like arithmetic and logical operations inside the computer.
3. **Storage:** It stores the data and the instructions for future execution.
4. **Output:** It generates the desired output after executing the instructions and processing the input data.

The various **characteristics** of a computer are:

1. It can perform complex calculations with speed and generate accurate results.
2. It has high processing speed and can execute millions of instructions in one second.
3. It can store large amounts of data and information which can be easily retrieved whenever required.
4. It can interact with users through its user interface, and provide required information within a fraction of a second.
5. It can be used for many hours, days and months continuously, without compromising on the work quality.
6. Its role is versatile, that is, it can be used for commercial use (data processing), scientific use (computing numerical data), office and educational use (word processing), communicating messages (e-mail, messenger), animation and industrial use (image processing) and multimedia purposes (voice recognition).

1.2 Evolution of Computers and Computer Generations

For computing purposes in the ancient era, various techniques were adopted such as abacus (a bamboo frame consisting of beads), Pascaline, which is a numerical wheel calculator (containing six movable dials to calculate eight-figured sums having base 10). The real onset of computers started in 1856, when Charles Babbage succeeded in devising Analytical Engine for printing the results of complex mathematical calculations, such as polynomials, trigonometric functions, etc. This was the first device to operate on conditional statements, which generated different results each time the operation is performed. Moving on, he further developed these machines and contributed immensely to the world of computers. Hence, he is also known as the father of computers.

The first general-purpose electronic computer called Electronic Numerical Integrator and Computer (ENIAC) was introduced in the year 1946 by three scientists, Joh von Neumann, John Presper Eckert and John W. Mauchly. It was designed to calculate trajectories of bombs and perform other artillery-related calculations. The high processing speed of ENIAC enabled it to perform 5000 additions and subtractions and 386 multiplications in just one second. However, ENIAC was very expensive and larger in size as compared to present-day computers.

Following the success of ENIAC, the machine was made simpler and more powerful by Eckert and Mauchly, who devised another machine called Electronic Discrete Variable Automatic Computer (EDVAC). It was a multipurpose computer which had internal memory that could store both data and program. This allowed programs to be saved in the memory allocated to them. Unlike its predecessor, EDVAC worked on binary data rather than decimal codes. A mercury tube was given an electronic pulse, which sprung back or forth to be regained when required. This on/off capability was useful as the data was stored in binary form (0's and 1's).

In 1940s, a complete and fully operational regular stored-program electronic digital computer called Electronic Delay Storage Automatic Calculator (EDSAC) was developed. The first programs run by EDSAC were table of squares and list of prime numbers.

In spite of the above-mentioned advancements, the devices were still very expensive and not reachable by the common man. In 1970s and 1980s, however, the International Business Machines (IBMs) developed computers suited for individual use. These computers came to called personal computers (PCs). They were also referred to as desktop computers as they could easily be placed on a desk/table.

The classification of computers into various generations is based on major developments in technology used for building these machines. The five generations of computers are discussed as follows:

1. **First generation computers:** These computers were used in the period 1945–1955. In these computers, thousands of vacuum tubes were used as switching devices for internal circuits and magnetic drums for memory. These vacuum tubes are large in size and generate a lot of heat. The best example of the first generation of computers is ENIAC as was discussed previously. These computers could understand only machine language (binary code of 0's and 1's) and could solve only one problem at a time. The machine language was translated into assembly language (mnemonic codes or symbols) using a compiler; while the assembly language was converted back to machine language using an assembler. This translation and re-translation was time-consuming, and hence the processing speed of these computers was low. Moreover, these computers were bulky, produced a lot of heat and had limited storage capacity.
2. **Second generation computers:** These computers were used in the period 1956–1963. In these computers, instead of vacuum tubes, transistors were used. This reduced the amount of heat produced, and the computers became smaller in size. With the use of transistors, use of electricity was reduced, the calculations became faster and more accurate. Moreover, these included primary memory and secondary memory for storing data and programs. These computers were programmed using assembly language instead of machine language. Examples include PDP-8, IBM 1401, CDC 1604.
3. **Third generation computers:** The computers were developed in the period 1964–1970. In these computers, integrated circuits (ICs) were used to replace transistors. An IC consisted of various components used in the internal circuitry, such as diodes, transistors, resistors, capacitors, etc., which are fabricated and integrated onto a silicon-composed material known as a chip. The use of ICs reduces the amount of heat generated further as the heat produced could destroy the internal circuitry. In these computers, the user interaction with the computer was through keyboards and monitors interfaced with an operating system which allowed different applications to run at the same time. These computers were smaller, cheaper and thus more accessible to a mass audience. Initially, this technology enabled integration of about 10 components onto a single chip and was referred to as small-scale integration (SSI) technology. Further, hundreds and thousands of components could be integrated on a single chip which were referred to as medium-scale integration (MSI) and large-scale integration (LSI) technologies, respectively. These computers were programmed using high level languages. Examples include IBM 370, NCR 395, PDP-11.

   Integrated circuits are further classified based on the way in which they are mounted on top of printed circuit boards (PCBs).

   - **Through-hole mounted:** In this technique, the pins (leads) are inserted through the holes of the PCB on one side and soldered to conductors on the other side. For example, dual-in-package (DIP). Points on the chip are connected to the package pins to establish I/O connections with the other devices. Transformers and heat-sinked power semiconductors can be mounted by this technique.
   - **Surface-mounted:** In this technique, the components are mounted directly onto the surface of the PCB. The components using this technology have smaller pins or no pins at all and are smaller in size as compared to components used in through-hole technology. For example, capacitors and resistors are surface-mounted on USB flash drive's circuit board.
4. **Fourth generation computers:** These computers were developed in the period 1971–1995. In these computers, **very large scale integration (VLSI)** technology, developed by Intel chip manufacturer by which millions of components could be integrated on a single chip, was

used in form of microprocessors. A microprocessor is a single chip device that contains all the circuit elements required to perform the arithmetic, logic and control functions of the computer. These computers had such a user-friendly interface that even non-technical users could run applications such as word processing and spreadsheets. As these computers used microprocessor chip, they were very small in size, more powerful, faster and cheaper. These computers were programmed using high level languages, in integrated development environment (IDE). Examples include Apple II, Altair 8800, Cray-1, Macintosh.

5. **Fifth generation computers:** These computers belong to the period 1995 and beyond. In these computers **super large scale integration (SLSI)** was used, with the microprocessor containing more than millions of components integrated onto a single chip. This enabled the computers to cater to large memory requirements and reduced their size considerably. This led to designing of portable computers such as laptop, PDA, smartphones, tablets, etc. With the implementation of Internet and its services and optical disk technology, the computers became faster, cheaper and very efficient in processing just about any given task.

   Also, this generation of computers uses **parallel processing technique** through which several instructions can be processed simultaneously instead of serial execution. This increases the processing speed. Examples include Intel dual core microprocessor, AMD K10, etc. Further enhancements were made by various scientists and researchers by adopting the concept of **artificial intelligence** so that the computers have some knowledge of the real world, understand the spoken language, translate different foreign languages and assist human beings in various ways. In this regard, many techniques for pattern recognition, language processing, speech recognition, inference making, knowledge-based management functions have been developed. These include Expert System (ES), Natural Language Processing (NLP), speech and voice recognition, and Robotics.

Solved Problems

1. *Explain the evolution of computers.* **(AU 2009, 2010, 2012, 2013, 2014)**

Solution: Refer to this section, and explain the history of computers followed by the five generations.

2. *Expand ENIAC, EDVAC, and EDSAC?*

Solution: Electronic numerical integrator and computer (ENIAC); electronic discrete variable automatic computer (EDVAC); electronic delay storage automatic calculator(EDSAC)

3. *What are the major components of first and second generation computers?*

Solution: Vacuum tubes were used in first generation computers for circuitry, whereas transistors were used in second generation computers. First generation used magnetic drums for memory; whereas in the second generation magnetic core technology was used.

4. *List some important hardware and software technologies of the fifth generation computers.* **(AU 2014)**

Solution: The hardware technologies used in fifth generation computers include SLSI, optical disk technology, Internet and its services, designing portal computers, such as PDA, laptop, smartphones, tablets, etc.

The software technologies implemented include parallel processing technique and artificial intelligence.

1.3 Classification of Computers

Computers can be classified on the basis of their size, data-processing capacity, memory and application areas. They can be further categorized as anolog or digital based on the type of signal received by the computer. The size of a computer may vary from palm-size hand-held device to room-size super computers. Based on size and computing speed, computers are broadly classified into four types which are discussed as follows:

1. **Microcomputers:** These are the smallest in the category of computers and are generally used by individuals for their personal use. Their processing speed and storage capacity is quite low as compared to other types of computers.

   The microcomputers have their own processor; input, output and storage devices. The processor is used to carry out the arithmetic and logical operations, input device is used to provide data or instruction, output device is used to display the output generated by the computer and storage device is used to keep the data and instructions for future use. Apart from these, a power cable and other cables are required to connect the system.

   These are also known as personal computers because they are developed and designed for personal use. A personal computer may also be connected to a network, so that many users can share their data and resources. One of the first and most popular personal computers was the Apple II, introduced in 1977 by Apple Computers. IBM's first microcomputer was designed in 1981 and was named as IBM-PC. Nowadays, these computers are inexpensive, use very little power, do not require special wiring, are easy to use, stable and reliable; hence they have become a necessity of modern lifestyle. These computers are widely used by individuals for programming, gaming, watching movies, listening to songs or maintaining database and accounts of small business units. The most popular types of personal computers are IBM-PC and Apple PC. The IBM-PC and other compatible PCs use the Windows operating system; whereas Apple PCs use the Macintosh operating system (MacOS).

The personal computers or microcomputers are further classified as follows:

- **Desktop computer:** This is the most common type of microcomputers or personal computers. It is a standalone personal computer that can be placed on top of a desk. It consists of three primary components: an input device like keyboard and mouse; an output device like monitor and printer and a system unit consisting of central processing unit (CPU), memory, hard disk, etc. These computers are small and inexpensive, so they are very popular for personal use. They can be used to manage small databases, play games, learn programming, communicate using internet, watch movies, etc. There are many manufacturers of desktop computers such as HP Compaq, IBM, HCL, ACER, DELL, APPLE, LENOVO, etc.
- **Laptop:** It can also be used for similar purposes as the desktop computers, because it has all the features of a desktop computer. The advantages of the laptop are that it can be carried anywhere; does not require direct power supply; can work and operate on the battery backup; and due to small size, it can be put into the briefcase just like a notebook. Therefore, the laptop is also known as the notebook. However, one disadvantage of laptops is that their batteries need to be recharged every few hours. The flexibility of carrying the laptop anywhere, working anytime and the portability increases its cost, so the laptop is costlier than the desktop computer. The notebook has gained significant popularity in recent times. There are many manufacturers of laptop computers who are also manufacturers of desktop computers such as HP Compaq, IBM, HCL, ACER, DELL, APPLE, LENOVO, etc.
- **Handheld computers:** These are small computers which can be fit into the palm of the hand and are also known as palmtop computers or pocket computers. The personal digital assistant (PDA) is a popular handheld computer. This is a portable computer not much bigger than an appointment book, which can be operated using a digital pen or stylus instead of keyboard or mouse. It has a small monitor to view the output; but it has limited storage capacity. However, external cards can be used to increase storage capacity to store data and programs.

  The handheld computers can be connected to larger computers for exchanging data or to the printer for taking hardcopies of the output. A PDA can function as a cellular phone, fax sender and personal organizer. Casio and Apple are some of the manufacturers of PDA. The Newton MessagePad introduced in 1993 was the first PDA. Some other examples of PDAs include Franklin eBookMan and Casio Cassiopeia.

2. **Mainframe computers:** The mainframe computers can handle processing of many users at a time; therefore, they are defined as multiuser, multiprogramming, high-storage and fast-processing computers generally used in centralized and extensive database manipulations. They have large capacity of data storage and very high processing speed. These computers can communicate with multiple users at the same time through the terminals connected to a central computer or a server through satellite link. These terminals may be dumb terminals consisting of I/O devices only, or intelligent terminals consisting of I/O devices as well as the processor. The terminals do not have storage facility; they use the large disk of the mainframe computer for data storage. Further, these terminals need not be in the same room in which the mainframe computer is located, but can be operated remotely also, that is, from a different room, building, city or even country. They are very expensive large in size and require a very large clean room with air conditioner.

   The mainframe computers are used in organization such as big hospitals; government agencies; insurance companies; universities; banks, etc., to manage high volume of data; and where many people require frequent access to the same data. Some examples of mainframe computers include CDC 6600, MEDHA, Sperry, DEC, S/390, VAX 8000, HP, HCL and IBM ES000 series.

3. **Mini computers:** These computers came into existence in mid-1960s, when it was observed that many tasks do not require such high-end computing facility as possible with mainframe computers were very costly. Mini computers are as powerful as mainframe computers, but limited number of terminals (ranging from 4 to 200) can be connected to them. The mini computers support multiprocessing, where multiple users can be connected through their terminals. They also have the high processing speed and storage capacity, but comparatively lower than the mainframe computers. They are much less expensive and also smaller than mainframe computers. These are generally used as servers in medium and small sized businesses, colleges, government departments, real-time applications, etc. Mini computers do not require air conditioning, and can be operated at room temperature. Some examples of mini computers include PDP 11, IBM 8000 series, VAX 7500 and AS/400. The storage and processing capabilities of a mini computer lies between mainframe and microcomputer, which is discussed next.

4. **Super computers:** These are most powerful computers which can carry out trillions of instructions per second. These computers were specifically designed and developed to be more powerful than the computers of 1980s to solve problems that require intensive numerical computations. These machines have the highest processing speed because many processors are used in parallel. The speed of super computers is generally measured in FLOPS (floating point operations per second). These are the biggest and most expensive computers; even bigger than mainframe computers, so they are used in large organizations, research laboratories, aerospace centers, nuclear research centers, etc. Examples of super computers include Cray-1, Cray-2, Cyber 205, CDC, ETA 10, ETA 20, IBM 3090, Intel ASCI Red. India has also developed its super computer named as PARAM. It was assembled by C-DAC (Centre for Development of Advanced Computing) in Pune. The latest super computer of PARAM series is PARAM Padma in India. China's Tianhe is also one of the recent super computers to be developed.

Solved Problems

1. *What are the factors needed to classify computers?* **(AU 2009)**

Solution: Computers can be classified based on size, shape, processing speed, cost and type of use.

2. *What are super computers? Give examples.* **(AU 2010)**

Solution: Super computers are the most powerful computers which can perform trillions of instructions per second. These machines have the highest processing speed because so many processors are used in parallel to solve the problem. The speed of the super computers is generally measured in FLOPS (Floating Point Operations Per Second). These are the biggest and most expensive computers; even bigger than mainframe computers, so they are used in large organizations, research laboratories, aerospace centers, nuclear research centers, etc. Examples of super computers include Cray-1, Cray-2, Cyber 205, CDC, ETA 10, ETA 20, IBM 3090, Intel ASCI Red. India has also developed its super computer named as PARAM. China's Tianhe is also one of the recent super computers developed.

3. *Explain different types of computers.* **(AU 2009)**
or What is the classification of computer? **(AU 2011, 2013)**

Solution: Refer to this section, explain about super computers, mainframe computers, mini computers and microcomputers. Briefly mention the types of microcomputers.

4. *What are mainframe computers? Give the name of any one mainframe computer.* **(AU 2012)**

Solution: Mainframe computers are the second largest and expensive computers. They have large capacity of data storage and very high processing speed. The mainframe computers can handle processing of many users at a time; therefore, they are defined as multiuser, multiprogramming, high-storage and fast-processing computers generally used in centralized and extensive database manipulations. These computers can communicate with multiple users at the same time through the terminals connected to a central computer or a server through satellite link. These terminals may be dumb terminals consisting of I/O devices only, or intelligent terminals consisting of I/O devices as well as the processor. The mainframe computers are used in organization such as big hospitals; government agencies; insurance companies; universities; banks to manage high volume of applications; and where many people require frequent access to the same data. Some examples of mainframe computers include CDC 6600, MEDHA, Sperry, DEC, S/390, VAX 8000, HP, HCL and IBM ES000 series.

5. *Distinguish between analog and digital computers.* **(AU 2010, 2013)**

Solution: Analog and digital computers differ based on the type of data processed by them. Analog computers accept linear combinations of voltage amplitude (or pressure, temperature, currents, etc.) as inputs, process these inputs and give outputs also in the same analogous form. For example, speedometer in the car. Digital computers accept inputs in the form of higher (i.e., 1) or lower (i.e., 0) voltage state, process these and give a digital output sequence. For example, personal computers, Mac computers.

Also, digitally stored data has many advantages as it is not affected by undesirable voltage fluctuations (called noise) as in case of analog signals; it can be stored more compactly and reproduced with greater accuracy and clarity.

1.4 Basic Computer Organization

To perform various operations as mentioned in the introduction of this chapter, the computer system allocates responsibilities among its various hardware components. The hardware of the general-purpose computer consists of input units, central processing unit, output units and the memory unit also called storage unit. The block diagram of the general-purpose computer is shown in Fig. 2.

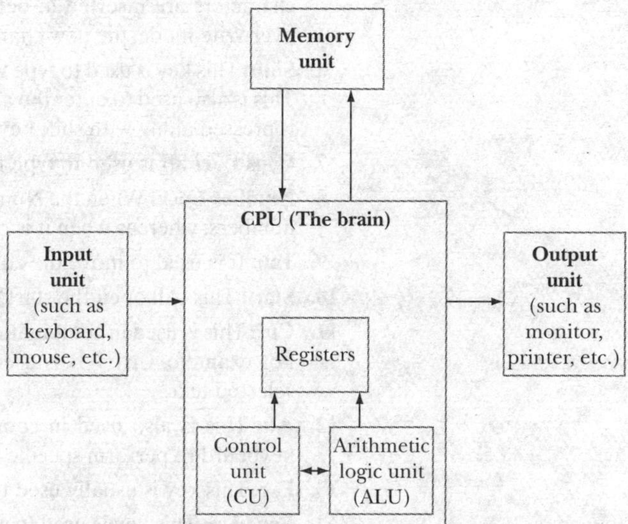

Figure 2 Basic structure of a computer.

The input/output (I/O) devices or peripherals are used so that the computer system can interact with the external environment. The input devices are used to feed data and the instruction by the user, the central processing unit and convert the given input into a computer-understandable form; and the output devices convert the processed result into a user-understandable form.

1.4.1 | Input Devices

The function of an input device is to take the data from the user in the raw form for further processing. The input devices commonly used are: keyboards, mouse, scanner, joysticks, microphones, digital cameras, scanners, etc. Some of these are discussed as follows:

1. **Keyboard:** It is the most common input device attached to all personal computers. It consists of several keys

TABLE 1

Keyboard Keys and their Description

Keys	Description
Alphanumeric keys	These consist of alphabets, numbers and special characters +, –, <, parenthesis, brackets, etc., and are used to enter text data and numbers, mathematical and logical operators and special characters.
Numeric keypad	It is located on the right side of the keyboard. It is used to quickly enter the numerical data and for use of frequently used mathematical operators. It consists of keys having numbers from 0 to 9, mathematical operators +, –, *, /, Enter key and Num Lock key. The numeric keypad becomes active when the Num Lock is set on.
Cursor movement keys	The arrow keys are used to move the cursor in the indicated direction such as up, down, left and right.
Function keys	These are 12 in number labeled from F1, F2, F3, … F12. The functions of these keys depend on the currently active application program; except the F1 button which is usually used for help option.
Special-function keys	These keys are used to perform special functions. There are various special keys on the keyboard, but the most common ones are described as follows: 1. **Enter:** To execute the command. 2. **Spacebar:** To insert space at the current cursor position. 3. **Backspace:** To delete the previous character from the current cursor position. 4. **Delete:** To delete a character at the current cursor position. 5. **Insert:** To toggle between insert and overwrite mode during data entry. In the insert mode, the characters are inserted in between and the existing characters are shifted to right; whereas in overwrite mode, the new character replaces the current character. 6. **Shift:** This key is used to type the upper character of the keys on which two characters are printed. This is also used to enter the alphabet is capital letters (if Caps Lock is not on) when the alphabet is pressed along with shift key. 7. **Caps Lock:** It is used to type the alphabets only in capital letters when it is on. 8. **Number Lock:** When the Num Lock key is on, it activates the number keypad and allows to type numbers; whereas when it is off, the same keypad is used for movement of the cursor. 9. **Tab:** It is used to move the cursor to the next tab position. 10. **Start:** This will open the start menu of the Windows operating system. 11. **Ctrl:** This is used in combination of other keys to provide extended functionality of the keyboard. For example, Ctrl + B is used to boldface the selected text and Ctrl + C is used to copy the selected text. 12. **Alt:** This is also used in combination of other keys to provide extended functionality of the keyboard to perform specific tasks. 13. **Esc:** This key is usually used to cancel the operation to be performed by the given command. 14. **Page Up:** This key is used to scroll up page-wise. 15. **Page Down:** This key is used to scroll down page-wise. 16. **Home:** This key is used to place the cursor before the first character of the start of the line. 17. **End:** This key is used to place the cursor at the right of the end character of the line.

mounted on a board. Each key has a specific function. The keys can be categorized into various categories, such as alphabet key, number key, special key, functions key, etc. The keyboard is used to give text input to the computer by pressing correct combination of keys. It starts typing the text from the current position of the cursor which may be indicated by a vertical bar, blinking line or an underscore. The keyboard generally contains a total of 101–104 keys. The different types of keys and their functions are described in Table 1.

2. **Mouse:** It is another input device that is used with the microcomputer. It has two or three buttons and a center-mounted scroll wheel on its top. The mouse rolls on a small ball at the bottom of the mouse. The left button of the mouse is used to select the object by pointing. Single clicking and double clicking on the object will start the object. The clicking depends on the mouse settings. The mouse is also used to drag and drop the selected object by selecting the object through single click of the left button, keeping it pressed, moving to the selected location, and then releasing it. The right button offers many options depending on the application currently being used. The center-mounted scroll wheel is used to move the cursor in all directions. It requires a smooth, dust-free surface for its movement, and the cursor moves in the direction in which the ball

rotates. The cursor moves very fast with the mouse giving more freedom to work in any direction. Nowadays, optical mouse is used in which an optical sensor is used to sense the motion instead of a rolling ball. The surface on which the mouse is moving is illuminated by a red light emitting diode (LED). The mouse provides a better, faster and easier way of selecting the object and moving the cursor as compared to the keyboard. The mouse is used for various purposes such as drawing an object in MS Word or Paint.

3. **Trackball:** It is also an input device which resembles the mouse. The difference is that in a mouse, the movement of the cursor requires the movement of the mouse also; whereas, in a trackball, the ball moves while the trackball as a whole remains stationary. The ball of the trackball can be rotated around 360° using fingers to control the movement of the cursor. It comes in varying sizes like big and small and shapes such as ball, button and square.
4. **Light pen:** It is a pen used to select the object or position directly on the computer screen. It is similar to mouse in functioning, except that we can point to the object using this pen for selection. The pen consists of photosensitive transducer in a small tube that converts the light emitted from the screen into an electrical signal when the pen is moved on the screen. These signals are then carefully converted into digital format, and this interrupt is used to identify the position of the light pen pointing on the screen. The light pen is used to draw diagrams, graphics, computer aided design (CAD), pictures or for menu selection directly on the computer system.
5. **Joystick:** It is a pointing device that moves in all directions and controls the speed of the cursor. Its physical design consists of a vertical stick attached to a plastic base. It contains one or two buttons that are used to select the option pointed by the cursor. The joystick moves the graphic cursor in the direction in which the stick is moved. It is primarily used with video games, computer games, training simulators, flight simulator, CAD/CAM systems and in controlling robots.
6. **Touch screen:** This is a special kind of input device where selection of the object, position or menu options is done by touching the screen using a fingertip or some other object. The touch screen consists of the glass panel with sensors and infrared beam or ultrasonic acoustic waves. When the user places his/her fingertip on the screen, the infrared beam or the ultrasonic acoustic wave is interrupted and this helps in identifying the position of the fingertip. So the object or the position is selected when a finger touches that object or the position on the screen. It is very useful for selecting data from small databases; therefore it is frequently being used in smart phones, mobile devices and computers used in ATMs, airline and railway reservation counters, hospitals, supermarkets, etc.
7. **Scanner:** It is an input device that uses a source of light for scanning a paper document, and converting it into digital form. Therefore, it is also known as an optical scanner. It simply scans the paper document and converts it into electronic form so that computer can understand it. The scanned documents are generally saved as an image, which can only be modified or edited if the utility software and optical character recognition software to edit the image is installed on the system.

   The quality of the scanned image depends on the resolution of the scanner, that is, higher resolution means better quality of the scanned document. This is a very useful device because the complete document is scanned and saved as a single graphical image. For example, we can scan important documents such as our certificates and send through e-mail, or take the printout, etc. The scanners are further classified as: flatbed scanner and handheld scanner.
8. **Digital camera:** It is a camera in which photographs or videos are stored in digital format either in its internal memory or in external memory cards. The photographs taken and saved may be transferred to the computer through a connecting cable which in turn may be copied into the hard disk, pen drive, CD or DVD. A digital camera takes pictures by converting the light passing through the lens on the front into electrical charges, and finally into a digital image using a charge coupled device (CCD). It can store many photographs which can be selected for future use or can be deleted. The photographs can be manipulated by adding some special effects; cropping; adjusting color, textures, contrast using an image editing software. Digital cameras are now available at reasonable prices with various features such as autofocus, zoom, etc.
9. **Speech input device:** Speech recognition is one such technology which provides the facility of communication with the computer by means of speech instead of typing. This technological feature is particularly useful for people with vision or other disability. The audio data is processed by speech recognition software installed on the computer system, and that instructs the computer or program to react accordingly. The speech recognition softwares are broadly classified into two categories: Speaker dependent and speaker independent.

1.4.2 | Output Devices

The output generated by the computer after processing the raw data is sent to the output devices, which are basically the hardware components used to store the softcopy (in electronic form) or hardcopy (in printed form) of the output. These devices are connected to the computer system using cables or wireless network. Some of them come in-built with the computer system. A number of output devices are available and these are discussed as follows.

1.4.2.1 *Monitor*

This is the most commonly used output device with the computer system to produce visual display. It is also known as the output screen or display device and comes in different types and sizes. Their size is measured diagonally from corner to corner. The desktop monitors are available in sizes 14, 15, 17, 19, 21, 24 and 27 inches and the laptop and tablet monitors are available in the sizes between 13 and 20 inches. The monitors are mainly of two types based on color of display:

1. **Monochrome monitor:** It uses only two colors to display the output and only one color to display the text. These are very bulky monitors and are now rarely used with the computer system.
2. **Color monitor:** It uses 256 colors to display the output. The color combination depends on the graphics card fitted inside the computer (motherboard), such as CGA, EGA,VGA, SVGA, etc.

Computer monitors are also classified on the basis of technology used for displaying the output. They are as follows:

1. **Cathode ray tube (CRT) monitor:** The CRT monitors are very heavy and big in size; therefore, they occupy more space. They use the cathode ray, a glass tube and a projector with phosphorescent dots to create pixels that make up display images. These types of monitors consume more power.
2. **Liquid crystal display (LCD) monitor:** The LCD monitors are very lightweight, flat and smaller in size; therefore, they occupy less space. They use LCD or plasma technology, electronically charged chemicals or gases and a glass panel to display the output. These types of monitors consume less power and are used with notebook, smart phones, mobile phones, etc.
3. **Light emitting diode (LED) monitors:** These monitors are similar to LCD monitors, and use light-emitting diodes for video display. The problem with LCD monitors is that on viewing from a certain angle, the images are not clearly visible. This problem is solved through LED backlighting. These monitors use blue LED lights with a yellow phosphorous coating to imitate white light, and are more energy-efficient than LCDs.
4. **Thin film transistor (TFT) monitors:** The technology used in these monitors is similar to LCD displays. However, in these monitors, chemical vapor deposition technique is used, by which very thin glass is coated with electrically conductive metal, without losing its transparency. These monitors have the thinnest display screens, and are also called active-matrix LCDs. Nowadays, widescreen display screens for monitors and television screens with aspect ratio 16:9 are becoming more popular than standard screens having aspect ratio of 4:3.
5. **Plasma display monitors:** In these monitors, there are two glass plates, one containing horizontal conductors, and the other containing vertical conductors. These two glass plates are filled with neon or xenon gas. An electric current passed through a pair of horizontal and vertical conductors causes the neon or xenon gas to glow. Though these monitors can produce high quality color display, but they are bulky and consume more power as compared to LCDs.

1.4.2.2 Printers

Printer is the hardware output device that is used to produce the hardcopy of the output. It prints the output on paper. Every printer connected with the system requires software to be installed on the system, before taking the hardcopy of the output. This software is called as driver of the printer, which actually converts the data sent to printer into the form understandable by the printer. The printers are externally connected to the computer system using appropriate cables.

There are different types of printers available in the market. The quality of the printer is primarily determined by its resolution, which is measured in dot per inch (dpi). The printer will produce better quality of the hardcopy of the output if the resolution is high. If the resolution of any printer is 300 it means 9,000 dpi (300 horizontal × 300 vertical) can be printed by the printer. The speed is also a measure of the quality of a printer. The speed is generally measured in characters per second (cps) or lines per minute (lpm). Printers can be broadly classified into two categories: Impact printers (e.g., dot matrix printer) and non-impact printers (e.g., inkjet and laser printers)

1. **Impact printer:** This printer physically strikes on the paper using needles and the ribbon of the printer to produce the hardcopy of the output. The impact printer prints a character or a line at a time. The **dot matrix printer** is the oldest impact printer that uses needles to strike on the ribbon and page to produce the hardcopy. It can be used to print multiple copies of the same document using carbon. It is not expensive and its maintenance cost is also very low; therefore, it is most commonly used to print low-quality and high-volume applications. It is used to generate the payroll sheet, invoice, accounting, etc. The dot matrix printer can print alphanumeric characters, special characters, characters of different sizes, characters of different font, graphics, charts, etc. The limitation of the dot matrix printer is that it can print in black and white only. The speed of the dot matrix printer may vary from 200 cps to 600 cps and it is normally available in two sizes – 80 column and 130 column printers. Other impact printers in use include Daisy wheel printer, chain/band printer and drum printer.
2. **Non-impact printer:** These printers do not physically strike on the paper, instead they use spray technique or magnetic field generation technique to print the output. Inkjet and laser printers fall under this category of printers.
    - **Inkjet printers:** These are slower than the dot matrix printer in speed, but produce better quality of hardcopy. They do not use the ribbon, but a separate cartridge is attached with the printer that can be changed or refilled according to the requirement. The inkjet printer uses spray technique to produce the hardcopy of the output. These printers are very expensive although they produce high-quality output.

- **Laser printer:** These printers are non-impact printers with built-in RAM, ROM and microprocessor to provide the highest quality output. They are expensive but provide the quality output at faster speed. Their resolution varies from 400 dpi to 1200 dpi and 6–25 pages per minute. Laser printers do not print character to character, instead they store the complete page in the memory and then print the complete page itself. Therefore, laser printers are used for high quality printing at faster speed.

1.4.2.3 CD/DVD/Floppy Disk

The compact disk (CD), digital versatile disk (DVD), floppy disk, pen drive, memory cards, etc., are secondary memory storage devices where the data can be saved for future use (refer subsection "Secondary Memory" for details). These can be considered both as input as well as output devices.

1.4.2.4 Plotter

A plotter is an output device that is basically used for drawing the graphical output such as maps, charts, blueprint of buildings, car parts or ships. It uses automated pens of four different colors cyan, magenta, yellow and black. The plotter looks similar to a printer in its functioning, but draws continuous and accurate lines using pen. The plotters are very much used in printing the design for computer aided design (CAD) and computer aided manufacturing (CAM) applications. The design is sent to the plotter via a graphics card, and then the plotter creates the design using automated pens. They are expensive and very slow in speed and not able to produce the solid fills. There are two basic types of plotters: Drum plotter and flatbed plotter.

1.4.2.5 Speakers/Headphones

Speakers and headphones are output devices used for audio data. The audio sound is sent to the sound card placed on the motherboard or in an expansion slot, which converts the digital signal into analog before sending it to the speaker or the headphone for delivering the sound. The quality of the audio sound depends on the quality of the sound cards. The audio output is required for various purposes such as listening to songs, watching movies, for announcement in airlines, banks, railways, video conferencing and hospitals.

1.4.3 | Central Processing Unit

The central processing unit (CPU) is used to execute program instructions and process data fed inside the computer system with input devices. Since CPU is the central unit of the computer, it is responsible for processing of the input data, controlling and managing the operations of the computer and generating the desired output. Therefore, it is also known as the brain of the computer and is the main component of any computer. It consists of control unit (CU), arithmetic logic unit (ALU) and registers.

1.4.3.1 Control Unit

The control unit is one of the important components of the CPU, and it is responsible for the proper execution of the instructions. The execution of instructions is performed by the CPU in sequence of four steps given as follows:

1. First CPU fetches the instruction issued by the user/program from the memory.
2. It decodes the instruction.
3. It executes the instruction.
4. It stores the result back into the memory or sends it to the output device.

The CU uses the registers for temporary storage of data and instructions, and it also uses the ALU to perform the arithmetic and logical operations. Therefore, the control unit controls and coordinates the overall operations of the computer. It also coordinates with the input and output devices to control the flow of data and information.

1.4.3.2 Arithmetic and Logical Unit

The ALU is a combination of arithmetic and logical unit. The arithmetic unit (AU) is used to perform fundamental arithmetic operations such as addition, subtraction, multiplication and division on the input data. The logical unit (LU) is used to perform logical operations such as equality comparison, less than, less than or equal to, greater than, greater than or equal to, logical AND, logical OR, logical NOT on the input data. The logical operations are performed by using combination of various logic gates such as AND, OR and NOT.

The ALU coordinates with the control unit for the instruction to be executed, and with the registers for temporary storage and retrieval of data. The result of operation can be temporarily sent to the registers, or it can be sent to the output device by the CPU.

1.4.3.3 Registers

Registers are special-purpose high-speed temporary storage areas for holding data, addresses and instructions during processing of the instructions. There are several registers used by the CPU, each for serving specific purposes. The registers work under the control unit of the CPU and they are not referenced by their addresses; rather they are directly accessed, therefore they operate at a higher speed.

The size of each register is called the word size and is determined by its functions. For example, the control unit gets the address of the instruction to be executed next from a register called the program counter and allows it to be executed by the CPU. The next instruction address is immediately placed in the program counter and the instruction must fit into the size of the program counter. The registers are available in different sizes from 8 bits, 16 bits, 32 bits, 64 bits, etc. The size of the register specifies how many bits can be manipulated by the CPU at a time. For example, 8-bit register can manipulate 8 bits of data at a time. Some of the important registers are described in Table 2.

TABLE 2

Important Registers and their Functionality

Register Name	Functionality
Program Counter (PC)	The program counter is used to keep track of the address of the next instruction to be executed in sequence.
Accumulator (AC)	The accumulator is used to store the result of the ALU temporarily.
Instruction Register (IR)	This register keeps the instruction fetched recently, and to be decoded by the control unit.
Memory Address Register (MAR)	The memory address register is used to hold the address of the next location in memory to be accessed.
Memory Buffer Register (MBR)	The memory buffer register acts as a buffer for the data fetched from the memory and being transferred to the CPU, or the data coming out of the CPU after processing to be transferred to the memory.
Data Register (DR)	The data register is used to store the operands and the data.

1.4.4 | Memory or Storage Unit

CPU receives input data and instructions from the input devices and the program. It performs the arithmetic and logical operations on the received data as per the instructions and produces the output. The processing of input data and instructions requires storage area because some of the intermediate results have to be stored somewhere; and later this result is retrieved for subsequent operations. The storage area for instructions and data to be processed is called the memory. Therefore, the memory is the internal storage area in the computer.

Each memory location has a unique address and the smallest unit of data is called a bit (0 and 1). The collection of 8 bits is called a byte, and collection of 4 bits is called a nibble. The CPU can retrieve these stored data in the form of byte and instruction quickly. The memory can be broadly categorized into two categories, primary memory and secondary memory.

1.4.4.1 Primary Memory

The primary memory is also called as the main memory and is of two kinds: read only memory and random access memory.

Read Only Memory: In read only memory (ROM), data is recorded on an integrated circuit by the manufacturer. Once the data has been recorded, it cannot be changed. The content of ROM can be read but it cannot be modified; hence the name is read only memory. It is designed to perform a specific function that is not changed, and generally instructions are required for initializing the devices stored in ROM. For example, ROM is used in most computers to hold the basic input and output system (BIOS) so that the computer's hardware such as hard disks, RAM, I/O ports and peripherals are recognized when the computer is switched on; and then the operating system is loaded.

The computer does not function if its ROM is damaged. This is a non-volatile memory, that is, the contents are not lost even when the power is turned off. ROM chips are used not only in computers, but in most other electronic items such as washing machines, microwave ovens, calculators, laser printers, media players, etc. It is not limited to electronic chips but include, CDROM and DVD ROM. The ROM is categorized into various types such as:

1. **Programmable read only memory (PROM):** This is a kind of ROM that has not been pre-recorded by the manufacturer, but is supplied empty. The user of this ROM can store programs on it using a special tool. Once the empty ROM is programmed, it behaves like any other ROM, that is, it cannot be rewritten.
2. **Erasable programmable read only memory (EPROM):** This is a ROM which has not been pre-recorded by the manufacture, but it is supplied empty. The user of this ROM can store programs on it using a special tool. Once the empty ROM is programmed, it can be rewritten repeatedly after erasing the previously written entire contents using ultraviolet light of specific frequency. EPROM is more expensive than PROM.
3. **Electrically erasable programmable read only memory (EEPROM):** This is a ROM which has not been prerecorded by the manufacture, but it supplied empty. The user of this ROM can store programs on it using a special tool. Once the empty ROM is programmed, it can be rewritten repeatedly after erasing the previously written contents using electric charge. This kind or ROM requires erasing the entire previously written content, but it allows erasing one byte at a time before writing the new content onto it. The EEPROM is more expensive than PROM, but it need not be removed from computer for rewriting. This is the most flexible type of ROM, which is now commonly used for storing BIOS programs.

Random Access Memory: This is the primary memory from where data and instructions can be retrieved in a random manner using a unique memory address. Hence, the name is random access memory (RAM). It is a volatile memory in which the contents are lost once the power is turned off. This kind of memory is used to store the data temporarily during the computer operations.

The data and instructions are brought into the temporary memory, that is, RAM, from the secondary memory whenever CPU needs to process it. The RAM can be both read from and written onto. Its size is measured in megabytes (MB) or in gigabytes (GB). For example, 64 MB RAM, 256 MB RAM, 1 GB RAM, 2 GB RAM, etc. The RAM is mainly of two types: static RAM and dynamic RAM.

1. **Static random access memory (SRAM):** It is a volatile memory based on traditional transistors using flip–flop gates to hold data as long as the power is on. It is very fast; therefore, they are used in cache memory. The SRAM takes more space and is expensive, but it is easy to use. It does not need to be refreshed periodically and synchronizes itself with the timing of CPU.
2. **Dynamic random access memory (DRAM):** It is a volatile memory based on the capacitors that hold data as long as the power is on. The DRAM is refreshed periodically due to discharging of capacitors. This refreshing is happens automatically, and due to the time consumed in refreshing, the DRAM is slow as compared to SRAM. It is inexpensive and takes less space; therefore, DRAM is used as the main memory.

1.4.4.2 Secondary Memory

The secondary memory are the storage devices in which the data can be stored for longer duration, and it is not lost even when the power is turned off. This memory has greater storage capacity than the primary memory. Also, it is inexpensive, but slow. There are two types of access to stored data in secondary storage devices:

1. **Sequential access** through which data can be retrieved or accessed in the order it was stored. It is useful when there is need to process timesheets or salary slips based on records entered at scheduled intervals. The storage device used for sequential access is **magnetic tape**. It consists of a plastic ribbon coated with iron oxide or chromium dioxide containing magnetized and non-magnetized regions where data can be stored. The stored data can be overwritten by new set of data. It is 50 to 2400 ft long and 1/2 to 1/4 inch wide.
2. **Direct access** through which we can randomly access any particular record at any time without worrying about the sequence in which it was stored. It is useful when we need to access any particular information from a person's record, such as date of birth, or account balance, etc. The various storage devices used for direct access are grouped into three:
   - **Magnetic disks:** These consist of a thin circular metal or plastic plate coated with iron oxide containing magnetized and non-magnetized regions as in case of magnetic tapes. Binary code containing 0's and 1's (generally EBCDIC) is used for storing data. Also, as in case of magnetic tapes, the existing data can be overwritten with new data. These magnetic disks can be of two types.

     (a) *Floppy disks*: These consist of a flat circular plastic material coated with magnetic oxide (or iron oxide) enclosed in a protective square jacket cover made of vinyl. Their sizes range from 3.5 to 5.25 inches. However, due to lower reliability and smaller storage capacity, these have been replaced with better devices such as the hard disk, pen drive, etc.

     (b) *Hard disks*: These offer offline secondary storage for the computers used today. These are composed of solid metal platter (like aluminium) and their sizes range from 1 to 14 inch diameters (with 1.0, 2.5 and 3.5 inch diameters being most common). There are three types of hard drives: Zip or Bernoulli disk (single hard disk enclosed in plastic cartridge capable of storing 8 to more than 500 GB of data); Disk pack (consisting of two or more hard disk platters mounted one below the other on a single central shaft and which can be separated from each other depending upon the data to be used; these are capable of storing few hundred GB to several thousand GB of data); and the Winchester disk (consisting of two or more hard disk platters mounted one below the other on a single central shaft like disk pack, but which are sealed together and cannot be separated from each other; these are capable of storing few GB to few TB of data).
   - **Optical disks:** These consist of a magnetic or plastic disk with highly reflective material coating. In these disks, laser beam technology is used to read/write vast amounts data in limited space. There are various types of optical disks, such as:

     (a) *CD-ROM*: The compact disk-read only memory is a lustrous silver colored metal disk made of polycarbonate plastic coated with a thin layer of pure aluminium for reflective surface. These are about 5.25 inches in diameter and are capable of storing 650 to 700 MB of data. This stored data can only be read by the user, but not modified.

     (b) *Worm/CD-R disks*: The write once read many or compact disk-recordable has the same structure of a CD-ROM, but though data can be written only once, it can be read multiple times using a CD-R drive attached to a computer. These are generally used to make permanent records of data that can never be altered.

     (c) *CD-RW disks*: These compact disk-read/write disks are composed of metallic alloy layer; data can be erased and new data written on the disk multiple times. This is achieved by using an incident laser beam that changes the chemical property of metallic alloy layer during writing process and changes the reflectivity at the desired areas. These have some limited cycles by which data can be erased and new data can be written onto the disks.

     (d) *DVD*: The digital video (or versatile) disk has greater storage capacity than CD, and can be used to store large multimedia data like audio and video. The density of spots where data is stored by laser beam is much higher (about 4.5 times) that of CD, which enables packing of more and more data bits in every inch. These are capable of storing 4.7 to 8.5 GB of data.

- **Memory storage devices:** These are solid-state (electronic) devices composed of EEPROM chips, and that do not involve any mechanical component for operation. These devices have high reliability and are very durable;hence,these have nowadays become the preferred means of transferring and storing data. The various types of memory storage devices are as follows:

  (a) *Flash drive*: Also known as pen drive, it is of compact size of that of a pen or even smaller coming in all types of stylish designs. Data can be transferred from one computer to another by simply plugging the device into the universal serial bus (USB) port of the computer. Data can be written, read and modified using these drives.

  (b) *Memory cards*: These are flash memory based cards, even smaller in size than pendrives, with storage capacity ranging from few MB to several GB. In contrast to pen drives, which can be used in computers and laptops, the memory cards can be used in other digital devices also such as mobile phone and digital cameras.

1.4.4.3 Cache Memory

The cache memory is a SRAM placed between the CPU and the main memory, and when CPU needs any data or instruction for processing, it first searches the cache memory. If the required data or instruction is found in the cache memory, it is retrieved by the CPU for processing. Otherwise, the main memory is searched for the same information. The most frequently used instructions and data are placed in the cache memory; therefore, the overall speed of the computer is increased.

Depending upon the type of data that cache memory holds, it is classified as:

1. **Instruction cache:** This cache only holds instructions.
2. **Data cache:** This cache only holds data.
3. **Unified cache:** This cache holds both instructions and data.

There are different levels of cache memory that are discussed as follows:

1. **L1:** This level of cache memory is the fastest and usually comes within the processor chip itself. Its size ranges from 8 KB to 64 KB. It uses the SRAM (static RAM) instead of the slower DRAM (dynamic RAM).
2. **L2:** This level of cache is placed between the L1 and RAM. Its size is larger than L1 and ranges from 64 KB to 4 MB).
3. **L3:** This cache is found on the motherboard rather than the processor, and is placed between the RAM and L2 cache.

If all the three levels of cache are present in the system, then data is fetched in the order: L1 → L2 → L3 → RAM. This means if data is not present in L1, L2 would be checked followed by L3 and then RAM.

1.4.4.4 Memory Hierarchy

The computer requires different kinds of memory for its proper functioning. Since the fast memories are very expensive, they cannot be used in excess. There is a hierarchy of memories considering their speed and cost. The registers are the fastest storage devices; even faster than the cache memory (SRAM), which is faster than the main memory. The primary or main memory is faster than the secondary memory. The hierarchy of various types of memory is shown in Fig. 3.

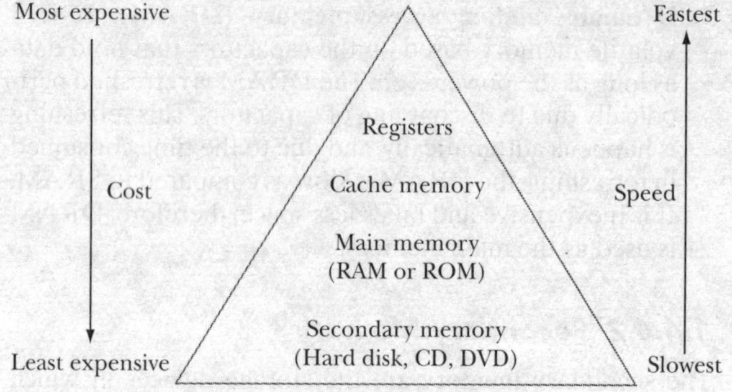

Figure 3 Memory hierarchy.

Solved Problems

1. *Differentiate between primary memory and secondary memory.*

Solution: Primary memory is located within the CPU, is expensive and has low storage capacity, whereas secondary memory is located outside the CPU, is cheaper and has high storage capacity. The examples of primary memory include RAM, ROM, cache, while that of secondary memory include hard disk, CD, etc.

2. *Differentiate between RAM and ROM.*

Solution: Random access memory (RAM) is a volatile memory used for temporary storage, and needs to be refreshed constantly, whereas read only memory (ROM) is non-volatile and used for permanent storage of data. RAM is made of flip-flops and allows reading as well as writing of data, whereas ROM is made of diodes and enables only reading of data. RAM allows faster data retrieval than ROM.

3. *Out of SRAM and DRAM, which one is faster? Justify your answer.*

Solution: Static random assessable memory (SRAM) is the cache memory placed between the CPU and the main memory. When CPU needs any data or instruction for processing, it first searches the cache memory. SRAM does not need to be refreshed constantly unlike dynamic random assessable memory (DRAM), and hence is faster

1.5 Types of Number Systems

Number systems are of two types: Positional and non-positional. In ancient times, an additive approach was used for counting the number items; this additive approach is also called *non-positional number system*. In this system, we have symbols representing numbers, for instance, I for 1, II for 2, III for 3, and so on; thus we find that each symbol is representing the same value regardless of its position. Arithmetic operations are difficult to perform on these number systems; hence new number systems called positional number systems came into existence. In *positional number systems*, only a few symbols called digits are used to represent numbers. Depending upon the position these digits occupy, different numbers are represented. The number represented by each digit is determined based on three considerations – the digit itself, the position occupied by it and the base (or radix) of the number system.

Numbers have arbitrary bases. Some of the base systems used in computing are base 2 (binary), base 10 (decimal), base 8 (octal) and base 16 (hexadecimal). The base of a number system defines the range of values a digit may have. For instance, in the decimal system the digit may have one of the 10 possible values (0, 1, 2, 3, 4, 5, 6, 7, 8 and 9), while the binary system can have only one of the two possible values (0 and 1). Hence, binary, decimal, octal and hexadecimal number systems belong to positional number systems.

In the language of computers, these digits are called bits. In weighted number systems, the bit can be the most significant bit or least significant depending upon the weight it carries. Usually, the leftmost bit is the most significant bit (MSB), and the rightmost bit is the least significant bit (LSB).

Other number systems are octal and hexadecimal number systems which have base values 8 and 16, respectively. These base values indicate that the octal number system has 8 possible values (0, 1, 2, 3, 4, 5, 6, 7) and hexadecimal number system has 16 possible values (0, 1, 2, 3, 4, 5, 6, 7, 8, 9, A, B, C, D, E, F). Table 3 compares binary, decimal, octal, hexadecimal and binary numbers.

TABLE 3

Comparison between Different Number Systems

Binary (Base = 2)	Decimal (Base = 10)	Octal (Base = 8)	Hexadecimal (Base = 16)
0	0	0	0
1	1	1	1
10	2	2	2
11	3	3	3
100	4	4	4
101	5	5	5
110	6	6	6
111	7	7	7
1000	8	10	8
1001	9	11	9
1010	10	12	A
1011	11	13	B
1100	12	14	C
1101	13	15	D
1110	14	16	E
1111	15	17	F
10000	16	20	G

Notice the manner in which increments occur in decimal and binary systems (Table 4):

TABLE 4

Addition of 0's and 1's in Decimal and Binary Number Systems

Decimal	0 + 0 = 0	0 + 1 = 1	1 + 0 = 1	1 + 1 = 2
Binary	0 + 0 = 0	0 + 1 = 1	1 + 0 = 1	1 + 1 = 10

1.5.1 Conversion between Number Systems

The general form of finding the decimal value of a number in any base k system is given by

$$\text{Value} = \sum_{i=0}^{n-1} b_i\, k^i \tag{1.1}$$

where b_i is the digit at position i, k is the base of the given number system, n the number of digits to the left of the base point, respectively.

1. **Decimal to binary conversion:** Consider the decimal number $(23)_{10}$ where the value at the base indicates the base value of the number system. Here, 10 indicates that 23 is a number in decimal base system. To convert $(23)_{10}$ to base 2, that is, binary number system, we adopt the following method:

   Step 1: Divide 23 by 2 and note the remainder as 1.

   Step 2: Divide quotient 11 by 2 and note the remainder as 1.

   Step 3: Divide the quotient 5 and note the remainder as 1.

   Step 4: Divide the quotient 2 and note the remainder as 0.

   Step 5: Divide the quotient 1 and note the remainder as 1.

   Now, reading the remainders from bottom to top, we get the corresponding binary value as $(10111)_2$.

2. **Binary to decimal conversion:** Consider the binary number $(10011)_2$. To convert it to base 10, that is, decimal number system, we adopt the polynomial method. The binary number can be represented as follows, to get:

$$\begin{aligned}(\underset{4\,3\,2\,1\,0}{10011})_2 &= 1\times 2^4 + 0\times 2^3 + 0\times 2^2 + 1\times 2^1 + 1\times 2^0 \\ &= 16 + 0 + 0 + 2 + 1 = (19)_{10}\end{aligned}$$

where the powers of 2 are the positions of the digits in the binary number starting from 0 from right to left. We can also use Eq. (1.1) for this conversion, with $k = 2$, $n = 5$, $i = 0$ to 4 and $b_i = 0$ or 1.

$$\text{Decimal value} = \sum_{i=0}^{5-1} b_i\, 2^i \qquad (1.2)$$

3. **Octal to binary conversion:** Consider the octal number $(26)_8$. To convert it to base 2, that is, binary number system, we can divide $(26)_8$ into two octal numbers $(2)_8$ and $(6)_8$. Now, referring to Table 3, we can find the corresponding binary numbers for 2 and 6 as $(010)_2$ and $(110)_2$. Placing them together, we get binary form of $(26)_8 = (010110)_2$.
4. **Binary to octal conversion:** Using similar method illustrated in point (3), we can convert the binary number $(001110)_2$ into octal system by dividing the binary number into groups of three as $(001)_2$ and $(110)_2$. Now, these binary numbers correspond to octal numbers $(1)_8$ and $(6)_8$, respectively. Hence, placing them together, we get the corresponding octal form of $(001110)_2 = (16)_8$.
5. **Hexadecimal to binary conversion:** Consider the hexadecimal number $(B6)_{16}$. To convert it to base 2, that is, binary number system, we can divide $(B6)_{16}$ into two hexadecimal numbers $(B)_{16}$ and $(6)_{16}$. Now, referring to Table 3, we can find the corresponding binary numbers for B and 6 as $(1011)_2$ and $(0110)_2$. Placing them together, we get binary form of $(B6)_{16} = (10110110)_2$.
6. **Binary to hexadecimal conversion:** Using similar method illustrated in point (5), we can convert the binary number $(01011110)_2$ into hexadecimal system by dividing the binary number into groups of four as $(0101)_2$ and $(1110)_2$. Now, these binary numbers correspond to hexadecimal numbers $(5)_{16}$ and $(E)_{16}$, respectively. Hence, placing them together, we get the corresponding octal form of (01011110)2 = $(5E)_{16}$.
7. **Octal to decimal conversion:** On modifying Eq. (1.1) in terms of octal representation, we get

$$\text{Decimal value} = \sum_{i=0}^{n-1} b_i\, 8^i \qquad (1.3)$$

Consider conversion of octal number $(768)_8$. This number can be represented as:

$$(\underset{2\,1\,0}{768})_8 = 7\times8^2 + 6\times8^1 + 8\times8^0 = 448 + 48 + 8 = (504)_{10}$$

where the powers of 8 are the positions of the digits in the binary number starting with 0 from right to left.

8. **Decimal to octal conversion:** Consider the decimal number $(465)_{10}$. To convert $(465)_{10}$ to base 8, that is, octal number system, we adopt the following method:

Step 1: Divide 465 by 8 and note the remainder as 1.

Step 2: Divide quotient 58 by 8 and note the remainder as 2.

Step 3: Divide quotient 7 by 8 and note the remainder as 7.

Now, reading the remainders from bottom to top, we get the corresponding octal value as $(721)_8$.

9. **Hexadecimal to decimal conversion:** On modifying Eq. (1.1) in terms of hexadecimal representation, we get

$$\text{Decimal value} = \sum_{i=0}^{n-1} b_i\, 16^i \qquad (1.4)$$

Consider conversion of octal number $(B84)_8$. This number can be represented as:

$$(\underset{2\,1\,0}{B84})_8 = 11\times16^2 + 8\times16^1 + 4\times16^0$$
$$= 2816 + 128 + 4 = (2948)_{10}$$

where the powers of 16 are the positions of the digits in the binary number starting from 0 from right to left. Here we have referred to Table 3, for decimal number corresponding to hexadecimal number B.

10. **Decimal to hexadecimal conversion:** Consider the decimal number $(8371)_{10}$. To convert $(8371)_{10}$ to base 16, that is, hexadecimal number system, we adopt the following method:

Step 1: Divide 8371 by 16 and note the remainder as 3.

Step 2: Divide quotient 523 by 16 and note the remainder as 11.

Step 3: Divide quotient 32 by 16 and note the remainder as 0.

Step 4: Divide quotient 2 by 16 and note the remainder as 2.

Now, reading the remainders from bottom to top, we get the corresponding hexadecimal value as $(20B3)_{16}$.

11. **Octal to hexadecimal conversion:** For this conversion, we need to first convert octal into binary number, and then regroup them to get the corresponding hexadecimal number. For example, $(76)_8 = (111110)_2 \approx (00111110)_2 = (3E)_{16}$.
12. **Hexadecimal to octal conversion:** For this conversion, we need to first convert hexadecimal into binary number, and then regroup them to get the corresponding octal number. For example, $(3FA5)_{16} = (0011\ 1111\ 1010\ 0101)_2 \approx (011\ 111\ 110\ 100\ 101)_2 = (37645)_8$.

Solved Problems

1. *Find the hexadecimal and decimal equivalent of the number $(1110101101)_2$* **(AU 2010)**

Solution: For hexadecimal equivalent, the given binary number can be written as $(0011\ 1010\ 1101)_2$. On referring Table 3, the corresponding hexadecimal number is $(3AD)_{16}$.

For decimal equivalent, we use the polynomial method

$$(\underset{9\,8\,7\,6\,5\,4\,3\,2\,1\,0}{1110101101})_2 = 1\times2^9 + 1\times2^8 + 1\times2^7 + 0\times2^6 + 1\times2^5$$
$$+ 0\times2^4 + 1\times2^3 + 1\times2^2 + 0\times2^1 + 1\times2^0$$
$$= 512 + 256 + 128 + 1 + 32 + 1 + 8 + 4 + 1 + 1$$
$$= (944)_{10}$$

2. *Find the binary equivalent of the number $(108.625)_{10}$* **(AU 2010)**

Solution: For the conversion, we divide the given number into integer part $(108)_{10}$ and fractional part $(0.625)_{10}$, and then convert them separately into corresponding binary representations.

(a) Integer part: We divide 108 repeatedly by 2 and note the remainder in each division.

Divide 108 by 2 and note the remainder as 0.
Divide quotient 54 by 2 and note the remainder as 0.
Divide quotient 27 by 2 and note the remainder as 1.
Divide quotient 13 by 2 and note the remainder as 1.
Divide quotient 6 by 2 and note the remainder as 0.
Divide quotient 3 by 2 and note the remainder as 1.
Divide quotient 1 by 2 and note the remainder as 1.

Now, reading from bottom to top, we get the binary representation as $(1101100)_2$.

(b) Fractional part: We multiply 0.625 repeatedly by 2 and note the integer part, and continue multiplying only the fractional part by 2, again noting the integer part in each case till no fractional part is left.

Multiply 0.625 by 2 to obtain 1.25. Note the integer part as 1.
Multiply 0.25 by 2, to obtain 0.5 and note the integer part as 0.
Multiply 0.5 by 2 to obtain 1.0 and note the integer part as 1.

Now reading from top to bottom, we get the binary representation as $(0.101)_2$

Now, combining the binary representations in (a) and (b) parts, we get the binary representation of $(108.625)_{10}$ as $(1101100.101)_2$.

3. *Find the octal equivalent of the number $(10111001100.1101011)_2$.* **(AU 2010, 2012)**

Solution: The given binary number can be represented in groups of 3 as $(010111001100.110101100)_2$. Now, referring to Table 3, the conversion is as follows:

010	111	001	100.	110	101	100
2	7	1	4	6	5	4

Hence, the octal number is $(2714.654)_8$.

4. *With examples illustrate the conversion of decimal to binary, octal and hexadecimal systems.* **(AU 2010, 2012)**

Solution:

(a) Decimal to binary conversion: Consider the conversion of 3.248×10^4 into single precision floating point binary number. First, we express the decimal number as 32480. The corresponding binary number is $(111111011100000)_2$, which can be expressed in binary fraction as $1.11111011100000 \times 2^{14}$.
The floating point number can be expressed in 32-bit format. These 32 bits are divided as follows:

Sign	Exponent	Mantissa
1 bit	8 bits	23 bits

Sign: Since the MSB is always 1, it will not occupy the bit position.
Exponent: The biased exponent is obtained in binary form by adding excess as 127 to it. Hence, we obtain 14 + 127 = 141, the binary representation of 141 is $(10001101)_2$.
Mantissa: Now, the fractional part in 23-bit form is $(11111011100000000000000)_2$.
Hence, the single precision floating point binary number is

Sign	Exponent	Mantissa
0	10001101	11111011100000000000000

(b) Decimal to octal conversion: Consider the conversion of $(153.5129)_{10}$ to its octal equivalent. We divide the decimal number into two parts, the integral part 153 and the fractional part 0.5129, and convert each part in the following way:

Integral part: We repeatedly divide 153 by 8 and note the remainders as 2, 3 and 1, which gives us the octal number $(231)_8$.

Fractional part: We repeatedly multiply the fractional parts (0.5129, 0.1032, 0.8256, 0.6048) by 16 and note the integral parts as 4, 0, 6, 5, which gives the octal number $(4065)_8$.

Thus, the octal equivalent of $(153.5129)_{10}$ is $(231.4065)_8$.

(c) Decimal to hexadecimal conversion: Consider the conversion of decimal number 1723.256 to hexadecimal number. We divide the decimal number into two parts, the integral part 1723 and the fractional part 0.256, and convert each part in the following way:

Integral part: We repeatedly divide 1723 by 16 and note the remainders as 6, 11 and 11, which gives us the hexadecimal number $(6BB)_{16}$.

Fractional part: We repeatedly multiply the fractional parts (0.256, 0.096, 0.536, 0.576, 0.216) by 16 and note the integral parts as 4, 1, 8, 9, which gives the hexadecimal number $(4189)_{16}$.

Thus, the hexadecimal equivalent of (1723.256) is $(6BB.4189)_{16}$.

5. *(a) Convert the decimal fraction 0.4375 to binary number.* **(AU 2010)**

Solution:

Step 1: The integer part is 0, hence, the binary equivalent of 0 is 0.

Step 2: In the fractional part, we repeatedly multiply 0.4375 by 2 and note the integer part, and continue multiplying only the fractional part by 2, again noting the integer part in each case till no fractional part is left.

- Multiply 0.4375 by 2 to obtain 0.875. Note the integer part as 0.
- Multiply 0.875 by 2, to obtain 1.75 and note the integer part as 1.
- Multiply 0.75 by 2 to obtain 1.5 and note the integer part as 1.
- Multiply 0.5 by 2 to obtain 1.00. Note the integer part as 1.
- Now reading from top to bottom, we get the binary representation of $(0.4375)_{10}$ as $(0.0111)_2$

6. *Convert hexadecimal number A5B to octal number. Explain each step involved in conversion.* **(AU 2010)**

Solution:

Step 1: Convert hexadecimal into binary number by consulting Table 3 in the chapter:

$$(A5B)_{16} = (1010\ 0101\ 1011)_2$$

Step 2: Regroup them into groups containing three digits each:

$$(A5B)_{16} = (1010\ 0101\ 1011)_2 = (101\ 001\ 011\ 011)_2$$

Step 3: Refer to Table 3 again, and write the corresponding octal numbers:

$$(A5B)_{16} = (1010\ 0101\ 1011)_2 = (101\ 001\ 011\ 011)_2$$
$$= (5133)_8$$

7. *Convert the decimal number 59.8125 into binary and octal.* **(AU 2010)**

Solution:

Step 1: For the integer part, 59, we repeatedly divide the number by 2 and note the remainder in each case.

- Divide 59 by 2 and note the remainder as 1
- Divide 29 by 2 and note the remainder as 1
- Divide 14 by 2 and note the remainder as 0
- Divide 7 by 2 and note the remainder as 1
- Divide 3 by 2 and note the remainder as 1
- Divide 1 by 2 and note the remainder as 1

Now, reading from bottom to top, we get the binary equivalent of the integer part 59 as $(111011)_2$

Step 2: For the fractional part, we repeatedly multiply 0.8125 by 2 and note the integer part, and continue multiplying only the fractional part by 2, again noting the integer part in each case till no fractional part is left.

- Multiply 0.8125 by 2 to obtain 1.625 and note the integer part as 1.
- Multiply 0.625 by 2, to obtain 1.25 and note the integer part as 1.
- Multiply 0.25 by 2 to obtain 0.5 and note the integer part as 0.
- Multiply 0.5 by 2 to obtain 1.00 and note the integer part as 1.
- Now reading from top to bottom, we get the binary representation as $(0.1101)_2$

Step 3: Now, we combine binary equivalents of both integer and fractional parts to obtain the binary equivalent of decimal fraction $(59.8125)_{10}$ as $(111011.1101)_2$.

8. *Find the decimal equivalent of the binary number $(10110011)_2$* **(AU 2013)**

Solution

The decimal equivalent is found by representing the binary number as follows:

$$\underset{76543210}{(10110011)_2} = 1\times2^7 + 0\times2^6 + 1\times2^5 + 1\times2^4 + 0\times2^3 + 0\times2^2 + 1\times2^1 + 1\times2^0$$
$$= 128 + 0 + 32 + 16 + 0 + 0 + 2 + 1 = (179)_{10}$$

9. *Convert $(756)_{10}$ to octal and hexadecimal.* **(AU 2013 Suppl.)**

Solution

For conversion into octal system, we divide $(756)_{10}$ by 8 successively till we get 0 as quotient.

Step 1: Divide 756 by 8 and note the remainder as 4.

Step 2: Divide quotient 94 by 8 and note the remainder as 6.

Step 3: Divide the quotient 11 by 8 and note the remainder as 3.

Step 4: Divide the quotient 3 by 8 and note the remainder as 3.

Thus, reading the remainders from bottom to top, we get the corresponding octal value as $(3364)_8$.

For conversion into octal system, we divide $(756)_{10}$ by 16 successively till we get 0 as quotient.

Step 1: Divide 756 by 16 and note the remainder as 4.

Step 2: Divide quotient 47 by 16 and note the remainder as 15.

Step 3: Divide the quotient 2 by 16 and note the remainder as 2.

Thus, reading the remainders from bottom to top, we get the corresponding hexadecimal value as $(2F4)_{16}$.

10. *Convert the decimal number 698.125 into the binary and octal equivalent.* **(AU 2013)**

Solution

For the conversion, we divide the given number into integer part $(698)_{10}$ and fractional part $(0.125)_{10}$, and then convert them separately into corresponding binary representations.

(a) Integer part: We divide 698 repeatedly by 2 and note the remainder in each division.

- Divide 698 by 2 and note the remainder as 0.
- Divide quotient 349 by 2 and note the remainder as 1.

- Divide quotient 174 by 2 and note the remainder as 0.
- Divide quotient 87 by 2 and note the remainder as 1.
- Divide quotient 43 by 2 and note the remainder as 1.
- Divide quotient 21 by 2 and note the remainder as 1.
- Divide quotient 10 by 2 and note the remainder as 0.
- Divide quotient 5 by 2 and note the remainder as 1.
- Divide quotient 2 by 2 and note the remainder as 0.
- Divide quotient 1 by 2 and note the remainder as 1.
- Now, reading from bottom to top, we get the binary representation as $(1010111010)_2$.

(b) Fractional part: We multiply 0.125 repeatedly by 2 and note the integer part, and continue multiplying only the fractional part by 2, again noting the integer part in each case till no fractional part is left.

- Multiply 0.125 by 2 to obtain 0.25. Note the integer part as 0.
- Multiply 0.25 by 2, to obtain 0.5 and note the integer part as 0.
- Multiply 0.5 by 2 to obtain 1.0 and note the integer part as 1.
- Now reading from top to bottom, we get the binary representation as $(0.100)_2$
- Now, combining the binary representations in (a) and (b) parts, we get the binary representation of $(698.125)_{10}$ as $(1010111010.100)_2$.

1.6 Signed Binary Numbers

In the previous sections, we dealt with unsigned binary numbers. There is another set of binary numbers called signed binary numbers, which are binary numbers containing a positive or negative sign. In this section, we would discuss the methods used to represent signed binary numbers. The following methods are used:

1. **Signed magnitude:** This is also referred to as sign and magnitude, and is most familiar when converting base 10 positive or negative number to base 2 binary representation. Consider $(+12)_{10}$ and $(-12)_{10}$. The corresponding binary representations in 8-bit format will be $(00001100)_2$ and $(10001100)_2$. Note that the leftmost bit is used for sign, which takes up value 0 for + and 1 for –.
2. **One's complement:** The negative number is represented by changing all 1's to 0's and all 0's to 1's. Consider $(+4)_{10}$ and $(-4)_{10}$. The corresponding binary representations in 8-bit format will be $(00000100)_2$ and $(11111011)_2$. Note that the leftmost bit is 1 for negative sign. This representation is commonly used in arithmetic calculations.
3. **Two's complement:** The two's complement is formed by first taking the one's complement of the number and then adding 1 to it. Consider $(+15)_{10}$ and $(-15)_{10}$. The corresponding binary representation in 8-bit format for $(+15)_{10}$ is $(00001111)_2$. Now taking the one's complement, we get $(11110000)_2$. To obtain two's complement, we add 1 to the one's complement, that is, $(11110000)_2 + 1 = (11110001)_2$. If we try to obtain the two's complement of a negative number, we will arrive at a negative number. This representation is commonly used in conventional computers.
4. **Excess representation:** In this representation, the number considered unsigned by adding another number known as excess or bias to the given number. Consider $(+6)_{10}$ and $(-6)_{10}$. Let the excess be 128, then the two numbers after addition become $(+6 + 128 = 134)_{10}$ and $(-6 + 128 = 122)_{10}$. The corresponding binary representations in 8-bit format are $(10000110)_2$ and $(01111010)_2$, respectively.

Solved Problem

1. *Illustrate the process of addition and subtraction in 1's and 2's complement systems with suitable examples.* **(AU 2010, 2012)**

Solution:

Consider addition and subtraction of $(+13)_{10}$ and $(-13)_{10}$. We first represent them in their binary representations using 1's complement and 2's complement methods separately, and then carry out the operations.

(a) For 1's complement form, $(+13)_{10}$ is represented as $(00001101)_2$ and $(-13)_{10}$ as $(11110010)_2$. Now, adding the binary numbers, we get

$$\begin{array}{r} (+13)_{10} = (00001101)_2 \\ +(-13)_{10} = (11110010)_2 \\ \hline (0)_{10} = (11111111)_2 \end{array}$$

Note that +0 and –0 are the same, so $(00000000)_2$ and $(11111111)_2$ are also the same, with the latter being the 1's complement.
Now, for subtracting, we take one's complement of the negative number again as $-(-13) = (+13)_{10}$; so $-(-13)_{10}$ can be represented as same as $(+13)_{10}$ in this case, that is,

$$\begin{array}{r} (+13)_{10} = (00001101)_2 \\ -(-13)_{10} = (00001101)_2 \\ \hline (26)_{10} = (00011010)_2 \end{array}$$

(b) For 2's complement form, $(+13)_{10}$ is represented as $(00001101)_2$ and $(-13)_{10}$ as $(11110010 + 1)_2 = (11110011)_2$. Now, adding the binary numbers, we get

$$\begin{array}{r} (+13)_{10} = (00001101)_2 \\ +(-13)_{10} = (11110011)_2 \\ \hline (0)_{10} = (00000000)_2 \end{array}$$

Note that the carry out in the leftmost position is discarded in 2's complement addition.
Another example is illustrated for better clarity. For subtraction of $(-5)_{10}$ and $(+2)_{10}$, we have their binary representations as follows:
$(+5)_{10} = (00000101)_2$, its 1's complement is $(11111010)_2$ and its 2's complement to obtain binary representation of $(-5)_{10}$ is $(11111011)_2$
Now, $(+2)_{10} = (00000010)_2$. For subtraction, we have to multiply by –1 to obtain $-(+2)_{10} = (-2)_{10}$. Hence, the 1's

complement is $(11111101)_2$ and its 2's complement is $(11111110)_2$.
Now, the subtraction of $(-5)_{10}$ and $(+2)_{10}$, and hence, the addition of $(-5)_{10}$ and $(-2)_{10}$ is as follows:

$$\begin{array}{r} (-5)_{10} = (11111011)_2 \\ -\,(+2)_{10} = (11111110)_2 \\ \hline (-7)_{10} = (11111001)_2 \end{array}$$

The carry generated from the MSB is rejected.

1.7 Binary Arithmetic Operations

In this subsection, we will perform the various arithmetic operations. Some of these operations, were noticed in previous sections.

1. **Binary addition:** Referring to Table 4 that highlighted the binary additions of 0's and 1's, we can easily perform binary additions.
2. **Binary subtraction:** In the section of signed binary numbers, by taking 1's and 2's complements to obtain the negative binary number, we were in fact multiplying the respective numbers by –1. On adding the 1's or 2's complement of a binary number to another binary number, we are actually performing binary subtractions.
3. **Binary multiplication:** The rules for binary multiplication are as follows

$0\times0=0$	$0\times1=0$	$1\times0=0$	$1\times1=1$

For multiplication of fractional binary numbers, the binary point is placed before the same number of digits as in the sum of the digits to the right of the binary point in the multiplicand and the multiplier.
4. **Binary division:** The rules for binary division are as follows:

$0\div0=0$	$0\div1=0$	$1\div0=0$	$1\div1=1$

If the result obtained by dividing the divisor with the dividend is negative, the divisor is shifted to one place to the right and added back to the negative number.

Solved Problem

1. *(a) Add binary numbers $(10011.10)_2$ and $(00110.11)_2$.*
   (b) Subtract the binary number $(100.10)_2$ from $(001.11)_2$.
   (c) Multiply $(110.10)_2$ with $(110.11)_2$ using binary multiplication.
   (d) Divide $(1000101)_2$ by $(1100)_2$

Solution:

(a) The binary addition is carried out as follows:

$$\begin{array}{r} 10011.10 \\ +\,00110.11 \\ \hline 11010.01 \end{array}$$

This addition can be verified by converting the binary numbers in decimal number system as $17.5 + 8.75 = 26.25$.

(b) The binary subtraction is as follows:

$$\begin{array}{r} 100.10 \\ -\,001.11 \\ \hline 10.11 \end{array}$$

This subtraction can be verified by converting the binary numbers in decimal number system as $4.5 - 1.75 = 2.75$.

(c) The binary multiplication of $(110.10)_2$ with $(110.11)_2$ is carried out as follows:

$$\begin{array}{r} 110.10 \\ \times\,110.11 \\ \hline 11010 \\ 11010\times \\ 00000\times\times \\ 11010\times\times\times \\ 11010\times\times\times\times \\ \hline 101011.1110 \end{array}$$

This multiplication can be verified by converting the binary numbers in decimal number system as $6.5\times6.75 = 43.875$.

(d) The binary division of $(1000101)_2$ by $(1100)_2$ gives the answer as $(101.11)_2$.

$$\begin{array}{r} 101.11 \\ 1100\,)1000101.000(\\ \underline{1100} \\ 10101 \\ \underline{1100} \\ 10010 \\ \underline{1100} \\ 1100 \\ \underline{1100} \\ 0000 \end{array}$$

This division can be verified by converting the binary numbers in decimal number system as $69 \div 12 = 5.75$.

1.8 Octal and Hexadecimal Arithmetic Operations

The addition and subtraction operations in octal and hexadecimal number systems proceed in a similar manner. In case the result is an invalid value, that is, greater than 8 in case of octal and greater than 16 in case of hexadecimal, then 8 and 16 are subtracted from the result, respectively. Each time 8 or 16 is subtracted, the carry is increased by 1.

In case of subtraction, the 7's or 8's complement in case of octal and 15's or 16's complement in case of hexadecimal number systems are used to express the negative numbers. These complements are then added to the positive number to obtain the sum. If a carry is produced in this addition, then the carry in the LSB is added to the sum, else the 7's (or 8's) and 15's (or 16's) complement of the sum is taken to obtain the correct result.

Solved Problems

1. *(a) Add octal numbers $(747)_8$ and $(857)_8$.*

   (b) Subtract octal number $(153)_8$ from $(253)_8$.

Solution:

(a) The addition can be done as follows:

Step 1: $7 + 7 = 14$, we subtract $14 - 8 = 6$, and carry 1.

Step 2: $1 + 4 + 5 = 10$, we subtract $10 - 8 = 2$, and carry 1.

Step 3: $1 + 7 + 8 = 16$, we subtract $16 - 8 = 8$, and carry 1.

Step 4: The carry is written as such, that is, 1.

Hence, we obtain the result as $(1826)_8$

(b) The subtraction $(153)_8 - (253)_8$ can be done as follows: First, we determine the 7's complement of $(253)_8$ as $777 - 253 = (524)_8$. This is then added to $(153)_8$ to obtain $(677)_8$. If there was carry, it should be added to the sum. Since there is no carry, we take 7's complement of the sum to obtain the difference as $777 - 677 = (100)_8$.

2. *(a) Add the hexadecimal numbers $(D5)_{16}$ and $(4D)_{16}$.*

   (b) Subtract $(B02)_{16}$ and $(98F)_{16}$

Solution:

(a) To add hexadecimal numbers, the following steps are performed:

Step 1: $5 + D$ (i.e., 13) = 18, which is subtracted with 16 to get sum 2 and carry 1.

Step 2: $1 + D$ (i.e., 13) + 4 = 18, which is subtracted with 16 to get sum 2 and carry 1.

Step 3: Carry is written as such, that is, 1.

Hence, we get the sum as $(122)_{16}$

(b) To carry out the subtraction $(B02)_{16} - (98F)_{16}$, we take 15's complement of $(98F)_{16}$ as $(15 - 9)\ (15 - 8)\ (15 - F)$ to get $(670)_{16}$, which is added to $(B02)_{16}$ to obtain the sum as 172 and carry 1. This carry is added to obtain the difference as $(173)_{16}$.

1.9 Coding Standards to Represent Stored Data

A binary code consists of a group of binary bits. These codes are used to represent decimal numbers (BCD) or alphabetic characters (ASCII, EBCDIC, Unicode).

1.9.1 | Binary Coded Decimal (BCD)

The binary coded decimal (BCD) is a 4-bit number representation used to store each digit from 0 to 9. For example, $(1020)_{10}$ is stored as 0001 0000 0010 0000 in BCD. This type of coding is used in business applications and calculators. However, we can see that storage space is wasted as 4 bytes are used for storage of $(1020)_{10}$. To minimize this wastage, BCD numbers are packed to occupy 2 bytes as shown: $(1020)_{10}$ is represented as 0010000 00100000 in packed BCD.

1.9.1.1 BCD Arithmetic Operations

The arithmetic operations addition, subtraction, multiplication and division follow the same method as used for binary numbers. These operations can be performed by first operating with binary numbers and then converting the answer into BCD.

1. **BCD addition:** In certain cases, where the result becomes greater than 1001 (i.e., 9) and is an invalid entry, a correction term needs to be added to the result to generate a carry bit and cause the sum to become valid. This correction term is 0110 (i.e., 6). The reason for adding 6 is that there are 16 possible 4-bit BCD values (since $2^4 = 16$), out of which only 10 values are valid (i.e., 0000 through 1001).
2. **BCD subtraction:** The positive sign in BCD is represented as 0000 and the negative sign is represented as 1001. For obtaining the negative value of the number, the 10's complement is taken, which is obtained by first taking the 9's complement of the number and then adding 1.

Solved Problems

1. *Add the BCD Numbers 00010110 and 00010101*

Solution: The addition is performed as follows:

```
  00010110
+ 00010101
----------
  00101011
```

This corresponds to 2 and 11 in decimal format, however, we cannot have the value exceeding 1001 (i.e., 9). Hence, 0110 (i.e., 6) is added to the result.

```
  00101011
+ 00000110
----------
  00110001
```

which is the BCD of decimal 31. This can be verified by writing the decimal equivalents of the BCDs, $16 + 15 = 31$.

2. *Subtract the decimal number 95 from 45 using 9's complement method.*

Solution: The number 95 in BCD is represented as 1001 0101 and the number 45 is expressed as 0100 0101. Now since we have to carry out subtraction of $45 - 95$, we need to take the 9's complement of 95.

The 9's complement of 95 is obtained as follows: $99 - 95 = 4$. Now, by placing the negative sign BCD representation to the left of the BCD representation of 4, we obtain the BCD representation of -95 as 0000 0100.

Now, the subtraction 45 – 95 is carried out by addition of 0100 0101 and 0000 0100 as follows:

```
  0000 0100 0101
+ 1001 0000 0100
----------------
  1001 0100 1001
```

This, the sign 1001 represent negative number. Now, converting this result to the decimal format gives 949. Now, taking 9's complement of this number, we get 999 – 949 = 50, which verifies the subtraction 45 – 95 = –50.

1.9.2 Extended Binary Coded Decimal Interchange Code (EBCDIC)

The limitation of the BCD code in representing 64 different characters in 6-bit code was overcome by a researcher who decided to extend the code to an 8-bit code which could be used to represent 256 characters. This new 8-bit code was termed as extended binary coded decimal interchange code (EBCDIC). The 256 characters in the EBCDIC code include printable as well as non-printable characters (e.g., spaces), and have not been assigned completely. New characters can still be assigned to the code. To represent the 8-bit code, it is divided into two 4-bit codes (representing the zone and digit) each represented by a hexadecimal number. This representation helps in reduction of memory space required to store the data. For example, A in EBCDIC code is 1100 0001, where 1100 is the zone and 0001 is the digit. The hexadecimal equivalent of which is C1. In EBCDIC coding, characters **A to I** are represented by a common zone 1100 and digits from 0001 to 1001; **J to R** by common zone 1101 and digits from 0001 to 1001; **S to Z** by a common zone 1110 and digits from 0010 to 1001; **numerals 0 to 9** by common zone 1111 and digits from 0000 to 1001.

Solved Problem

1. *Write the EBCDIC coding for GOOD in binary and hexadecimal notations. How many bytes are used to store this word in EBCDIC coding?*

Solution: The characters in GOOD can be represented as:

EBCDIC	G	O	O	D
Binary	1100 0111	1101 0110	1101 0110	1100 0100
Hexadecimal	C7	D6	D6	C4

Since each character in EBCDIC requires 1 byte for representation and there are four characters in GOOD, so four bytes are required for storage.

1.9.3 American Standard Code for Information Interchange (ASCII)

The ASCII standard codes were published by the American National Standards Institute (ANSI) in 1963 and revised thereafter to include new characters. There are two types of ASCII codes: ASCII-7 which is a 7-bit code to represent 128 characters (printable and non-printable) and ASCII-8 which is an 8-bit code to represent 256 characters (printable and non-printable).

The ASCII code can be represented in binary and hexadecimal forms as follows: **Uppercase characters A to Z** are represented as 0100 0001 (binary) or 41 (hexadecimal) to 0101 1010 (binary) or 5A (hexadecimal); **lowercase characters a to z** are represented as 0110 001 (binary) or 61 (hexadecimal) to 0111 101 (binary) or 7A (hexadecimal); **numerals 0 to 9** are represented as 0011 0000 (binary) or 31 (hexadecimal) to 0011 1001 (binary) or 39 (hexadecimal).

1.9.4 Unicode

In spite of detailed coding standards adopted in form of ASCII and EBCDIC, a need arose for a universal coding standard which could include the characters of English as well as other languages. This encoding standard provides a unique number for every character, without being specific to the platform, language or program. It defines codes for special characters, mathematical symbols, technical symbols and diacritics, and enables transfer of multilingual data across different systems all over the world without the risk of corruption.

1.10 Computer Applications

1. **Education:** Computers play a vital role in education. Computer labs are present in almost every school and the subject is part of school and college curricula. Books are available online in the form of e-books, and online tutorials are available to enhance the knowledge of the concerned. Working professionals continue to enhance their qualifications by means of distance learning programs available online.

   The Internet provides an opportunity to the students, faculty and research scholars to search for research papers and books because it is a huge database of information. The different application software like PowerPoint and flash are very helpful in making the lectures student-friendly. Computers are also frequently used in education institutes for storing students' personal as well as academic records, question banks; for online tests, comparative result analyses, video conferencing; for delivering online lectures; for conducting online examinations; for learning through animations, for searching information, etc.

2. **Multimedia and Animation:** Multimedia is an integration of different content forms, such as text, graphics, animations, audio and video effects to develop effective presentations and to provide a completely interactive interface through a computer system. Animation is a part of multimedia, in which the graphics and images move. Multimedia applications require computerized and electronic devices to record and play. Multimedia-based learning is becoming increasingly popular in education industry because it is very useful in making classroom-teaching more interesting and interactive. The multimedia-based applications are actively used in advertisement and entertainment industries. Cartoon

films are also animation-based films, which are very popular among people. These applications have the disadvantage that they require a sophisticated high-end computer systems and trained persons. Also, these applications and the computer systems are costly, not easy to configure and also end up in slower processing.

3. **Healthcare or in medicine:** The hospitals is use computers to keep the patients' personal information, prescriptions, billing information and their medical history in the computer. The doctors can also immediately consult their counterparts abroad in case of emergencies. Complex surgeries or operations are also being performed with the help of the computers. There are various medical equipment such as emergency alarm systems, X-ray machines, infrared cameras, CT scanners, etc., which are operated by computers. Further, medical e-books, journals can also be downloaded online.

4. **Remote Sensing:** This is a technique of acquiring and transporting spectral, spatial or temporal information by means of radiation about an object from a distance, without coming in physical contact with the object. The most common use of remote sensing technology is to monitor the Earth's weather for forecasting and in radar for sending and receiving signals to the pilot of an aircraft, aeroplane or the airbase.

   In this technique, data is transferred by using electromagnetic radiation (EMR), which travels from its source to the target. A remote sensor is required to collect and record this EMR, which in turn is transmitted to a receiving and processing station. At this station, the data are processed and interpreted to extract information about the target. The sensors are the usually wireless devices placed away from the source and target.

   Remote sensing is classified as active remote sensing and passive remote sensing, depending on the source of reflection of radiation.

   - *Passive remote sensing*: When the reflection of radiation is caused by a natural source of energy, that is, the Sun and it is observed by the sensor.
   - *Active remote sensing*: When the reflection of radiation is caused by an artificial source of energy like a radar system.

   The remote sensing technique is useful and applied in the field of satellite, due to which the number of satellite missions has increased in last few decades. It is also used in agriculture for benefits of the farmer, in forestry, geology, searching natural resources, weather forecasting, etc.

5. **Geographic Information System (GIS):** It is a system of hardware, software, data and trained people used for mapping and analyzing things related to a specific location on the Earth. The computer system used may be a simple desktop system, workstation or designated server. There is an input system to feed the geographic input for processing and analysis, and an output system to take the hardcopy of the map or other geographic data. The GIS software consists of tools needed to acquire, store, analyze, manipulate and display geographic information.

   The GIS application also uses database management system to store and manipulate the geographic data. The specific data may be retrieved and manipulated by using a query. Creation of geographic database is very difficult, expensive and time-consuming process, and it requires the trained and skilled persons to operate it. The geographic data comprises geographic features and the corresponding attribute information. There are many different GIS software packages available today.

   The GIS systems are very useful in determining policy on land reforms to ensure land balance, creating smart maps, solving complicated problems and developing a reliable, timely and cost-effective way of agricultural planning. The GIS are also used in the fields of healthcare, forests, industry and transportation, etc. Some of the GIS packages commercially available are ARC/INFO, PAMAP, MAPINFO, GRASS, ISRO-GIS and GRAM.

6. **Bioinformatics:** This term is made up of two words "bio" and "informatics". It is a combined study of biology, mathematics, statistics, and computer technology. Bioinformatics is a new emerging field of research where computer and various software tools are used to store and analyze the biological information. The BLAST and FASTA are very popular molecular biology packages used for sequence analysis and modeling of the molecules.

   Also, it is being used in various fields such as drug designing, drug development, molecular medicine, forensic analysis, crop improvement, DNA mapping, medical research, gene therapy, genomics, proteomics, 3D modeling, DNA sequences analysis, pattern recognition, computational genomics, waste cleanup, evolutionary studies, biotechnology, etc.

7. **Computer games:** These are very popular nowadays. These come pre-installed with computer systems and can be bought separately as CDs. These games require a good graphics card and sound card.

POINTS TO REMEMBER

1. **Basic operations** of a computer are **input**, **process** and **control**, **storage** and **output**.
2. Computer generations.

Time period	1945–1955	1956–1963	1964–1970	1971–1995	Beyond 1995
Generation	First	Second	Third	Fourth	Fifth
Component used	Vacuum tubes	Transistor	Integrated circuits (ICs)	Very-large scale integration (VLSI) technology for microprocessor chip	Super large scale integration (SLSI) and concept of artificial intelligence

3. Computers can be classified into **super computers** (e.g., Cray-1, Cray-2, Cyber 205, CDC, ETA 10, ETA 20, IBM 3090, Intel ASCI Red, PARAM, Tianhe), **mainframe-computers** (e.g., CDC 6600, MEDHA, Sperry, DEC, S/390, VAX 8000, HP, HCL and IBM ES000 series), **mini computers** (e.g., PDP 11, IBM 8000 series, VAX 7500 and AS/400), **microcomputers** which comprise desktop computers and laptops (e.g., HP Compaq, IBM, HCL, ACER, DELL, APPLE, LENOVO) and handheld computers (e.g., Franklin eBookMan and Casio Cassiopeia).
4. Basic computer organization includes **CPU** (comprising registers, control unit and arithmetic logic unit), **input unit** (e.g., keyboard, mouse, joystick, trackball, scanner, touch screen, speech recognition, etc.), **output unit** (e.g., monitor, printer, plotter, speakers and headphones, etc.) and **memory unit** [comprising primary memory (RAM, ROM), secondary memory (magnetic disks, optical disks, memory storage devices) and cache memory.
5. **Number systems, conversions and coding standards:** The corresponding values in different number systems and the coding used to store decimal number 56 are as follows:

Number Systems				Coding Standards		
Decimal	Binary	Octal	Hexadecimal	BCD	EBCDIC	ASCII
56	111000	70	38	0101 0110	1111 0101 1111 0110	0011 1000
Method	By successive division by 2 and noting the remainder in each case from bottom to top.	Grouping binary form into groups of three and referring to Table 3.	Grouping binary form into groups of four and referring to Table 3.	Taking binary equivalent of decimal digits 5 and 6 separately and expressing them in 4-bit format.	Taking EBCDIC equivalent of hexadecimal numbers 3 and 8 separately and expressing them in 16-bit format.	Taking ASCII-8 equivalent of hexadecimal numbers 38 expressing them in 8-bit format.

6. **Applications** of computers can be found in various fields such as bioinformatics, healthcare/medicine, education, geographic information systems and remote sensing, multimedia, animation and computer gaming.

REVIEW QUESTIONS

1. Define computer?
2. What are the basic operations of the computer? (AU 2013)
3. List out the characteristics of computer? (AU 2009, 2010, 2011, 2013)
4. Define CPU and ALU?
5. Define VLSI?
6. What are the applications of computers?
7. Who invented the integrated circuits?
8. Explain about the block diagram of the computer in detail. (AU 2008–2014)
9. Explain in detail about the components of CPU.
10. List out the features of all generations of computer with their advantages and disadvantages. (AU 2010, 2013, 2014)
11. Write a note on classification of computers. (AU 2009)
12. Explain briefly the various computers used initially before the personal computers came into existence.
13. Explain how multiplication and division of binary numbers can be done using arithmetic shift operation.
14. Explain about the integrated circuits in detail.
15. Define non-positional number systems.
16. What are the types of positional number systems?
17. Define binary, decimal, octal and hexadecimal number systems. (AU 2009)
18. Define MSB and LSB.
19. What is the procedure to find out binary subtraction using complementary method?
20. Define 1's complement and 2's complement.
21. With suitable example, show how multiplication operation can be performed by additive approach?
22. What are the rules for binary addition, subtraction, multiplication and division?
23. What are the types of number system conversions?
24. List out the procedure for BCD addition.
25. Write a note about the monitors and its types.
26. What are the different types of output devices?
27. What is a printing device and what are its types?
28. List the similarties and differences between 7-bit and 8-bit ASCII codes.
29. What are the types of input devices?
30. Describe various types of memories used in computers.
31. Define secondary storage and discuss its types.
32. What is magnetic storage?
33. What is dynamic memory?
34. What is primary storage and its components.
35. What is a CPU? What are its functions?
36. Explain in detail about storage devices.
37. Explain briefly about audio visual input/output devices.
38. What are various types of coding standards adopted to represent stored data.

COMPUTING ASSIGNMENTS

1. Convert the following binary numbers into decimal:
   (a) 111001 (b) 00101 (c) 101110 (d) 110010
2. Convert the following hexadecimal numbers into decimal:
   (a) 93A (b) 6BA (c) 3B9 (d) 28D
3. Convert the following octal numbers intodecimal:
   (a) 773 (b) 7373 (c) 1267 (d) 6347
4. Convert the following decimal numbers into hexadecimal:
   (a) 7793 (b) 2389 (c) 2079 (d) 676
5. (a) Add the BCD numbers 01100111 and 01010011.
   (b) Convert the decimal number 4019 into hexadecimal number.
6. (a) Convert the decimal number 250 into octal number.
   (b) Divide the signed number 01100100 by 00011001.
   (c) Determine the decimal value of signed binary number 01010110 expressed in 2's complement form.
7. (a) Subtract the hexadecimal number 173 from BCD.
   (b) Subtract the decimal number 75 from 25 using 9's complement method.
   (c) Convert the binary number 1011100.10101 to decimal number.
8. (a) Convert $(850)_{10}$ to binary number.
   (b) Multiply the signed numbers 0101011 and 11000101.
9. (a) Convert the decimal fraction 0.75 to binary number.
   (b) Subtract the hexadecimal number 0B from C3.
10. (a) Convert $(5C2)_{16}$ to decimal number.
    (b) Multiply the signed number 01001101 by 00000100.
    (c) Add the hexadecimal numbers DF and AC.
11. (a) Subtract 55 – 35 using 10's complement method.
    (b) Convert the decimal fraction 186.9028 to binary number.
    (c) Subtract signed numbers 00001000 – 00000011.
12. Determine the decimal value of signed binary number 00010111 expressed in 1's complement form.
13. (a) Subtract 110 – 320 using 10's complement method.
    (b) Convert $(10010.111)_2$ into its decimal equivalent.
    (c) Convert hexadecimal number AC5.4D to octal number.
14. (a) Subtract signed numbers 11100111 – 00010011.
    (b) Convert the binary number 11110.11011 to hexadecimal number.
    (c) Subtract 125 –110 using 9's complement method.
15. (a) Subtract 101010 from 111000 using 2's complement method.
    (b) Convert the binary number 1011110 to octal number.
16. (a) Add the BCD numbers 00101110 and 001101111.
    (b) Convert the decimal number 3.298×10^5 into a single precision floating point binary number.
17. Using binary notation, write the EBCDIC code for "FUNDAMENTALS".
18. (a) Convert the hexadecimal number 6BB.4189 to decimal number.
    (b) Express +39 and –39 in 1's complement form and 2's complement form.
19. (a) Add the hexadecimal numbers 4C and 3A.
    (b) Divide 1111010 by 1110.
    (c) Convert decimal number 9673 to BCD number.

Problem Solving through Algorithms, Flowcharts and Pseudocodes

2

LEARNING OBJECTIVES

After completing this chapter, you will be able to understand the following:

- Problem formulation and planning a computer program.
- Steps involved in developing a program.
- Introduction to algorithms, flowcharts and pseudocodes.
- Characteristics and categorization of program control structures.
- Program methodology – top-down and bottom-up approaches.
- Generations of programming languages.
- Programming models – unstructured, procedural, and modular.

2.1 Introduction

We know that the computer is an electronic device that can perform various tasks with great speed and accuracy. We also know that the computer system consists of hardware, software and users who operate the system. Now the question arises that how does the user instruct the computer to perform some task? The instructions are passed by means of a program. There are several programming languages and using any of these languages, the users can instruct the computer to perform some specified task. The computers also need to be instructed about how the task is to be performed.

2.2 Problem Formulation and Planning a Program

A program is defined as the set of instructions written in a proper syntax and in a certain order to perform some specific task. Now before compiling these set of instructions, the following requirements must be kept in mind:

1. **Problem formulation:** The problem to be solved or the task to be performed should be understood thoroughly, and the following requirements should be analyzed:
   - The instructions to be performed can be ideated by reading the problem statement.
   - The input data required.
   - The output data to be generated.
2. **Setting up algorithms/designing flow charts:** The logic for solving the problem should be planned by charting the sequence in which instructions should be given. This can be done in two ways:
   - Written stepwise in English-like statements using algorithms.
   - Pictorial representation using flowcharts.
3. **Planning a program:** A program is defined as the set of instructions written in a proper syntax and in certain order to perform a task. The coding of programs is done by:
   - Selecting the appropriate programming language for expressing the instruction.
   - Converting the pseudocode or flowchart instructions into the programming language based on a predefined structure called the syntax.
   - Once the program is coded in the programming language, it is tested to rectify errors, and once all the errors are rectified, it is ready for implementation.

Solved Problem

1. *Explain in detail the various stages involved in planning a program.* (AU 2007 Suppl., 2010)

Solution: Refer to the section above.

2.3 Steps for Program Development

The basic steps involved in the development of a program are as follows:

1. **Defining the problem:** It is important to be first define the problem or set of problems and define clear objectives to solve the problem(s).
2. **Requirement analysis:** After defining the problem, it is split into several small problems and the possible solutions to these problems are analyzed. The solution that is feasible practically and economically is chosen.
3. **Designing algorithms:** The solution is outlined in form of tasks to be performed and steps to be carried out in sequential order.
4. **Algorithm testing:** Some sample data is run though the steps of the algorithm to check its correctness. Any logical errors found are rectified. This step is very important before converting the algorithm into program code. Usual data as well as data with certain exceptions are tested to check variance in both the cases.
5. **Coding:** In this phase, the actual program coding is done. Once the initial code is written, it is checked against design and specification requirements and updated accordingly to maintain consistency.
6. **Testing:** The developed program is tested on the grounds of functionality, performance, business logic and data accuracy. A program compiler is used to compile the program and a list of errors is generated. These errors are checked and rectified one by one. The required changes are incorporated in the coding and the testing process is repeated to ensure that all changes have been incorporated and that no inadvertent discrepancy is introduced during updation. More complex the program, more rounds of testing are required. After testing, the work is started on the functional environment or user interface.
7. **Documentation:** This documentation is done throughout the various phases. It contains the internal design structure of the program and other details required for running the program by any user. During its lifetime, the program can be implemented by many programmers; therefore, it is better to document the changes and understand the logic behind the changes.
8. **Implementation:** The program is installed on the end user's machine and user is briefed about the proper working of the program. The feedback from various users is collected and the changes are incorporated to enhance the program's functionality.
9. **Maintenance, enhancement and evolution:** The program is updated periodically for it to be reliable and long-lasting. Also, the existing program is relooked upon in view of emerging and evolving technologies. The new technical and functional requirements are implemented accordingly and new versions of the existing program are developed.

2.4 Problem Solving Techniques

The computer is used to solve real-life problems which are first identified and for which a solution is then designed before being programmed for a computer. There are various problem-solving tools and techniques, namely algorithms, flowcharts and pseudocodes, to design the solution of a computational problem as a logical sequence of instructions.

In order to solve a computational problem, it is necessary to consider the various factors involved in solving the problem.

1. Since the computer has a limited memory, the first requirement is the consideration of memory space and its efficient utilization, called the space complexity of the program.
2. Time required in solving the computational problem is called time complexity of the program.
3. Selection of programming languages in which the problem-solving tool can be implemented.

The computational problem can be solved by using different problem-solving tools; however, the selection of efficient tools is very important so that it reduces the space utilization and time utilization for that problem.

2.4.1 | Algorithms

An algorithm is defined as a sequence of instructions to solve a computational problem. These instructions are applied on some raw data called the input, and the solution of the problem produced is called the output. The characteristic features of an algorithm are:

The characteristics of an algorithm are as follows:

1. Each instruction in an algorithm should be unambiguous.
2. The steps of an algorithm should be written in sequence, and there should not be any uncertainty about which step should be followed next.
3. The steps should not be repeated infinitely, they must reach their concluding state; that is, they must terminate after executing certain number of instructions.
4. The algorithm must not be open-ended, and its description must be finite.
5. The algorithm should be general enough to deal with any contingency.

Algorithm is written in a sequence of steps and once developed; it should also be tested manually and redefined if needed. The following example shows the use of algorithm to solve the problem of finding roots of a quadratic equation. $ax^2 + bx + c = 0$.

1. Start
2. Read three numbers a, b and c
3. Calculate D from the equation $D = b^2 - 4ac$.
4. Check if $(D < 0)$, then print "roots are imaginary" and stop.
5. Otherwise calculate roots x1 and x2 using the formula

$$x1=(-b+\sqrt{(b^2-4ac)})/(2a)$$
$$x2=(-b-\sqrt{(b^2-4ac)})/(2a)$$

6. Print roots x1 and x2
7. Stop

2.4.2 | Flowcharts

A flowchart is a pictorial and a very structured representation of the algorithm. The algorithm is represented graphically using different shapes representing different program constructs and the lines connecting them show the flow of control. Most commonly used symbols for flowchart are shown in Fig. 1:

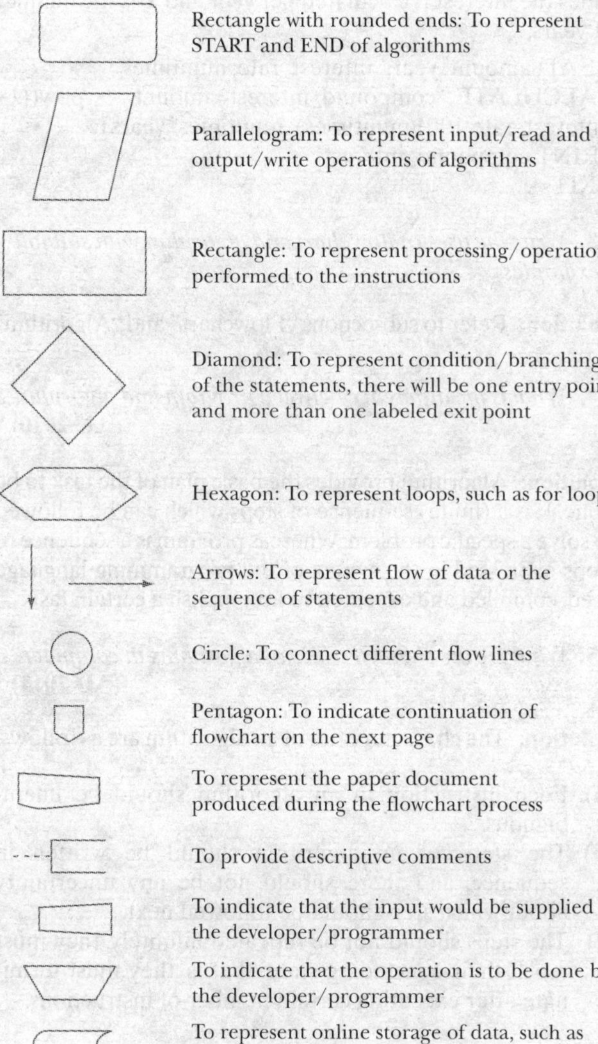

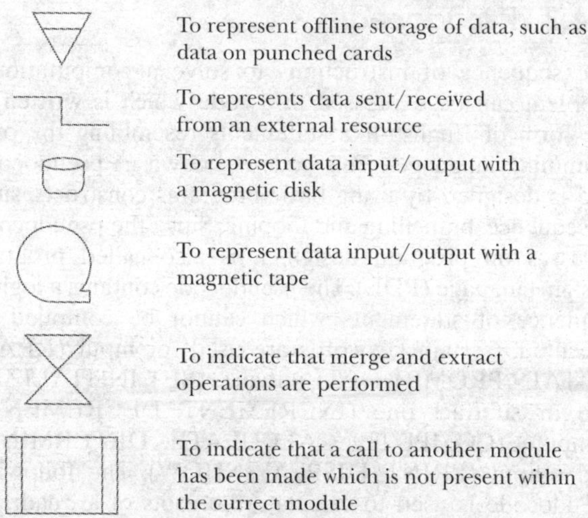

Figure 1 Flowchart symbols.

The characteristics of a flowchart are as follows:

1. The flowchart must have a clearly represented logical start and finish.
2. Since these are graphical representations of the code, they are better in communicating the logic of the statements, and easier to convert into a programming code.
3. The symbols and arrows are helpful in reducing the amount of errors, as well as detect the exact position where errors can take place.
4. However, for complex problems, the flowcharts need to be very extensive and it is cumbersome to design such extensive flowcharts.
5. Any update or modification in the statements would result in complete re-designing of the flowchart.

The flowchart corresponding to the algorithm for finding roots of quadratic equation $ax^2 + bx + c = 0$ is shown in Fig. 2:

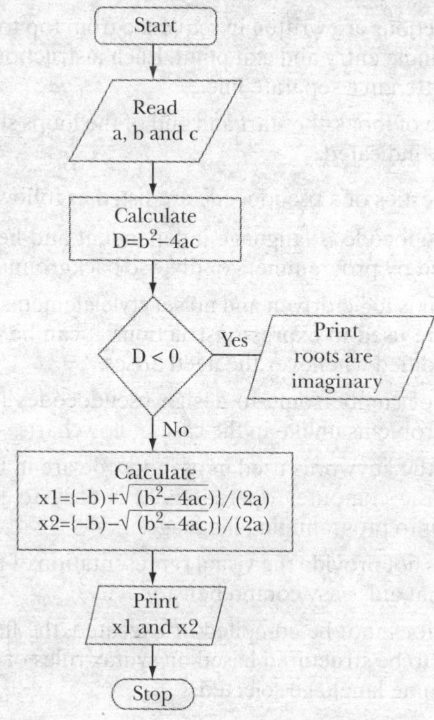

Figure 2 Flowchart for calculating roots of quadratic equation. **(AU 2013)**

2.4.3 Pseudocodes

The sequence of instructions to solve a computational problem can be expressed in a code which is written in the form of English-like statements resembling the programming languages. This code is known as pseudocode and is designed by using basic programs constructs, such as sequence, branching and looping. Since the pseudocode focusses on program design, it is also called program design language (PDL). The pseudocode contains a logical sequence of statements which cannot be compiled or executed. Certain keywords are used for input (READ, OBTAIN, PROMPT, GET), initialize (SET, INITIALIZE), add or subtract one (INCREMENT, DECREMENT), compute (COMPUTE, CALCULATE, DETERMINE) and output (PRINT, DISPLAY, SHOW). The following pseudocode is used to calculate the roots of a quadratic equation.

```
READ a, b and c
CALCULATE D=b²–4ac
CHECK if (D<0)
   PRINT "roots are imaginary"
   EXIT
Otherwise
CALCULATE roots x1 and x2 using the formula
   x1=(–b+√(b²– 4ac) )/(2a)
   x2=(–b–√(b²– 4ac) )/(2a)
PRINT roots x1 and x2
EXIT
```

The guidelines for writing a pseudocode are as follows:

1. The statements must be concise, program independent and in simple English.
2. Keywords such as READ, PRINT, etc. should be capitalized.
3. Instructions are written in sequence from top to bottom with single entry and exit point. Each instruction should be written in a separate line.
4. In case of loops, the start and end of the loops should be clearly indicated.

The properties of a pseudocode are listed as follows:

1. A pseudocode is language independent and hence can be used by programmers of diverse backgrounds.
2. Since it is logic-driven and no set style elements or symbols are used to express instructions, it can be updated or modified whenever the need arises.
3. It is not cumbersome to design pseudocodes for complex problems unlike in the case of flowcharts.
4. Since the keywords used in pseudocode are in line with the basic computer operations, it is easy to translate them into programming languages.
5. It does not provide the visual representation of the solution that aids easy comprehension.
6. Since it cannot be compiled or executed, the final code needs to be structured based on syntax rules of the programming language selected.

Solved Problems

1. *(a) What is pseudocode?* **(AU 2009, 2013)**

(b) What are the guidelines and benefits of pseudocode. **(AU 2013)**

(c) Write two characteristics of pseudocode. **(AU 2014)**

Solution:

(a) The sequence of instructions to solve a computational problem can be expressed in a code which is written in the form of English-like statements resembling the programming languages. This code is known as pseudocode and is designed by using basic programs constructs, such as sequence, branching and looping. The pseudocode contains a logical sequence of statements which cannot be compiled or executed.

(b), (c) refer to the section above.

2. *Write a pseudocode for calculating compound interest.* **(AU 2009)**

Solution: The formula for compound interest is $FV=P*(1 + r/n)^{Y*n}$ where FV is the future value, P is the present value (principal amount), r is the interest rate, n is the number of times the interest is calculated per year and Y is the number of years.

```
READ amount, years, interest_rate, numtimes
CALCULATE compound_interest=amount * pow((1+
(interest_rate/100)/numtimes), numtimes*years)
PRINT compound_interest
EXIT
```

3. *Write the uses of flowchart and algorithm with suitable examples.*

Solution: Refer to subsections "Flowchart" and "Algorithm".

4. *What is the difference between program and algorithm.* **(AU 2010)**

Solution: Algorithm provides the basic plan of the task to be done. It is a (finite) sequence of steps which can be followed to solve a specific problem. Whereas program is a sequence of steps expressed in the syntax of the programming language used, compiled and executed to accomplish a certain task.

5. *What are the characteristics of algorithms in computer?* **(AU 2011)**

Solution: The characteristics of an algorithm are as follows:

(a) Each instruction in an algorithm should be unambiguous.

(b) The steps of an algorithm should be written in sequence, and there should not be any uncertainty about which step should be followed next.

(c) The steps should not be repeated infinitely, they must reach their concluding state; that is, they must terminate after executing certain number of instructions.

(d) The algorithm must not be open-ended, and its description must be finite.

(e) The algorithm should be general enough to deal with any contingency.

6. *Explain guidelines for preparing flowcharts, benefits and limitation of flowcharts.* **(AU 2010)**

Solution: The guidelines for preparing flowchart are as follows:

(a) The flowchart should have a logical start and stop.

(b) Standard flowchart symbols should be used for input, output, decision, start, stop operations.

(c) Intersection of flow lines should be avoided to obtain a chart with better clarity.

(d) Connector symbols should be used in complex flowcharts to reduce the extensive nature of flowcharts.

The benefits of flowcharts are as follows: **(AU 2013)**

(a) As these are graphical representations of the code, they are better in communicating the logic of the statements, and are easier to convert into a programming code.

(b) The symbols and arrows are helpful in reducing the amount of errors, as well as detect the exact position where errors can take place.

The limitations are as follows:

(a) For complex problems, the flowcharts need to be very extensive and it is cumbersome to design such extensive flowcharts.

(b) Any update or modification in the statements would result in complete re-designing of the flowchart.

7. *Write an algorithm for finding sum and average of n numbers. Also state the properties of a good algorithm.* **(AU 2010)**

Solution: The algorithm for finding sum and average of *n* numbers is as follows:

1. Start
2. Read n, a1, a2, ..., an
3. Set sum=0
4. Set i=1
5. Calculate sum = sum + ai
6. Set i=i+1
7. Is i>n else goto Step 5
8. Calculate average=sum/n
9. Print sum and average
10. Stop

The properties of a good algorithm are as follows:

(a) Each and every instruction should be precise and unambiguous.

(b) All steps in the algorithm should be written in sequence.

(c) The language used in the instructions should be like English.

(d) The steps should not be repeated infinitely and the algorithm should terminate at some point.

(e) The desired result should be obtained from the algorithm as soon as it terminates.

8. *What is pseudocode? How does it differ from flowchart? Write a pseudocode to add up all the even numbers between 0 and 100 and print the result.* **(AU 2010)**

Solution: Refer Problem 1 for the first part.

The advantages of pseudocode over flowcharts are as follows:

(a) As it is logic-driven and no set style elements or symbols are used to express instructions, the pseudocode can be updated or modified whenever the need arises unlike flowcharts.

(b) It is not cumbersome to design pseudocodes for complex problems unlike flowcharts.

The pseudocode to add all the even numbers between 0 and 100 and print the result is as follows:

```
SET i=2
SET sum=0
LOOP
  sum+=i
  i+=2
UNTIL i<=100
PRINT sum
```

9. *Explain with diagram symbols used in flowchart and the basic design structures in flowchart.* **(AU 2011)**

Solution: Refer subsection "Flowcharts" and Fig. 1.

10. *Write the pseudocode to add two matrices.* **(AU 2012)**

Solution:

```
READ row, col
SET i=0, j=0
LOOP
  READ a[i][j], b[i][j]
  c[i][j]=a[i][j]+b[i][j]
  PRINT c[i][j]
  j=j+1
UNTIL j<col
  i=i+1
UNTIL i<row
```

11. *Write an algorithm to find the sum of the following series 1 + 5 + 9 + 13 + ... 20 terms.* **(AU 2008 Suppl.)**

Solution:

1. Start
2. Set sum=1 and n=1.
3. Check if (n<=20)

4. n=n+1
5. sum=sum+4
6. Goto Step 3
7. Print sum
8. Stop

12. *(a) Draw a flowchart to find the maximum among the three numbers.* **(AU 2009 Suppl., 2013)**

(b) Write an algorithm to find the maximum among the given three numbers. **(AU 2009 Suppl., 2013)**

Solution:

(a) The flow chart is:

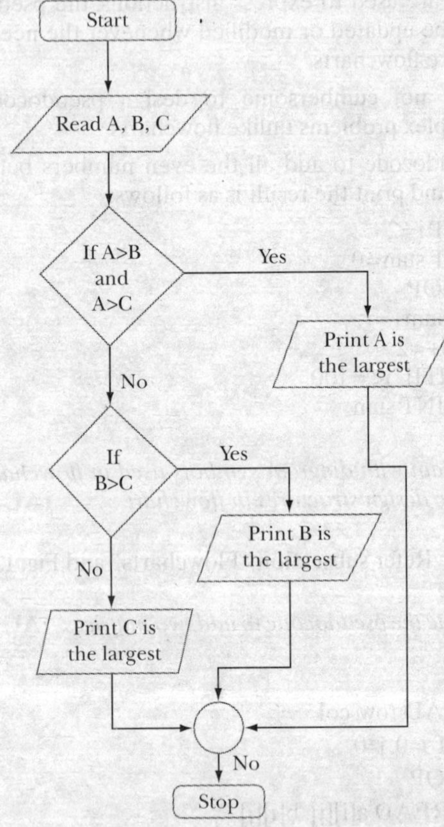

(b) The algorithm is as follows:

1. Start
2. Read three numbers x, y and z
3. If x > y and y > z goto step 6 else goto step 4
4. If y > z goto step 7 else goto step 5
5. Print z is the maximum among the three numbers and goto step 8
6. Print x is the maximum among the three numbers and goto step 8
7. Print y is the maximum among the three numbers and goto step 8
8. Stop

2.5 Program Control Structures

Once the set of instructions have been designed, some program statements need to be developed that drive the control of the entire program, that is, to determine the order in which the statements are to be executed, by evaluating the statements and executing them depending upon the result. These program statements are called control structures. There are three types of control structures: sequence, selection and repetition control structures.

2.5.1 | Sequence

In this control structure, the statements are written in the sequence they need to be executed in. For example, the following pseudocode shows how two numbers A and B are multiplied and their product is stored in the variable called Product, which is displayed.

```
READ A and B
CALCULATE Product=A*B
PRINT Product
EXIT
```

2.5.2 | Selection

In this control structure, options of branching or decision making are provided to the program, that is, it allows the program to choose between two or more alternate paths when it approaches the conditional statement. For example, the following flowchart is used to determine whether a given number is odd or even (Fig. 3).

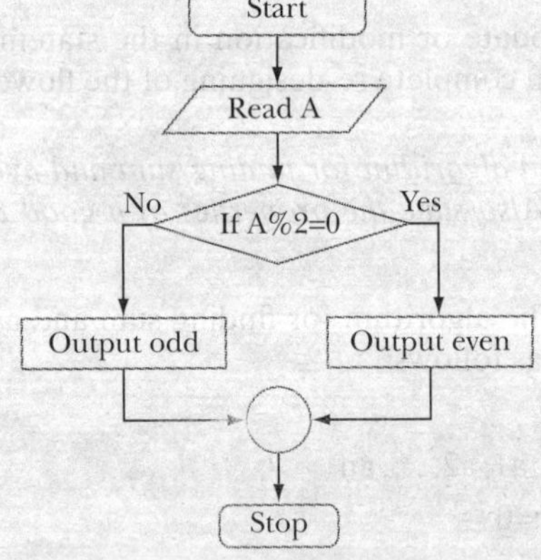

Figure 3 Flowchart to determine if number is odd or even.

In the figure, % is the modulus operator, which finds the remainder of the division of A by 2.

2.5.3 | Repetition (or Iteration)

In this control structure, an interruption is caused in the normal sequence of the code, and the user is redirected to a previous set of statements, thus forming a loop. With looping, the unnecessary repetition of statements is avoided, and the loop can be executed a defined number of times. For example, the following flowchart is used to find the factorial of a number (Fig. 4).

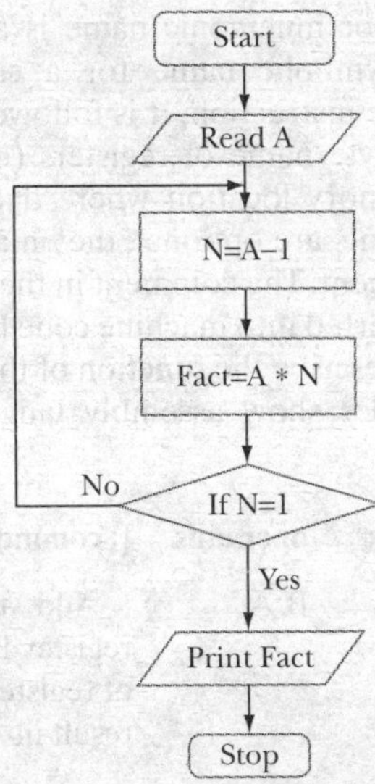

Figure 4 Flowchart to determine the factorial of a number. (AU 2008 Suppl.)

Solved Problem

1. *Explain sequence logic, selection logic and iteration logic design structure in pseudocode.* **(AU 2011)**

Solution:

(a) **Sequence logic:** The following pseudocode shows how two numbers A and B are multiplied and their product is stored in the variable called Product, which is displayed.

```
READ A and B
CALCULATE Product=A*B
PRINT Product
EXIT
```

(b) **Selection logic:** The following pseudocode is used to determine whether a given number is odd or even.

```
READ A
CHECK IF A%2=0
    PRINT "odd"
ELSE
    PRINT "even"
EXIT
```

(c) **Iteration logic:** The following pseudocode is used to find the factorial of a number.

```
READ A
SET N=A–1
LOOP
   CALCULATE Fact=A*N
   N=N–1
UNTIL N>1
PRINT Fact
EXIT
```

2.6 Evolution of Programming Languages

A number of programming languages have been developed over the past few decades to perform computational operations for scientific, engineering, mathematical and other applications. According to the history of development of programming languages, they are mainly classified into machine language, assembly language and high-level language (Fig. 5).

2.6.1 First Generation Languages (Machine Language)

The computer can be considered as a digital electronic device which can understand only two states of operations: on and off. The on state is represented by binary number 1 and off state is represented by binary number 0. Therefore, the first generation of programming language was based on the binary modes 0 and 1; and hence is called machine language. It is a low-level language and its instructions can be divided into two parts:

1. **Opcode:** It stands for operation code and it instructs the computer to perform a specific operation.
2. **Operand:** It specifies the location of the input or output in the memory, or the location from where the input is to be read or where output is to be kept.

Machine language is understood and program statements are directly processed by the computer because they are written in binary form of 0's and 1's. There is no need of any translator like compiler or assembler. The machine language is machine dependent because the instructions

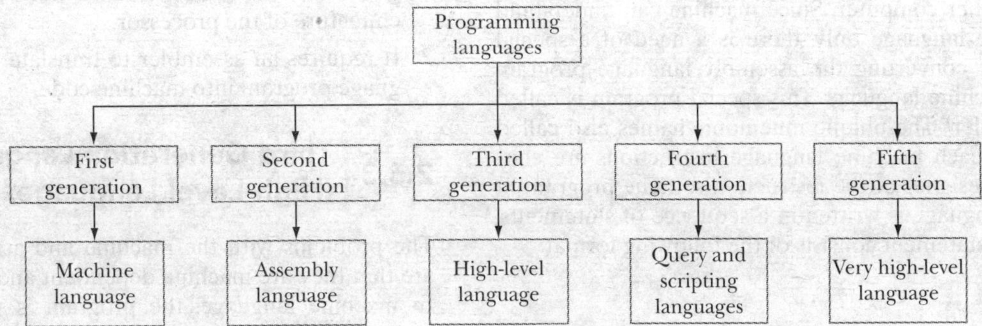

Figure 5 Categorization of programming languages.

are hardware dependent. So, different machine languages would be required for the computers with different versions of Pentium processors. Nowadays, machine language is rarely used because it requires a computer system hardware expert and lots of instructions.

2.6.1.1 Advantages of Machine language

1. The program is directly processed and does not require any translator.
2. Since the instructions are written in binary code (0s and 1s), they are processed at a high speed.

2.6.1.2 Disadvantages of Machine Language

1. It is difficult to understand and learn because instructions are written in binary code only.
2. It requires a hardware expert to write the program.
3. It is fast in execution, but writing a program is time-consuming and there is also possibility of many errors.
4. The language is machine dependent, so a code written for some task on one machine cannot be used for the same task on another machine, due to different hardware configuration.

2.6.2 Second Generation Languages (Assembly Language)

To overcome the problems associated with first generation (machine) language, the second generation of programming language was developed in 1950s. This is known as the assembly language. It is also a low-level programming language in which a unique name called mnemonic is assigned to the each machine language instruction, so that instructions became easier to remember. The mnemonic name is generally a three-character abbreviated name for the binary-coded instruction, which itself describes the function of the instruction. For example, the mnemonic name ADD describes that it performs addition; MOV is responsible for moving the data from one memory location to another; MUL performs multiplication; etc.

Instructions in assembly language are generally very simple. They are easier to remember because instead of remembering the sequence of 0s and 1s of machine language instruction, it is simpler to remember the mnemonic name. However, the instructions are still machine dependent, that is, the instructions are system hardware specific. Thus, the instructions developed for one computer may not run on another computer. Since machine can understand the machine language only, there is a need of a special program for converting the assembly language program into the machine language. This special program is called the "assembler". The unique mnemonic names also called opcode for each machine language instructions are chosen by the designer of the instruction set. The program in assembly language is written in a sequence of statements, where each statement consists of the following format:

Syntax

```
[label]     opcode/mnemonic     operand/data
section     [; comments]
```

The opcode or mnemonic name is a three-character long (usually) symbolic name for a single executable machine language instruction. It is followed by the zero or more than one byte name of registers (operands) or the addresses of memory location where data is stored. The label and comments are optional; they may or may not be used in the statement. The comment in the statement is not executed or converted into machine code by the assembler; it is just used to describe the function of the statement. The following examples show assembly language codes and their description.

[Label]	opcode	operands	[; comments]
Start	ADD	B, A	; Add the content of register B to the content of register A, and put the result in A

[Label]	opcode	operands	[; comments]
	MOV	BC, 45h	; Move the hexadecimal number 45 into the register named "BC"

[Label]	opcode	operands	[; comments]
	MOV	B, C	; Move the content of register C into the register B

[Label]	opcode	operands	[; comments]
	CMP	B, 0	; Compare content of register B with 0

2.6.2.1 Advantages of Assembly Language

1. Each instruction has a unique mnemonic name, which is easier to understand, remember and use.
2. Probability of errors is reduced compared to machine language.
3. It is reliable and has minimal overhead compared to machine language.
4. The program is processed quickly because each opcode is directly translated into a single machine code.

2.6.2.2 Disadvantages of Assembly Language

1. It is machine dependent because the mnemonics are given by the designer of instruction set based on the architecture of the processor.
2. It requires an assembler to translate the assembly language program into machine code.

2.6.3 Third Generation Languages (High-Level Language, 3GLs)

The problems with the machine and assembly languages are that they are machine dependent and difficult to learn. In machine language, the program is written in binary code whereas in assembly language the program is written using symbolic mnemonics which are again dependent on the computer's architecture. Therefore, a need for a more natural and easy-to-understand language was felt. This led scientists and developers to develop high-level language, which is also said to be the third generation language.

The instructions of the high-level language are words/phrases in English so, program writing in this language is easier for the programmer. This language is also portable, that is, the program written in high-level language can be executed on any computer with no change in coding or with small changes. This allows the programmer to concentrate on the development of the programs, rather than on the architecture of the computer. The different 3GLs have their own syntax, but they are similar to English phrases; therefore they can easily be learnt and used.

Since the program written in high-level languages cannot be understood by the computer, a translator is required that converts the program into the machine language. This translator is called compiler. A single statement of high-level language corresponds to the many machine and assembly language instructions. There may be various mathematical, relational, logical, etc., operators used with the instruction of high-level language. For example, instead of writing ADD, a more familiar + symbol is used. There are many third generation languages developed over the past few years such as Pascal, FORTRAN (FORmula TRANslation), COBOL (COmmon Business Oriented Language), Ada, C, C++, JAVA, etc.

2.6.3.1 Advantages of High-Level Language

1. The instructions of the high-level languages are similar to English words/phrases; therefore, the user can write the program easily and use the computer more efficiently.
2. The user does not need to know the hardware details before writing the program in high-level language.
3. Writing a program using high-level language requires less time and it is easy to maintain.
4. The high-level language program developed on one machine can be easily executed on another machine with the required translator without any difficulty.

2.6.3.2 Disadvantages of High-Level Language

1. The high-level language requires a compiler to translate the high-level language program into machine code.
2. It requires more memory.
3. It is not domain specific.

2.6.4 Fourth Generation Languages (4GLs)

The programmers working on third generation languages are required to specify not only what is to be done but also the procedure to complete the task. The procedure consists of sequence of instructions to be executed in certain order. Therefore, the third generation languages are also said to be procedure-oriented languages. The third generation languages are not domain specific and it requires the trained programmers to work on it. The 4th Generation Language (4GL) are domain specific, which allows us to specify only what is to be done without specifying how it is to be done. Therefore, the 4GLs are also said to be non-procedural languages. For example in structured query language (SQL), we need to specify the attributes and the conditions to be satisfied without specifying how to interact with the actual database. Therefore, the programmer with a limited programming ability can also develop applications using 4GLs. Generally, the 4GLs are used to solve problems from other applications. Some examples of 4GLs are: SQL, Progress 4GL, Ingres 4GL, Focus, Fox-Pro, Power Builder, Metafont, IDL-PV, APL, CSP, Mathematica, Iris, AVS. The 4GLs with specific application domain are listed in Table 1.

TABLE 1

The 4GLs with Specific Application Domain

Domain	4GLs
Relational database query	SQL, Progress 4GL, Ingres 4GL, Focus
General use	Fox-Pro, IBM-Rational Enterprise Generation Language, Power Builder
Report generation	Report Builder, Oracle Reports, report program generator (RPG), NATURAL
Database manipulation	Procedural language/structured query language (PL/SQL), ABAP, FOCUS, IDL, MATLAB
Web development	Wave Maker
Data management	Statistical analysis system (SAS), (statistics and data) stata and statistical product and service solutions (SPSS), etc.

The programming in 3GL is slow, time consuming and error prone. The 4GLs are designed to reduce these drawbacks of 3GL. Also, the 4GLs are user friendly, easy to use and reduce the cost of the software development.

2.6.5 Fifth Generation Languages (Very High Level Languages)

These languages exist only in theory based on what can be predicted for the near future. It is predicted that these languages would be able to process natural or native languages of the users. Through developments in artificial intelligence and other technological advances, it would be possible to pass a set of instructions to the computer directly without the need of any programming languages. However, there has not been any concrete understanding regarding these languages, and many products are still in developmental phase. Some of the products based on this category of languages are Siri in IPhone 4S.

Solved Problem

1. *Write notes on high-level languages and low-level languages.* **(AU 2007 Suppl.)**

Solution: Refer to the subsections fifth generation and first generation languages.

2.7 Program Methodology

Programming methodology deals with the analysis, design and implementation of programs. There are two ways of designing a program (algorithm) in software development process: Top-down and bottom-up.

These two approaches play a key role in the software development process. Although the top-down and bottom-up designs are two different methodologies of the program design, the real-world software design approaches usually implement a combination of the two. This is because both of them define the system by describing all of the interaction between the procedures.

2.7.1 | Top-Down Approach

Top-down approach is a method of program design that leads from generalization to specialization. This design essentially starts with the description of the overall system and then breaks it down into subsystems. Each subsystem is again broken down into more subsystems until we reach to the refined subsystem, which cannot be broken down further. Top-down approach consists of a hierarchical structure which contains the description of the subsystem at each lower level. The hierarchical or tree-like structure is shown in Fig. 6.

The top level of the hierarchical structure contains the description of the overall system and each sublevel consists of a system module. The top–down approach starts with a specification and definition of the main procedure (i.e., the complex piece of the main program) which are then recursively divided into successively smaller pieces of subprograms (Fig. 6).

The main program consists of all the major functions and the subprogram consists of the requirement of all these functions, and this process is repeated. The top-down approach supports the modular design of program design by separating the lower levels from the higher levels. This makes the software design easy and less time consuming, because each module may be prepared by different persons and the errors can be easily identified. The top-down approach is preferred by software designers because of the above-mentioned reasons; and it is also not necessary to define the lower level design in advance as required by the bottom-up approach. However, the use of top-down approach requires the designer or the system analyst to have the detailed understanding of the system. Top-down approach is usually possible only when one programmer has a clear idea of the problem and the method to solve it.

2.7.2 | Bottom-Up Approach

The bottom-up approach is a reversal of the top-down approach. In this approach, the design of the program starts with the description of the lowest level procedures, and then moves up towards more and more complex procedures using these already defined low level procedures. Hence this approach starts with the specific details and moves up to the general details. This design methodology continues until all levels of the system are connected in a hierarchical structure to form the entire system.

2.8 Programming Models

One style of program writing may not be efficient for all kinds of applications. For instance, the programming style for business data processing may be different from the programming style for engineering applications. For example, the object-oriented programming (OOP) style may be suited for any real-world application and the logical style is suitable for program logic inference. Therefore, there must be different programming models (paradigms) for different application domains. The major programming models are procedural or imperative, object-oriented, functional and logical. A computer programmer should be aware of all the programming style so that the model can be selected according to the application domain before developing the program. These have different scope of applicability. The different programming models are discussed as follows.

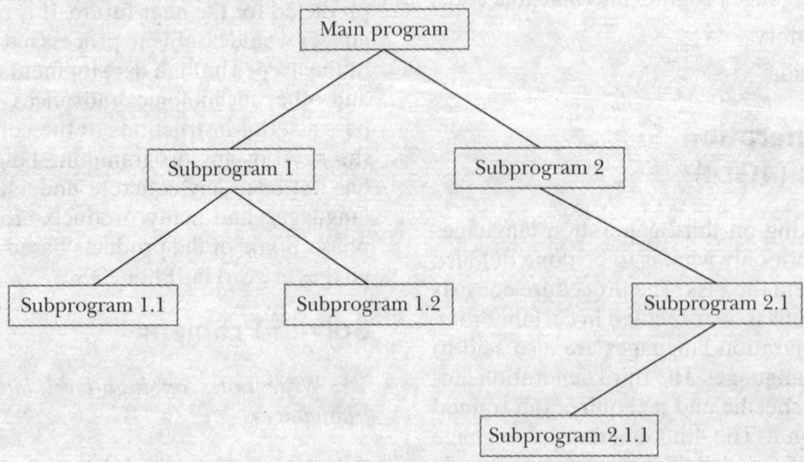

Figure 6 Schematic diagram of top-down approach.

2.8.1 | Unstructured Programming

This type of programming is also called functional and declarative (logic) programming style. In this model, the program is written as a collection of formulas, which are predefined for computing a value. The formulas are mutually related to each other. The most popular functional language is LISP (LISt Programming). The formulas take some inputs and generate the outputs. Hence in functional programming paradigm, the instructions are issued in the form of formulas with specified input arguments, which are executed to generate the output.

The declarative language is a symbolic language that uses some facts, rules (usually called as axioms) and principle of logical reasoning to prove the theorem. In other words, we can say that based on the given statements which are assumed to be true and known as facts and using the rule of logical reasoning, the new statements are deduced. So the inference rules are used and deduced to prove the theorem. Prolog (programming logic) is the most popular declarative/logic language.

Both the functional and declarative languages are domain-specific. The functional programming is used for symbolic processing of the knowledge; and logic programming is used for the inference mechanism in deductive databases. Both the languages are usually recursive, interpretive and find applications in various areas such as artificial intelligence expert systems and natural language processing.

2.8.2 | Structured Programming

2.8.2.1 Procedural Programming Model

The procedural programming model is the oldest programming paradigm which follows the top-down design approach. This is also known as imperative paradigm. In this approach, the focus is on the processing so algorithms are needed to perform the desired computation. The main function calls other functions or procedures by passing the required data to the function or procedure. In procedure-oriented languages, the emphasis is on doing the things or we can say the emphasis is on the action. The data on which the action is taken or performed is of least importance. These languages have been an avid choice for the programmers because the large program is divided into a number of small subprogram using functions, so that the handling of such programs is easy. They are also suitable for scientific applications development because there are many built-in scientific functions, such as log, cos, sin, etc.

In this approach, we have a single program (normally a main function), which itself is divided into small pieces called procedures or functions to perform specific tasks as shown in Fig. 7. The main program consists of a sequence of instructions and procedure/function calls. These functions consist of sequence of instruction that perform some specific tasks with clearly defined interfaces to interact with the other functions. Each statement in the function tells the computer to do something, that is, get some input, perform some operation or display the output. Even when we use a simple mathematical operator (*, +, –, /), a call

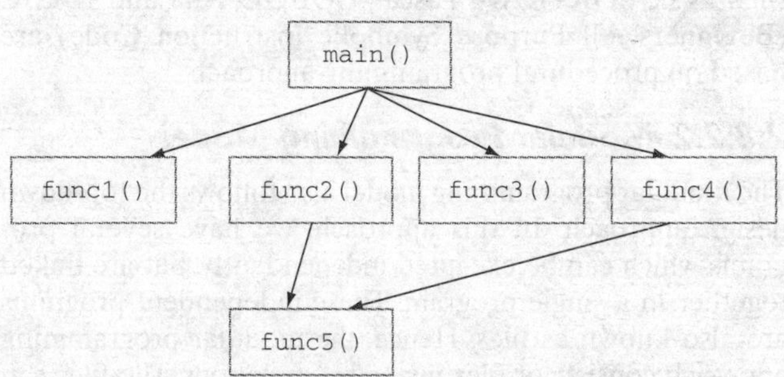

Figure 7 Procedure-oriented programming approach.

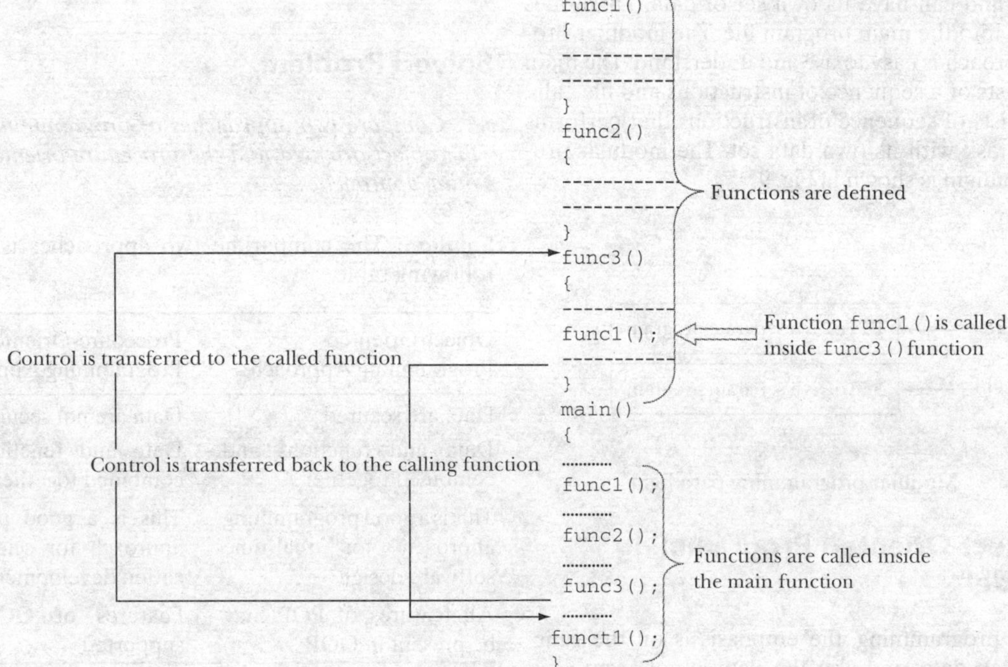

Figure 8 Transfer of control across the functions inside the program.

is made to an already written procedure corresponding to the operator to perform the specific operation. Hence, a procedural program consists of many procedures designed to perform some specific task. When these procedures are called, the control is transferred to the called procedure and it is executed. After finishing the execution, the control comes back to the called procedure as shown in Fig. 8.

However, there are various shortcomings to these languages also. As the programs grow larger and more complex, this approach begin to show signs of strain and fails to give the desired results in terms of bug-free and reusable programs. Another problem with this approach is that the data defined inside the function (local) or procedure cannot be accessed from outside the function. To make the data accessible to all the functions, they are declared outside all the functions (globally) so that any function can manipulate the data. As many functions access the same data, the important data may be lost anytime. Several functions can access the data; therefore, the way data is arranged or organized is very crucial, the arrangement of data cannot be changed without modifying all the functions that access it. Hence, in the procedure-oriented programming (POP), the procedures/programs are said to be active agents and the data are said to be passive agents. Programming languages such as C, FORTRAN, Pascal, COBOL, Ada and BASIC (Beginners All Purpose Symbolic Instruction Code) are based on procedural programming approach.

2.8.2.2 Modular Programming Model

The modular programming model also follows the top-down design approach. In this approach, we have several programs which can be executed independently, but are linked together in a single program. These independent programs are also known as files. Hence, the modular programming approach consists of files instead of functions. The files can be executed independently, but functions cannot be executed independently. We can say that one program is a collection of many programs linked together. Each file can perform the specified task and can have its own set of data. These files are integrated into the main program file. The modular programming approach is easy to use and understand. The main program consists of a sequence of instructions and file calls. Each file consists of sequence of instructions that performs some specific task with its own data set. The modular programming paradigm is shown in Fig. 9.

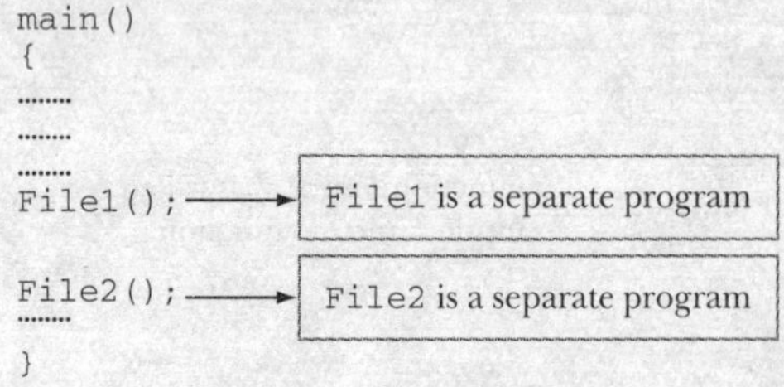

Figure 9 Modular programming paradigm.

2.8.3 Object-Oriented Programming Model

In procedural programming, the emphasis is on the functions rather than data, and also the data is not secured in this approach. The object-oriented programming approach (OOP) eliminates these weaknesses of procedure-oriented programming (POP) approach by combining the data and the function that work on it into a single unit called class. So the data is secured from the outside world because data can be changed by the associated function only.

OOP is implemented on the real-world entities called objects that have some characteristics and behavior (Fig. 10). For example, a box that has some color, price (characteristics) may be empty or filled (behavior) with the candies. These objects form the basic units of construction of object-oriented programs. An object comprises both passive data and active function. The data describes the state, and function describes the behavior of the object. Objects are independent of each other and they communicate with each other by asking for services provided by other objects, rather than sharing as in case of procedural programming.

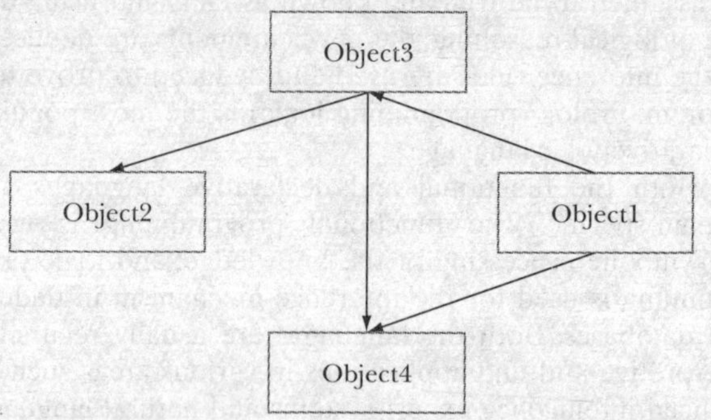

Figure 10 Object-oriented programming approach.

The class is a collection of objects with the same structure and behavior. Objects communicate with each other by passing messages which may be interpreted as a procedure or a function. OOP follows the bottom-up design concept. The terms that are commonly associated with OOP are class, object, encapsulation, data abstraction, inheritance, polymorphism and data hiding. Some of the languages that support OOP features include C++, Smalltalk, Java and Ada.

Solved Problem

1. *Compare two approaches of programming languages, the object-oriented and the procedure-oriented programming approaches.*

Solution: The compari.he two approaches is given in the following table.

Object-Oriented Programming Approach	Procedure-Oriented Programming Approach
Data are secured	Data are not secured
Data and functions and combined together	Data and functions are not combined together
This is a good programming approach for real-time software design	This is a good programming approach for scientific application development
All features of POP may be present in OOP	Features of OOP are not supported

(Continued)

Object-Oriented Programming Approach	Procedure-Oriented Programming Approach
We can define an abstract data type which describes all objects of a class	We cannot define an abstract data type
We can define an abstract data type which describes all objects of a class	Many functions can access the same data
Bottom-up design concept is followed	Top-down design concept is followed
Objects are created and communication is done by sending messages to them.	Communication is done by parameters and return values
Objects exchange *messages* with each other.	*Data* are exchanged between *procedures* under control of a main program.

(*Continued*)

POINTS TO REMEMBER

1. **Program** is defined as the set of instructions written in a proper syntax and in a certain order to perform some specific task.
2. **Logical analysis** through **algorithms, flowcharts** and **pseudocodes**

	Algorithm	Flowchart	Pseudocode
Definition	It defined as a sequence of instructions in English-like language used to solve a computational problem.	It is a pictorial and a very structured representation of the algorithm.	It is a sequence of instructions to solve a computational problem expressed in a code which is written in the form of English-like statements resembling the programming languages.
Guidelines	(a) Precise and unambiguous instructions. (b) Steps in sequence. (c) English-like language. (d) Steps should not be repeated infinitely and the algorithm should terminate to give the desired result. (e) General enough to deal with any contingency	(a) The flowchart should have a logical start and stop. (b) Standard flowchart symbols should be used for input, output, decision, start, stop operations. (c) Intersection of flow lines should be avoided to obtain a chart with better clarity. (d) Connector symbols should be used in complex flowcharts to reduce the extensive nature of flowcharts.	(a) One statement per line. (b) English-like language. (c) Capitalize initial keywords (d) Steps in sequence. (e) Indent to show loop/structure (f) End structure and then the pseudocode.
Advantages	(a) Explicit instructions in a form understandable by any person with or without programming knowledge can understand. (b) Basic instructions which can be expressed in various forms such as flowcharts and pseudocodes.	(a) Graphical representations of the code, they are better in communicating the logic of the statements, and easier to convert into a programming code. (b) Symbols and arrows are helpful in reducing the amount of errors, as well as detecting the exact position where errors can take place.	(a) It is language independent, can be used by programmers of diverse backgrounds. (b) Since it is logic-driven and no set style elements or symbols are used to express instructions, it can be updated or modified whenever the need arises. (c) It is not cumbersome to design pseudocodes for complex problems unlike in the case of flowcharts. (d) Since the keywords used in pseudocode are in line with the basic computer operations, it is easy to translate them into programming languages.
Disadvantages	Algorithms cannot be as such used by programmers, They need to be made more effective by converting them into flowcharts and pseudocodes.	(a) For complex problems, the flowcharts need to be very extensive and it is cumbersome to design such extensive flowcharts. (b) Any update or modification in the statements would result in complete re-designing of the flowchart.	(a) It does not provide the visual representation of the solution that aids easy comprehension. (b) Since it cannot be compiled or executed, the final code needs to be structured based on syntax rules of the programming language selected.

3. **Program control structures:** Program statements need to be developed that drive the control of the entire program, that is, to determine the order in which the statements are to be executed, by evaluating the statements and executing them depending upon the result. These are of three types – **sequence**, **selection** and **repetition** control structures.
4. **Evolution of programming languages:** Five categories are first generation languages (**machine language**), second generation languages (**assembly language**), third generation languages (**high-level language**), fourth generation languages (**4GLs**) and fifth generation languages (**very high level language**)
5. **Program methodology:** It deals with the analysis, design and implementation of programs. There are two ways of designing a program (algorithm) in software development process.
   - **Top-down approach** is a method of program design that leads from generalization to specialization. This design essentially starts with the description of the overall system and then breaks it down into subsystems.
   - **Bottom-up approach** is a reversal of the top-down approach. In this approach, the design methodology starts with the description of the lowest level procedures, and then moves up towards more and more complex procedures using the low level procedures which are already defined. Hence this approach starts with the specific details and moves up to the general details.
6. **Programming models**
   - **Unstructured programming:** the program is written as a collection of formulas, which are predefined for computing a value.
   - **Structured programming:** These are of three types
     (a) *Procedural programming models*: In this approach, a single program (normally a main function), which itself is divided into small pieces called procedures or functions to perform specific tasks.
     (b) *Modular programming models*: In this approach, we have several programs which can be executed independently, but are linked together in a single program.
     (c) *Object-oriented programming models*: In this approach, we combine data and the function that work on them into a single unit called class. So the data is secured from the outside world because data can be changed by the associated function only.

REVIEW QUESTIONS

1. Define program.
2. Define algorithm. How can you measure the quality of algorithm?
3. What is a flowchart? What is need for flowchart symbols?
4. What is pseudocode? Explain how it can be designed and its benefits and limitations.
5. Describe briefly about flowchart and its types.
6. (a) Describe briefly about the advantages of flowcharts.
   (b) Describe pseudocode with its advantages and disadvantages. (AU 2009 Suppl.)
   (c) Enlist the advantages of algorithm. (AU 2012)
7. Write down steps involved in writing a program to solve a problem. (AU 2010)
8. List the general characteristics of writing pseudocode. (AU 2009)
9. Give examples each for first, second, third and fourth generation languages.
10. What are the different program design techniques? Which one is preferred by the software engineers and why?
11. What are the differences between top-down and bottom-up program designs?
12. Distinguish between machine language and assembly language.

PROGRAMMING ASSIGNMENTS

1. Write an algorithm to compute the factorial of a number n. (AU 2012)
2. Draw a flowchart to find the highest marks in a set of a marks. (AU 2012)
3. What are the essential properties of an algorithm? Develop an algorithm Fibonacci series upto 100. (AU 2007 Suppl.)
4. Draw a flowchart to find the sum of first n natural numbers. (AU 2008 Suppl.)
5. Draw a flowchart to find a factorial of a given number. (AU 2008 Suppl.)
6. Draw a flowchart to compute the salary of an employee in a company. Assume that there are two types of employees in the company: daily wages and regular. Salary is calculated as the number of hours worked (wages per hour for daily wagers and basic pa+ (%DA + basic pay)/100 + HRA + medical allowance for regular employees. Sketch the flow of your design for a regular employee with basic pay = 5000, % of DA = 75% and HRA = 500. (AU 2010)
7. Draw a flowchart to multiply two matrices. (AU 2009)
8. Write the pseudocode to multiply two matrices. (AU 2009)
9. What is an algorithm? Write an algorithm to print even numbers from 2 to 100. (AU 2009)
10. Write an algorithm to find the maximum among the given three numbers. Draw a flowchart for your algorithm. (AU 2009 Suppl.)

C Programming Basics 3

LEARNING OBJECTIVES

After completing this chapter, you would be able to understand the following:

- Overview of C with C Character Set, identifiers, keywords.
- Various types of constants, variables and data types used in C.
- Operators, their properties, types and precedence.
- Formatted and unformatted input and output functions.
- Structure of the C program.
- Statements used in C – decision-making, branching and looping statements.

3.1 Introduction

The C programming language was developed by Dennis Ritchie and Brian Kernigan at AT&T Bell laboratories in 1972. It has the following features:

1. It has a combination of the virtues of high-level and structured programming languages and the functionality of assembly languages.
2. It is suitable for use in application as well as system software and is portable across various platforms.
3. It is efficient, fast, reliable and highly portable, and can run under various operating systems such as MS DOS, UNIX, etc. C compiler is required to compile the C programs and generate the desired output.
4. It is a modular and structured programming language like FORTRAN and PASCAL and unlike the older unstructured languages such as BASIC and COBOL, in which a problem can be broken into several tasks that are dealt with in separate function blocks or modules. In the final program, all these modules are linked together to produce the solution.
5. It supports user-defined data types, which enables greater flexibility in programming.
6. It enables dynamic memory allocation by creating a reference variable for any data type. This reference variable is called pointer and it stores the data value as well as the memory address of the variable. Programmers can access these memory addresses directly and carry out bit-level manipulation of the data stored in those addresses. This eliminates the need to make multiple copies of the same data, and hence reduces the amount of memory allocated to store each copy separately.

The applications of C are as follows: C programming language finds use in business as well as scientific/academic fields, since it provides various types of operators, control statements for solving different types of problem sets, allows manipulation of data at the lowest level (bit), etc. C is used in system software such as operating systems, compilers, interpreters, etc. and in application software such as verification software, test code, simulators, etc.

Solved Problem

1. *What are the main features and applications of C language?* **(AU 2011)**

Solution: Refer to the section above.

3.2 C Character Set and Tokens

The **C Character Set** is a set of valid characters (93 characters) that the language can recognize. All characters other than letters (alphabets) and numerals are treated as special characters. In C, the uppercase and lowercase letters are distinct so it is case sensitive; and hence there are 52 letters (26 lowercase and 26 uppercase) in all. It consists of the following:

1. **Letters (alphabets):** Lowercase a…z (26 characters), uppercase A…Z (26 characters).
2. **Digits:** 0…9 (10 characters).
3. **Special characters:** ~ (tilde)` ! @ # $ % ^ & * ( ) _ (underscore) – + = | \ { } [ ] : ; " ' <> , . ? / (31 characters).
4. **White spaces:** Blank space (\b), horizontal space (\t), carraige return (\r), new line (\n), form feed (\f).

The small individual units that make up the C program are called **tokens**. These are identifiers, keywords, constants (integer, floating point, character and string constants), operators and other symbols as discussed in the following subsections.

3.2.1 | Identifiers

Identifier is the fundamental building block of a program and is a combination of permissible characters. In other words, identifier is a name given to different parts of the program such as variables, functions, arrays, etc. There are certain rules to name an identifier:

1. An identifier name can have alphabetic letters, digits and underscores.
2. An identifier name cannot start with a digit.
3. A declared keyword or reserve word cannot be used as a variable name.
4. There is no set maximum length for an identifier.

Valid examples are city, age, basic-pay, mark, num1, num2, etc.
Invalid identifiers are basic pay, 1 price, $ amount, break, etc.

3.2.2 | Keywords

There are some identifiers in C which have predefined meaning to the compiler. These identifiers are called keywords. We cannot use the keyword as a variable name and it is mandatory that all the keywords should be in lowercase letters. The C keywords are listed in Table 1.

Out of these keywords, auto, register, static, extern, const, volatile, signed, unsigned, short and long are called qualifiers. These standard qualifiers change the meaning of certain aspects of data type declaration, such as lifetime (auto, register, static, extern); modifiability (const, volatile); sign (signed, unsigned); size (short, long).

TABLE 1

C Keywords

auto	break	case	char	class	const
continue	default	delete	do	double	else
enum	extern	float	for	goto	if
int	long	register	return	short	signed
sizeof	static	struct	switch	typedef	union
unsigned	virtual	void	volatile	while	

3.2.3 | Constants

Constants are the fixed data values that do not change their values during the execution of a program. These are also called literals. A constant must be initialized at the time of declaration. C allows many types of constants which are discussed next. The types of constants are as shown below:

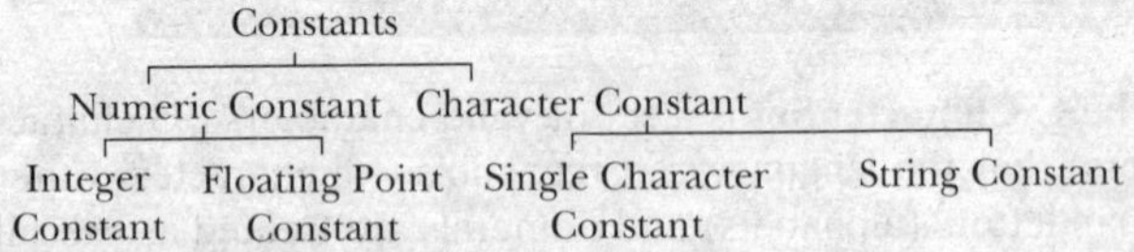

- Constants
  - Numeric Constant
    - Integer Constant
    - Floating Point Constant
  - Character Constant
    - Single Character Constant
    - String Constant

3.2.3.1 Integer Constants

Integer constants are whole numbers without any decimal part. These can be positive or negative. These require 2 to 4 bytes of memory. C allows three types of integer constants:

1. **Decimal integer constants:** It is a number without decimal point and it should not begin with 0 (zero). For example, 0, +47, –179, 22009 are a decimal integer constant.
2. **Octal integer constants:** It begins with leading 0 (zero). For example, 0, 047, 0174, 0240 is an octal integer constant.
3. **Hexadecimal integer constants:** It begins with leading 0x (uppercase or lowercase). For example, 0x12 is a hexadecimal integer constant.

For instance, the decimal integer constant 16 has the corresponding octal and hexadecimal constants as 020 and 0x10, respectively.

3.2.3.2 Floating Point Constants

Floating point numbers contain decimal point. They are the real numbers in mathematics. Also, as integers, these numbers can be positive or negative. For example `-0.96, 179.42` is a floating point constant. In case the real number is in exponential form, it is expressed as mantissa and exponent, with the letter "e" (or "E") separating the two. The mantissa can be a floating point number or integer but the exponent should be an integer. For example, `3.18E4, 12e-2.`

3.2.3.3 Character and String Constants

One or more characters enclosed within single quotes (e.g., 's') form a character constant. The single quote is not part of the characters. So to represent a single character constant, we must use single quotes and to represent a string, we must use double quotes. Hence, 'a' and "a" are different. The first one is a character constant, and the second one is a string (collection of two characters – a and null) terminated by null character. Every character is assigned a numeric value called an ASCII (American standard code for information interchange) value. String constants automatically end with a null character "\0". A single space, word or a group of words between the double quotes is a C string constant. The double quote is never considered as a part of the string constant.

String constants: One or more characters enclosed within double quotes (e.g., "s") form a string constant. To represent a string, we must use double quotes. Hence, 'a' and "a" are different. The first one is a character constant, and the second one is a string (collection of two characters – a and null) terminated by null character. String constants automatically end with a null character "\0". A single space, word or a group of words between the double quotes is a C string constant. The double quote is never considered as a part of the string constant

3.2.3.4 Symbolic Constants

These constants are similar to variables in terms of definition, but once initialized, their values cannot change. The following keywords are used to define symbolic constants:

1. **#define:** It is preprocessor directive for defining symbolic constants. For example, `#define sum 10;`
2. **const:** Using the const keyword, symbolic constants can be defined. For example, `cons tint sum = 10;`
3. **enum:** Using enum keyword a constant of user defined data type can be defined. For example, `enum (x, y, z);` where x = 0, y = 1 and z = 2.

3.2.4 | Variables

A variable is an identifier whose value changes during the execution of the program. In other words, we can say that variable is a name given to some part of memory location. Variable names are unique and follow the same rules for naming as for identifiers.

1. A variable name has a fixed length of 1 to 31 characters as per ANSI standard.
2. The variable should not be a keyword in C (given in Table 1).
3. The first character of a variable should always be an alphabet.
4. Special characters except _ (underscore) cannot be part of the variable name.
5. The variable name can have a combination of lowercase and uppercase alphabets, but are case sensitive; that is, name and Name are treated as different variables.

Examples include `total, num5, total_amt.`

3.2.4.1 Declaration and Initialization of Variables

All variables used in a C program must be declared in the beginning of the program before they are used. This declaration prepares the compiler to recognize the variable name and allocate memory depending upon data type of the variable. The values stored in the variables undergo changes during the execution of the program. A variable can be declared anywhere in the C program. Before its first reference, a variable is declared as follows:

Syntax

```
Specifiers data_type variable_name;
```

For example, `int sample;`
Here the variable name sample can hold whole numbers (integers) only. To declare signed or unsigned variable, place these modifiers before the data types as

```
signed int sample;
```

Variables can be assigned values or initialized in the declaration statement itself, or they can be assigned separately. For example,

```
int age = 6;
```

or

```
int age;
age=6;
```

Another method of initializing variables is called dynamic initialization in which the variables are assigned values at run time. For example,

```
void main()
{
int r = 4;
float area_sphere=(4/3)*(22/7)*r*r'
printf("Area of sphere=%f",area_sphere);
}
```

Here the expression of area_sphere is evaluated and the value is assigned to area_sphere at run time.
There are different types of variables:

1. **Global variables:** These are declared outside all functions (including the main() function), and are globally available to all functions, that is, can be used anywhere in the program.
2. **Local variables:** These are declared within a function block and are available for use in that function block only, and not anywhere else.
3. **Constant variable:** For a variable to remain unchanged during the course of the program, it is declared as constant using the keyword const. For example,
   `const int a=5;`
4. **Volatile variables:** These variables can be changed anytime during the program or by any other external program. For example,
   `volatile int a;`

3.2.5 Data Types

C supports various types of data that can be held by variables (Fig. 1). These are classified into three categories: (a) Built-in, (b) derived and (c) user-defined data types.

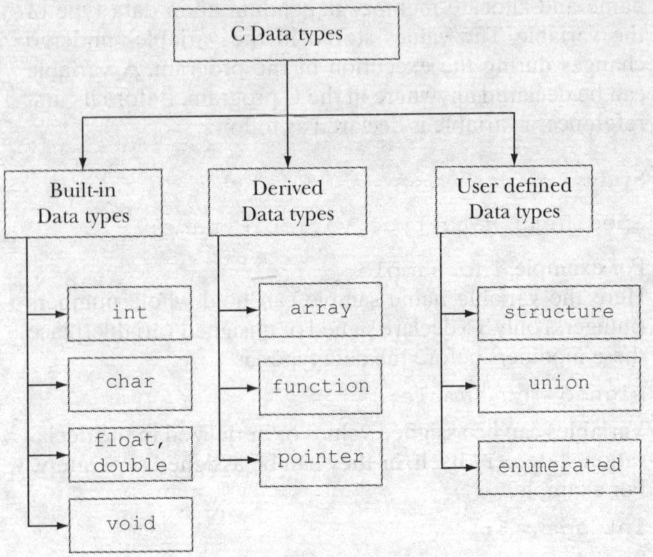

Figure 1 Data types in C.

3.2.5.1 Built-in Data Types

There are four types of built-in data types: (a) int stores the whole numbers, (b) float stores the decimal values, (c) char stores character values and (d) void. Except the void data type, all other built-in data types may have several modifiers such as signed, unsigned, long and short. The modifier short may be applied to integer and character data types and long can also be applied to double data type. Table 2 shows the size, range and format specifiers (used to print the formatted output onto the screen) for char, int, float and double data types with modifiers.

The "void" data type is generally used for the following purposes:

1. It specifies the return type of a function when the function is not returning any value.
2. It indicates an empty parameter list to a function when no arguments are passed.
3. A void pointer can be assigned a pointer value of any basic data type.

3.2.5.2 Derived Data Types

C also supports three types of derived data types. They are array, function and pointer. These are the data types which are basically derived from the built-in data types. Out of these, arrays are discussed the next chapter in the last section; the rest would be discussed in chapter 6.

3.2.5.3 User Defined Data Types

C also supports three types of user-defined data types. They are structure, union and enumerated data types. These data types are basically defined by the user and contain the built-in data type as their member. The structures and unions will be discussed in the next chapter.

TABLE 2

Built-in Data Types with Modifiers

Type	Approximate Size in Bytes	Range	Format Specifiers
char type			
`char`	1	–128 to 127	`%c`
`signed char`	1	0 to 255	`%c`
`unsigned char`	1	–128 to 127	`%c`
int type			
`int`	2	–32768 to 32767	`%d`
`unsigned int`	2	0 to 65535	`%u`
`signed int`	2	–32768 to 32767	`%d`
`short int`	2	–32768 to 32767	`%d`
`unsigned short int`	2	0 to 65535	`%u`
`signed short int`	2	–32768 to 32767	`%d`
`long int`	4	–2147483648 to 2147483647	`%ld`
`signed long int`	4	–2147483648 to 2147483647	`%ld`
`unsigned long int`	4	0 to 4294967295	`%lu`
float type			
`float`	4 (precision = 7)	3.4e–38 to 3.4e+38	`%f`
double type			
`double`	8 (precision = 15)	1.7e–308 to 1.7e+308	`%lf`
`long double`	10 (precision = 19)	3.4e–4932 to 1.1e+4932	`%lf`

enumerated Data Type

It is a user-defined data type which is used to attach numbers to names. It is used only when we know all possible values (a variable can take) in advance.

Syntax

```
enum tag{enumeration list} variable list;
or
enum tag{enumeration list}
tag variable name;
```

For example, we know that switch can operate only in two modes, on or off, so we can define an enumerated data type for this as

```
enum operation{OFF,ON};
```

Here a variable of operation data type can hold either on or off. Other values cannot be assigned to this particular variable. These data values are also attached with numbers. By default the numbering starts from 0, therefore for the above example 0 is assigned to off and 1 is assigned to on. The next number in the sequence is 1, if more values are there then the next value will be assigned the number 2 then 3 and so on. We can either use the name or the number value for operation type variable to hold. Let us take one more enumeration declaration

```
enum weekdays{Sun,Mon,Tue,Wed,Thurs,Fri,
Sat};
```

We know in advance that there are only seven days in a week, so we can define an enumerated data type "weekdays" which can have only one of the values from the above set at a time. The numbers for these enumerated values are assigned as Sun=0, Mon=1, Tue=2, Wed=3, Thurs=4, Fri=5, Sat=6. Instance of an enumerated type can be declared in a program. For example,

```
weekdays cal;
if (cal==3)
printf("Wednesday");
```

Since by default, the compiler assigns value 1 to Mon (starting from 0), therefore the condition is true. To set the number sequence from 1 instead of 0, it has to be specified in the variable declaration itself, as shown in the following example.

```
enummonth{Jan=1,Feb,Mar,Apr,May,June,July,
Aug,Sep,Oct,Nov,Dec};
```

typedef Data Type

C allows us to give a different name to the data type "keywords" by using typedef. The typedef does not create a new data type but it simply gives a new name to the existing data type. It does not replace the standard C data type name but rather adds the new name along with the already existing type name.

Syntax

```
typedef datatype newname;
```

For example, `typedef int whole;`
Here onwards we can use whole instead of int. This statement instructs the compiler to recognize whole as an alternative name for int. Now we can define an integer variable using whole as `whole a=8;`

3.2.5.4 Type Conversion

The compiler will always return the result in the data type in which the arguments are declared. However, in certain cases like addition of two integers, it is desired that the result be in float data type. For this purpose, the concept of type conversion is implemented.

Type conversion by the compiler is done in two ways:

1. **Automatic:** When an expression consists of more than one type of data element, the C compiler converts the smaller (memory size) data type element to a larger data type element. This process is known as implicit or automatic conversion. For example

   ```
   double x;
   int y = 4;
   float z = 5.5;
   x = y * z;
   ```

   When two operands of different type are encountered in the same expression, the variable having data type of lower priority is converted to the one with higher priority. The order of data types is

   `long double > double > float > long > int > char`

   The int value of y is converted to type float and stored in a temporary variable before being multiplied by the float variable z. The result is then converted to double type so that it can be assigned to the double variable x.

2. **Typecasting:** C also allows to change the data type by using typecast operator. Using this operator, the programmer can convert one data type into another by explicitly mentioning the type in the expression. It may be noted here that type casting can only be done on the right hand side the assignment statement.

   ```
   doubleT_Sal, bonus;
   float salary;
   T_Sal = double (salary) + bonus;
   ```

   Initially variable salary is defined as float but for the above calculation it is first converted to double data type and then added to the double variable bonus.

Solved Problems

1. *Define with examples integer and floating type of data in C language.* **(AU 2011)**

Solution: Refer to the section above.

2. *Differentiate between signed and unsigned integers.* **(AU 2010)**

Solution: The signed integer represents both positive and negative numbers indicated by a positive or negative sign, whereas an unsigned integer represents positive numbers (including 0) only.
The range of values for a signed integer is from –32767 to +32767, whereas for the unsigned integer, the range is from 0 to 65535.

3. *Explain different data types in C with suitable examples.* **(AU 2009, 2013)**

Solution: Refer to the section above.

4. *What do you mean by C Tokens?* **(AU 2010 Suppl.)**

Solution: The small individual units that make up the C program are called **tokens**. These are identifiers, keywords, constants (integer, floating point, character and string constants), operators and other symbols.

5. *Give an example for enumerated data type.* **(AU 2008 Suppl.)**

Solution: The following is an example of an enumerated data type:

```
enum boolean{False,True};
```

where boolean data type can have two values 0 for false and 1 for true.

6. *Describe the purpose of qualifiers const and volatile.* **(AU 2005 Suppl.)**

Solution: The qualifier const added before the variable name indicates that it is a constant variable, and it cannot change during the course of the program. The qualifier volatile added before the variable name indicates that the variable can be changed at any time in the program or by an external program accessing it.

3.3 Operators and Expressions

Operators and expressions are used to denote computations in a program. Operator is a symbol such as +, –, etc. operating upon two variables or constants (called operands); an expression is the combination of operands (variables/constants) and operators written according to the syntax of the programming language. For example, (x – y)* 5 = 4 is an expression.

3.3.1 | Types of Operators

Operators can be classified as follows:

1. **Based on number of operands:** Unary, binary or ternary operators.
2. **Based upon the nature of operation:** Arithmetic, relational, logical, assignment, increment/decrement, conditional, bitwise and special operators.

3.3.1.1 Arithmetic Operators

The arithmetic operators are generally binary operators as they require two variables to be evaluated. These are the basic operators for any programming language. The list of arithmetic operators is given in Table 3. When division operation between two integers is performed, it will always produce an integer value. The modulus operator (%) for obtaining the remainder in a division operation is used between integer numbers only.

For example, if a and b are integers, and the values of a = 10 and b = 4. We have the following results:

```
a+b is 14,    a/b is 2
a–b is 6,     a%b is 2
a*b is 40,
```

TABLE 3

Arithmetic Operators

Operator	Meaning	Example	Associativity
=	Initialize	a=b, the value of b is assigned to a	Right to left
+ and +=	Addition	a+=b means a=a+b	Left to right (+) Right to left (+=)
– and –=	Subtraction	a–=b means a=a–b	Left to right (–) Right to left (–=)
* and *=	Multiplication	a*=b means a=a*b	Left to right (*) Right to left (*=)
/ and /=	Division	a/=b means a=a/b	Left to right (/) Right to left (/=)
% and %=	Modulus (remainder)	a%=b means a=a%b	Left to right (%) Right to left (%=)
–(unary)	Unary minus	–a	Right to left

3.3.1.2 Relational Operators

The relational operators are used to compare the value between two variables. The answers of these expressions are true or false. The list of relational operators is given in Table 4.

TABLE 4

Relational Operators

Operator	Meaning	Example	Associativity
<	Less than	a<b	Left to right
<=	Less than or equal to	a<=b	Left to right
>	Greater than	a>b	Left to right
>=	Greater than or equal to	a>=b	Left to right
==	Equal to	a==b	Left to right
!=	Not equal to	a!=b	Left to right

Example: if a=10, b=4, then a < b is false; a > b is true; a<=b is false; a>=6 is true; a==b is false; a|=b is true.

3.3.1.3 Logical Operators

These operators are used to combine two or more conditional expressions in a statement. The list of logical operators is given in Table 5. The logical operators are called Boolean operators.

3.3.1.4 Bitwise Operator

These operators are used to perform bitwise operations. These operations are performed on the bits of the binary pattern of the numbers. The list of bitwise operators is given in Table 6.

Example: if a = 10, b = 4, then a > b && b > 2 is true; a > 5 || b < 2 is true; a < 5 && b < 2 is false; a < 5 || b < 2 is false; a > 5 && b < 2 is false; a > 5 || b > 2 is true.

3.3.1.5 Special Operators

Apart from all these operators that we have seen so far, C provides some special operators. For example, the increment (++) and decrement (--) operators. These come in two varieties: they may either precede or follow the operand. The prefix version comes before the operand and the postfix version comes after the operand. The two versions have the same effect on the operand, but they differ by when they take place in an expression. The prefix increment or decrement operator follows "change then use" rule. They first change the value of their operand, and then use the new value in evaluating the expression. The postfix increment or decrement operators follow "use then change"

TABLE 5

Logical Operators

<table>
<tr><th>Operator</th><th>Meaning</th><th>Associativity</th><th>Remarks</th></tr>
<tr><td>&&</td><td>Logical AND</td><td>Left to right</td><td>It will produce true when both operands produce true values.</td></tr>
<tr><td>||</td><td>Logical OR</td><td>Left to right</td><td>It will produce true when atleast one of the operands produce true value.</td></tr>
<tr><td>!</td><td>Logical Not</td><td>Right to Left</td><td>It will produce the negation value of the operand.</td></tr>
</table>

Example:

TABLE 6

Bitwise Operators

<table>
<tr><th>Operator</th><th>Meaning</th><th>Example</th><th>Associativity</th></tr>
<tr><td>& and &=</td><td>Bitwise AND</td><td>a &= b means a = a & b</td><td>Left to right (&)
Right to left (&=)</td></tr>
<tr><td>| and |=</td><td>Bitwise OR</td><td>a |= b means a = a | b</td><td>Left to right (|)
Right to left (|=)</td></tr>
<tr><td>^ and ^=</td><td>Bitwise XOR</td><td>a ^= b means a = a ^ b</td><td>Left to right (^)
Right to left (^=)</td></tr>
<tr><td>>> and >>=</td><td>Bitwise right shift</td><td>a >>= b means shift all bits in a b number of places to the right and store the result in a</td><td>Left to right (>>)
Right to left (>>=)</td></tr>
<tr><td><< and <<=</td><td>Bitwise left shift</td><td>a>>= b means shift all bits in a b number of places to the left and store the result in a</td><td>Left to right (<<)
Right to left (<<=)</td></tr>
<tr><td>~</td><td>Bitwise complement</td><td>~a means $\bar{a}$, all 1's to 0's and all 0's to 1's</td><td>Right to left</td></tr>
</table>

rule. They first use the value of their operand in evaluating the expression and then change the operand's value. The postfix or prefix operators are unary operators. They have higher precedence over prefix increment/decrement operators. Table 7 provides the special operators in C.

TABLE 7

Special Operators

Operator	Meaning	Example	Associativity
++	Incrementer	a++ means post-increment (use then change) for example, if a = 2 then a++ will give 3 but 2 will be used first ++a means pre-increment (change then use) for example, if a = 2 then ++a will give 3 and 3 will be used	Left to right Right to left
--	Decrementer	a–– means post-decrement (use then change) ––a means pre-decrement (change then use)	Left to right Right to left
*	Value at address	*p will display the value at the address contained in the pointer variable p	Right to left
&	Address of	&p will display the address of p	Right to left
`sizeof()`	Size of	Displays the size of the argument specified within the parenthesis (can be variable or data type)	Right to left
?:	Ternary operator	`z?a:b` If z is true (not zero), then a is returned otherwise b is returned. It is an alternative to the simple `if-else` statement. Example, for a = 2 and b = 3 (a>b)? a;b will return 3	Right to left
,	Comma	a,b means a then b. It is used in separating the multiple declaration or initialization or updation in a for loop	Right to left
[]	Array element reference	a[b] to refer to the bth element of array a.	Left to right
()	Function call	a() to call the function a. a(b) to call function a and pass argument b.	Left to right
.	Dot operator	a.b to access the member b of structure a.	Left to right
->	Pointer to structure	a->b to access member b of structure a using pointer	Left to right

The referencing and deferencing operators are used to access the memory location of a variable. These are discussed as follows.

1. **Referencing operator (&) or Address of operator:** This operator is a unary operator used to create a reference variable which can provide an alias for an existing variable. This means to represent that variable, two variable names can be used. It returns the address of the variable following it.

   Syntax

   ```
   data_type & reference_variable =
   variable_name;
   ```
   For example,
   ```
   r = &sample;
   ```
   where r will hold the address of sample, that is, 1001.
   Now if we use
   ```
   printf("%d", ptr);
   ```
   The output will be `1001`
   Now, for the `statement r1=&sample1;`
   the statement `printf("%d", ptr1);`
   will give output as `2001`.

2. **Deferencing operator (*) or value at operator/ indirection operator:** Indirection operator that returns the contents stored at the memory location (address). This is also called value at operator or dereference operator. This operator can be represented by a combination of * with a variable. This operator is a unary operator and is used to declare a pointer pointing to a variable. It stores the value at the address of the variable.

   For example, suppose p holds the address of sample
   ```
   int sample=15;
   p=&sample
   printf("%d", *p);
   ```
   The output will be the content at p, that is, 10. *p is read as "the value at the address contained in p" or the "value at p". In case of declaring a pointer to a variable, the pointer would hold the memory address of the pointer. For pointers to structures and unions, C provides two member dereferencing operators.

   (a) *** operator:** This operator is used to access a member using an object and a pointer to that member.

(b) **->* operator:** This operator is used to access a member using a pointer to the object and a pointer to that member.

3.3.1.6 Trigraph Characters

These are a sequence of three characters (trigraph sequence) with the first two characters being question marks (??) and the third character can be any of the characters in ANSI C trigraph sequences. These are usually employed when the keyboard does not support special characters like square brackets, etc. For example, ??= corresponds to # number sign; ??(corresponds to left bracket ([); ??) corresponds to right bracket (]); ??< corresponds to left curly brace ({); ??> corresponds to right curly braces (}); ??! corresponds to vertical bar (|); etc.

3.3.2 | Properties of Operators

Certain properties associated with operators are as follows:

1. **Precedence:** This property defines the order in which the operations should be performed. Certain operators have higher priority than other operators, example, * has higher priority over +. This is further discussed in Table 8.
2. **Associativity:** The property which defines whether the computation should be from left to right (L → R) of the expression or from right to left (R → L) depending upon the precedence of the operators.

TABLE 8

Operator Precedence

Operator	Precedence
`++, --`	Highest
`++, --, sizeof, !, -,+`	↑
`*, /, %`	
`+, -`	
`<, <=, >, >=`	
`==, !=`	
`&&`	
`||`	
`?:`	
= and other assignment operator	
, Comma operator	Lowest

3.3.3 | Escape Sequence

C also supports some non-graphic characters, which cannot be typed directly from the keyboard. These non-graphic characters can be represented by using escape sequences. An escape sequence is represented by a backslash (\) followed by one or more characters. Table 9 presents some escape sequences.

TABLE 9

Escape Sequences

Sequence	Task
`\a`	Alert a bell character
`\n`	New line
`\t`	Horizontal tab
`\b`	Backspace
`\r`	Carriage return
`\f`	Form feed
`\v`	Vertical tab
`\\`	Backslash
`\'`	Single quote
`\"`	Double quote
`\0` (zero)	Null character
`\?`	Question mark
`\o`	Octal value
`\x`	Hexadecimal value

3.3.4 | Expressions using Operators in C

The combination of operators and operands form expressions. The evaluation of expressions are based on the precedence and associativity of operators. The expressions having a combinations of smaller expressions are called compound expressions. The following examples are used to apply the concepts discussed in previous sections and evaluate expressions.

1. 20.0 – 2/6 + 3 = 20.0 – 0 + 3 = 8.0
2. 3.0*4/6 + 6 = 12.0/6 + 6 = 2.0 + 6.0 = 8.0
3. 3.0*4% 6 + 6 = 12.0 % 6 + 6 = invalid expression
4. 10.0 + 10/2 + 4.3 = 10.0 + 5 + 4.3 = 21.8
5. (20–2)/6 + 3 = 18/6 + 3 = 3 + 3 = 6

Solved Problems

1. *Write assignment statements in C to evaluate the following expressions: (a)* $Side = \sqrt{a^2 + b^2 - 2abcos(x)}$ *and (b)* $Area = \pi r^2 + 2\pi rh$. **(AU 2005 Suppl.)**

Solution:

(a)
```
float a, b, x, side;
side = (a^2 + b^2 - 2*a*b*cos(x))^(1/2);
```

(b)
```
float r, h, area;
area = 3.14*r^2 + 2*3.14*r*h;
```

2. *Write a C statement for the following expressions. (a) a = 5 <= 8 && 6!=5 and (b) a = b++ + ++b where b = 50.* **(AU 2010)**

Solution:

(a)
```
int a=((5<=8)&&(6!=5));
```

(b)
```
int b=50;
int a=(b++) + (++b);
```

3. *(a) Differentiate between operator and operand.* **(AU 2005 Suppl.)**

(b) Describe the various types of operators supported by C. **(AU 2005 Suppl., 2013, 2014)**

Solution: Operator is a symbol such as +, –, etc. operating upon two variables or constants. The variables or constants on which operators act upon are called operands. The various types of operators supported by C are arithmetic operators, relational operators, logical operators, bitwise operators and special operators. For details, refer to the respective subsections above.

4. *Differentiate between relational and logical expressions.* **(AU 2005 Suppl.)**

Solution: Relational expressions involve relationships between two variables/constants and evaluate to true or false depending upon the relationship. The various relational operators are >, <, <=, >=, == and !=. For example, Is 5 > 4 evaluates to true.

Logical expressions involve logical relationship between two expressions (which can be relational expressions). The evaluation of the logical expression depends upon the evaluation of the individual expressions it is composed of. There are three logical operators, && (AND), || (OR) and ! (NOT). The && operator evaluates to true if both the expressions are true; the || operator evaluates to true if either of the expressions is true and the ! operator evaluates to true if the condition is false. For example, 5 > 3 && 5 < 10 evaluates to true.

5. *What are the roles of << and >> operators in C?* **(AU 2009 Suppl.)**

Solution: Both << and >> operators are bitwise operators and have associativity from left to right. An example for each is a<<n and a>>n, respectively. In the first expression, the << operator acts as a bitwise left shift operator causing shift of all bits in operand "a" to the left by n positions. In the second expression, the >> operator acts as a bitwise right shift operator causing shift of all bits in operand "a" to the right by n positions.

6. *Write the following conditions using "?:" operator.*

$$Salary = \begin{cases} 4x + 100 \text{ for } x < 40 \\ 300 \text{ for } x = 40 \\ 4.5x + 150 \text{ for } x > 40. \end{cases}$$

(AU 2009)

Solution:

```
Salary = x < 40? 4x + 100 : x = 40? 300:4.5x
+ 150
```

7. *Evaluate the expressions (a) 2*3/12*8/4 and (b) 10.0+15/2+4.3.*

Solution:

(a) `2*3/12*8/4 = 6/12*8/4=0*8/4=0/4=0`

(b) `10.0+15/2+4.3 = 10.0+7+4.3=21.3`

8. *Write any four escape sequences in C.* **(AU 2013)**

Solution: Refer to Table 9.

3.4 Structure of a C program

The simple structure of C program is as follows:

Syntax

```
Preprocessor directives
Global variable declaration if any
Global constant declaration if any
void main()
{
/*comments*/
local variable declaration;
statements;
function call (parameters);
}
User-defined function (arguments)
{
Function body
}
```

The various components of the C program in the syntax are as follows:

1. **Preprocessor directives:** These directives (e.g., #include) are used to include the header files, that is the files containing all the definitions and prototypes in the current program. For example, stdio.h is used to include the prototypes and definitions of all the standard input and output functions.
2. **Global variable declaration:** This includes declaration for variables that need to be used in more than one function.
3. **Global constant declaration:** This includes declaration for global constants using # define. For example # define N 2.
4. **main():** Every program in C needs to have a main() function. The return type of main() can be void or int. In case of int, return(0) statement is included at the end of the program.
5. **Comments:** A comment is a statement or a set of statements inserted in the program body to make reading and understanding of a program much more pleasant. A comment is a sequence of characters beginning with a forward slash asterisk combination (/*) and ending with comment delimiter (*/). A compiler does not understand the contents of the comment and ignores it. A comment can appear anywhere in the program.
6. **Local variable declaration:** All local variables of respective data types are declared in the beginning of the main() function. These variables can only be used in the main function as they are declared locally.
7. **Statements:** The various types of input, output and control statements follow after declaration of variables.
8. **Function call():** Using this statement, a user-defined function is called into action. The function call can be

with or without any arguments; in the latter case, parameters can be passed from the main function to the user-defined function. Once the function body terminates, the control is passed to the main function again.

3.4.1 | Compilation and Linking Processes

A C program typically goes through six steps: Creation, Preprocessing, Compilation, Linking, Loading and Execution.

1. **Creation:** This is the first phase which has editor to create a C program. We can make a necessary correction using the editor and save the program on a secondary storage device, such as hard drive. C source code file names often end with the .c extension which indicates that file contains C source code. An editor widely used on UNIX systems is vi editor. We can use simple text editor or notepad to write a C program.
2. **Preprocessing and compiling:** In a C system, a preprocessor program executes automatically before the translation compiler phase begins. The C preprocessor obeys commands called preprocessor directives, which are required to indicate certain manipulations performed before compilation. The compiler translates the C program into machine language code which is referred to as object code.
3. **Linking:** A C program typically contains reference functions and data defined elsewhere, such as the standard libraries or in the private libraries of programmers assigned to a project. The object code produced by the compiler, therefore, contains gaps. A linker helps in linking the object code with the code for the missing functions to produce an executable file.
4. **Loading:** Before executing a program, it must be placed in memory. The loader takes executable file from disk and transfers it to memory. The additional components from shared libraries supporting the program are also loaded.
5. **Execution:** In this final phase, under the control of its CPU, the program is executed one instruction at a time.

Debugging: The compiler displays a list of errors, if any, which need to be rectified in the program. These are called **compile-time errors** and are indicative of syntactical or logical errors in the source code. Once the errors are rectified, the program is compiled again, and if no errors are identified by the compiler, the program enters the run mode in which the executable object code is loaded into the main memory and the program is executed. Sometimes, we come across errors in the program execution in which case the desired result as per the coded program is not obtained. These errors are **run-time errors**, and could be due to various reasons, such as division by zero in evaluation of an expression, stack overflow, etc.

3.4.2 | Execution of a C Program

When the C program is created, the program needs to be written in C editor. The filename must have a ".C" extension. Once the program is ready for compilation, the entire source code of the program is translated into object code by the compiler and stored in a filename with extension .obj. The compiler links all the functions and operators with their respective header files with the main() function. After compilation, it displays a list of errors, if any, which need to be rectified in the program. These are called compile-time errors and are indicative of syntactical or logical errors in the source code. Once the errors are rectified, the program is compiled again, and if no errors are identified by the compiler, the program enters the run mode in which the executable object code is loaded into the main memory and the program is executed. Sometimes, we come across errors in the program execution in which case the desired result as per the coded program is not obtained. These errors are run-time errors, and could be due to various reasons, such as division by zero in evaluation of an expression, stack overflow, etc.

Solved Problems

1. *What is the basic structure of C program?* **(AU 2010, 2011)**

Solution: Refer to the section above.

2. *What is meant by debugging?* **(AU 2007 Suppl.)**

Solution: The process of detecting errors and rectifying them is called debugging. There are various types of errors such as compile time errors and run time errors.

3. *What is the need to compile a program?*

Solution: Compiling helps to identify syntax errors in erroneous case, in normal case it converts the higher level language into an intermediate level object file.

4. *How are library files are linked to source files?*

Solution: Linker performs linking of the library files to source code after compilation and just after the result of execution.

5. What is a compiler?

Solution: A compiler is used to convert high-level language into machine language. It compiler converts the complete program in a single go and then displays the list of errors if any.

3.5 Managing Input and Output Operations

The input/output operations in C are carried out by standard library functions. These functions are of two types: (1) Formatted functions [scanf(), printf(), etc.] and (2) unformatted functions [getch(), getche(), getchar(), gets(), putch(), putchar(), put(), etc.].

3.5.1 | Formatted Functions

These functions are called formatted as the format is specified while reading or displaying the data using format specifiers (see Table 2). These functions work on all data type variables and are of the following types:

1. **scanf():** To read input data from the keyboard at run time. The format of the data being input needs to be specified in the scanf statement using format specifiers.

   Syntax

   ```
   int scanf(const char * format_string; &arg_1,
   &arg_2,...);
   ```

   For example, `scanf(%d %f %s, &a, &b, &c);` where % indicates that a conversion specification follows. In some cases field width can be specified for a number to be read, for example `scan (%2d %3d; & num1, & num2);` then if 50456 is the input by user, 50 will be assigned to num1 and 456 to num2.
2. **printf():** To display the output in the data format specified by the programmer using format specifiers.

   Syntax

   ```
   int printf(const char * format_string; arg_1,
   arg_2,...);
   ```

   For example, `printf(Area of circle is: %f,area);`
3. **sscanf():** This function is used to scan a string passed as the first parameter. The standard C library functions used for writing to the output device. It writes into the screen according to the format as described. It also contains conversion specification.

   Syntax

   ```
   int sscanf(const char *str, const char
   *format_string, &arg_1, &arg_2,...);
   ```
4. **sprintf():** This function is used to write a formatted text into an array of characters.

   Syntax

   ```
   int sprintf(const char *str, const char
   *format_string, arg_1, arg_2,...);
   ```
5. **fscanf():** To read a set of data values from the file. For example, `fscanf(f2, "%d %f", &i, &f);` where f2 is the file pointer pointing to the file opened in reading mode.
6. **fprintf():** To write a set of data values onto the file. For example, `fprintf(f1, "%d %f\n",i,f);` where f1 is the file pointer pointing to the file opened in reading mode.

To read the input from the input device and display the output on the output device rather than files, two standard keywords used are stdin and stdout. For example, `fprintf(stdout, "%f \n", f);`

3.5.2 | Unformatted Functions

These functions are called unformatted as the format is not specified while reading or displaying the data. These functions work on character data type variables only. Format specifiers are not used in these functions as they treat all data as character type. These are of three types:

1. **Character input/output functions:** These functions are used to read and display one character at a time.
   - **getchar():** This function is used to read a character that is input during the runtime. It returns the character which reads from the keyboard. Enter key needs to be pressed after each character.

     Syntax

     ```
     int getchar(void);
     ```

     For example,

     ```
     #include<stdio.h>
     #include<conio.h>
     void main()
     {
     getchar();
     }
     ```
   - **putchar():** This function is used to write the data which is specified in the argument char to standard output device (stdout). It returns the character which is given in the argument.

     Syntax

     ```
     int putchar(int char);
     ```

     For example,

     ```
     #include<stdio.h>
     #include<conio.h>
     void main()
     {
     putchar(b);
     }
     ```

     The output is

     ```
     b
     ```
   - **getch():** This function is used to get one character at a time from console but it does not echo to the screen. It returns the alphanumeric character read from the keyboard.

     Syntax

     ```
     int getch(void);
     ```

     For example,

     ```
     #include<stdio.h>
     #include<conio.h>
     void main()
     {
     getch();
     }
     ```
   - **getche():** This function is used to read alphanumeric data from console and echo it to the screen. It returns the alphanumeric characters read from the keyboard.

     Syntax

     ```
     int getche(void);
     ```

     For example,

     ```
     #include<stdio.h>
     #include<conio.h>
     void main()
     {
     getche();
     }
     ```

     If the user input is x, then output is x.

     x ← input
     x
   - **putch():** This function displays any alphanumeric characters to the standard output device, one character at a time. It returns the character which is given in the arguments.

Syntax

```
int putch(int char);
```

For example,

```
#include<stdio.h>
#include<conio.h>
void main()
{
putch(a);
}
```

The output is

```
a
```

2. **String input/output functions:** These functions are used to read the entered string and display it onto the screen.

   - **gets():** This function is used to read a line from stdin and store it into the string pointed by str. It stopped when newline character is read or when Enter key is pressed. It returns pointer to a string. Spaces are accepted as part string inlike scanf().

Syntax

```
char *gets(char *str);
```

For example,

```
#include<stdio.h>
#include<conio.h>
void main()
{
gets();
}
```

   - **puts():** This function displays a string to the output device. It does not include the null character and also append the newline character.

Syntax

```
int puts(const char *str);
```

For example,

```
#include<stdio.h>
#include<conio.h>
void main()
{
puts("Hello");
}
```

The output is

```
Hello
```

   - **cgets():** To read string from the keyboard input. It requires character pointer as an argument. For example, `cgets(char *p);`
   - **cputs():** To display string onto the screen. It requires character pointer as an argument. For example, `cputs(char *p);`

3. **File input/output functions:** These functions are used to read and write characters/strings into files. Out of these, the formatted functions fscanf() and fprintf() have been discussed under formatted functions.

   - **getc():** To read a character from the file. For example, `c=getc(fp2);` where fp2 is the file pointer pointing to the file opened in reading mode. It returns EOF as soon as end of file is reached.
   - **putc():** To write a character onto the file. For example, `putc(c,fp1);` where fp1 is the file pointer pointing to the file opened in writing mode. It returns EOF as soon as end of file is reached.
   - **getw():** To read an integer from the file. For example, `i=getw(fp2);`
   - **putw():** To write an integer onto the file. For example, `putw(i,fp1);`
   - **fgets():** To read a string from the file pointed by the file pointer and copy the string to a memory location referred by the array. For example, `fgets(text, 50,fp);` where fp is the file pointer and 50 is the length of the string text.
   - **fputc():** To write a string to an opened file pointed by the file pointer. For example, `fputs(text, fp);` where fp is the file pointer and text is the string.

Solved Problems

1. *Explain with example unformatted input and output statements in C language.* **(AU 2005 Suppl., 2011)**

Solution: Refer subsection on unformatted functions.

2. *Explain briefly the formatted and unformatted I/O functions in C.* **(AU 2007 Suppl., 2012, 2013)**

Solution: Refer to the section above.

3. *What is the output of the following code?* **(AU 2005 Suppl.)**

```
#define scanf "%s is character";
main()
{printf(scanf,scanf);
}
```

Solution: The code will result in error as the format specifier is not mentioned in the printf statement. On including the format specifiers as

```
printf("%s, %s",scanf,scanf);
```

the output will be

```
%s is character %s is character.
```

4. *Differentiate between getchar() and scanf() functions for reading strings.* **(AU 2005 Suppl., 2009)**

Solution: Both functions are used to read one character at a time from the keyboard, however, in case of scanf(), the input is formatted as specified by the format specifier.

5. *Write a C program to implement the expression* $((m+n)/p-m)*m)$, *where* $m=4, n=6, p=8$. **(AU 2012)**

Solution

```
#include <stdio.h>
#include <conio.h>
int main()
```

```
{
float m,n,p,result;
printf("\n Enter value of m:");
scanf("%f",&m);
printf("\n Enter value of n:");
scanf("%f",&n);
printf("\n Enter value of p:");
scanf("%f",&p);
result=(((m+n)/p-m)* m);
printf("\n    Result    on    substituting
values  of  m,n  and  p  in  the  expression
((m+n)/p-m)*m):%.2f",result);
getch();
}
```

The output is

```
Enter value of m: 4
Enter value of n: 6
Enter value of p: 8
Result on substituting values of m,n and
p in the expression ((m+n)/p-m)*m): -11.00
```

6. *Write a program to read the numbers 50.21 and –23.73, round them off to the nearest integers and print out the results in integer form.* **(AU 2008 Suppl.)**

Solution

```
#include<stdio.h>
#include<conio.h>
#include<math.h>
void main()
{
float x,y;
printf("Enter the values of x and y");
scanf("%f %f", &x, &y);
printf("The values after rounding off are");
x=floor(a);
y=ceil(b);
printf("%d %d",x,y);
}
```

Here, floor() and ceil() are functions defined in math.h header file used for floating point operations.

7. *Write a program to print the various types of constants in C.*

Solution:

```
#include<stdio.h>
#include<conio.h>
void main()
{
const int a=1;
const float b=5e-6;
const char c='x';
printf ("a=%d b=%df c=%c",a,b,c);
getche()
}
```

The output is

```
a=1   b=0.0000000005   c=x
```

8. *Write a program to display the names of current month using enumerated data types.*

Solution:

```
#include<stdio.h>
#include<conio.h>
void main()
{
enummonth{Jan=1,Feb,Mar,Apr,May,June,July,
Aug,Sep,Oct,Nov,Dec};
enum month current_month;
printf("Enter  the  current  month  as  an
integer between 1 and 12:");
scanf("%d", &month);
printf("The current month is %s",
current_month);
}
```

The output is

```
Enter  the  current  month  as  an  integer
between 1 and 12: 5
The current month is May
```

9. *Write a program to obtain the average of five numbers in integer and float data types using type conversion.*

Solution:

```
#include<stdio.h>
#include<conio.h>
void main()
{int sum;
sum=1+5+6+8+9;
int average=sum/5;
printf("The  average  in  integer  form  is
%d",average);
average=(float)sum/5;
printf("The   average   in   float   form   is
%f",average);
}
```

The output is

```
The average in integer form is 5
The average in float form is 5.8
```

Here, the variable `sum` is converted into float data type. But after that statement, the sum will remain of int data type.

10. *Write a program to get a string and display it using functions.*

Solution:

```
#include <stdio.h>
#include <conio.h>
void input_output string()
{
char str[100];/*character array, discussed
in Chapter 4*/
printf("Enter the string:\n");
```

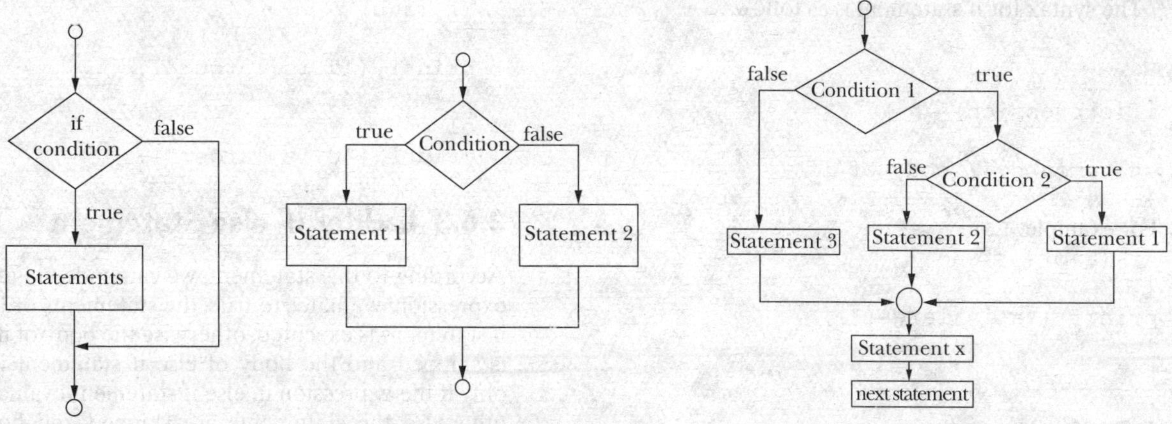

(a) "if" control structure flowchart. (b) if-else control structure flowchart. (c) Ladder if–else control structure flowchart.

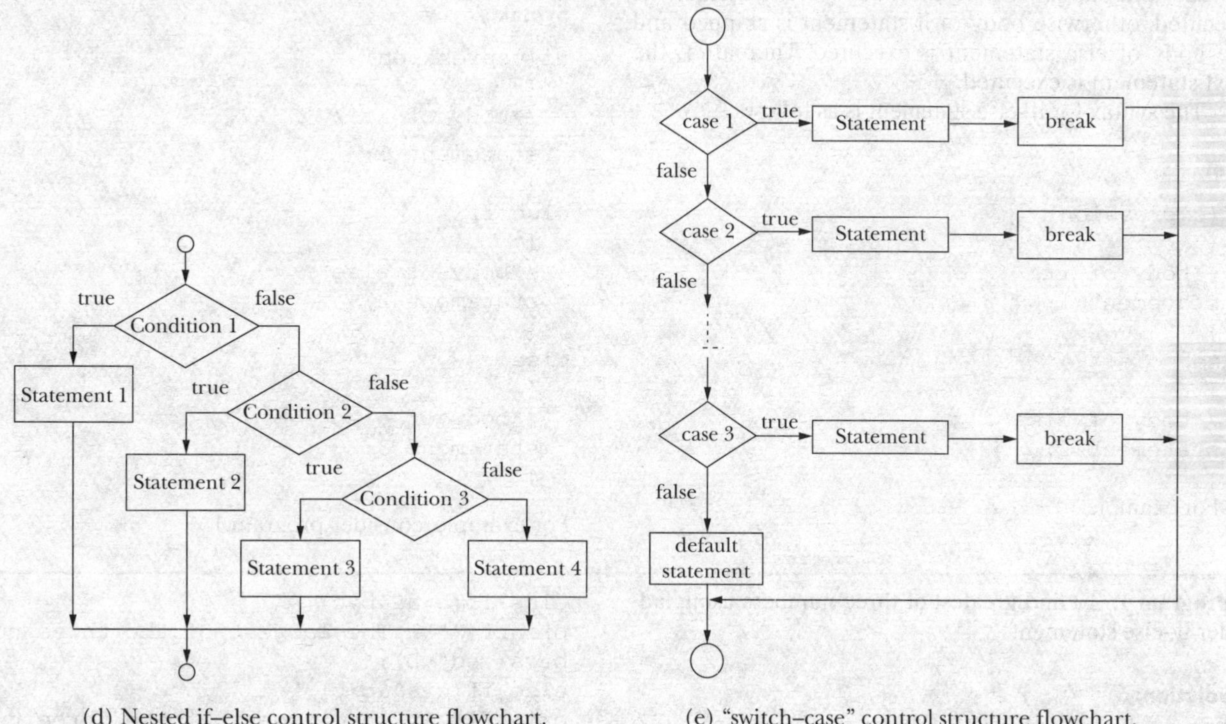

(d) Nested if–else control structure flowchart. (e) "switch–case" control structure flowchart.

Figure 2 Flowchart structures for if, if-else, ladder if-else, nested if-else and switch-case statements.

```
gets(str);
puts(str);
}
void main()
{
input_output string();
}
```

3.6 Decision Making Statements

In these type of statements, the execution of body (statements) depends on the test condition. If the condition evaluates to true, one set of statements are executed otherwise another set of statements are executed. These statements are also called decision constructs, because they allow choosing the set of statements for execution depending upon expression's truth value. C provides various types of selection statements, such as if; if–else; nested if; switch–case, nested switch, etc. Some of them are discussed in the following subsections. The flowchart representation of these statement is shown in Fig. 2.

3.6.1 | If Statement

According to this statement, that if the expression evaluates to true, the statements or the body of if statement is executed, otherwise body of if statement is skipped and execution continues with the next statement.

The syntax for if statement is as follows.

Syntax

```
if(expression)
{
statements; /*body of if*/
}
```

For example

```
if (a>b)
{
printf ("a is larger");
}
```

3.6.2 | If–else Statement

According to this statement, if the expression evaluates to true, the statements or the body of if statement is executed, otherwise body of if statement is skipped and the body of else statement is executed. Thereafter, the next statement is executed.

The syntax for if–else statement is as follows:

Syntax

```
if(expression)
  {
  /*body of if*/
  statement 1;
  }
else
  {
  /*body of else*/
  statement 2;
  }
```

For example

```
if (a>b)
{
printf ("a is larger");
}
else
printf ("b is larger");
```

3.6.3 Ladder if–else Statement

According to this statement, we can understand that if the expression evaluates to true, the statements or the body of if statement is executed, otherwise the body of if statement is skipped and the body of else if statement is executed only if the expression in else if statement evaluates to true, otherwise the statements are skipped and body of else statement is executed.

The syntax for ladder if–else statement is as follows:

Syntax

```
if(expression)
  {
  /*body of if*/
  statement 1;
  }
else if
  {
  /*body of else*/
  statement 2;
  }
else
  {
  /*body of else*/
  statement 3;
  }
```

For example, consider program 1

Program 1: To find greatest of three numbers using ladder if–else statement.

Solution:

```
include <stdio.h>
#include <conio.h>
int main()
{
int a,b,c;
printf("Enter three different numbers:");
scanf("%d %d %d",&a,&b,&c);
if(a>b&&a>c)
printf(""\n The largest of the three num-
bers: %d",a);
else if(b>a&&b>c)
printf(""\n The largest of the three num-
bers: %d",b);
else if(c>a&&c>b)
printf(""\n The largest of the three num-
bers: %d",c);
else
printf("\nInvalid input");
getch();
}
```

Output

```
Enter three numbers: 5, 7, 3
The largest of the three numbers: 7
```

3.6.4 | Nested if–else Statement

According to this statement, we can understand that if the expression evaluates to true, the statements or the body of if statement is executed. Again in the if statement inside the if construct, the statement after if is executed when it evaluated to true, otherwise the statement after else is executed. If the expression in the parent if statement evaluates to false, then the entire if construct is skipped and body of else statement is executed. For example consider program 2.

The syntax for nested if–else statement is as follows:

Syntax

```
if(expression)
  {
  statement 1;/*body of if statement*/
  if(expression)
      statement 2;
  else
      statement 3;
  }
else
  {
  statement 4;
  }
```

Note: When C programs are executed in Linux operating system, then statements like `#include<conio.h>`, `clrscr()` would not work.

3.6.5 | switch-case Statement

This statement is used to test multiple conditions for the same variable or expression in a program and execute statements accordingly. The switch statement takes a variable or expression of integer data type as its argument. The argument is evaluated and matched with the conditions in the case statement. If none of the case conditions match, then the statements in the default section is executed. The syntax for the switch case construct is as follows:

Syntax

```
switch (variable or expression)
{
case constant A:
statement;
break;
case constant B:
statement;
break;
default:
statement;
}
```

Note that each case statement is terminated by a ":" instead of a ";" and `break;` statement is used to exit from each case construct. If no break statement is used, all the case statements are executed in the top-down order.

Program 2: To check whether the entered number is even or odd and whether it is divisible by 4 or not.

```
#include<stdio.h>
#include<conio.h>
void main()
{
int number;
printf("Enter any number: ")
scanf("%d", &number);
if(number%2==0)
printf ("The number is even");
  if(number%4==0)
/*using nested if-else statement*/
    printf("It is divisible by 4");
  else
    printf("It is not divisible by 4");
else
printf("The number is odd and not
divisible by 4");
}
```

Output

```
Enter any number: 48
The number is even
It is divisible by 4
```

Program 3: To determine whether a number is "odd" or "even" and print the message. **(AU 2008 Suppl.)**

```
#include<stdio.h>
#include<conio.h>
void main()
{
int x;
char a,b;
a="Even";
b="Odd";
printf("Enter a number: ");
scanf("%d", &x);
switch(x)
{
case 0:
printf ("%c",a);
break;
case 1:
printf("%c",b);
break;
default:
switch(x%2)
{
case 0:
printf("Even number");
default:
printf("Odd number");
}
}
getche()
}
```

Output

```
Enter a number: 0
Even number
Enter a number: 7
Odd number
```

Program 4: To check whether the given year is leap or not using ternary operator.

```
#include<stdio.h>
#include<conio.h>
void main()
{
int y,leap;
clrscr();
printf("Enter any year:");
scanf("%d",&y);
leap=(y%400==0)?:(y%100!=0)
?(y%4==0)?1:0:0;
if(leap==1)
printf("The given year is leap year");
else
printf("The given year is not leap year");
}
```

Output

```
Enter any year: 1998
The given year is not leap year
```

3.6.6 | Nested switch-case Statement

An inner switch construct can be contained part of the outer switch statement.The same variables and constants can be used in the two switch constructs. For example, consider program 3.

3.6.7 | Using Ternary Operator

The ternary operator discussed in the subsection "Types of Operators" can be used in to form a conditional decision making statement as shown in program 4.

3.6.8 | Combination of Conditional Statements

The code in program 5 shows a combination of ladder if–else and switch statements. The *switch* statement is used to validate and select an operation upon the users input choice, simulating a simple calculator, and the nested if statement is used to display the result of the operation according to the option selected from the menu of choices.

Program 5: To simulate a simple calculator using switch and ladder if–else statement.

```
#include<stdio.h>
#include<conio.h>
void main()
{
int menu,n1,n2,total;
printf("Enter two numbers:");
scanf("%d %d", &n1, &n2);
printf("Enter the choice of operation:\n");
printf("1=Addition\n");
printf("2=Subtraction\n");
printf("3=Multiplication\n");
printf("4=Division\n");
scanf("%d", &menu);
switch(menu)
{
case 1: total=n1+n2; break;
case 2: total=n1-n2; break;
case 3: total=n1*n2; break;
case 4: total=n1/n2; break;
default: printf("Invalid option
  selected\n");
}
if(menu==1)
printf("Addition of %d and %d gives
  %d\n",n1,n2,total);
else if(menu==2)
printf("Subtraction of %d from %d gives
  %d\n",n1,n2,total);
else if(menu==3)
printf("Product of %d and %d gives
  %d\n",n1,n2,total);
else if(menu==4)
printf("Division of %d by %d gives
  %d\n",n1,n2,total);
}
```

Output

```
Enter two numbers: 5, 4
Enter the choice of operation:
1=Addition
2=Subtraction
3=Multiplication
4=Division
2
Subtraction of 5 from 4 gives 1
```

Solved Problems

1. *Compare if–else statement with switch statement?* **(AU 2009 Suppl.)**

Solution: The differences between if–else and switch statements are given in the following table

if–else Statement	switch Statement
Apart from equalities, other relational operators can also be used with if–else statement	switch variable can test only for equal values
if expression can be of float type	switch variable cannot be of float type
Logical operators can be used with if–else statement	Logical operators cannot be used with switch statement
if–else expression can accommodate more than one value. For example, `if(a>0 && a<5)`	Each switch case expression must be a single value. For example, `switch(flag)`

2. *Explain any two constructs used for decision making. Give an example for each and explain the working of the construct.* **(AU 2009)**

Solution: The two constructs are if–else and switch. Refer to the section above for explanation and examples.

3. *What will be the outputs for the following program, when the value of i is 5 and 10?* **(AU 2012)**

```
void main()
{
int i ;
scanf ("%d", &i) ;
if (i=5)
printf ("Five") ;
}
```

Solution: The output will be `Five`. When user enters value of i as 5, then "Five" is displayed. When user enters value of i as 10, no message is displayed.

3.7 Looping and Branching Statements

3.7.1 Looping Statements – for, while and do-while

The iterative or looping statements are used when we want to repeat a set of statements for certain number of times. The number of iterations depends on the test condition. A set of statements are repeated again and again till the condition is true. As soon as the condition becomes false, the repetition stops. The set of statements that are repeated is called the body of the loop. C offers various kinds of looping statements, such as for loop; nested for; while loop; do-while loop. The flowchart representations of these statements is given in Fig. 3.

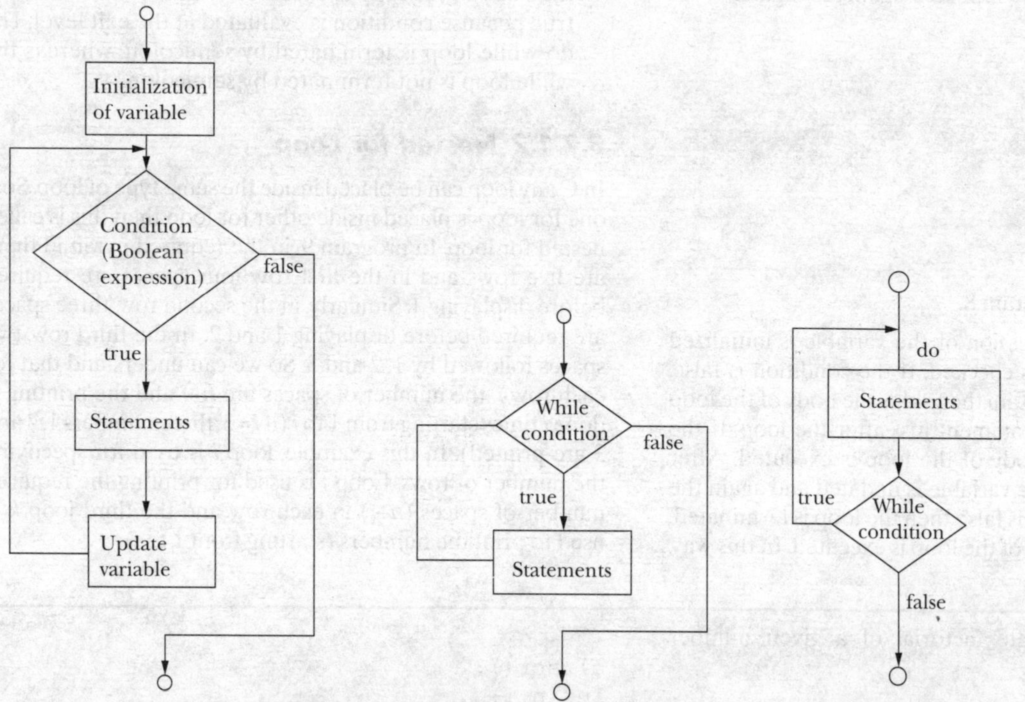

(a) for repetition structure flowchart. (b) While repetition structure (c) do–while repetition structure flowchart.

Figure 3 Flowchart structures for for, while and do-while loops.

1. In **for loop**, the body of the loop is executed for the fixed number of iterations as long as the condition is true.

   Syntax

```
for (initialization;condition;updation)
{
/*body of the loop*/
Statements;
}
```

   For example, see program 6.

2. In the **while loop**, the condition is evaluated at the entry level of the loop. If the condition evaluates to true then only the statements of the loop body are executed otherwise the loop is not executed at all. So, the while loop is called an entry controlled loop.

   Syntax

```
initialization;
while(condition)
{
statements;
updation;
}
```

   For example, see program 7.

3. In **do-while loop**, the body of the loop is executed first and then the condition is checked. So, the do-while loop is also called an exit controlled loop. In do-while loop the body of the loop is executed at least once even if the condition is false. As long as the condition is true, the loop statements will be repeated again and again.

   Syntax

```
initialization;
do
{
statements;
updation;
}
while(condition);
```

   For example, see program 8.

In general, first the expression or the variable is initialized and then the condition is checked. If the condition is false, the loop terminates. Program then skips the body of the loop and comes to the next statement just after the loop. If the condition is true, then body of the loop is executed. After execution of the body, the variable is updated and again the condition is checked. If it is false then the loop is terminated, otherwise again the body of the loop is executed. In this way, the loop is executed again and again till the condition is true. We know that the condition can be any valid C expression including the value of a variable, a unary or binary expression, or the value returned by a function. The body of the loop may contain a single or a compound statement.

3.7.1.1 Comparison of for, while and do-while looping statements

1. **for vs. while vs. do-while:** In for loop, the body of the loop is executed for a fixed number of iterations as long as the condition is true. In the while loop, the condition is evaluated at the entry level of the loop. If the condition evaluates to true then only the statements of the loop body are executed otherwise the loop is not executed at all. So, the while loop is called an entry controlled loop. In do-while loop, the body of the loop is executed first and then the condition is checked. So, the do-while loop is also called an exit controlled loop. In do-while loop, the body of the loop is executed at least once even if the condition is false. As long as the condition is true, the loop statements will be repeated again and again.
2. **for vs. while:** The while loop is similar to the for loop. The difference is in using the sequence of the three expressions. Another difference is that if we know the fixed number of iterations then we may use the for loop. However, if we do not know the number of iterations before starting the loop, then while loop is used.
3. **while vs. do-while:** In while statement, the condition is checked at the entry level. If it is true then body of the loop is executed. In do-while statement, at least once the body of the loop is executed even if condition is not true because condition is evaluated at the exit level. The do-while loop is terminated by semicolon, whereas the while loop is not terminated by semicolon.

3.7.1.2 Nested for Loop

In C any loop can be placed inside the same type of loop. So if one for loop is placed inside other for loop then this is called nested for loop. In program 9, in the required pyramid there are five rows and in the first row four spaces are required before displaying 1. Similarly, in the second row, three spaces are required before displaying 1 and 2. In the third row, two spaces followed by 1, 2 and 3. So we can understand that for each row i, the number of spaces are $n-i$ and the printing is done i times starting from 1 to i (if i=3, three numbers 1, 2 and 3 are printed). In this example, loop i is used for specifying the number of rows. Loop j is used for printing the required number of spaces ($n-i$) in each row and the third loop k is used to print the numbers (starting from 1 to i).

Program 6: To calculate factorial of a given number using the for loop.

```
#include<stdio.h>
#include<conio.h>
void main()
{
clrscr();
int n,i;
long double factorial=1;
```

(*Continued*)

```
printf("Enter the number whose factorial
is required:");
scanf("%lf", &n);
if(n==0)
{
printf("The factorial of 0 is 1");
}
for(i=1;i<=n;i++)
{
factorial=factorial*i;
}
printf("Factorial of %d=%lf",n,factorial);
getche();
}
```

Output

```
Enter the number whose factorial is
required: 20
Factorial of 20=2.432902e+18
```

Program 7: To print the Fibonacci series using while loop. **(AU 2014)**

```
#include<stdio.h>
#include<conio.h>
void main()
{
clrscr();
int first=0,second=1,next;
int n,i;
printf("Enter the number of terms in the
series: ");
scanf("%d", &n);
printf(" *** The Fibonacci series ***");
printf("%d \t %d",first,second);
i=3;
while(i<=n)
{
next=first+second;
printf("%d\t",next);
first=second;
second=next;
i++;
}
getche();
}
```

Output

```
Enter the number of terms in the series: 7
 *** The Fibonacci series ***
0     1     1     2     3     5     8
```

Program 8: To check whether the given number is palindrome using the do-while loop.

```
#include<stdio.h>
#include<conio.h>
void main()
{
clrscr();
int orinum,chnum,rev=0,digit;
printf("Enter the number: ");
scanf("%d", &orinum);
chnum=orinum;
do
{
digit=chnum%10;
rev=rev*10+digit;
chnum=chnum/10;
}while(chnum!=0);
if(orinum==rev)
{
printf("Number is palindrome");
}
else
{
printf("Number is not palindrome");
}
getche();
}
```

Output (First run)

```
Enter the number: 123
Number is not palindrome
```

Output (Second run)

```
Enter the number: 262
Number is palindrome
```

Program 9: To print the pyramid of numbers by using nested for loop.

```
#include<stdio.h>
#include<math.h>
void main()
{
clrscr();
int n,i,j,k;
printf("Enter the number of rows in the
pyramid: ");
scanf("%d", &n);
for(i=1;i<=n;i++)
{
  for(j=1;j<=n-i;j++)
  {
  printf(" ");
```

(Continued)

```
  }
  for(k=1;k<=i;k++)
  {
  printf("%d",k);
  }
  printf("/n");
}
getche();
}
```

Output

```
Enter the number of rows in the pyramid: 5
    1
   12
  123
 1234
12345
```

Program 10: Write a C program to count the letters in a sequence of characters. **(AU 2013)**

```
#include<stdio.h>
#include<conio.h>
void main()
{
clrscr();
char A[10];
int i,count;
printf("Enter the string:\n");
gets(A);
for(i=0;A[i]!='\0';i++);
//Last value of i will be equal to the
length of the string
{
count = i;
}
printf("The number of letters in the
string entered is: %d", count);
}
```

Output

```
Enter the string:
today is sunday
The number of letters in the string entered
is: 15
```

3.7.2 Branching Statements – break, continue, goto and exit

3.7.2.1 break Statement

The break statement causes an exit from a loop. It is used to terminate the execution of the loop statements. It terminates the loop in which it is written and transfers the control to the immediate next statement outside the loop. The break statement is normally used in the switch conditional statement where each case block must contain break statement, otherwise the control will be transferred to the subsequent case blocks also [Fig. 4(a)].

Syntax

```
{
/*body of decision making statement or looping
statement*/
break;
}
```

In the program 11, the while loop is used for five iterations. In the body of the loop, the first two statements are displayed as it is but the third printf statement is not executed because before that statement break statement is used which terminates the loop, and so the immediate next statement after the while loop is executed.

3.7.2.2 continue Statement

The continue statement is used to execute the loop statements to predetermined number of iterations (till the condition is true) even if it finds the error after the continue statement. The continue statement does not update the looping variable [Fig. 4(b)]. The continue statement is used for the reverse operation of the break statement.

Syntax

```
{
/*body of decision making statement or looping
statement*/

continue;
}
```

In program 12, when we enter 6, then the if statement becomes true and displays the message "The number is greater than or equal to five" and executes the continue statement which will continue the loop with the previous value of $i=3$ and it will continue with the same value of *i* again when we give the number 7. So when continue statement is executed, it does not update the *i*. That is why, we can see here that the loop is executed six times instead of four times.

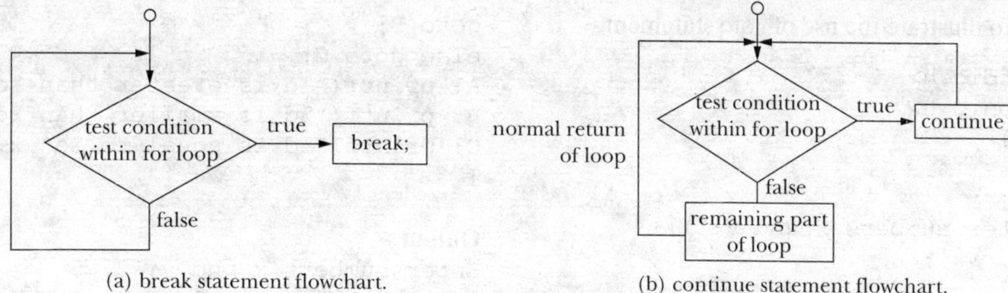

Figure 4 Flowchart structures for break and continue statements.

Program 11: To demonstrate the break statement.

```
#include<stdio.h>
void main()
{
clrscr();
int i;
i=1;
while(i<5)
{
printf("This is sample program/n");
printf("To test the break statement/n");
break;
printf("control never comes here/n");
i++;
}
printf("This is the next statement after break");
getch();
}
```

Output

```
This is sample program
To test the break statement
This is the next statement after break
```

Program 12: To demonstrate the continue statement.

```
#include<stdio.h>
#include<conio.h>
void main()
{
clrscr();
int i,number;
i=1;
while(i<5)
{
printf("Enter the number: ");
scanf("%d", &number);
if(number>=5)
{
printf("The number is greater than or equal to five/n");
continue;
}
printf("The number is: %d/n",number);
i++;
}
getch();
}
```

Output

```
Enter the number: 2
The number is: 2
Enter the number: 3
The number is: 3
Enter the number: 6
The number is greater than or equal to five
Enter the number: 7
The number is greater than or equal to five
Enter the number: 2
The number is: 2
Enter the number: 3
The number is: 3
```

3.7.2.3 goto Statement

This statement passes unconditional control to another part of the same program. The syntax of the goto statement is as follows:

Syntax

```
goto label;
```

where a label is a name that can be given to any statement in the program.

3.7.2.4 exit Statement

The exit statement is used to terminate the execution of the program. This statement will take you out of the program. It is used when we want to stop the execution of the program depending on some condition. When we use the exit() statement, we have to include either process.h or stdlib.h file. This is a library function of C.

Syntax

```
exit(int);
```

Program 13: To illustrate the use of goto statement.

```
#include<stdio.h>
#include<conio.h>
void main()
{
int x,y;
printf("Enter numbers x and y:");
scanf("%d", &x);
if (x>y)
goto A;
else if(x<y)
goto B;
else goto C;
A: printf("%d is greater than %d",x,y);
B: printf("%d is smaller than %d",x,y);
C: printf("%d is equal to %d",x,y);
}
```

Output

```
Enter numbers x and y: 2, 5
2 is smaller than 5
```

Solved Problems

1. *With an example, state the purpose of break and continue statements.* **(AU 2007 Suppl., 2014)**

Solution: The break statement is used to terminate the execution of the loop statements. It terminates the loop in which it is written and transfers the control to the immediate next statement outside the loop.
The continue statement is used to execute the loop statements to predetermined number of iterations (till the condition is true) even if it "finds the error".
Refer to the programs given in the above section.

2. *Write a C program to print the number 10 ten times, the number 9 nine times and so on.* **(AU 2009)**

Solution:

```
#include<stdio.h>
#include<conio.h>
void main()
{
int i,a;
a=10;
A: for(i=0;i<a;i++);
{printf("%d", a);
}
a—;
goto A;
}
```

3. (a) *Write a code segment using for statement to print numbers from 10 down to 1.* **(AU 2014)**

(b) *Write the same code using while loop* **(AU 2010)**

Solution:

(a)
```
void main()
{
int a=10;
int i;
for(i=0;i<10;i++)
{
printf("%d",a);
a—;
}
```

(b)
```
void main()
{
int a=10;
print a;
while a<10
{
a—;
print a;
}
```

4. *State the differences between entry controlled loop and exit controlled loop.* **(AU 2007 Suppl., 2008)**

Solution: The break statement is the exit controlled loop, and is used to terminate the loop and takes control outside the loop. The continue statement is the entry controlled loop, and is used to take control to the beginning of the loop.

5. *Write a C program that reads a number and display whether the number is prime or not.* **(AU 2010)**

Solution:

```
#include<stdio.h>
#include<conio.h>
void main()
{
int i,n,check=0;
clrscr();
printf("Enter a number:");
scanf("%d",&n);
if(n==0||n==1)
{
printf("The number is neither prime nor composite");
}
for(i=2;i<=n;i++)
{
if(n%i==0)
check++;
}
if(check==1)
printf("The entered number is a prime number");
else
printf("The entered number is not a prime number");
getch();
}
```

The output is

```
Enter a number: 45
The entered number is not a prime number
```

6. *Write a program using while loop to reverse the digits of a given number.* **(AU 2008 Suppl., 2009)**

Solution:

```
#include<stdio.h>
#include<conio.h>
void main()
{
int n,a,b=0;
printf("Enter the number: ");
scanf("%d", &n);
while(n>0)
{
a=n%10;
n=n/10;
b=(b*10)+a;
}
printf("The number after reversing the dig-
its is %d",b);
}
```

3.8 Solving Simple Scientific and Statistical Problems

C language can be used to solve scientific problems, such as conversion of temperature from Fahrenheit to Celsius and vice versa, and statistical problems such as computing mean, variance, mode, median, range, etc., for a given set of data. The programs for solving such problems are given as follows.

Program 14: To find the area of various shapes using switch–case.

```
Solution
#include<stdio.h>
#include<conio.h>
#include<math.h>
void main()
{
clrscr();
int choice;
printf("1. For area of circle /n");
printf("2. For area of rectangle /n");
printf("3. For area of triangle /n");
printf("Enter choice:/n");
scanf("%d", &choice);
switch(choice);
{
case 1:
{
float radius,areac;
printf("Enter the radius of the circle: /n");
scanf("%f",&radius);
areac=3.14*radius*radius;
printf("Area of circle = "%f", areac);
}
break;
case 2:
{
float length,breadth,arear;
printf("Enter the sides of the rectangle:
/n");
scanf ("%d%d", &length, &breadth);
arear=length*breadth;
cout<<"The area of the rectangle: "<<arear;
}
break;
case 3:
{
float sidea,sideb,sidec,s,areat;
printf("Enter the three sides of the tri-
angle: /n");
scanf("%f%f%f",&sidea, &sideb, &sidec);
s=(sidea+sideb+sidec)/2;
areat=sqrt(s*(s-sidea)*(s-sideb)*(s-
sidec));
printf("The area of a traingle: %f");
}
break;
default:
{
printf("Enter the proper choice");
}
getch();
}
```

Output

```
1. For area of circle
2. For area of rectangle
3. For area of triangle
Enter choice: 1
Enter the radius of the circle: 2
Area of circle = 12.56
```

Program 15: Write a function to computer the highest common factor of integer numbers m and n. Use this function to find the highest common factor of integer numbers a and b.

```
Solution:
#include<stdio.h>
#include<conio.h>
int main()
{
int m,n,r=1;
clrscr();
printf("\nEnter the first number\t");
```

(Continued)

```
scanf("%d", &m);
printf("\nEnter the second number\t");
scanf("%d", &n);
do
{
r=m%n;
m=n;n=r;

}while(r!=0);
printf("\nH.C.F. of the given number is\t"%d", m);
getch();
return 0;
}
```

Output

```
Enter the first number     150
Enter the second number   45
H.C.F. of the given number is   15
```

Program 16: To find the sum of the series $1^2 + 2^2 + 3^2 + \ldots + n^2$

```
#include<stdio.h>
#include<conio.h>
void main()
{
int n,i,sum=0;
clrscr();
printf("Enter the value of n \n");
scanf("%d", &n);
for(i=0;i<=n;i++)
{
sum=sum+i*i;
}
printf("\nThe sum of squares is\t %d", sum);
getch();
}
```

Output

```
Enter the value of n
5
The sum of squares is    55
```

Program 17: Write a C program to convert centigrade to Fahrenheit and vice versa.

```
#include <stdio.h>
#include <conio.h>
int main()
{
float Celsius, Fahrenheit, Fahrenheit_1, Celsius_1;
printf("Enter the temperature in Fahrenheit: ");
scanf("%f", &Fahrenheit);
Celsius = (100.0 / 180.0) * (Fahrenheit - 32);
printf("Celsius temperature is: %8.1f C\n\n\a", Celsius);
printf("Enter the temperature in Celsius: ");
scanf("%f", &Celsius_1);
Fahrenheit_1 = 32 + (Celsius_1 * (180.0 / 100.0));
printf("Fahrenheit temperature is: %5.1f F\a", Fahrenheit_1);
getch();
}
```

Output

```
Enter the temperature in Fahrenheit: 101
Celsius temperature is:  38.3 C

Enter the temperature in Celsius: 25
Fahrenheit temperature is:       77.0 F
```

Program 18: Write a C program to compute the following function: $S = (x^2 + x^4 + \ldots + x^{2n})$ = Sqrt(x) * (1–power(x,n))/(1–x). Trace the program for the values x = 2 and n = 5.

(AU 2010 Suppl.)

Solution:
(Result is approximate not accurate)

```
#include<stdio.h>
#include<math.h>
#include<conio.h>
int main(){
int n,i,x;
double total = 0.0,result;
printf("\nEnter number of terms n:");
scanf("%d",&n);
printf("\nEnter value of x:");
scanf("%d",&x);
for(i=2;i<=n;i++){
if(i%2==0)
{
total=total+pow(x,i);
}
}
printf("\nLHS=%f",total);
result sqrt(x)*(1-pow(x,n))/(1-x);
printf("\nRHS %f",result);
getch();
}
```

Output

```
Enter number of terms n:5
Enter value of x:2
LHS = 20.000000
RHS = 43.840620
```

Program 19: Write a C program to calculate the simple interest.

```
#include<stdio.h>
#include <conio.h>
int main(){
float principle, noOfYears, rate;
double  simpleInterest;
printf("\n Calculate Simple Interest:");
printf("\n ——————————————————— ");
printf("\n Enter principle amount : ");
scanf("%f", &principle);
printf("\n Enter no of years : ");
scanf("%f", &noOfYears);
printf("\n Enter rate of interest : ");
scanf("%f", &rate);
simpleInterest = (principle * noOfYears *
rate)/100;
printf("\n    Simple    interest    :    %f
",simpleInterest);
getch();
}
```

Program 20: Write a C program to calculate compound interest.

The formula for calculating Compound Interest is given below:
FV = P * (1 + r/n)t*n
where FV is the future value, P is the present value (principal amount), r is the interest rate, n is the number of times the interest is calculated per year and t is the number of years.

```
#include <stdio.h>
#include <math.h>
#include <conio.h>
int main()
{
double amount;
double years;
double interest_rate;
double numtimes;
double compound_interest;
printf("\n Program to Calculate Compound
Interest");
printf("\n  ———————————————————————
——— ");
printf("\n Enter Principal Amount:");
scanf("%lf",&amount);
printf("\n Enter Number of Years:");
scanf("%lf",&years);
printf("\n Enter Interest Rate:");
scanf("%lf",&interest_rate);
printf("\n Enter the number of times the
interest is compounded per year: ");
scanf("%lf",&numtimes);
compound_interest  =  amount  *  pow(  (1  +
(interest_rate / 100) / numtimes ), num-
times * years);
printf("\n      Compound        Interest      =
%lf\n",compound_interest);
getch();
}
```

Output

```
Program to Calculate Compound Interest
———————————————————————————
Enter Principal Amount: 2000
Enter Number of Years: 5
Enter Interest Rate: 2
Enter the number of times the interest is
compounded per year: 2
Compound Interest = 3581.695393
```

Program 21: Write a program to find the roots of the quadratic equation.

```
#include<stdio.h>
#include<conio.h>
#include<math.h>
int main()
{
clrscr();
float a,b,c,d,r,r1,r2;
printf("\nEnter  the  coefficient  of  X^2
term\t");
scanf("%f",&a);
printf("\nEnter   the   coefficient   of   X
term\t");
scanf("%f",&b);
printf("\nEnter  the  coefficient  of  con-
stant term\t");
scanf("%f",&c);
if(a!=0)
{
d = b*b - 4*a*c;
if(d==0)
{
r1=r2=(-b/(2*a));
printf("\nThe roots are real and equal");
printf("\nThe First root is\t%f",r1);
printf("\nThe Second root is\t%f",r2);
}
```

(*Continued*)

```
else if(d>0)
{
r=sqrt(d);
r1=((-b+r)/(2*a));
r2=((-b-r)/(2*a));
printf("\nThe roots are real and distinct";
printf("\nThe First root is\t%f",r1);
printf("\nThe Second root is\t%f",r2);
}
else
{
r=sqrt(-d);
r1=(-b/(2*a));
r2=((-d)/(2*a));
printf("\nThe roots are not real");
printf("\nThe real part is\t%f",r1);
printf("\nThe imaginary part is\t%f",r2);
printf("\nComplex form is\t%f + i%f",
r1,r2);
}
}
else
prinf("\n Sorry it is not a quadratic
equation");
getch();
return 0;
}
```

Output

```
Enter the coefficient of X^2 term 5
Enter the coefficient of X term 28
Enter the coefficient of constant term 15
The roots are real and distinct
The First root is 5.0
The Second root is 0.6
```

Program 22: To display a pyramid of numbers and then print the reverse pyramid of numbers

```
#include<stdio.h>
#include<conio.h>
#include<math.h>
void main()
{
clrscr();
int n,i,j,k,l;
printf("Enter the number of rows in the
pyramid: ");
scanf("%d",&n);
printf("The pyramid is\n");
for(i=1;i<=n;i++)//loop for number of rows
{
for(j=1;j<=n-i;j++)  // loop to print
spaces
{
printf(" ");
}
for(k=1;k<=i;k++)//loop to print numbers
in each row
{
printf("%d",k);//For n = 5, it prints 1,
2, 3, 4, 5 and so on
}
for(l=i-1;l>=1;l--)//loop to print num-
bers in reverse
{
printf("%d",l);//For n = 5, it prints 5,
4, 3, 2, 1 and so on
}
printf("\n");
}
printf("The reverse pyramid is\n");//Loop
for the reverse pyramid
for(i=n;i>0;i--)
{
for(j=0;j>i-n;j--)//Loop to print spaces
printf(" ");
for(k=i;k<=2*i-1;k++)
printf("%d",k);//For n = 5, it prints 5,
6, 7, 8, 9 and so on
for(l=2*i-2;l>=i;l--)
printf("%d",l); //For n = 5, it prints 8,
7, 6, 5 and so on
printf("\n");
}
getch();
}
```

Output

```
Enter the number of rows in the pyramid: 5
The pyramid is
    1
   121
  12321
 1234321
123454321
The reverse pyramid is
567898765
 4567654
  34543
   232
    1
```

Program 23: To find if entered number is an Armstrong number

```
#include <stdio.h>
int main()
{
int number, sum = 0, temp, remainder;
printf("Enter an integer\n");
scanf("%d",&number);
temp = number;
while( temp != 0 )
{
remainder = temp%10;
sum = sum + remainder*remainder*remainder;
temp = temp/10;
}
if ( number == sum )
printf("Entered number is an armstrong
number.\n");
else
printf("Entered number is not an armstrong
number.\n");
return 0;
}
```

Output

```
Enter an integer
371
Entered number is an Armstrong number.
```

Program 24: Write a program in C to check whether a given number is divisible both by 7 and 11.

```
#include<stdio.h>
#include<conio.h>
void main()
{
int number;
printf("Enter any number: ")
scanf("%d", &number);
if(number%7==0)
{
printf("The number is divisible by 7");
        if(number%11==0)
  printf("It is also divisible by 11");
else
  printf("It is not divisible by 11");
}
else
printf("The number is neither divisible
by 7 nor by 11");
}
```

Output

```
Enter any number: 77
The number is divisible by 7
It is also divisible by 11
```

POINTS TO REMEMBER

1. The **C programming language** was developed by Dennis Ritchie and Brian Kernigan at AT&T Bell laboratories in 1972.
2. **C Character Set** is a set of valid characters (93 characters) that the language can recognize:
   - **Letters (alphabets):** Lowercase a…z (26 characters), uppercase A…Z (26 characters).
   - **Digits:** 0…9 (10 characters).
   - **Special characters:** ~ (tilde)` ! @ # $ % ^ & * ( ) _ (underscore) - + = | \ { } [ ] : ; "' <> , . ? / (31 characters).
   - **White space:** Blank space (\b), horizontal tap (\t), carraige return (\r), new line (\n), form feed (\f).
3. **Constants** in C are the fixed data values that never change their values during the execution of a program. These are also called literals; these include the following types: **integer** constants, **floating point** constants, **character** and **string** constants
4. **Variable** is an identifier whose value changes during the execution of the program and which identifies a certain part of the memory location to hold some specified type of information. The different types of variables are **global, local, constant** and **volatile** variables.
5. C supports various **types of data** that can be held by variables. These are categorized in to three categories: **Built-in** (int, char, float, double, void); **derived** (array, function, pointer, reference) and **user-defined** data types (structure, union, enumerated).
6. **Operator** is a symbol such as +, −, etc. operating upon two variables or constants (called operands); an **expression** is the combination of operands (variables/constants) and operators written according to the syntax of the programming language. The various types of operators are **arithmetic, relational, logical, assignment, increment/decrement, conditional, bitwise** and **special** operators.

7. C also supports some non-graphic characters, which can be represented by using **escape sequences** by a backslash (\) followed by one or more characters
8. The **various components** of the **C program** in the syntax are **preprocessor directives, global variable declaration, main()** function, **comments** enclosed in /* and */, **statements, function call()**.
9. C offers **formatted** [`scanf()`, `printf()`, `fscanf()`, `fprintf()`] and **unformatted input/output** functions [`getch()`, `getche()`, `getchar()`, `gets()`, `putch()`, `putchar()`, `puts()`, `cgets()`, `cputs()`, `getc()`, `putc()`, `getw()`, `putw()`, `fgets()`, `fputs()`].
10. **Control statements:** The statements used in C are of the following types **decision making** statements (`if`, `if-else`, `ladder if-else`, `nested if-else`, `switch-case`, `nested switch-case`), **looping** statements (`for`, `while`, `do-while`, `nested for`) and **branching** statements (`break`, `continue`, `goto`, `exit`).

REVIEW QUESTIONS

1. State and explain the various data types supported by "C" languages. (AU 2007 Suppl., 2009 Suppl.)
2. List the rules that are to be followed while declaring variables. (AU 2007 Suppl.)
3. What are the different operators available in C? Explain with examples. (AU 2010)
4. List the bitwise operators supported by C. (AU 2007 Suppl.)
5. Explain the need and types of various looping constructs. Give an example for each and explain the working of the construct. (AU 2009, 2014)
6. Compare in terms of their functions, while and do-while. Give examples (AU 2005 Suppl., 2008 Suppl., 2010 Suppl., 2013)
7. Define C tokens, identifiers and keywords data types and its types.
8. What are the input and output functions in C. (AU 2007 Suppl., 2013)
9. Explain in detail about operators in C program with examples?
10. Explain in detail about conditional and looping statements in C program with example?
11. Illustrate the use of getc(), putc(), fprintf(), fscanf() with suitable examples. (AU 2008 Suppl.)
12. Explain the data types, operators with precedence and expressions in C language. (AU 2009 Suppl.)
13. With examples, explain the statements used for selection, and iteration in C. (AU 2009 Suppl.)
14. List out the rules involved in formatting an identifier (AU 2010)
15. What is a global variable?
16. Describe the basic structure of a C program.
17. What is meant by type conversion?
18. With example describe the structure of (a) if–else statement, (b) nested if–else statement, (c) switch statement in C language. (AU 2011)
19. What is the difference between if–else, ladder if–else and nested if–else statements?
20. Explain the following conditional statements, nested if–else statement and switch-case statement. (AU 2010)
21. Discuss about the bitwise and logical operators in C. (AU 2013)
22. Write the syntax of "for contruct" in C. Give an example. (AU 2013)
23. What are constants? Explain the various types of constants in C. (AU 2013)

PROGRAMMING ASSIGNMENTS

1. Write a program to swap two numbers without using third variable.
2. Write a program to find the area and circumference of a circle.
3. Write a program to find the biggest of two numbers using ternary operator.
4. Write a program to convert Celsius to Kelvin and Kelvin to Celsius.
5. Write a program to calculate the simple interest.
6. The numbers in sequence 1, 1, 2, 3, 5, 8, 13, 21 are called Fibonacci numbers. Write a program to print the first *m* Fibonacci numbers. (AU 2008 Suppl.)
7. Write a program to check whether the given number is palindrome or not.
8. Write a program to find the number of and the sum of all integers greater than 200 and less than 400 that are divisible by 6. (AU 2005 Suppl.)
9. Write a program to count the letters in a sequence of characters. (AU 2009, 2013)
10. Write a program to generate Fibonacci series upto 200. (AU 2012)
11. Write a program to compute and print a table of factorials for a given integer. (AU 2010 Suppl.)

Arrays and Strings 4

LEARNING OBJECTIVES

After completing this chapter, you will be able to understand the following:

- Need for arrays and their types – One-dimensional, two-dimensional and multidimensional.
- Declaration and Initialization of arrays.
- Accessing array elements.
- Input/Output operations on arrays.
- String as a character array.
- Ways to initialize string variables.
- Input/Output operations of strings.
- Standard library string functions to manipulate strings.

4.1 Introduction

An array is a sequentially arranged collection of data items of the same data type, such as int, char, float or any user-defined type like structure. The array elements are stored in consecutive memory locations; therefore, they are linear data structures. In other words, an array is a collection of similar items which are referred by a common name, which is the name of the array.

There are two types of arrays:

1. **One-dimensional array:** It is the simplest form of an array, sometimes called a list. It is a collection of items of the same data type.
2. **Multidimensional array:** It is also a collection of items of the same data type where each data item is also an array of fixed size. **Two-dimensional array** is a simple case of multidimensional array where each element of the array is a one-dimensional array itself. So we can say that two-dimensional array is a collection of one-dimensional arrays.

Solved Problems

1. *What is an array?* **(AU 2013, 2014)**

Solution:

Array is a collection of items of the same data type. The data type can be int, char, float or any user-defined type such as structure or class. For example, marks[5] represents the marks of a student in 5 subjects.

2. *Write any four features of arrays.* **(AU 2013)**

Solution:

(a) Array is a sequentially arranged collection of data items of the same data type, which may be int, char, float or any user-defined type, such as structure.

(b) The items of an array are referred by a common name. A specific element in an array is accessed by an index.

(c) Arrays are linear data structures because elements are stored in consecutive memory locations.

(d) In the contiguous memory locations, the lowest address is used to store the first element and the highest for the last element.

4.2 One-Dimensional Array

4.2.1 Declaration of One-Dimensional Array

The one-dimensional array is defined by specifying its name, size and data types of the items. The elements of a one-dimensional array can be accessed using a single subscript. The general format in C for defining one-dimensional array is

Syntax

```
storage_class data_type array_name[size];
```

For example,

```
int arr[7];
```

Here, the storage class specifies the scope of the array variables. The storage class can be external, static or auto. The storage class specifier is optional. If it is not used then compiler automatically takes it as auto. The array name is the name of the array which follows the same naming conventions as for a variable. The size must be an integer value or integer constant (without any sign) that specifies the number of elements which are to be stored into the array. The size can be directly given as integer number or as an expression that evaluates into an integer. We cannot use the variable name in place of size. It must be a constant. The array must be declared before using it in the program, like other variables.

```
float arr[5];
```

Here arr is an array which can hold five data items of float type. These items are stored into consecutive memory locations. Array elements are accessed by their index or subscript. The index numbering starts from 0. So, the five elements are stored in the following manner.

1.2	arr[0]
3.5	arr[1]
6.2	arr[2]
7.8	arr[3]
9.1	arr[4]

or

1.2	3.5	6.2	7.8	9.1
arr[0]	arr[1]	arr[2]	arr[3]	arr[4]

In a similar manner we can declare an integer array

```
int X[5];
```

1	2	3	4	5
X[0]	X[1]	X[2]	X[3]	X[4]

The array elements are accessed and modified by using their index or subscript.

4.2.2 Initialization of One-Dimensional Array

Array elements can also be initialized just like simple variables. The general format for initialization of array elements is as follows:

Syntax

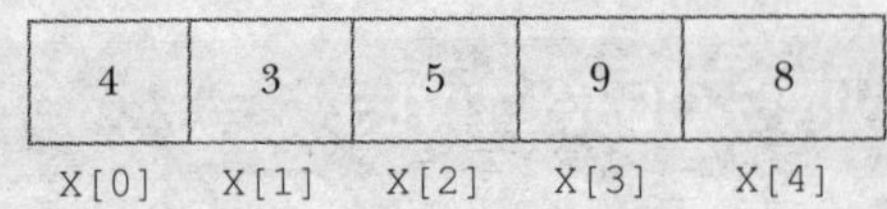

```
storage_class  data_type  array_name[size]=
{value1,value2…value size};
```

The initial values may be enclosed in the {} curly braces and they are separated by comma. For example,

```
int X[5]={4, 3, 5, 9, 8};
```

The elements of array X are initialized as follows

4	3	5	9	8
X[0]	X[1]	X[2]	X[3]	X[4]

We know that the index of an array always starts with 0, so first element is represented by X[0], second by X[1] and so on. It is not necessary that all the elements of the array should be initialized. For example,

```
int X[5]={4, 3, 5};
```

The elements of array X are initialized as follows

4	3	5	0	0
X[0]	X[1]	X[2]	X[3]	X[4]

Though only three elements of an array X are initialized, the memory is allocated to five elements; therefore the remaining two elements are initialized to 0.

In Program 1, different arrays of int and float types are initialized. We know that the array index starts from 0 so all the elements are displayed by using the loops starting from 0. Some elements of the arrays are not initialized, so the compiler takes their values as zero by default.

Program 1: To initialize the array elements and display them.

```
#include<stdio.h>
#include<conio.h>
#define max 5;
void main()
{
clrscr();    /* to clear screen */
int X[5]={4,3,2,1,9};
float Y[5]={1.1,3.2,2.2,0.9,4.1};
int A[5]={10,20,30};
float B[5]={10.1,2.5,29.3};
int i;
printf("** ARRAY X **");
for(i=0;i<5;i++)
{
printf("\nDisplay value of X[%d]: %d",
i,X[i]);
}
printf("\n** ARRAY Y **");
for(i=0;i<5;i++)
{
printf("\nDisplay value of Y[%d]: %d",
i,Y[i]);
}
printf("\n** ARRAY A **");
for(i=0;i<5;i++)
{
printf("\nDisplay value of A[%d]: %d",
i,A[i]);
}
printf("\n** ARRAY B **");
for(i=0;i<5;i++)
{
printf("\nDisplay value of B[%d]: %d",
i,B[i]);
}
getche();
}
```

Output

```
** ARRAY X **
Display value of X[0]:4
Display value of X[1]:3
Display value of X[2]:2
```

(Continued)

Note: When C programs are executed in Linux operating system, then statements like `#include<conio.h>; clrscr();`would not work.

```
Display value of X[3]:1
Display value of X[4]:9
** ARRAY Y **
Display value of Y[0]:1.1
Display value of Y[1]:3.2
Display value of Y[2]:2.2
Display value of Y[3]:0.9
Display value of Y[4]:4.1
** ARRAY A **
Display value of A[0]:10
Display value of A[1]:20
Display value of A[2]:30
Display value of A[3]:0
Display value of A[4]:0
** ARRAY B **
Display value of B[0]:10.1
Display value of B[1]:2.5
Display value of B[2]:29.3
Display value of B[3]:0
Display value of B[4]:0
```

Solved Problems

1. *Write a C program to get an array of N inputs and perform the search operation. Print the number of occurrences of a given element with their position.* **(AU 2007 Suppl.)**

Solution:

```
#include<stdio.h>
#include<conio.h>
#define max 10;
void main()
{
clrscr();
int X[max],i,item,a;
a=0;
for(i=0;i<max;i++)
{
printf("Enter "<<"X["<< i<<"]"<<" element");
scanf("%d",&X[i]);
}
printf("The item to search: ");
scanf("%d",&item);
for(i=0;i<max;i++)
{
if(X[i]==item)
{
a=a+1;
printf("\nItem found at %d position",i+1);
}
else
printf("\nItem not found");
getch();
}
printf("The number of occurrences of %d in the array is %d",item,a);
getch();
}
```

The output is

```
Enter X[0] element 21
Enter X[1] element 21
Enter X[2] element 22
Enter X[3] element 35
Enter X[4] element 28
Enter X[5] element 29
Enter X[6] element 26
Enter X[7] element 23
Enter X[8] element 26
Enter X[9] element 11
The item to search: 23
Item is found at 8 position
The number of occurrences of 23 in the array is 1
```

2. *Write a C program to find the largest and smallest number in the given array.* **(AU 2010 Suppl.)**

Solution:

```
#include<stdio.h>
#include<conio.h>
int main()
{
int a[30],smallest,largest,n,i;
printf("Enter the number of elements in the array: ");
scanf("%d", &n);
printf("Enter the elements");
for(i=0;i<n;i++)
{
scanf("%d", &a[i]);
if(i==0)
{
smallest=largest=a[i]
}
If(a[i]<smallest)
smallest=a[i];
else if(a[i]>largest)
largest=a[i];
}
printf("The largest element is %d and the smallest element is %d",largest,smallest);
getch();
}
```

3. *Write a program to sort the given set of numbers in ascending order.* **(AU 2013)**

Solution:

```
#include<stdio.h>
#include<conio.h>
void main()
{
clrscr();
int list[10], num1, num2;
```

```
int i, j, temp, n;
printf("Enter number of list items: ");
scanf("%d", &n);
cout<<"Enter the list: ";
for(i=0;i<n;i++)
{
scanf("%d",&list[i]);
}
for(i=0;i<n-1;i++)//sorting the list
{
num1=list[i];
pos=i;
for(j=i+1;j<n;j++)//finding the smallest
{
if(num1>list[j])
{
num1=list[j];
pos=j;
}
}
temp=list[i]; //interchanging the smallest
element with the first element
list[i]=list[pos];
list[pos]=temp;
}
printf("The sorted list is: ");
for(int i=0;i<n;i++)
{
printf("%d",list[i]);
}
}
```

Output

```
Enter number of list items: 4
Enter the list: 1,4,5,2
The sorted list is 1 2 4 5
```

Note: For descending order the step is `if (num1 < list[j]){...}` and the rest of the program is same.

4.3 Multidimensional Arrays

Multidimensional arrays are defined in similar way as one-dimensional arrays. The number of square brackets is more (a pair for each subscript is required) in multidimensional arrays. There will be two pairs of square brackets for two-dimensional arrays, three pairs for three-dimensional arrays and so on. The general syntax for declaration of multidimensional array is as follows:

Syntax

```
storage_class data_type array_name [Dim1]
[Dim2]...[Dimn];
```

where `Dim1, Dim2,..., Dimn` are the dimensions of the array.

4.3.1 | Two-Dimensional Arrays

These are the simplest form of the multidimensional arrays where there are two dimensions only. The syntax to define two-dimensional arrays is

Syntax

```
storage class data_type array_name [row]
[col];
```

The syntax is same as for multidimensional arrays. Here, only two dimensions are required where the first dimension refers to the number of rows and the second dimension refers to the number of columns. It is just like a matrix in mathematics. For example,

```
char student[10][5];
```

Here student is a two-dimensional array of char type. The student array contains name of 10 students where each name can have maximum 5 characters. We can say that it is a one-dimensional array (of names); that is, each element itself is a one-dimensional array (of maximum 5 characters). So there will be a total of 50 characters in the array student. If a two-dimensional array X[m][n] is present then this array can contain $m \times n$ elements.

The multidimensional array is usually processed in row major order. Therefore, first all the columns of row 1 are processed then the columns of row 2 and so on. So in C, usually two loops are required to process the elements of two-dimensional arrays.

Initialization of Two-Dimensional Array Elements

We can initialize the two-dimensional array in the same manner as one-dimensional array. For example,

```
int X[3][4]={1,2,4,5,9,6,7,9,10,13,14,15}; or
X[3][4]={{1,2,4,5},{9,6,7,9},{10,13,14,15}}
```

The array X can contain 12 (3 rows × 4 columns) elements so all the 12 elements are assigned the initial values. It is not necessary to initialize all the elements. For example

```
int X[3][4]={1,2,4,5,9,6,7,9};
```

Here 8 elements are assigned the initial values. Rest of the values are initialized to 0 by default. The assignment is always done in row major order; that is, initially the first row is initialized, then second row is initialized, then third and so on. If we want to change the order of initialization then we can use the extra {} braces. For example,

```
int X[3][4]={{1,2,4},{5,9,6,7},{9}};
```

In this example, the first three elements of row one are initialized; the last element is initialized to 0 by default. All the four elements of the second row are initialized. Only one element of the third row is initialized and rest of the three elements is initialized to 0 by default.

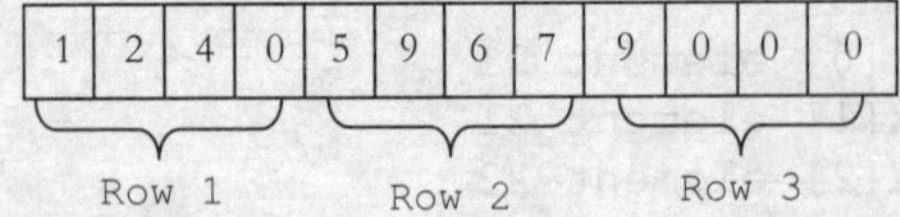

In Program 2, we are using three two-dimensional arrays of 3 × 2 dimensions. All the six elements of array X are initialized, where only first four elements (each element of first two rows) of matrix Y are initialized. Matrix Z is not initialized but its elements are read from the user and then displayed.

Program 2: To initialize the two-dimensional array elements and display them.

```
#include<stdio.h>
#include<conio.h>
void main()
{
clrscr();
int X[3][2]={9,2,1,3,4,6};
int i,j;
int Y[3][2]={4,3,1,2};
int Z[3][2];
printf("Display elements of X \n");
for(i=0;i<3;i++)
{
  for(j=0;j<2;j++)
  {
  printf("%d  ",X[i][j]);
  }
printf("/n");
}
printf("\nDisplay elements of Y \n");
for(i=0;i<3;i++)
{
  for(j=0;j<2;j++)
  {
  printf("%d  ",Y[i][j]);
  }
printf("/n");
}
printf("/nEnter elements of Z\n");
for(i=0;i<3;i++)
{
  for(j=0;j<2;j++)
  {
  scanf("%d  %d", &i, &j);
  }
}
printf("\nDisplay elements of Z\n");
for(i=0;i<3;i++)
{
  for(j=0;j<2;j++)
  {
  printf("%d  ",Z[i][j]);
  }
printf("/n");
}
getch();
}
```

Output

```
Display elements of X
9  2
1  3
4  6
Display elements of Y
4  3
1  2
0  0
Enter elements of Z
4  4  4  0  3  0
Display elements of Z
4  4
4  0
3  0
```

Solved Problems

1. *Differentiate between one-dimensional and two-dimensional arrays.*

Solution:

One-dimensional array	Two-dimensional array
It is a collection of data items of the same data type, and is used to store and manage data in linear mode.	It is a collection of data items of the same data type where each data item is also a one-dimensional array. It is used to store and manage data in tabular mode.
One index value is required to access the element. For example, a[0] refers to the first element.	Two index values are necessary to access the element. For example, a[1][2] refers to the element in the first row and second column.
In C, the syntax for declaration of one-dimensional array is `storage_class data_type array_name [size];` where size represents the number of elements in the array.	In C, the syntax for declaration of two-dimensional array is `storage_class data_type array_name [Dim1] [Dim2];` where Dim1 and Dim2 indicate number of rows and columns, respectively.
In C, one for loop is required to process the elements of one-dimensional arrays.	In C, usually two for loops are required to process the elements of two-dimensional arrays.

2. *Write a C program to find the addition of two matrices.* **(AU 2013, 2014)**

Solution:

```
#include <stdio.h>
#include <conio.h>
int main()
{
int  i,j,m1[100][100],m2[100][100],m3[100]
[100],m,n,sum;
printf("Enter values of n and m to set
order m x n of both the matrices");
scanf("%d %d",&n,&m);
printf("Enter elements of 1st matrix");
for(i = 0;i < n;i++)
{
for(j = 0;j < m;j++)
{
scanf("%d",&m1[i][j]);
}
}
printf("Enter elements of 2nd matrix");
for(i = 0;i < n;i++)
{
for(j = 0;j < m;j++)
{
scanf("%d",&m2[i][j]);
}
}
printf("Matrix after addition of two matri-
ces is -- \n");
sum = 0;
for(i = 0;i < n;i++)
{
for(j = 0;j < m;j++)
{
sum = m1[i][j] + m2[i][j];
m3[i][j] = sum;
printf("%d\t",m3[i][j]);
}
printf("\n");
}
getch();
}
```

3. *Write a C program to get a matrix as input and perform the following operations:*
(a) Add all diagonal elements.
(b) Find the transpose of a given matrix. **(AU 2007 Suppl.)**

Solution:

```
#include<stdio.h>
#include<conio.h>
void main()
{
int X[20][20],Y[20][20],i,j,m,n,sumdgl;
printf("Enter dimensions m and n: ");
scanf("%d %d", &m, &n);
for(i=0;i<m;i++)
{for(j=0;j<n;j++)
{scanf("%d", &X[i][j]);
}
sumdgl=0;
for(i=0;i<3;i++)
{for(j=0;j<3;j++)
{
if(i==j)
{sumdgl=sumdgl+X[i][j];
}
Y[i][j]=X[j][i];
}
}
printf("The sum of the diagonal elements is
%d",sumdgl);
printf("The transpose of the matrix is/n");
for(i=0;i<3;i++)
{for(j=0;j<3;j++)
{
printf("%d", &Y[i][j]);
printf(" ");
}
printf("/n");
}
```

4. *Write a program to perform the multiplication of two matrices.*

Solution:

```
#include<stdio.h>
#include<conio.h>
void main()
{
clrscr();
float X[3][3],Y[3][3],Z[3][3];
int i,j,rowx,colx,rowy,coly;
printf("Enter dimensions of the matrix X:
");
scanf("%d, %d",&rowx,&colx);
printf("Enter dimensions of the matrix Y:
";
scanf("%d, %d",&rowy,&coly);
if(colx!=rowy)
{
printf("\nMatrix multiplication is not
possible");
getch();
exit(1);
}
else
{
printf("Enter elements for matrix X\n");
for(i=0;i<rowx;i++)
{
for(j=0;j<colx;j++)
{
scanf("%f",&X[i][j]);
```

```
}
}
printf("Enter elements for matrix Y\n");
for(i=0;i<rowy;i++)
{
for(j=0;j<coly;j++)
{
scanf("%f",&Y[i][j]);
}
}
for(i=0;i<rowx;i++)
{
for(j=0;j<coly;j++)
{
Z[i][j]=0;
for(int k=0;k<colx;k++)
Z[i][j]=Z[i][j]+X[i][k]*Y[k][j];
}
}
printf("The resultant is\n");
for(i=0;i<rowx;i++)
{
for(j=0;j<coly;j++)
{
printf("%f  ",Z[i][j]);
}
printf("\n");
}
getche();
}
```

4.4 Strings and String Functions

String is a sequence of characters that is created as a single data item.

We know that string constants are declared within double quotes. In an extension to arrays, string can also be expressed in the form of character array. Each string is terminated by a null character "\0" which takes one byte for its storage. Hence, the string length would be the number of characters (which take one byte each) plus one byte for null character.

4.4.1 Declaration of Character Array (String)

The string or character array is a collection of characters. This character array is also declared in the same manner as integer or float array is declared. The general syntax for declaring a character array is

Syntax

```
Storage_class data_type array_name[size];
```

The difference between character array and other type of array is that the character array is always terminated by a null character ('\0'). The null character is represented by a backslash followed by zero. The null character is very important because it refers to the end of a string. For example,

```
char name[10];
char city[15];
```

Here name is an array of 10 characters. Actually we can store only 9 characters in name because last location (space) is required to store the null character. The compiler automatically initializes a null character at the end of each character array by default. Therefore, we must declare the size of the character array one more than the actual number of characters we want to store, leaving room for the null character; otherwise on displaying the string, the output will be the desired string followed by some garbage value.

An array of string is a two-dimensional array where first dimension determines the number of strings and the second dimension determines the number of characters in each string. For example

```
char empname[5][10];
```

Here empname can have 5 elements (name) of length 10 characters.

For example, empname `[0] [10]`
`[1] [10]`
`[2] [10];`

4.4.2 Initialization of Character Array (String)

The character array can also be initialized in same manner as integer or float arrays are initialized. The only thing that we must remember is that the character array always terminates with the null character so we must keep an extra space for null character. For example

```
char day[7]={'M','O','N','D','A','Y','\0'};
```

When we initialize the character array, it is not necessary to mention the size. The C compiler automatically takes it equal to the number of characters assigned. So we can initialize the above array name as follows

```
char name[]={'M','O','N','D','A','Y','\0'};
```

We know that the character constants are always represented by using single quotes, and the characters must be separated by a comma. Character array may also be initialized in the following manner.

```
char name [] = "MONDAY";
```

We can also initialized the two-dimensional array in the same manner:

```
char month [5][10] = {"January", "February",
"March", "April", "May"};
```

In the Program 3, the character array is initialized in two ways. Either we can assign the value for individual position as is done for junname in this program, or we can give the string at once within double quotes as is done for stuname. When values are assigned to individual elements, then a space must be made for null character and that should also be assigned to the last character of the string.

Program 3: To demonstrate the initialization the character array.

```
#include<stdio.h>
#include<conio.h>
#include<string.h>
void main()
{
clrscr();
char name[15];
char stuname[]="Mona";
char junname[]={'S','t','u','t','i',
'i','\0'};
int i,len=0,lenR=0;
printf("Enter the name:");
gets(name);
for(i=0;stuname[i]!='\0';i++)
len=len+1;
for(i=0;name[i]!='\0';i++)
lenR=lenR+1;
int lenj=strlen(junname);
printf("\nName initialized string: %s",
stuname);
printf("\nThe number of characters in %s
is: %d",stuname,len);
printf("\nName read: %s",name);
printf("\nThe number of characters in %s
is %d",name,lenR);
printf("\nName initialized string (character):
%s",junname);
printf("\nThe number of characters in %s
is %d",junname,lenj);
getch();
}
```

Output

```
Enter the name: Ram Naik
Name initialized string: Mona
The number of characters in Mona are: 4
Name read: Ram Naik
The number of characters in Ram Naikare: 7
Name initialized string(character): Stuti
The number of characters in Stuti are: 5
```

Reading strings from terminal: scanf() can be used with "%s" format specification to read a string of characters. For example,

```
char empname[20];
scanf ("%s", empname);
```

4.4.3 | String Standard Functions

There are various built-in functions which are frequently used with the character array. These functions are defined in `string.h` so we must include that file whenever we want to use such functions. Some of the functions are given in Table 1. In the program following the table, the built-in library function `strlen()` is used to find the length of a string as in the previous program, `strcpy()` is used to copy the string from source to destination and `strcmp()` is used to compare two strings.

TABLE 1

Some Frequently Used String Library Functions

Function	Syntax	Description	Example
strlen	strlen(string)	This function determines the length of a string not including null character.	int len=strlen(justname);

strcpy and strncpy	strcpy (dest,source)
	strncpy (dest, source, length)
		This function copies the source string into destination string, where source and destination both must be character arrays.
		The strncpy function copies one string into another upto a specified length indicated in the argument.
			char dest;
			int length;
			char source[ ]= "ABC";
			strcpy(dest,source);
			strncpy(dest, source, length);

strcmp and stricmp	strcmp(S1,S2); stricmp(S1, S2);	The comparison starts with the first character of the string and continues until a corresponding character differs or end of string is reached. The stricmp function does not discriminate between two strings if the characters are same, but the case is different.	strcmp("Monday", "monday"); Produce 1 if s1!=s2 Produce 0 if s1=s2 strcmp returns 1, whereas stricmp returns 0.
strlwr and strupr	strlwr(string); strupr(string);	It converts all uppercase characters to lowercase. It converts all lowercase characters to uppercase.	strlwr("Monday"); The output is monday. strupr ("Monday"); The output is MONDAY.

(Continued)

strdup	strdup(string);	It duplicates the string	
strchr and strrchr	strchr(string, ch); strrchr (string, ch);	It finds the first occurrence of character ch in the string. It finds the last occurrence of character ch in the string.	strchr ("Monday", 'o');
strstr	strstr(S1, S2);	It finds the first occurrence of a given string in another string.	strstr("Monday", "on");
strcat and strncat	strcat(dest, source); strncat(dest, source, length)	It appends the destination string to the source string. The strncat function appends the strings upto specified length.	strcat("Today is ", "Monday");
strrev	strrev(string);	It reverses the order of characters in the given string.	strrev("Monday");
strpbrk	strpbrk(S1, ch);	It displays the rest of characters of a string after the first occurrence of the specified character.	strpbrk("Monday", "d");

Program 4: To find the length of strings, copy and compare the strings using string library function.

```
#include<stdio.h>
#include<conio.h>
#include<string.h>
void main()
{
clrscr();
char S1[]="SUNDAY";
char S2[]="TUESDAY";
printf("copy TUESDAY into SUNDAY: %s\n",str
cpy("SUNDAY","TUESDAY"));
printf("The length of string is:
%d\n",strlen("SUNDAY"));
difference=strcmp("sunday","tuesday");
if(difference==0)
{printf("The strings are identical");
}
else
{printf("The strings are not identical");
printf("copy S2 into S1:
%s\n",strcpy(S1,S2));
printf("The length of S2 string is:
%s\n",strlen(S2));
printf("Comparison of two strings S1 and
S1: %d\n",strcmp(S1,S1));
getch();
}
```

Output

```
Copy TUESDAY into SUNDAY: TUESDAY
The length of string is: 6
The strings are not identical
Copy S2 into S1: TUESDAY
The length of S2 string is: 7
Comparison of two strings S1 and S1: 0
```

Solved Problems

1. *List and discuss the various string operations.* **(AU 2007 Suppl.)**

   or Explain the function (a) strlen(), (b) strcpy(), (c) strcat(), (d) strcmp() with examples. **(AU 2011)**

Solution: Refer Table 1.

2. *How are strings stored in C language?* **(AU 2009 Suppl.)**

Solution: Strings are stored in the memory in form of ASCII codes. The number of bytes used to store strings is equal to the number of characters plus the null character, which requires 1 byte.

3. *What is the ASCII value for the null character?*

Solution: The ASCII value of null character is "0".

4. *Write a program to reverse a string.* **(AU 2014)**

Solution:

```
#include<stdio.h>
#include<conio.h>
#include<string.h>
void main()
{
clrscr();
char str[100];
printf("Enter the string to be reversed:
");
gets(str);
strrev(str);
printf("The reverse order of the entered
string is \n%s\n",str);
}
```

The output is

```
Enter the string to be reversed: ABCD
The reverse order of the entered string is
DCBA
```

Note: Alternately without the string library function, the string can be reversed as can be seen in the laboratory manual.

5. *To find the length of an entered string without using strlen()*

Solution:

```
#include<stdio.h>
#include <conio.h>
void main()
{
char str[100];
int len=0;
printf("\nEnter a string:");
gets(str);
while(str[len]!='\0')
{
len++;/*to calculate the length of string*/
}
printf("\nThe length of the string %s is
%d",str1,len);
}
```

6. *To concatenate two strings and print the result and the length of the resultant string without using string library functions.*

Solution:

```
#include<stdio.h>
#include<conio.h>
#include<string.h>
main()
{
char str1[100], str2[100];
int i, len=0, temp;
printf("Enter the first string: \n");
gets(str1);
printf("\nEnter the second string: \n");
gets(str2);
for(i=0; str1[i]!='\0'; i++)
len++;
temp=length;
for(i=0; str2[i]!='\0'; i++)
{
str1[temp]=str2[i];
temp++;
}
str1[temp]='\0';
printf("\nThe string after concatenation
is:\n");
puts(str1);
for(i=0;str1[i]!='\0';i++)
{
count++;
}
printf("\nThe length of the concatenated
string is: %d",count);
getch();
}
```

7. *Write a program to copy the string from one variable to another variable without using standard library string functions.*

Solution:

```
include<stdio.h>
#include<conio.h>
void main()
{
char a[100],b[100];
int i;
printf("\nEnter the string: ");
gets(a);
i=0;
while(s1[i]!=NULL')
{
b[i]=a[i];
i++;
}
b[i]= '\0';
printf("\nThe copied string is %s: ",b);
getch();
}
```

8. *Write a program to compare one string with another without using standard library string functions.*

Solution:

```
include<stdio.h>
#include<conio.h>
void main()
{
char a[100],b[100];
int i, temp;
printf("\nEnter the first string: ");
gets(a);
printf("\nEnter the second string: ");
gets(b);
i=0;
temp=0;
while(a[i]!=NULL&&b[i]!=NULL)
{
if(a[i]=b[i]);
{
i++;
temp++
}
}
if(temp==0)
printf("\nThe two entered strings are not
equal");
else
printf("\nThe two entered strings are
equal");
getch();
}
```

POINTS TO REMEMBER

1. C provides a data structure, **the array**, which stores a fixed-size sequential collection of elements of the same type and referred to a common name.
2. **Array** is a collection of items of same data type. The data type may be int, char, float or any user-defined data type such as structure. These are of two types, **one-dimensional** and **multidimensional** (two-dimensional, etc.)
3. Like other variables array must be explicitly declared so that the compiler may allocate space for them in memory.
4. An element can be accessed by **indexing** the array name.
5. Strings are a sequence of characters.
6. String constants are declared within double quotes. Each string is terminated by a null character "\0" which takes one byte for its storage.
7. C supports a wide range of functions that manipulate null-terminated strings such as **strcpy(), strcmp(), strlen(), etc.**

REVIEW QUESTIONS

1. Explain how the data are stored in an array.
2. Explain briefly about strings in C.
3. Explain the significance of array? What are the different types of arrays?
4. Explain the need for array variables. Describe the following with respect to arrays: Declaration of array, two-dimensional array and accessing an array element. (AU 2005 Suppl.)
5. What is the importance of NULL character in a string?
6. Distinguish between the character array and integer array.
7. Describe the following with respect to arrays: Declaration of array, two-dimensional array and accessing an array element.
8. How are string variables initialized?
9. Write a note on the string library functions? How are they useful?
10. What is the difference between strcmp() and stricmp() functions?
11. Explain any four format strings with examples. (AU 2013)
12. Name any two library functions used for string handling. (AU 2014)

PROGRAMMING ASSIGNMENTS

1. Write a program to find the first and second biggest element from the given array of integers. (AU 2009 Suppl.)
2. Write a program to sort the elements of an n × n matrix and to display the elements in the following pattern: (AU 2007 Suppl.)

   5 4 3
   6 1 2
   7 8 9

3. Write a program to read m × n matrix and to check whether the element of the last column of each row is the sum of the elements of the other columns in that row. (AU 2007 Suppl.)
4. Write a program to check whether the given matrix is orthogonal ($AA^T = 1$) or not.
5. Write a program to concatenate two strings.
6. Write a program to count the letters in a sequence of characters using strlen function.
7. Write a program using array to calculate the mean, standard deviation and variance of the given elements.
8. Write a program to find the number of duplicate elements and remove the duplicate elements from the list.
9. Write a program to find the position of (a) an element in an array and (b) character in a string.
10. Write a program to find the average male height and average female heights in the class.

Functions and Pointers

5

LEARNING OBJECTIVES

After completing this chapter, you will be able to understand the following:

- User defined functions – declaration and definition.
- Different types of parameter passing methods for functions.
- Types of functions based on return type and function call.
- Solving problems recursively using functions.
- Handling of character strings.
- Standard string functions.
- Pointers and dynamic memory allocation.

5.1 Introduction

A complex program has large number of instructions that need to be executed. For better management, these programs are split into a number of modules with each module having some specific set of instructions to be executed. Such modules are called **functions** and are the building blocks of C programming. A function is an assignment or a task that must be performed to complement the other part(s) of a program. There are various types of functions based on the tasks accomplished by them – user defined, system-defined (standard library and string, etc.) and functions, which will be discussed in the subsequent sections of the chapter. The functions that are supplied to user are usually in the following categories: those built-in with the operating system and written in C language and those supplied with the programming environment.

The **advantages** of the functions are as follows:

1. They can be created and tested in the program once; however, they can be used wherever necessary.
2. They are easy to understand a program and may reduce the size of the program. except inline functions
3. They provide easy means to identify and rectify errors. If there is need to change the calculation, the change is made at one place, and on recompilation everything gets updated.
4. Modularity is implemented as the activity inside the function does not impact code outside the function.
5. The local variables are contained within the function and valid only as required.

Solved Problem

1. *Explain the needs and benefits of using functions.* (AU 2014)

Solution: Refer to the section above.

5.2 User Defined Functions

Any function defined by the user to carry out operations to solve a particular problem is called a user-defined function. In C, main() itself is a user-defined function that invokes other functions in the program to perform various tasks. A function can be invoked from other parts of the program. Usually, if some sequence of instructions is repeatedly appearing in a program then a function can be defined for that particular sequence rather than repeating it again. Also, the function may or may not return a value to the calling function; therefore there is no difference between a function and a subroutine (procedure) in C.

5.2.1 | Declaring a Function

The function declaration is also called the function prototype. When a function is defined before the function call in the program, then the function prototype is not required. However, a function declaration is required if its definition is appearing after the function call (i.e., after the main function). The function prototype or the first statement of the function definition (depending upon its appearance in the program) is a very useful in C as the compiler checks whether the number and data type of parameters are matching with their usage in the function body. If they do not match, it generates an error. The general syntax for declaring the function is as follows:

Syntax

```
return_type function_name (individually
declared parameters);
```

A function has a return type, function name, a pair of parentheses containing zero or more parameters and a body. The *return type* is any C data type which describes that the function will return the value of *return type* from the body of the function to the calling function. But if the function *return type* is `void`, then it specifies that the function is not returning any value and so there is no need of the return statement. The *function name* is any valid identifying name given to the function. The name is generally made relevant to operation performed by the function. For example, if function is written to find the *least* number then the function name may be given as *least*. The *parameters* are the variables of same or different types which are passed from the calling function to the called function. Here it is important to note that each variable of the parameter list must be declared independently inside the parenthesis. For example, `Sum(int num1,num2)` will give an error, so we must define it as `Sum(int num1, int num2)`. Parameter list may or may not contain variables. If there is no parameter then *`void`* may be written.

5.2.2 | Defining a Function

A function definition is a declaration that contains the function body. Actually, it tells the program what statements are to be executed and how they are executed. The syntax of a function definition is as follows.

Syntax

```
return_type function_name (para1, para2,
...paran)
{
body of the function;
}
```

where `para1, para2,...paran` is the parameter list separated by commas.

The parameter list contains the individually declared variables separated by comma. A function definition may or may not have any parameters. If it does not contain any parameter then we may write `void` in the parenthesis. A function definition, just like a function declaration, must have a return type. If a function does not return any value then we must write `void` as the return type. A body of a function consists of a single statement or a combination of statements (compound statements) enclosed between pair of `{}` braces. In the body, *`return`* is a keyword. The return statement returns the value that the function would return to the calling function. The data type of this value must be same as the function return type and after returning a value, it terminates the function. If the function does not return a value, the *`void` return type* is used. A function may contain several return statements but only one (the first one encountered during execution) of them is executed.

There are two ways that a function terminates execution and returns to the caller. It occurs when the last statement in the function is executed and the functions ending curly brace is encountered. Also, it may contain one return statement or several return statements.

Program 1: To demonstrate the use of return statement.

```
#include<stdio.h>
#include<conio.h>
int square(int);//declaration of a function
int main()
{
int a,b;
clrscr();
printf("\nEnter the value to square\t");
scanf("%d",&a);
b=square(a);//function call
printf("\nSquare of the given number
is\t %d",b);
getch();
return 0;
}
int square(int x)//definition of a function
{
return (x*x);//function returns value
}
```

Output

```
Enter the value to square 7
Square of the given number is 49
```

Note: For C programs executed in Linux operating system, `clrscr(); #include<conio.h>;` would not work.

5.2.3 | Function Call

If a function is being used by a program then it needs to be called for execution. When a function is called, the program execution control is transferred to the function; the body of the function is executed and then the control returns to the statements following the function call. A function is called in two ways:

1. `function_name(actual parameters);`
2. `variable/expression = function_name(actual parameters);`

In the first case function is called by providing the function name, followed by the actual parameters. In this case function does not return a value. In the second case also the function is called by providing function name. The value returned by that function is stored in some variable of the same type as of function return type or it may be used in some expression. For example, in the following sample program two functions factorial and factorial1 are declared. The first function (factorial) does not return any value so return type is void. The second function returns a value of type long int.

5.2.3.1 Actual and Formal Parameters

The parameters written within parenthesis when a function is called are known as actual parameters. The parameters

Program 2: To calculate the factorial of a given number using both ways of function calling.

```
#include<stdio.h>
#include<conio.h>
void main()
{
clrscr();
int n;
long f;
printf("Enter the number whose factorial
 is required:");
scanf("%d",&n);
if (n ==0)
printf("The factorial of 0 is 1");
void factorial(int); /*function prototype*/
printf("\n**The function is called in first
way**");
factorial(n);/*first method of function call*/
long  int  factorial1(int);   /*function
prototype*/
printf("\n**The  function  is  called  in
second way**");
f=factorial1(n);/*second method of function
call*/
printf("\nThe factorial of %d = %d",n,f);
getch();
}
void factorial(int num1)/*function definition
{
long int fact=1;
for(int i=1;i<=num1;i++)
{
fact=fact*i;
}
printf("\n The factorial of %d = %d",
num,fact);
}
long int factorial1(int num2)/*function
definition*/
{
long int fact=1;
for(int i=1;i<=num2;i++)
{
fact fact*i;
}
return(fact);
}
```

Output

```
Enter the number whose factorial is
 required:5
**The function is called in first way**
The factorial of 5 = 120
**The function is called in second way**
The factorial of 5 = 120
```

written in the header while defining a function are called formal parameters. Thus, formal parameters are associated with defining of a function and actual parameters with calling of a function. The formal parameters become active when the function is called and they exist only within the function, hence they are local in nature. We can give the same name to the actual and formal parameters, but their scopes are different. Formal parameters are available only in the function definition and actual parameters are available in the calling function. In the following program, n is an actual parameter whereas num1 and num2 are formal parameters.

Calling function can pass parameters to the called function in two ways; by value and by reference. These two modes of calling a function are explained and illustrated in Fig. 1.

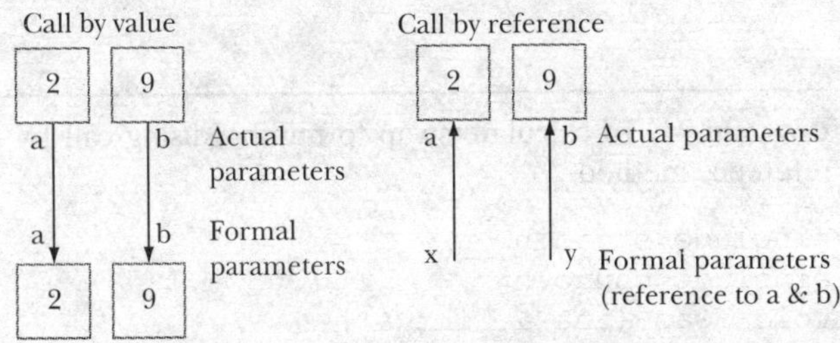

Figure 1 Parameter passing by call by value and call by reference methods.

Program 3: To demonstrate call by value type of function calling.

```
#include<stdio.h>
#include<stdlib.h>
#include<conio.h>
void swap(int,int);
int main()
{
int a=2,b=9;
printf("\nThe  a  value  before  swap  is\t
%d",a);
printf("\nThe  b  value  before  swap  is\t
%d",b);
swap(a,b);
printf("\nThe  a  value  after  swap  is\t
%d",a);
printf("\nThe  b  value  after  swap  is\t
%d",b);
getch();
return 0;
}
void swap(int a,int b)
{
int temp;
temp=a;
a=b;
b=temp;
}
```

(Continued)

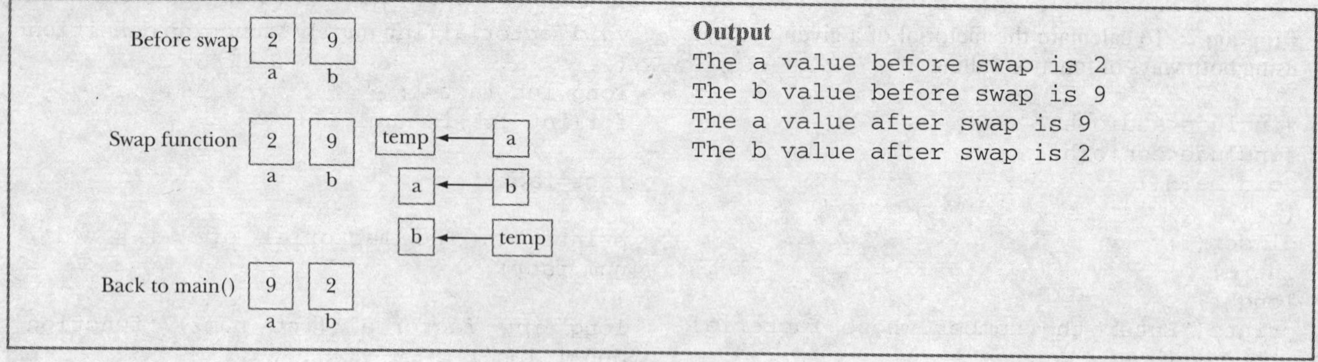

Output

```
The a value before swap is 2
The b value before swap is 9
The a value after swap is 9
The b value after swap is 2
```

5.2.3.2 *Call by Value*

In this mode of parameter passing the values of actual parameters are copied into formal parameters (temporary variables). The function does not have access to the actual parameters (original values) and can work only on the copies of the values created as formal parameters. In this method, changes made in the formal parameter do not get reflected in the actual parameter even if the names of actual and formal parameters are same. So this method is useful when we want to keep the values of actual parameters intact.

5.2.3.3 *Call by Reference*

In this mode of parameter passing instead of passing the value to a function, a reference or the alias to the actual parameter is passed. Therefore, the actual parameters can be accessed by two names, the original name and the alias or reference name. When a function is called then the formal parameter becomes a reference to the actual parameter. In this method of parameter passing, actual parameters are referred by another name (formal parameter), therefore the changes made in the formal parameters are reflected in the actual parameters. This implies that call by reference is useful when we want to change the values of the actual parameters in case formal parameters change their values. This can be easily understood considering the following example: Suppose a class of BE Ist Semester is scheduled in Room Number 42. To refer to the location, we can use two different names (BE Ist Semester and Room Number 42). So in call by reference method, if we make any change to Room Number 42 it means we are making a change in the name BE Ist Semester.

Program 4: To calculate swap to number using call by reference method.

```
#include<stdio.h>
#include<conio.h>
void swap (int &, int &);
void main()
{
clrscr();
int a=2,b=9;
printf("\nThe a value before swap is\t
%d",a);
printf("\nThe b value after swap is\t
%d",b);
swap(i,j);
printf("\nThe a value before swap is\t
%d",a);
printf("\nThe b value after swap is\t
%d",b);
}
void swap (int &x, int &y)/*&x and &y are
reference variables */
{
int temp;
temp=x;
x=y;
y=temp;
}
```

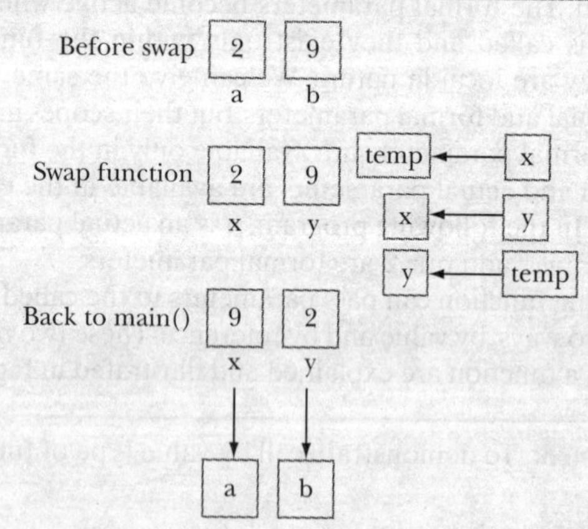

Output

```
The a value before swap is 2
The b value before swap is 9
The a value after swap is 9
The b value after swap is 2
```

Solved Problems

1. *Write notes on actual and formal parameters* (AU 2007 Suppl.)

Solution: There are two types of parameters associated with functions. They are:

(a) **Actual parameter:** The parameters associated with function call are called actual parameters.

(b) **Formal parameter:** The parameters associated with the function definition are called formal parameters.

The formal parameters become active when the function is called and they exist only within the function, hence they are local in nature. We can give the same name to the actual and formal parameters, but their scopes are different. Formal parameters are available only in the function definition and actual parameters are available in the calling function.

2. *What is the need for declaring function prototype?* (AU 2007 Suppl., 2014)

Solution: A function declaration introduces the function name to the program. It tells about the return type, the number and type of parameters and their sequence to the program. It differs from the function definition in the term that it has no body. The parameter's name is optional in the function prototype but its data type is must. Prototype declaration must match with the function header of the function definition. When a function is called the compiler compares the function to its prototype to determine whether the number and type of parameters are matched or not. If they do not match, it generates an error. The general syntax for the prototype is as follows.

Syntax

```
return_type function_name (para1, para2,...
paran);
```

where `para1, para2,...paran` is the parameter list separated by commas.

3. *What is the need for user defined functions?* (AU 2011)

Solution: In addition to standard library functions, we require functions defined by the user to solve certain problems in a certain manner. These functions are called user defined functions, and have the following syntax:

```
return_type function_name (parameter list)
{
body of the function;
}
```

Each function definition must have a return type. If a function does not return any value then we must write `void` as the return type. A body of a function consists of a single statement or a combination of statements (compound statements) enclosed between pair of `{}` braces.

4. *What is call by value?* (AU 2011, 2014)

Solution: It is a mode of parameter passing where the values of actual parameters are copied into formal parameters (temporary variable). The function does not have access to the actual parameters (original values) and can work only on the copies of the values created as formal parameters. In this method, changes made in the formal parameter do not get reflected in the actual parameter even if the names of actual and formal parameters are same. So this method is useful when we want to keep the values of actual parameters intact.

5.3 Types of Functions based on their Return Type and Function Call

The various types of functions used are the following:

1. **`void` function:** It does not require any parameter to pass and it does not return any value.

2. **`void` function with parameters:** A function which is called with some parameters and *does not* return any value is called `void` function with parameters.

3. **Function with parameter and with return type:** A function which is called with some parameters and *does* return a value is called function with parameters and with return type. For example, `int sum(int a, int b);`

4. **Nested function:** Since there is no restriction in C for calling the number of functions in a program, a function in C may call another function and such functions are called multifunctions or nested functions.

5. **Function with default arguments:** C allows us to assign default value to function parameters so that a function can also be called without specifying all its parameters. All such parameters which are not specified must be provided some initial values in the function declaration. Whenever a function is called without specifying a parameter, the program will automatically assign default values to the parameters from the function declaration. The default values are specified at the time of the function declaration and should not be repeated in the function definition. The default values to the parameters must be added from right to left. Any argument cannot have a default value unless all parameters appearing on its right have their default values. We cannot assign a default value to a particular parameter in the middle. For example, `int func(int x, int y, int z=5);`

6. **Function with constant parameters:** Functions can have constant parameters just like any program can have constant variables. When a function is having constant parameters it is meant that the function cannot change the value of these parameters in the body. So to make the parameter constant a keyword `const` is used before the parameter. For example, `float area(int r, const int pi=3.14);`

5.3.1 | Recursion

Recursion is the ability of a function/procedure/algorithm to repeatedly call itself until a certain condition is met. Such a condition is called the base condition. A function which calls itself directly or indirectly is called a recursive function. This method of calling a function by itself is called recursion. The following conditions must be satisfied for using recursion:

1. There must be some base condition for which the function does not call itself.
2. Each time, the function calling should lead to the base condition

Recursion can be direct (when the function calls itself directly) or indirect (when the function calls another function which may eventually call the original function).
We can apply recursion to find the factorial of 6, in which case the following operations need to be carried out:

6! = 6*5!
5*4!
4*3!
3*2!
2*1!
1!
= 6*5*4*3*2*1 = 720

Hence, we can see that to find the factorial of 6 we are using 6*5! which means to calculate the factorial (of 6), we are again using factorial (of 5). This is recursion because function factorial calls itself. But for factorial of 1 it does not have to call itself; rather it uses the value 1 for factorial of 1. This is the base condition for factorial function and we can see here that each time function is called with a lesser (6, 5, 4, 3, 2, 1) value thus moving towards the base condition (factorial of 1 = 1).

Program 5: Recursive procedure to evaluate factorial of n.

```
#include<stdio.h>
#include<conio.h>
long int factorial(int);/*declaring it inside main is not wrong. But this is the best practice*/
void main()
{
clrscr();
int fact,N;
printf("Enter the value of N:");
scanf("%ld",&n);
if(n==0)
{printf("The factorial of 0 is 1");
}
fact=factorial(n);
printf("The factorial of given number is: %ld", fact);
getch();
}
long int factorial(int num)
{
if(num==1)
{
return(1);
}
else
{
return(num*factorial(num-1));
}
}
```

Output

```
Enter the value of n: 5
The factorial of given number is: 120
```

Iteration is generally used for repetitive computation in which each action is defined in terms of the previous result. It looks just like recursion, but this is not true. The above program by iterative method is shown in Program 6.

Program 6: Iterative procedure to evaluate factorial of n.

```
#include<stdio.h>
#include<conio.h>
void main()
{
clrscr();
int n;
long f;
printf("Enter the number whose factorial is required:");
scanf("%d",&n);
if(n==0)
{printf("The factorial of 0 is 1");
}
long int factorial1(int &);//function prototype
f=factorial1(n);/*call by reference*/
printf("\nThe factorial of %d is %d",n,f);
getch();
}
long int factorial1(int &num2)/*function definition*/
{
long int fact=1;
for(int i=1;i<=num2;i++)
{
fact=fact*i;
}
return(fact);
}
```

Output

```
Enter the number whose factorial is required:5
The factorial of 5 = 120
```

There are some differences between recursion and iterations as compiled in Table 1.

TABLE 1

Table 1 Comparison of recursion and iteration

Recursion	Iteration
When a function calls itself, it is called recursion.	In iteration, a set of statements is executed repeatedly until some specified condition is satisfied.
Recursion is based on the base condition; execution of statements moving towards the base condition.	Iteration is based on the initialization, termination condition, updation and execution.
Recursion is a top-down approach.	Iteration is bottom-up approach.
Recursion runs out of memory if base condition is not checked.	Iteration results in infinite loop if termination condition is not met.
Recursion takes more space to store new set of local variables.	Iteration does not take much time as compared to recursion.
Recursion is not efficient.	Iteration is efficient.
Every recursive algorithm can be converted into its iterative version.	Every iterative method cannot be converted into its recursive version.
For proper function recursion saves the return address.	Iterative method does not save the return address.

5.3.2 | Inline Functions

Function calling is a time-consuming process because when we call a function, the control is transferred to the function definition and after executing the function body, the control is transferred back to the immediate next statement in the calling function as shown in the Fig. 2.

It requires time to transfer the control. A solution to save this time is by declaring a function as inline. When we call inline function, the compiler replaces the function call statement with the corresponding function definition and in this manner the time required for transferring the control is saved. Inline function is defined simply by placing the keyword before the function declaration.

```
void main
{
double a , b;
a = cube(4.0)
b = cube(4. 9+7.1)
printf("The value of a is:" , a);
printf("The value of b is:" , b);
printf("%ld",cube (c++));
}

inline double cube (double  x)
{
return x * x * x;
}
```

Figure 2 The control transfer mechanism in function calling.

Syntax

```
inline return_type name of function
(parameter list);
```

When to use inline function: The inline functions are good for small function body because each time the function is called, the function call statement is replaced by the corresponding code of the called function, therefore it requires extra memory. Inline functions are never used for functions having large set of instructions.

Solved Problems

1. *What is recursion? Write a recursive procedure to evaluate factorial of N.* **(AU 2007 Suppl., 2008 Suppl., 2014)**

Solution: Recursion is an ability of a function/procedure/algorithm to repeatedly call itself until a certain condition called the base condition is met. A function which calls itself directly or indirectly is called a recursive function. This method of calling a function by itself is called recursion. The following conditions must be satisfied for using recursion:

(a) There must be some base condition for which function does not call itself.

(b) Each time, the function calling should lead to the base condition.

The recursive procedure to evaluate factorial of n is given in program 5.

2. *Write a C program to check whether the given year is leap or not.* **(AU 2009)**

Solution:

```
#include<stdio.h>
#include<conio.h>
void leap(int year);

void main()
{
int year;clrscr();
printf("Enter a year: ");
scanf("%d",&year);
leap(year);
}
voidleap (int year)
{
if(year%4==0&&year%100!=0||year%400==0);
printf("The given year is a leap year");
else
printf("The given year is not a leap year");
}
```

The output is

```
Enter a year: 1996
The given year is a leap year
```

3. *Define a C function to exchange the content of two variables.* **(AU 2009, 2013)**

Solution:

```
void interchange(int a, int b)
{
int i;
i=a;
a=b;
b=i;
printf("The values have been exchanged as
a=%d and b=%d", a,b);
}
```

4. *What are the different types of recursion?*

Solution: Recursion can be classified into two categories: *Direct recursion*, which occurs when the function calls itself directly, and *indirect recursion*, which occurs when the function calls another function that may eventually call the original function.

5. *Explain function with and without arguments with examples for each?* **(AU 2014)**

Solution:

A function is called in four ways based on arguments and return type:

(a) Function call without arguments and without return type: These are called void functions that do not require any parameter to pass and it does not return any value. For example,

```
#include<stdio.h>
#include<conio.h>
void add();
int main()
{
clrscr();
add();
getch();
return 0;
}
void add()//function definition without
arguments and without return type
{
int a,b,c;
printf("\nEnter the value of a\t");
scanf("%d",&a);
printf("\nEnter the value of b\t");
scanf("%d",&b);
c=a+b;
printf("\nThis sum is\t",c);
}
```

Output

```
Enter the value of a 5
Enter the value of b 8
This sum is 13
```

(b) Function call with arguments and without return type: void function with parameters is a function which is called with some parameters and *does not* return any value is called void function with parameters.

```
#include<stdio.h>
#include<conio.h>
void add(int,int);
int main()
{
int a,b;
clrscr();
printf("\nEnter the value of a\t");
scanf("%d",&a);
printf("\nEnter the value of b\t");
scanf("%d",&b);
add(a,b);
getch();
return 0;
}
void add(int a,int b)
{
int c;
c=a+b;
printf("\nThis result is\t",c);
}
```

Output

```
Enter the value of a 4
Enter the value of b 3
This result is 7
```

(c) Function call without arguments and with return type: A function is called without passing any arguments but it does return a value of specified return type.

```
#include<stdio.h>
#include<conio.h>
void add();
int main()
{
clrscr();
add();
getch();
return 0;
}
void add()
{
int a,b,c;
printf("\nEnter the value of a\t");
scanf("%d",&a);
printf("\nEnter the value of b\t");
scanf("%d",&b);
c=a+b;
printf("\nThis sum is\t",c);
}
```

Output

```
Enter the value of a 6
Enter the value of b 9
This sum is 15
```

(d) Function call with arguments and with return type: A function which is called with some parameters and *does* return a value is called function with parameters and with return type. The following example shows how it is called with arguments and return type.

```
#include<stdio.h>
#include<conio.h>
int add(int,int);
int main()
{
int a,b,c;
clrscr();
printf("\nEnter the value of a\t");
scanf("%d",&a);
printf("\nEnter the value of b\t");
scanf("%d",&b);
c=add(a,b);
printf("\nThis result is\t ",c);
getch();
return 0;
}
int add(int a,int b)//function definition
with arguments and with return type
{
return (a+b);
}
```

Output

```
Enter the value of a 5
Enter the value of b 2
This result is 7
```

5.4 Arrays and Functions

In C, it is possible to pass an entire array onto a function as parameter. An array name refers to the address of the first element or the base address. So when an array is passed to a function, it is sufficient to only pass address. Therefore, in cases where an entire array is passed, call by value method of parameter passing is not possible. It is always passed by reference. When an array is passed, no subscript or square brackets are required in the parameter list of the function call statement. The syntax for passing an array to a function is:

Syntax

```
data_type function_name(array_name[],size);/*
function declaration*/
function_name(array_name,size);/*function
call*/
data_type function_name(array_name[],size)/*
function definition*/
{
function body;
}
```

In declaration of function, array name is required followed by square bracket but size is optional. When an entire array is passed, the function can be called with only function name and array name if no extra arguments are passed. When we want to pass a two-dimensional array, there will be some changes in the syntax. The syntax would be as follows:

Syntax

```
data_type function_name(int array_name[]
[col], int size);/*function declaration*/
function_name (array_name);/*function call*/
data_type function_name(array_name[])/*
function definition*/
{
function body;
}
```

For example, `fn(double values[][4],int size);`

We can see that the second dimension of the two-dimensional array cannot be left blank when it is passed to a function, because a two-dimensional array is a collection of one-dimensional arrays. We can skip the first dimension. To call the function only array name is passed. Its dimension is not required.

Program 7: To insert an element at the given position in one-dimensional array using functions..

```
#include<stdio.h>
#include<conio.h>
void main()
{
clrscr();
int X[10], num,i,j,element,pos;
int insert(int pos, int element);
printf("Enter the size of the array:");
scanf("%d",&num);
printf("Enter the elements of the array\n");
for(i=0;i<num;i++)
scanf("%d",&X[i]);
printf("\nEnter the pos and the element to
insert:");
scanf("%d %d",&pos,&element);
printf("\nAfter insertion the elements of
the array are \n");
insert(pos, element);
}
int insert(int pos, int element)
{
int k;
for(int k=num;k>=pos;k--)
{X[k]=X[k-1];
X[k]=element;
}
for(i=0;i<=num;i++)
printf("%d ",X[i]);
getch();
}
```

Output

```
Enter the size of the array: 8
Enter the elements of the array
1 2 3 4 5 6 7 8
Enter the pos and the element to insert:
3 9
After insertion the elements of the array are
1  2  9  3  4  5  6  7  8
```

Solved Problem

1. *Write a C program to add two 3 × 3 matrices and display their sum.* **(AU 2013)**

Solution:

```
#include<stdio.h>
#include<conio.h>
void main()
{
int a[3][3], b[3][3],i,j;
void add(int a[3][3], int b[3][3]);
clrscr( );
for(i=0;i<=2;i++)
{
for(j=0;j<=2;j++)
{
printf("Enter the value for a[%d][%d]:
",i,j);
scanf("%d",&a[i][j]);
printf("Enter the value for b[%d][%d]:
",i,j);
scanf("%d",&b[i][j]);
}
}
printf("The sum of the two matrices is/n");
add(a,b);
}

void add(int a[i][j], int b[i],[j])
{
int c[3][3];
for(i=0;i<3;i++)
{
for(j=0;j<3;j++)
{
c[i][j]=a[i][j]+b[i][j];
printf("%d",c[i][j]);
}
printf("\n");
}
getch();
}
```

The output is

```
Enter the value for a[0][0]: 4
Enter the value for a[0][1]: 2
Enter the value for a[0][2]: 5
Enter the value for a[1][0]: 4
Enter the value for a[1][1]: 2
Enter the value for a[1][2]: 0
Enter the value for a[2][0]: 4
Enter the value for a[2][1]: 2
Enter the value for a[2][2]: 6
Enter the value for b[0][0]: 0
Enter the value for b[0][0]: 2
Enter the value for b[0][0]: 2
Enter the value for b[0][0]: 4
Enter the value for b[0][0]: 6
Enter the value for b[0][0]: 3
Enter the value for b[0][0]: 2
Enter the value for b[0][0]: 1
Enter the value for b[0][0]: 3
The sum of the two matrices is

4 4 7

8 8 3

6 3 9
```

5.5 Pointers

We know that variables are used to store values and these values are kept in the memory. We also know that every byte in the memory has an address; therefore, the values stored in the memory must have some address. A variable which holds the address of the value is called *pointer*. In other words, a pointer is a variable that can hold the address of other variables or address of a value. Therefore, using pointers we can access the memory locations and the data stored in those memory locations by indirect reference. Hence, pointers not only provide the access to the memory location, but also provide a method for dynamic memory allocation. They are the most useful and strongest feature of C. In fact, a pointer can point to any type of data item or a function.

5.5.1 | Pointer Declaration

A pointer is also a variable, therefore, the declaration of a pointer variable is similar to that of a normal variable except for the addition of the unary * character. This symbol informs the compiler that the variable is a pointer variable. The * (asterisk) means "pointer to". The syntax for pointer declaration is

Syntax

```
data_type * pointer variable;
```

Here, pointer variable is the name of the pointer, and the data type may be any C data type such as int, float, char, etc. The asterisk symbol may be placed anywhere between the data type and the pointer variable. So the pointer declaration is based on the data type of the variable it points to. For example,

```
int *ptr;
int sample=15;
char *ptr1;
char sample1='x';
```

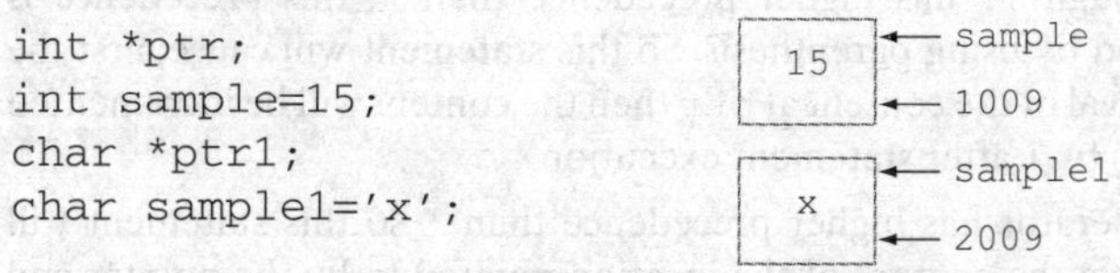

In the above example, `ptr` is a pointer to the integer, so it can hold the address of the integer type of data. sample is an integer type of variable which contains the value 15. So, `ptr` can hold the address (let it be 1009) of sample. Also, `ptr1` is a pointer to character, so ptr1 can hold the address (2009) of the char type of data sample1.

With pointers two types of operators are used: (1) Address of operator (&) and (2) value at operator (*).

5.5.1.1 Address of Operator

A unary operator that returns the address of the variable following it is known as "address of" operator. Since it is a unary operator, it requires only one operand and so it is represented by using the ampersand sign (&) followed by the variable name. For example,

```
ptr=&sample;
```

where `ptr` will hold the address of `sample`, that is, 1009. Now, if we use

```
printf("%d",ptr);
```

it will display the address of `sample` (1009 in this example). Let

```
ptr1=&sample1;
```

then `printf("%d",ptr1);` will display the address of `sample1` (2009 in the example)

5.5.1.2 Value at Operator

A unary operator that returns the contents stored at the memory location (address) is called "value at" operator. It is also called "indirection operator" or "dereference operator". This operator can be represented by a combination of * with a variable. For example if `ptr` holds the address of sample

```
ptr=&sample;
```

If we now write `printf("%d",*ptr);` then it will display the content at `ptr`, that is, 15. The (`*ptr`) is read as "the value at the address contained in `ptr`" or the "value at `ptr`". Here we must remember that both the pointer operators & and * have a higher precedence over all other arithmetic operators except the unary minus, with which they have equal precedence.

5.5.2 | Initializing Pointers

The pointer variable needs to be initialized and if the address of base data type variable is not assigned to the pointer variable, it may be initialized with null. It is important that the variable whose address is assigned to a pointer variable is declared first. The general rules for assigning value to the pointer variable are the same as that of any other variable data type. For example,

```
char X;
char *ptr1,*ptr2;
```

Here we can assign address of `char` variable to `ptr1` and `ptr2` so

1. `ptr1=&X;` the memory address of X is assigned to `ptr1`.
2. `ptr2=&X;` the memory address X is assigned to `ptr2`.
3. `*ptr1='Y';` the character Y is assigned to the location pointed by `ptr1`.

5.5.3 | Arithmetic Operations with Pointer

There are only two arithmetic operations possible with pointer variables:

1. addition of value (you may not add two pointers);
2. subtraction of value (you may not subtract two pointers).

Any other arithmetic operations like multiplication or division are not allowed with pointer variables. The addition of value to the pointer variable is performed according to the size of the base data type. For example,

```
ptr=ptr+5;
```

Since `ptr` is an integer pointer and integer number usually takes 2 bytes of storage so

```
ptr=ptr+5*(size of base data type)
ptr=ptr+5*2;
ptr=ptr+10;
ptr=1009+10;
ptr=1019;
```

So, when we add 1 to a pointer variable, we actually add the size of whatever the pointer is pointing at. Whenever the pointer is incremented by 1, it will point to the memory location of the next element of its base type. Similarly, when we decrement the will point variable by 1 (subtracting by 1), it will point to the location of the previous element of its base type. So, if we add 1 to `ptr`, it will point to the next integer number. Similarly, if we add 5 to the `ptr1`, then it will point to the location of sixth character (`ptr1` represents the 0th character). The pointer arithmetic is compiled into Table 2.

TABLE 2

Arithmetic Operations with Pointer Variables

Pointer Arithmetic	Equivalent to	Explanation
`ptr++`	`ptr=ptr+sizeof(data type)`	We are using post-increment operator which means "use then increment". So this statement will use original value of `ptr` and then `ptr` is incremented after statement execution.
`++ptr`	`ptr=ptr+sizeof(data type)`	We are using pre-increment operator which means "increment then use". So this statement will increment the original value of `ptr` and will be used in the statement.
`ptr--`	`ptr=ptr-sizeof(data type)`	We are using post-decrement operator which means "use then decrement". So this statement will use original value of `ptr` and then `ptr` is decremented after statement execution.
`--ptr`	`ptr=ptr-sizeof(data type)`	We are using pre-decrement operator which means "decrement then use". So this statement will decrement the original value of `ptr` and will be used in the statement.
`(*ptr)++`	`*ptr then *ptr=*ptr+1`	Although ++ has higher precedence than *, this precedence is altered by using parenthesis. So this statement will cause; first the retrieval of the content at `ptr` then the content will be incremented (post) by 1 after statement execution.
`*ptr++`	`*ptr then ptr=ptr+1`	++ operator has higher precedence than * so this statement will retrieve the content of the location pointed to by the pointer and then increment (post) `ptr` after statement execution. It is not similar to `(*ptr)++`.
`* ++ptr`	`ptr=ptr+1 then *ptr`	++ operator has higher precedence than * so this statement `*(++ptr)` will increment pointer and then retrieve the content of the new location pointed to by the `ptr`.
`++ *ptr`	`*ptr then *ptr=*ptr+1`	This statement will cause first the retrieval of the content at `ptr` then the content will be incremented (pre) by 1 before statement execution.

5.5.4 | Pointers and Arrays

5.5.4.1 Pointers and One-Dimensional Arrays

In C, arrays and pointers are closely related. The versatile use of pointers in C can be attributed to their ability to handle arrays. A pointer is an efficient tool to access elements of an array. In C the array name acts as a pointer because the array name always refers to the address of first element of the array. So we can say that array name is a pointer which holds the address of its first element. For example,

Address	1002	1004	1006	1008	1010
A[i]=	10	20	30	40	50

```
int A[5];
int *ptr;
```

`ptr=&A[0];` true because ptr is a pointer to integer so ptr will hold 1002

`ptr=A;` true because array name refers to the address of the first element, that is, `ptr=1002`

So `ptr=&A[0];` and `ptr=A;` are two equivalent statements. Now,

`printf("%d",ptr);` will show 1002.

`printf("%d",A);` will show 1002.

`printf("%d",A[0]);` will show the value 10.

`printf("%d",*A);` will show the value 10.

`printf("%d",(A+0));` will show 1002 (i.e., 1002 + = 1002).

`printf("%d",*(A+0));` will show value at 1002, that is, 10.

`printf("%d",A[0]);` will also show the value 10.

The last two statements produce the same output. Also consider the following two statements:

`printf("%d",(A+2));` will show 1006 (i.e., `1002+2*sizeof int=1002+2*2=1006`).

`printf("%d",*(A+2));` will show value at 1006, that is, 30.

`printf("%d",A[2]);` will also show the value 30.

Based on above examples we generalize the statement as `A[i]=*(A+i)=*(&(A)[0]+(i))`

Similarly, if `ptr=A;` then

`printf("%d",ptr);` will display 1002.

`printf("%d",*ptr);` will display 10.

`ptr++;`

`printf("%d",ptr);` will display 1004.

`printf("%d",*ptr);` will display 20.

The relation between array and pointer can be summarized as follows.

`ptr=1002`	`*ptr=`content at the address contained in `ptr (at 1002)=A[0]=10`
`ptr+1=1000+1*2=1002`	`*(ptr+1)=content at 1004=A[1]=20`
`ptr+2=1000+2*2=1004`	`*(ptr+2)=content at 1006=A[2]=30`
`ptr+3=1000+2*3=1006`	`*(ptr+3)=content at 1008=A[3]=40`
`ptr+4=1000+2*4=1008`	`*(ptr+4)=content at 1010=A[4]=50`

5.5.4.2 Pointers and Two-Dimensional Arrays

Array name always refers to the address of the first element: in one-dimensional array, the address of 0th element. In two-dimensional arrays, the 0th element is the element present in the 0th(first) row and 0th(first) column. We know that the two-dimensional array is a collection of one-dimensional arrays. For example,

```
int A[2][3]={{1,2,4},{5,8,3}};
```

Thus, A is a collection of two elements which themselves are arrays of three elements. Therefore array A is a collection of two one-dimensional arrays. Let us take

```
B[3]={1,2,4} C[3]={5,8,3};
```

then we can say that A is a collection of B and C and so

```
A[2]={B,C};
```

This array can be represented in row major order in the memory as

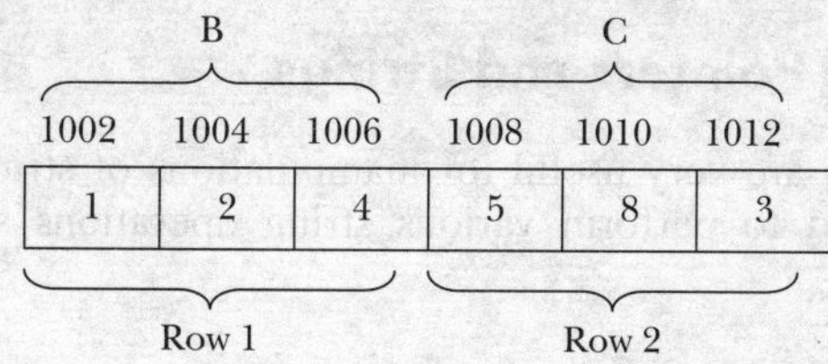

Now,

`printf("%d",A);` will display 1002.

`printf("%d",A+1);` will display the address of the next element of array A, that is, address of `A[1]` = 1008.

`printf("%d",*(A+1));` will display content at 1008, that is, a one-dimensional array C of three elements 5, 8 and 3.

`printf("%d",*(A+1)+1);` will display the address of the next element of array C, that is, 1010.

`printf("%d",(*(A+1)+1));` will display the content at 1010, that is, 8.

`printf("%d",A[1][1]);` will display the content of 1st row and 1st column, that is, 8.

We now establish the formula to access the element of two-dimensional array using pointers:

```
A[i][j]=*(*(A+i)+j)
```

if `int *ptr, ptr=A or ptr=&A[0][0]` then to access the contents `A[i][j]` we can use

```
A[i][j]=*(*(ptr+i)+j)
```

5.5.4.3 Pointers and Multidimensional Arrays

Consider an array

```
A[2][2][3]={
 {
 {1,2,4},
 {5,6,8}
 },
 {
 {11,7,3},
 {0,9,12}
 }
 };
```

then we can represent the allocation of memory for array A as follows:

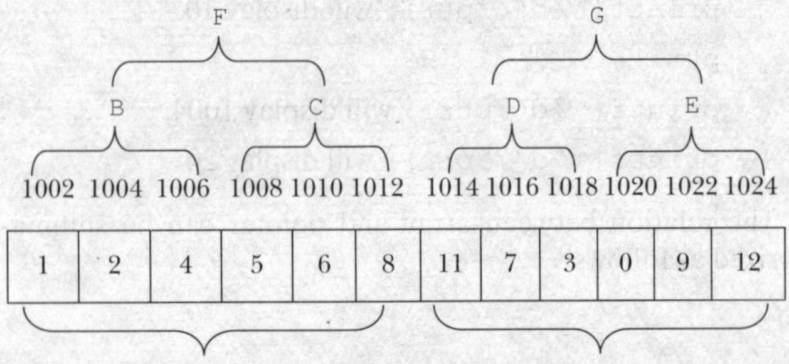

We can say that the three-dimensional array A is a collection of two-dimensional arrays. Here in this example array A is a collection of two-dimensional arrays, F and G, of dimensions 2 × 3 where each element of the two-dimensional arrays is a collection of two one-dimensional arrays of 3 elements. So F is a collection of B(1,2,4) and C(5,6,8)and G is a collection of D(11,7,3) and E(0,9,12). Now

`printf("%d",A);` will produce the base address, that is 1002.

`printf("%d",A+1);` will produce the address of the next element of A that is a two-dimensional array (G). So it will give you the base address of G, that is, 1014.

`printf("%d",*(A+1));` will produce the content at 1014, that is, a two-dimensional array (G). So it will give you the base address of G again that is 1014.

`printf("%d",*(A+1)+1);` will produce the address of the next element of G (at 1014), that is a one-dimensional array (E). So it will give you the base address of E, that is, 1020.

`printf("%d",*(*(A+1)+1));` will produce the content at 1020, that is, a one-dimensional array (E). So it will give you the base address of E again, that is 1020.

`printf("%d",*(*(A+1)+1)+1));` will produce the address of the next element of E (at 1020), that is 9. So it will give you the base address of 9 which is 1022.

`printf("%d",*(*(*(A+1)+1)+1));` will produce the content at 1022 that is an individual value 9.

`printf("%d",A[1][1][1]);` will also give us 9.

So for three-dimensional arrays we can give the following formula to access the contents:

```
A[i][j][k]=*(*(*(A+i)+j)+k)
```

Similarly we can formulate the formula for arrays having more than three dimensions.

5.5.4.4 Array of Pointers

We can declare array of pointers just like the array of built-in data type or the user-defined data types. The collection of pointers is called an array of pointers. Since each element of such an array is a pointer, it can hold the address of specified data type. So the array of pointers represents a collection of addresses. It is important to remember that the pointers must be of same type. The array of pointers may be declared as follows.

Syntax

```
data_type *array name [size];
```

Consider as an example

```
int *ptr[4];
```

Here each element of `ptr` array can hold the address of `int` variable. So if we have

```
int X[4]={9,3,2,0};
```

then we can assign the addresses of each element of X to the different elements of `ptr`. That is

```
ptr[0]=&A[0];
ptr[1]=&A[1];
ptr[2]=&A[2];
ptr[3]=&A[3];
```

We can assign the address of any integer to any element of `ptr` array, such as

```
int x1,x2,x3,x4;
ptr[0]=x1;
ptr[1]=x2;
ptr[2]=x3;
ptr[3]=x4;
```

The declaration for array of pointers to characters may be given as

```
char *ptr[row][col];
```

This is very useful when we deal with array of strings. This array of pointers can be passed to a function as shown:

```
display (msg, 61); //Function call
void display (char *ptr [][], int n, int m)
//Function definition
{
//Body of function
}
```

5.5.5 | Pointers and Strings

Pointers are very useful for manipulations of strings and are used to perform various string operations such as string copy, string length, string concatenate, string compare, etc. In fact we can easily exchange the position of strings in the array using pointers. There are two ways to initialize the character string:

1. **`char A[]= "Sample string";`** Here array contains 14 characters including NULL character (\0) and the array name refers to the base address, that is the address of the first element. Also the array name is a constant pointer and so we cannot the change the value of A. This implies that A = A + 1 is not allowed. We must note that though A + 1 is allowed but assignment of A + 1 back to A is not allowed because this will change the base address, which we cannot do.
2. **`char *ptr= "Sample string";`** Here character pointer `ptr` is declared which points to the first character of the string. Also `ptr` is a pointer variable, so we may change the value in it by using operators such as `ptr++` or `ptr--`.

5.5.6 | Pointers and Functions

Just like the normal arguments, functions can also have pointers as arguments. The general syntax for functions with pointers as arguments is as follows.

Syntax

```
return_type function_name(data_type
*variable1,data_type *variable2);
```

When we call a function we have to pass the address of the variable which can be stored in the corresponding pointer variables. In this mode of parameter passing, we pass the addresses to the function. It is similar to the call by reference in the sense that in this method also the changes in formal parameters are reflected in actual parameters.

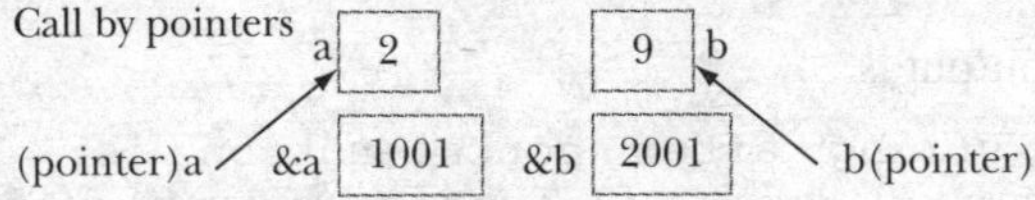

5.5.6.1 Function Returns Pointer

We already know that functions can return any data type. In a similar manner they can also return a pointer variable. The general syntax for pointer to function is as follows.

Syntax

```
return_type *function_name(parameters)
```

Here returntype is the data type of the value pointed to by the pointer which is returned by the function and functionname follows the usual rules of naming the identifiers. The list of parameters may consist of different types of parameters such as int, float, array, structure or even class.

5.5.6.2 Pointer to Function

We have pointer to int, float or char and in addition, we can define a pointer to a function? A pointer to function is just like a normal pointer. It contains the address of the function, that is, the value of pointer to function is the address of the function name. Since the name itself is a pointer, therefore it is a constant pointer. A pointer to a function is declared as a pointer to the data type by the function, such as void, int, float, etc. The general syntax for pointer to function is as follows.

Syntax

```
return_type  (*pointer  variable)(list  of
parameters);
```

The pointer variable is always enclosed in parenthesis otherwise C compiler would interpret it as a function which returns a pointer type value. Using pointer to function, the function is called as follows:

```
sum=(*ptr)(num1,num2)
```

where num1 and num2 are actual parameters and sum is a variable in which the function returns value. We must note here that declaring a pointer only creates a pointer. It does not create an actual function. We have to define the function separately for the task to be performed by the function. The pointers to functions can be used to refer to the function and they can also be used to pass a function as an argument to another function. Once a pointer to functions is declared, the address of the function is assigned to the pointer.

5.5.6.3 Pointer for Passing a Function to Another Function

By using the pointer to function technique, we can pass the function as argument to another function. The general syntax for passing a function to another function is as follows.

Syntax

```
return_type function_name((*pointerto
function),other parameters));
```

5.5.7 | Pointer to a Pointer

Pointer is a variable which can hold the address of other variable that may also be of pointer type.

```
int *ptr;
int X=15;
ptr=&X; (Let it be 1009)
```

Here `ptr` is a (pointer) variable. We can also hold the address of `ptr`. Let it be 2009. So we can define a pointer to hold the address of `ptr` as

```
ptr* ptr1
```

where `ptr` itself is a pointer to integer. Now we can write the above statement as

```
int **ptr1;
```

The pointer to a pointer is a form of multiple indirections and this indirection can be carried out to whatever extent desired.

`ptr1=&ptr;` **will assign 2009 to** `ptr1`.
`ptr=&X;` **will assign 1009 to** `ptr`.

Now using

`printf("%d",ptr1);` will display 2009.
`printf("%d",*ptr1);` will display the value at 2009 (i.e., 1009).
`printf("%d",*(*ptr1));` will display the value at 1009 (i.e., 15).

5.5.8 | Pointer to void

The pointer is a variable which can hold the address of some another variable of same type. In other words if ptr is a char pointer then it can hold the value of char type. So the address we put into the pointer must be the same type as the pointer. We cannot assign the address of a float variable to a char pointer. void pointer is a special type of pointer which can point to any data type. The void pointer is declared as follows:

```
void *ptr
```

Solved Problems

1. *Compare pointers and arrays*

Solution:

Pointer	Array
Pointer is a variable that holds an address.	Array is a collection of similar items.
Pointer is a variable so its value may be changed using ++ or –– operators.	Array name is constant so its value cannot be changed, that is arrayname++ or arrayname-- is not allowed.
The pointer variables generally appear on the left side of an assignment operator.	The array name cannot appear on the left side of an assignment operator because it is a constant.
It is not necessary that pointer should be an array.	Array name refers to the base address so it is a pointer to its first element.
Pointers do not allocate continuous memory blocks.	Array allocates continuous memory blocks.

2. *State the advantages of using pointers.* **(AU 2007 Suppl.)**

or What do you mean by a pointer? Mention its uses. **(AU 2010, 2013, 2014)**

Solution: A variable which holds the address of the value is called *pointer.*

Pointers are used for compact and efficient programming by providing reference variables to pass information between functions and their reference points. They also provide alternate ways to access an array element. Pointers provide efficient tools for manipulating dynamic data structures such as structures, linked lists, queues, stacks and trees.

3. *Write a C program to perform string operations using pointers.* **(AU 2007 Suppl.)**

(a) Find the length of a given string.
(b) String copy.
(c) String concatenate.

Solution:

(a) For the length of a given string:

```
#include<stdio.h>
#include<stdlib.h>
void main()
{
char *pt;
strlen(pt, "AFTERNOON");
printf("The length of the string is:%d",
pt);
}
```

The output is

```
The length of the string is: 10
```

(b) For string copy:

```
#include<stdio.h>
#include<stdlib.h>
void main()
{
char *pt;
pt=(char*)malloc(9);
strcpy(pt, "AFTERNOON");
printf("The copied content is: %s", pt);
}
```

The output is

```
The copied content is: AFTERNOON
```

(c) For string concatenate:

```
#include<stdio.h>
#include<stdlib.h>
void main()
{
char *pt1, *pt2, *pt3;
strcpy(pt1, "GOOD ");
strcpy(pt2, "AFTERNOON");
pt3=strcat(pt1,pt2);
printf("The string after concatenation is:
%s", pt3);
}
```

The output is

```
The string after concatenation is: GOOD
AFTERNOON
```

Note: For C programs to perform string operations without using library functions, but using Pointers, refer to Appendix A.

4. *Write an example program to access a variable through its pointer.* **(AU 2008 Suppl.)**

Solution:

```
#include<stdio.h>
#include<conio.h>
main()
{
int *pt, n;
printf("Enter value of n:");
scanf("%d",&n);
pt = &n;
printf("%d",*pt);
getch();
}
```

The output is

```
Enter value of n: 30
30
```

5. *Determine the output for the following printf statements:* **(AU 2012)**

```
main()
{char *ptr= "string"'
printf("%c", *ptr++);
printf("%.c", *(++ptr));
printf("%c", (*ptr)++);
printf("%c", ++*ptr);
}
```

Solution: The output is `srrn`. This is because in the initialization statement, ptr points to the first character of the string, that is, "s". Now, `*ptr++` gives output as "s" and the pointer variable gets incremented to t. Now, the expression `(*++ptr)` further increments the pointer variable to r and displays "r". Then, the expression `(*ptr)++` displays the pointer variable as "r" and then increments it to i. Finally, the expression `++*ptr` further increments the pointer variable to n and displays "n".

6. *Write a function using pointers to add two matrices and to return the resultant matrix to the calling function.* **(AU 2008 Suppl.)**

Solution:

```
int *multiply(int *a[3][3], int*b[3][3])
{
int *c[3][3];
int i,j,k,sum=0;
for(i=0;i<3;i++)
{
for(j=0;j<3;j++)
{
for(k=0;k<3;k++)
{sum=sum+*(&(a+i)+&(&(b+k)+j)
}
*(*c+i)+j)=sum
}
}
return (sum);
}
```

7. *Write a program in C to sort an array in ascending order using pointers.* **(AU 2013)**

Solution:

```
#include<stdio.h>
#include<conio.h>
void main()
{
clrscr();
int list[10],*ptr,*num1,*num2;
int i, j, temp, n;
cout<<"Enter number of list items: ";
scanf("%d",&n);
printf("Enter the list: ");
for(i=0;i<n;i++)
{
scanf("%d",&list[i]);
}
for(i=0;i<n-1;i++)/*sorting the list*/
{
for(j=i+1;j<n;j++)
{
num1=ptr+i;
num2=ptr+j;
if(*num1>*num2)
{
temp=*num1;
*num1=*num2;
*num2=temp;
}
}
}
printf("The sorted list is");
for(int i=0;i<n-1;i++)
{
cout<<list[i] << " ";
}
}
```

The output is

```
Enter number of list items: 4
Enter the list: 1,4,5,2
The sorted list is 1  2  4  5
```

8 *Write a program to concatenate two strings.*

Solution:

```
#include<stdio.h>
#include<string.h>
#include<stdlib.h>
void main()
{
char *pt1, *pt2, *pt3;
strcpy(pt1, "GOOD ");
strcpy(pt2, "AFTERNOON");
pt3=strcat(pt1,pt2);
printf("The string after concatenation is:
%s", pt3);
}
```

The output is

```
The string after concatenation is: GOOD
AFTERNOON
```

9 *Write a program to count the number of words in a string using pointers.* **(AU 2013)**

Solution:

```
#include<stdio.h>
#include<string.h>
#include<stdlib.h>
void main()
{
char *str;
int num=0
int pos=0;
```

```
printf("Enter the string/n");
gets(str);
while(*str!='\0')
{
if(pos==0);
{
pos=1;
++num;
}
printf("The number of words in the string
is: ", num);
}
```

The output is

```
Enter the string
today is sunday
The number of words in the string is: 3
```

5.6 Dynamic Memory Allocation

When the memory is allocated at compile time, it is called static memory allocation. The declaration of variables, arrays, structures, etc., that we have done so far, are examples of static memory allocation. The global and local variables are allocated memory during compile time. We cannot add global and local variables at run time. However we can allocate memory at run time also according to our requirement. This method of memory allocation is called dynamic memory allocation. The dynamic memory allocation provides more flexibility to the C programmer.

5.6.1 | Use of Dynamic Memory Allocation

The unallocated memory space that is used during the program execution for dynamic memory allocation is called free store or the memory heap. The free store can be managed by using malloc(), calloc(), free()and realloc() functions. The situation when we forget to release the memory which was dynamically allocated is called memory leak. If these functions are used then we need to include the files alloc.h and stdlib.h.

1. **malloc():** The memory may be allocated dynamically for the object using the operator malloc() function. The memory allocation for an object in this manner is called the dynamic memory allocation or run-time allocation.

   Syntax

   ```
   void* malloc(size);
   ```

   Typecasting in malloc() is required because the return value of malloc() is void (in ANSI compiler the return type of malloc() is char). In program 8, void pointer is converted into char pointer.

2. **calloc():** This function is used for allocating various block of memory and is declared with two arguments, the number of blocks to be allocated and the size of each block. This function is used in place of malloc(), in case we need to allocate memory for arrays and structures.

   Syntax

   ```
   void* calloc(number of blocks, size of
   block);
   ```

3. **free():** This function is used to release the memory which was dynamically allocated to avoid memory leak.

   Syntax

   ```
   free(pointer variable);
   ```

4. **realloc():** Sometimes the allocated memory can be more or less than the actual memory required. The realloc() function is used to reduce or enlarge the memory allocated by the malloc() or calloc() functions. It returns the address of the reallocated block that is different from the original address and returns null in case the block cannot be reallocated.

   Syntax

   ```
   realloc(string, size);
   ```

Program 8: To copy two strings and demonstrate typecasting using malloc().

```
#include<stdio.h>
#include<stdlib.h>
#include<string.h>
void main()
{
char *pt;pt=(char*)malloc(9);/*here mal-
loc is used to allocate 9 bytes of memory
to char pointer pt*/
strcpy(pt, "AFTERNOON");
printf("The copied content is:. s", pt);
}
```

Output

```
The copied content is: AFTERNOON
```

POINTS TO REMEMBER

1. **Functions:** A complex program contains a large list of instruction which is not easy to manage. Therefore, such programs are generally decomposed into different modules containing small sets of instructions that perform specific tasks. These modules are called functions.
2. **Return type:** It is any C data type which describes that the function will return the value of *return type* from the body of the function to the calling function.
3. **Types of functions:**
   - **Based on the tasks accomplished by them:** User-defined, standard library and string functions.
   - **Based on their return type and function call:** `void` function, `void` function with parameters, function with parameter and with return type, nested function, recursive function, inline functions, function with default arguments, function with constant parameters.

4. **Types of parameters:** Parameters associated with function call are called **actual parameters**. Parameters associated with the function definition are called **formal parameters**.
5. **Types of parameter passing methods** are **call by reference** and **call by value**.
6. **Arrays and functions:** The second dimension of the two-dimensional array cannot be left blank when it is passed to a function, because a two-dimensional array is a collection of one-dimensional arrays. We can skip the first dimension. To call the function only array name is passed. Its dimension is not required.
7. **Pointer:** A variable which holds the address of the value is called *pointer*.
8. **Dynamic memory allocation:** It is the method of allocating memory at run time. The unallocated memory space that is used during the program execution for dynamic memory allocation is called free store or the memory heap. The free store can be managed by using malloc(), calloc(), free() and realloc() functions.

REVIEW QUESTIONS

1. What is the need for functions? (AU 2014)
2. Write notes on pointers. (AU 2009)
3. Describe with example:
   (a) declaring a structure,
   (b) pointer to multidimensional array and
   (c) union. (AU 2011)
4. What character terminates all strings composed of character arrays?
5. Explain about the different parameter passing methods with examples. (AU 2009)
6. What are the operators exclusively used with pointers?
7. When is the function prototype not required?
8. What is a *return* statement in function and how many return statements can be used in a function?
9. What are the different types of parameters? Explain the different types of parameter passing.
10. What are the differences between array of pointers and pointer to the array?
11. What is the relationship between an array and a pointer?
12. Discuss about any eight built-in functions (AU 2013)
13. How is a poniter variable initialized? (AU 2013)
14. Explain call by reference with suitable examples. (AU 2014)

PROGRAMMING ASSIGNMENTS

1. Write a program to find the greatest number amongst three given numbers by using function with parameters and return value.
2. Write a program to find the sum of square of first *n* even natural numbers using function without parameter but with return type.
3. Write a program in C that reads a list of student records and count the number of male students in the list. (AU 2009 Suppl.)
4. Write a menu-driven program to add, subtract, multiply and divide complex numbers.
5. Write a program to read and display the following details of employees using pointers: ename, designation, age, dob (dd/mm/yyyy).
6. Write a program to convert a decimal number into binary number using functions.
7. Write a program to find the smallest and largest element of an array using dynamic memory management technique.
8. Write a program to find the duplicate elements and remove them from a list using pointers.
9. Write a program to evaluate the following series. (AU 2009, 2010, 2012)
$$e = 1 + \frac{1}{1!} + \frac{1}{2!} + \frac{1}{3!} + \frac{1}{4!} + \cdots + \frac{1}{n!}$$
10. Write a program to evaluate the following series. (AU 2013)
$$\sin(x) = x - \frac{x^3}{3!} + \frac{x^5}{5!} - \frac{x^7}{7!} + \cdots \frac{x^n}{n!}$$
11. Write a program to find the sum of the series. (AU 2009)
$$S = 1 - \frac{x}{1!} + \frac{x^2}{2!} - \frac{x^3}{3!} + \cdots \frac{x^n}{n!}$$

Structures and Unions

6

LEARNING OBJECTIVES

After completing this chapter, you will be able to understand the following:

- Structure and its distinction with union.
- Structure declaration and accessing structure elements.
- Initialization of structure.
- Array within structure and array of structure.
- Structure within structure.
- Passing structure to a function.
- Union and its distinction with structure.
- Storage classes.
- Preprocessor directives and Standard C library functions.

6.1 Introduction

Array is a collection of items of same data types and it cannot store items of different data type. Sometimes it is required to process together logically related data elements of different types. Structures are used for such situations. A structure is a collection of different types of data elements which are related together. The data items in a structure are called the members of the structure. In other words, similar or different data types can be grouped to form a structure to represent the single entity. For example, if we want to represent complex numbers in an array, then these have two types of components, real and imaginary (imag). Thus, a complex number has two types of integer numbers and can be represented as a structure.

The differences between array and structure are tabulated in Table 1.

TABLE 1

Differences between array and structure

Array	Structure
Array is a collection of similar data items	Structure may be a collection of similar or different data items
Array elements are accessed by their position in the array	Each structure elements have different name
Array name is not used as a data type	Structure name is used to define the variable of that type.
Memory is allocated at the time of array declaration	Memory is not allocated when structure is declared, but rather when the structure variable is declared
Array has a finite number of elements	Structure also has a finite number of elements
The entire array can be referred using array name because array name refers to the base address	The entire collection of elements can be referred using structure name.
An array of structure type may be defined.	A structure may contain an array as a member.

6.2 Structure Declaration and Accessing Structure Elements

The definition of a structure is specified with keyword struct followed by the name of the structure followed by data type specification of members enclosed in braces. The structure name is also called tag of the structure and the entire definition is terminated with semicolon. The general format for structure declaration in C is as follows.

Syntax

```
Struct                                                          keyword

structure_name          struct book .................. structure tag
{                       {
data_type field 1;      char title[20];.............. first member, a char array
data_type field 2;
 .                      char author[10];............. second member, a char array
 .
 .
 .                      char publication[20];........ third member, a char array
data_type field n;
} structure var_name;   int pubyear;................. fourth member,an int
                        float price.................. fifth member, float
                        }var_name;................... end of definition and declaration
                                                      structure variable var_name
```

The structure variable var_name can also be declared as follows: `struct book var_name;`

6.2.1 | Accessing Structures (Dot Operator)

The structure variable cannot read or write the values in the single command. For example, if X is a structure variable,

```
scanf("%d",&X);
```

This statement produces error since a single statement cannot read the values for all members of X.

Each member of a structure is accessed by using three components: a variable name followed by a dot, and then the member name. Once the structure variable is defined, its members can be accessed by using dot operator. For example,

1. `bdate.month=3;`
2. `X.price=240.90;`
3. `X.pubyear=2012;`

In (1), structure variable bdate is followed by a dot and the field name or member name (month). Similarly, in (2) and (3), the structure variable name X is followed by dot, then the member name (price or pubyear). The format for the dot operator is as follows:

Syntax

```
structure variable.member name;
```

6.3 Initialization of a Structure

The structure variable can be initialized in the same way as variables of other data types are initialized. The only thing that we must keep in mind when structure variable is initialized; the values assigned to the members must be in the same order in which they are declared in the structure. For example

```
book X ={"Computers","ABC","WILEY",
    2012,240.90};
```

Here X is a variable of book type whose members are initialized as

```
X.title="Computers"
X.author="ABC"
X.publication="WILEY"
X.pubyear=2012
X.price=240.90
```

Hence, the compiler not only allocates the memory but also stores value into the structure members (Fig. 1).

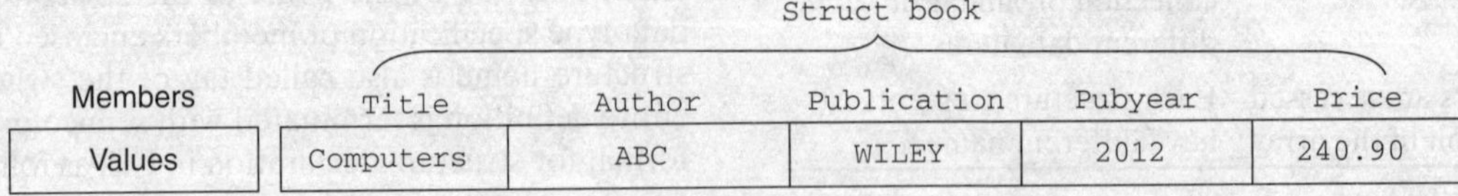

Figure 1 Memory allocation for a structure variable.

6.4 Array and Structures

6.4.1 | Array within Structures

Like the simple data type, an array can also be a member of a structure. In the previous subsection, we have seen that character arrays are members of the structure. When a structure consists of array elements, they are treated in the same way as normal arrays are treated. The array elements of a structure are also accessed by using the dot operator. For example,

```
struct student
{
int rollno;
char name[25];
char branch[15];
int marks[5];
int age;
}X;
```

Here the structure `student` contains three arrays: `name` and `branch` of character type, and `marks` of integer type. X is defined as a variable of `student` type. Now suppose we want to access the marks in different subjects scored by X then we have to write X `.marks[i]`, where `i` is an index value that can vary from 1 to 5 or from 0 to 4.

Program 1: To read and display student's information using array within structures.

```
#include<stdio.h>
#include<conio.h>
struct student
{
int rollno;
char name[20];
char branch[20];
int marks[5];
char result;
int age;
};
void main()
{
clrscr();
student X;
int total=0;
printf("Enter student information");
printf("\nEnter roll number of the stu-
dent: ");
scanf("%d",&X.rollno);
printf("Enter the name of the student: ");
gets(X.name);
printf("Enter the branch enrolled in: ");
gets(X.branch);
printf("Enter marks scored in five sub-
jects: \n");
for(int i=0;i<5;i++)
{
scanf("%d",&X.marks[i]);
}
printf("Enter the age of the student: ");
scanf("%d",&X.age);
for(i=0;i<5;i++)
{
total=total+X.marks[i];
}
float avg=total/5;
if(avg>=80)
X. result='H';
else
   if(avg>=70)
   X.result='F';
   else
   X.result='S';
printf("RESULT);
printf("\nRoll number: ",X.rollno);
printf("\nName: ",X.name);
printf("\nBranch: ",X.branch);
printf("\nMarks scored in five subjects:
\n");
for(i=0;i<5;i++)
{
printf("%d /t",X.marks[i]);
}
printf("\nAge: %d",X.age);
printf("\nOverall result: %d",X.result);
printf("\n(D: For distiction,F: first
division,S: second division)";
getch();
}
```

Output

```
Enter student information
Enter roll number of student: 101
Enter the name of student: Aryan Bose
Enter the branch of student: Civil
Engineering
Enter marks scored in five subjects:
88
98
86
85
95
Enter the age of the student: 21
RESULT
Roll number: 101
Name: Aryan Bose
Branch: Civil Engineering
Marks scored in different subjects:
88   98   86   85   95
Age: 21
Overall result: D
(D: For distinction, F: first division,
S: second division)
```

6.4.2 | Array of Structure

As we already know that an array is a collection of similar data items. It is possible to have an array where all elements are of the type struct and this collection of same structure type of variables is called array of structure.

Declaration

To declare an array of structure, we have to first define the structure and then we can define the array of that structure type.

```
struct student
{
int rollno;
char name[25];
char branch[15];
int marks[5];
int age;
};
student X[3];
```

Here X is an array of three student type data. This implies that each element of X will have rollno, name, branch, marks in five subjects and age. The elements of this array – X[0], X[1] and X[2] – will be structure variables of type student. We can represent X[3] graphically as follows:

To access the marks of the first student in the third subject, we have to write `X[0].marks[2];`

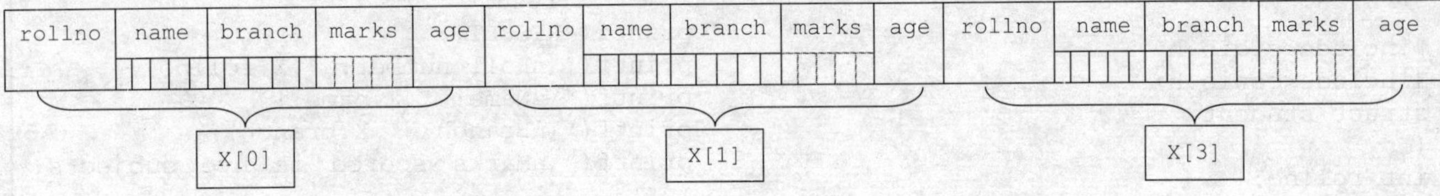

Initialization

An array of structures can be initialized in the same manner as a normal array is initialized. For example, let us define an array of the following structure:

```
struct book
{
char title[20];
char author[10];
char publication[20];
int pubyear;
float price;
};
book  X[2] {{"Computers",  "ABC",  "WILEY",
2012,240.90}, {"Mathematics", "DEF", "WILEY",
2013,290.40}}
```

Program 2: Read names and addresses using a structure and rearrange the data in alphabetical order of names and display.

```
# include<stdio.h>
#include<conio.h>
#include<string.h>
struct list
{
char name[20];
char address[100];
}listOfPeople[3];
void getData(int  number,  struct  list
listOfPeople[])
{
int i,j;
float total;
printf("\nEnter data\n");
for(i=1; i<=number; i++)
{
/*storing the data*/
printf("\nEnter name of person%d:",i);
scanf(" %[^\n]s",&listOfPeople[i].name);
printf("\nEnter address of person%d:",i);
scanf(" %[^\n]s",&listOfPeople[i].
address);
}
}
void  sortData(int  number,  struct  list
listOfPeople[])
{
int i,j;
struct list temp;
for(i=0;i<=number-1;i++)
{
for(j=i;j<=number-i;j++)
{
if(strcmp(listOfPeople[j].
name,listOfPeople[j+1].name)>0)
{
strcpy(temp.name,listOfPeople[j].name);
strcpy(temp.address,listOfPeople[j].
address);
strcpy(listOfPeople[j].
name,listOfPeople[j+1].name);
strcpy(listOfPeople[j].
address,listOfPeople[j+1].address);
strcpy(listOfPeople[j+1].name,temp.
name);
strcpy(listOfPeople[j+1].address,temp.
address);
}
```

```
}
}
}
void displayData(int number, struct list
listOfPeople[])
{
int i,j;
/*Displaying data*/
printf("\n Name\tAddress");

for(i=1; i<=number; i++)
{
printf("\n ");
printf("%s\t",listOfPeople[i].name);
printf("%s\t",listOfPeople[i].address);
}
printf("\n ---------------------------\n");
}
int main()
{
int number = 3;
printf("\n Names and Addresses");
printf("\n -------------------");
getData(number,listOfPeople);
sortData(number,listOfPeople);
printf("Displaying data\n");
printf("----------------------------\n");
displayData(number,listOfPeople);
getch();
}
```

Output

```
----------------------------------------
Names and Addresses
----------------------------------------
Enter data
Enter name of person1 :Mary
Enter address of person1 :31 A block, ABC
Apartments, Dehradun
Enter name of person1 :=George
Enter address of person1 :32 B block, DEF
Apartments, Delhi
Enter name of person1 :Julie
Enter address of person1 :31 C block, GHI
Apartments, Chennai

Displaying data
----------------------------------------

Name   Address
George 32 B block, DEF Apartments, Delhi
Julie  31 C block, GHI Apartments, Chennai
Mary   31 A block, ABC Apartments,
Dehradun
```

Solved Problems

1. *Can you assign a structure variable to another? If yes, when?*

Solution: Yes, if both the variables are of the same structure type.

2. *Write a C program to accept records of 20 states using array of structures. The structures should contain name of the state and number of engineering colleges, medical colleges, management colleges, science colleges. Calculate and display the total colleges in each state and the state which is having the highest number of colleges.* **(AU 2010 Suppl.)**

Solution:

```
#include<stdio.h>
#include<conio.h>
void main()
{
int i,j, maximum;
struct state
{
char name[15];
int number_engg, number_med, number_mgmt,
number_science, total;
} struct state S[20];
for(i 0;i<20;i++)
{
printf("Enter the state name, number of
engineering, medical, management and sci-
ence colleges: ");
scanf("%d %d %d %d",&S[i].number_engg,&S[i].
number_med,&S[i].number_mgmt,&S[i].
number_science);
S[i].total S[i].number_engg+S[i].number_
med+S[i].number_mgmt+S[i].number_science;
}
maximum S[0].total;
for(j 1;j<20;j++)
{
if(S[j].tot>maximum)
{maximum S[j].total;
}
}
printf("The total number of colleges in
each state is: ");
for(i=0;i<20;i++)
{
printf("State: %c/tTotal:/n %d",S[i].
name,S[i].total);
if(S[i].total maximum)
{
printf("The state having maximum number
of colleges is %c with colleges %d",S[i].
name,maximum);
}
}
```

6.5 Nested Structures

Structure is a collection of different data types. It may be int, float, char or array. When a structure is declared as a member of another structure, then it is called a nested structure. Structures can be nested to any depth. Let us take the previous structure declaration of student. Now one more information is required, the date of enrollment for each student in this case. Consider as an example, the date of enrollment as 20 May 2012. We can see that day (20) is an integer value, month (May) is a string and year (2012) is again an integer value; therefore, the date is a collection of three different types of elements, namely, day, month and year. The structure for date is defined as follows.

```
struct date
{
int day;
char month[10];
int year;
};
struct student
{
int rollno;
char name[20];
char branch[10];
int marks[5];
int age;
date enrolldate;
};
student X;
```

6.5.1 Accessing Nested Structure Members

In the above structure definition, `enrolldate` (structure variable) is a member of student, so student is called a nested structure. The members of the nested structure are also accessed by using the dot operator. To access the element of this nested structure; we have to use the dot operator twice:

```
X. enrolldate.day 04;/*04 is assigned to
day of enrollment*/

gets(X.enrolldate.month);/*To  read  month
of the enrollment*/

printf("%d",X.enrolldate.year);/*To   dis-
play year of enrollment*/
```

Solved Problem

1. *Define and declare a structure to store date, including day, month and year.* **(AU 2014)**

Solution: Refer the example in the above section

6.6 Structure and Function

The structure variables can also be passed to the function in two ways: call by value and call by reference just like other variables. When the structure variable is passed by using call by value, the actual parameters are not changed if formal parameters are changed. When the structure variables are passed by using call by reference, then the changes made in the formal parameters are also reflected in the actual parameters. The function can return a structure also. The structures are generally defined as global declaration, so that structure tag can be used in any function. Apart from passing the whole structure variable, we can also pass the individual structure elements in two ways: call by value and call by reference.

In the following program, for each student rollno, name, branch, marks in five subjects, bdate (DD/MM/YYYY), age, result are required. We can see that the date of birth is required in DD/MM/YYYY format, so we declare another structure for date. Therefore bdate is of date type. To access the members like day of date for first student we use `X[0].bdate.day;` We are using the display function to display the information for each student. Here we are passing array of structure variable X[2].

Program 3: To read and display the students' information using nested structure and function.

```
#include<stdio.h>
#include<conio.h>
struct date
{
int day;
char month[10];
int year;
};
struct student
{
int rollno;
char name[20];
char branch[20];
int marks[5];
date bdate;
int age;
char result;
};
void main()
{
clrscr();
student X[2];
int total=0;
void display(student []);
for(int j 0;j<2;j++)
{
printf(" ** Enter information for student
%d **",j%1);
printf("\nEnter roll number:");
scanf("+d",&X[j].rollno);
printf("Enter the name:");
gets(X[j].name);
```

```
printf("Enter the branch:");
gets(X[j].branch);
printf("Enter marks scored in different
subjects: \n");
for(int i=0;i<5;i++)
{
scanf("%d",&X[j].marks[i]);
}
printf("\n* Enter date of birth like 20
May 2012 *";
scanf("%d",&X[j].bdate.day);
gets(X[j].bdate.month);
scanf("%d",&X[j].bdate.year);
printf("Enter the age: ");
scanf("%d",&X[j].age);
for(i=0;i<5;i++)
{
total=total+X[j].marks[i];
}
float avg=total/5;
if(avg>=75)
X[j].result='D';
else
if(avg>=65)
X[j].result='F';
else
X[j].result='S';
}
display(X);
getch();
}
void display(student X[2])
{
clrscr();
for(int j=0;j<2;j++)
{
printf("\nRESULT FOR STUDENT %d",j+1);
printf("\nRoll number: %d",X[j].rollno);
printf("\nName: %c",X[j].name);
printf("\nThe branch: %c",X[j].branch);
printf("\nMarks scored in different sub-
jects: \n)";
for(int i=0;i<5;i++)
{
printf("%d\t",X[j].marks[i]);
}
printf("\n Date of Birth: ");
printf("%d - %d  %d",X[j].bdate.day,X[j].
bdate.month,X[j].bdate.year);
printf("\nAge: %d,X[j].age);
printf("\nOverall    result:    %d,X[j].
result);
}
printf("\n(D: For distinction,F: first
division,S: second division)");
}
```

Output

```
RESULT FOR STUDENT 1
Roll number: 101
Name: Meena
The branch: CSE
Marks scored in different subjects:
90 91 86 79 75
Date of Birth: 22-December-1991
Age: 21
Overall result: D
RESULT FOR STUDENT 2
Roll number: 102
Name: Arun
The branch: CSE
Marks scored in different subjects:
88 55 60 65 59
Birth date: 23-July-1992
Age: 20
Overall result: F
(D: For distinction, F: first division, S:
second division)
```

Solved Problem

1. *Can we pass a structure variable to a function? What are the ways to pass structure variable to a function?*

Solution: The structure variables can also be passed to the function in two ways (call by value and call by reference) just like other variables. When the structure variable is passed by using call by value, the actual parameters do not change even if the formal parameters are changed. When the structure variables are passed by using call by reference then the changes made in the formal parameter are also reflected in the actual parameter. The function can return a structure also.

6.7 Pointer to Structures

We have learnt that pointer can point to int, char, float and strings. In addition, a pointer can also be used to hold the address of a structure variable. So let us take the structure named student:

```
struct student
{
introllno;
char name[20];
int age;
} A;
```

Here A is a variable of structure "student" type. Now let us take a pointer to structure:

```
student *ptr;
```

This declaration is similar to the pointer declaration for other data type. The `ptr` can hold the address of A.

```
ptr=&A;
```

The members of the student A can be accessed by pointer `ptr` to the structure using arrow operator. For example, if we want to access the age of student A then we can access it in two ways (a) `ptr-/>age` and (b) `A.age`. Here we must note that when arrow operator is used then on the left side of the arrow operator (made up of a minus sign and a greater than sign, ->) there must be a pointer to structure and when dot operator (.) is used then on the left side of the dot operator there must be a structure variable. Structure pointers are very useful in -creating dynamic data structures such as linked list, stacks queues, trees, etc. We should also note that the member operator (.) has a higher precedence than the indirection operator.

Solved Problem

1. *Differentiate a pointer to structure from a pointer to integer.* **(AU 2009 Suppl.)**

Solution: Pointer to a structure is useful in accessing all the members of the structure using -> operator, whereas pointer to an integer has limited use as it contains the memory address of that integer only. For example,

```
struct item
{
char name[10];
int qty;
float price;
}*pt;
The pointer *pt can be used to access members of structure item as follows:
pt->name;
pt->qty;
pt->price;
```

The pointer `*ptr` to variable x can be assigned as follows: ptr=&x;

6.8 Unions

A union is similar to structure because it is also a collection of different types of data. The difference between the two is that union stores values of different types in a single location while each member of the structure has its own storage location. In union, space is reserved for the largest data type only. Therefore, union provides a way to manipulate different kinds of data in a single area of storage. If a new assignment is made, the previous value is automatically erased. The general syntax for union declaration is as follows

Syntax

```
Storage class union union_name
{
data_type member 1;
data_type member 2;
:::
data_type member n;
};
```

It can be noted that the syntax for defining union is similar to structure definition. The storage class may be auto, static or extern that is optional. The keyword to define a union is union and the identifier is union_name. It is also known as union tag.

The members of the union are accessed by using dot operator in the same way as it is used with the structure members. A dot operator is used in between the union name and member name. Syntactically, members of a union are accessed as

```
unionname.membername;
```

As in case of structures, members of the union are also accessed using the arrow operator as

```
union pointer->membername;
```

6.8.1 | Initialization of Union

In a union, it is not possible to initialize the members because at any given time only one member of union is active. When the union is declared as the member of a structure, it should not be the first member but the last one. because the union only holds a value for one data type which requires a larger storage than their members. In the following program the memory occupied by the union type variable X is 10 because the member which occupies the largest memory is the character array name of 10 characters. So, X is occupying 10 bytes. Now we are reading the input data for rollno, name and percentage in the sequence and the data stored is also displayed. From the output, we can see that rollno and name are not correctly displayed, but the percentage is correctly displayed because the last element for which we have given the data is percentage when we are reading. So all other values are erased and garbage value is displayed for those members (rollno and name).

Program 4: To display student's records using union.

```
#include<stdio.h>
#include<conio.h>
void main()
{
clrscr();
union example
{
int rollno;
float percentage;
char name[10];
};
example X;
printf("Memory occupied by X is:");
printf(sizeof(X));
printf("\nEnter information");
printf("\n\nEnter roll no:");
scanf("%d",&X.rollno);
printf("\nEnter Name:");
gets(X.name);
printf("\nEnter percentage marks:");
scanf("%d",&X.percentage);
printf("\nThe   result   after   execution
**\n");
printf("\nThe roll no: %d",X.rollno);
printf("\n\nName:");
puts(X.name);
printf("\n\nThe percentage marks: %d",X.
percentage);
printf("\n\nSize of X is still
%d",sizeof(X));
getch();
}
```

Output

```
Memory occupied X is:10
Enter information
Enter roll no: 101
Enter Name: Xavier
Enter percentage marks: 78.29
The result after execution **
The roll no:-27525
Name:Xavier
The percentage marks: 78.290001
Size of X is still 10
```

6.8.2 | Union and Arrays

6.8.2.1 Array within Union

Array can also be a member of a union. These arrays are treated in the same way as normal arrays. The array elements of a union are also accessed by using the dot operator. For example,

```
union example
{
int rollno;
int marks[5];
float percentage;
char name[10];
};
example X;
void main()
{
printf("Enter rollnumber, name and marks");
scanf("%d",&X.rollno);
gets(X[j].name);
for(i=0;i<5;i++)
{
scanf("%d",&X.marks[i]);
}
```

6.8.2.2 Array of Unions

By declaring array variables of type union, each element of the array is of type union. For example,

```
union sample
{
int a;
double b;
char c[15];
}x[3];
```

The members of the union can be accessed/ initialized as follows:

```
x[0].a=3;
x[1].b=1.23456;
x[2].c="Hello world";
```

As in the case of structures, members of the union are also accessed using the arrow operator as union pointer → member name;

6.8.3 | Union of Structures

Like nested structures, we can have one union within another union, or a union within a structure. This is illustrated in the following program.

Program 5: To demonstrate use of union of structures

```
#include<stdio.h>
#include<conio.h>
void main()
{
struct date
{ int year;
char day[10], month[12];
};
union week
{struct date set;
};
union week st;
st.set.year=2012;
st.set.day[10]= "Monday";
st.set.month[12]="November";
clrscr();
printf("\n %c", st.set.day[10]);
printf("\n %c", st.set.month[12]);
printf("\n %d", st.set.year);
```

```
}
```

Output

```
Monday
November
2012
```

To find size of structure and union, we have the following code:

```
union result
{
int marks;
char grade;
}
struct result1
{
char name[15];
int age;
union result res;
}
```

Using the statements

```
printf("Size of union:\n %d",sizeof(data.
res));
printf("Size of structure:%d",size
of(data));
```

we get output as

```
Size of union = 2;
Size of structure = 19;
```

Even though int and char require 2 and 1 bytes, respectively, union reserves 2 bytes as int takes more space than char.

6.8.4 | Anonymous Union

If we define a union without a name or tag then it is called anonymous union. In this union, the members are accessed directly by their name. In the following program, anonymous union is used, so the members of the union can directly be used. The program prints the name correctly but the value of sal is wrong because `gets(name);` statement is after `scanf("%f",sal);` which means that currently the value of name is read therefore name is valid.

Program 6: To demonstrate the use anonymous union.

```
#include<stdio.h>
#include<conio.h>
void main()
{
union
{
char name[10];
float sal;
};
clrscr();
printf("Enter the salary and name \n");
printf("Enter salary: ");
scanf("%f",&sal);
printf("\nEnter name: ");
gets(name);
printf("The name is: %c",name);
printf("\nThe salary is: %d",sal);
getch();
}
```

Output

```
Enter the salary and name
Enter salary: 20000
Enter name: S K Bose
The name is: S K Bose
The salary is: 4.544498e+30
```

Solved Problems

1. *Compare structures with union.*
(AU 2007 Suppl, 2013, 2014)

Solution: A union is similar to a structure in the sense that it is also a collection of different types of data. However, the difference between the two is that, union stores values of different types at a single location whereas in a structure each member has its own storage location. In union space is reserved for the largest data type only. Therefore union provides a way to manipulate different kinds of data in a single area of storage. For example, if two structure variables of structure `A` are declared as `A x,y;` then both the structure variables x and y will have different memory locations. However, if we declare two union variables of union `B` as `B x,y;` then the both the union variables `x` and `y` will have the same memory location.

Consider the following codes,

```
struct A
{
int x;
char y;
};
union B
{
int x;
char y;
};
void main()
{
A str_example;
B union_example;
str_example.x=3;
str_example.y='a';
union_example.x=3;
union_example.y='c';/* this will affect
the value of union_example.x";
printf("%d %s\n",str_example.x,
str_example.y);
printf("%d %s %f\n",union_example.x,
union_example.y);
}
```

Therefore, we can see that in structure we can modify x or without affecting the values of the others as each is stored in a different memory location. Whereas in a union, each element overlaps the others as they point to the same memory location. Modifying one renders the others undefined. The values of the two variables are same because memory location has 2 bytes (as int has 2 bytes and char has 1 byte).

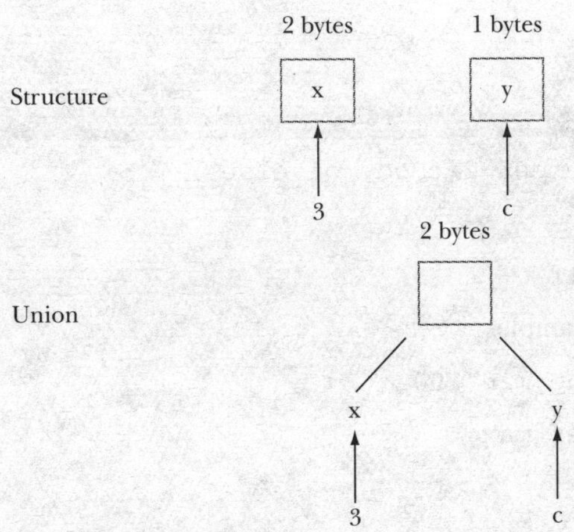

2. *What is the purpose of union in C programming?* **(AU 2008 Suppl.)**

Solution: A union stores values of different types in a single location. In union, space is reserved for the largest data type only. Therefore, union provides a way to manipulate different kinds of data in a single area of storage. If a new assignment is made, the previous value is automatically erased.

6.9 Storage Classes

Each variable declared in C programs is allocated a specific memory block from where it can be accesses. This block is called the area or scope of the variable and is defined by using storage classes. The storage class of a variable gives the following information to the compiler: (a) storage size of the variable, the initial value of the variable in case it is not initialized and (b) the scope of the variable and the duration of the variable in which it will be actively used throughout the program. There are four storage classes in C used to define variables. Four types of variables, constant, volatile, local and global variables were discussed in Chapter 3. Refer to those variables before going through the types of storage classes.

1. **auto:** All local variables that are defined inside a function are auto variables. The keyword auto is optional as by default all variables are treated as auto variables. The scope of the variable is localized to the function in which it is declared. For example,

```
void main()
{int a; /*local variable*/
}
```

2. **extern:** All global variables that are defined outside all function blocks to be used throughout the program are external variables. The compiler does not allocate memory while compiling the program as the memory is allocated in another module when they are declared. For example,

```
int a; /*global variable*/
void main()
{/*function body*/
}
```

In case both auto and extern variables have the same name, then priority is given to the auto variable first.

3. **static:** These can be global or local depending upon where the variable is declared. The keyword static is mandatory. Once the variable is declared static, its garbage value is set to null; it is initialized only once in the program, and the last change made to the static variable is retained the next time the program is executed. This helps in finding out how many times the function modifying the static variable has been called. For example,

```
void display();
void main()
{int static a;
a++;
display(a);
}
void display()
printf("\na=%d",a);
}
```

4. **register:** The keyword register implies that the values of the variables are stored in the registers in the central processing unit instead of the memory. Register access is faster than the memory access; however, there are only limited registers in the CPU. If the limit is exceeded, the compiler automatically treats the rest of the variables as automatic variables. For example, the float and double variables cannot be stored in the register as they require more than 16 bits for storage.

```
void main()
{
register int a=10
a--;
while(a!=null)
{printf("a=%d",a);
}
}
```

Solved Problem

1. *Explain, with examples, the different types of storage classes in C.*

(AU 2010 Suppl., 2013)

or Write notes on various storage classes supported by C languages.

(AU 2007 Suppl., 2009)

Solution: Refer to the section above.

6.10 Preprocessor Directives and Standard Library Functions

The standard C library is a library for C programming language specified by the American National Standards Institute C (ANSI C) and adopted by the International Organization for Standards (ISO). This library contains various features such as macros; type definitions; as well as string handling, mathematical, memory allocation, input and output functions.

6.10.1 | Preprocessor Directives

To avail the various macros and functions of the C library, certain directives should be used in the program. C offers preprocessor directives that are command lines used to operate preprocessors, which process the source code before passing it to the compiler, thus reducing the run time of the program. These are always initialized in the beginning of the program outside all functions, including main(). The hash (#) symbol is used for defining a preprocessor directive in a program. For example, #preprocessor directive. There are three types of preprocessor directives:

1. **Macro substitution directives:** These are used to define macro templates and their expansions to be used in the program.

Syntax

#define identifier substitute_value

For example, #define max 100 defines an identifier max and provides its substitution value as 100. So, the preprocessor will replace every occurrence of max in the program with the value 100.

To undefined a macro, the #undef directive is used. For example, #undef max 100;

2. **File inclusion directives:** These are used to include the functions and macros defined in specific header files.

Syntax

#include<filename>

where filename is the header file to be loaded, which contains the required macros/functions.

For example, #include<stdio.h>

3. **Compiler control directives:** These are used to select specific portions of the program for compilation based on certain conditions. The compiler then compiles that specific portion if the condition is satisfied. These are of various types, such as #ifidef, #else, #endif, #error, #ifndef, #line, #inline, etc. The syntax for some of the directives is given as follows:

Syntax

```
#define identifier substitute_value
#ifdef identifier
{
Statement 1;/*Body of ifdef*/
}
#else
{
Statement 2/*Body of else*/
}
#endif
```

For example,

```
#define min 100
#ifdef max
{
printf("The maximum value is 100");
}
#else
{
#error The maximum value is not defined
}
#endif
```

In the above example, ifdef checks where the identifier max has been defined with a substitute value, if not then the body of else directive is executed, in which the error directive is used to display the error message.

Another directive used is the #ifndef directive which works opposite to the ifdef directive. In the above program, if ifndef directive is used as #ifndef max, then even though the identifier max is defined, the body of else will be executed.

6.10.2 | Standard Library Functions

The standard library functions are predefined, compiled and placed in the C library in respective header files. For example, string functions are stored in string.h header file. Some standard library functions in the respective header files are as follows:

1. **stdio.h:** This header file contains core input/output functions, such as stdin (standard input device), stdout (standard output device), stderr (standard error output device), stdaux (standard auxiliary device), stdprn (standard printer).
2. **ctype.h:** This header file contains functions to check whether the entered character is alphanumeric

[isalpha()], uppercase [isupper()], lowercase [islower()], a digit [isdigit()], a letter or a digit [isalnum()], hexadecimal [isxdigit()]], a space [isspace()], a punctuation symbol [ispunct()], printable [isprint()], printable but not a space [isgraph()], control character [iscntrl()], ASCII code [isascii()].

3. **stdlib.h:** This header file contains numeric conversion functions (atof, strtof, etc.), pseudo-random numbers generation functions (rand, srand), memory allocation (malloc, realloc, calloc, free), process control functions (abort, exit, getenv, etc.).
4. **math.h:** This header file contains mathematical functions, such as power functions (sqrt, pow, etc.), trigonometric functions (sin, cos, tan, etc.), hyperbolic function (sinh, cosh, etc.), nearest integer floating point operations (ceil, floor, trunk, etc.), among others.
5. **string.h:** This header file contains string handling functions (gets, puts, etc.) as discussed in the previous section.
6. **time.h:** This header file defines data and time handling functions, such as time, clock, etc.

Apart from the above-mentioned header files, one header file exists which is not part of the C library but is used in old MS-DOS compilers for text–user interfaces. This header file is conio. The various functions defined under this header file are kbhit, getch, getche, ungetch, cgets, cscanf, putch, cputs and cprintf.

Note: List of header files and standard library functions have been provided in Appendix C.

Solved Problems

1. *Discuss about any eight built-in functions.* (AU 2013)

Solution: Some built-in functions are `stdin()`, `stdout()`, `stderr()`, `isalpha()`, `isupper()`, `islower()`, `malloc()`, `calloc()`, `sqrt()`, `pow()`, etc. Refer to the above subsection on standard library functions for details.

2. *Write any two preprocessor directives in C.* (AU 2014)

Solution: Two preprocessor directives are #define and #include. Refer to the above subsection on preprocessor directives for details.

POINTS TO REMEMBER

1. **Structure** is a collection of different types of data elements which are related together. The data items in a structure are called the members of the structure.
2. The data declared within the structure is called **member** and the structure name is called the **structure tag** which is a new data type. Memory is not reserved for the structure tags but is reserved when the variable of structure tag type is defined.
3. Members of structures are accessed using **dot operator**.
4. We can have array as a member of structure and can form an **array of structures**.
5. Structure variables can be initialized. There must be exact correspondence between the members and the initializing values. If some of the structure members are not initialized then the C compilers will automatically initialize them to 0.
6. One structure variable can be assigned to another variable of the same type but the other operations, such as comparison or not equal to, are not defined for similar structures.
7. A structure can be a member of another structure. This is **called nested structure.**
8. **Union** stores values of different types in a single location and each member of the structure has its own storage location. In union, space is reserved for the largest data type only.
9. **Storage classes:** The storage class of a variable gives the following information to the compiler: (a) storage size of the variable, the initial value of the variable in case it is not initialized and (b) the scope of the variable and the duration of the variable in which it will be actively used throughout the program. There are four storage classes in C used to define variables: auto, extern, static, register.
10. **Preprocessor directives:** The command lines used to operate preprocessors, which process the source code before passing it to the compiler, thus reducing the run time of the program. These are always initialized in the beginning of the program outside all functions, including main(). These are of three types, macro substitution, file inclusion and compiler control directives.
11. **Standard library functions:** Functions that are predefined, compiled and placed in the C library in respective header files. For example, stdio.h, ctype.h, stdlib.h, math.h, string.h, time.h.

REVIEW QUESTIONS

1. Can an array be a member of a structure? Give an example.
2. Explain about structures and unions with suitable examples. (AU 2009)
3. Describe with example: (a) declaring a structure, (b) pointer to structure and (c) union. (AU 2011)
4. What do you understand by nested structure? Give an example.
5. How the structure is initialized?
6. Can we have array of union like array of structure? Give example.

7. Declare a structure for an employee payroll slip containing Eno, Ename, Basic pay, HRA, DA, Gross, Income tax, Professional tax.
8. Explain the purpose of storage classes auto, extern, static and register with suitable example. (AU 2008 Suppl, 2013)
9. What is meant by a preprocessor? What are the different types of preprocessor directives?
10. Write the syntax of structure declaration and give and example. (AU 2013)
11. What is storage class? List and explain with example (AU 2014)
12. What is meant by C library? Define header file.

PROGRAMMING ASSIGNMENTS

1. Write a menu-driven program to add, subtract, multiply and divide complex numbers.
2. Write a menu-driven program to read distances in meter and centimeter, add and subtract two distances using structure and functions.
3. Write a program to print the bill details of 10 customers with the following data: Meter number, customer name, number of units consumed, bill date, last date to deposit and the city name. The bill is to be calculated according to the following condition:

No. of units	Charge
For first 100 units	₹0.75 per unit
For the next 200 units	₹1.80
For the next 300 units	₹2.75

4. Define a structure called student that would contain name, reg-no and marks of five subjects and percentage.
5. Write a program to read the details of name, reg-no and marks of five subjects for 30 students, calculate the percentage and display the name, reg-no, marks of 30 subjects and percentage of each student. (AU 2014)
6. Consider the following declaration and illustrate the application of sizeof operator to this structure.

```
struct
{
char name;
int num;
}student;
```

7. Write a program to find the size of union and the number of bytes reserved for it.

File Handling in C 7

LEARNING OBJECTIVES

After completing this chapter, you would be able to understand the following:

- Need for files for storing data.
- Basic terminologies associated with files.
- File streams and file structures.
- Types of file access methods.
- Input/Output operations on files and standard devices.
- Different operations on files.
- Error handling during file operations.
- Command line arguments.

7.1 Introduction

We have various input and output functions in C to read and display data, such as printf, scanf, etc. However, there are some limitations with these functions, such as

1. It is very difficult to handle large volume of data.
2. It is difficult to store the input data for future use.
3. It is difficult to store the output data for future use.
4. Some of the input data are in image form or in text form.
5. The data are stored into the main memory which has limited size.

To deal with such problems, there is a special kind of data structure called **Files**. A file is also called as an external data structure whereas other data structures we have discussed so far are called internal data structure. It handles the inputs and outputs to a program through disks. The file is a collection of records where each record may contain different fields. The records may be of same size or variable sizes. If the file contains all the records of the same size then it is said to be made up of a fixed length record. If file consists of records of different sizes then it is said to be made up of variable length records. The variable size of the records may be due the variable size of the field.

There are two types of files that are stored in the disk depending on the manner in which they can be stored and accessed: (a) Sequential files which can be stored and read sequentially and (b) random files in which data can be accessed and processed randomly.

7.2 Basic Terminology Associated with Files

The various terminologies used are as follows:

1. **Field:** It is the basic unit of the record which represents meaningful information about the record. This is characterized by the data type and size. For example, name, age, sex, roll number of any student.
2. **Record:** It is a collection of logically related fields (information) about any real-world entity. For example, student is a collection of logically related information such as name, age, sex, roll number, etc. Hence, any student may be defined by his/her name, age, sex and roll number.
3. **File:** A file is a collection of records. For example, a file of students of EEE branch or a file of all students in an institute.
4. **File organization:** It is concerned with the arrangement of records on the disks.
5. **Key field:** It is a field that contains unique value for each record, so the record in the file is uniquely identified by specifying the value of a particular field of the record.
6. **Index:** It is a pointer used to determine the location of the record in a file that satisfies some condition.

7.3 Types of Files

The files are classify into two categories, text (ASCII) files and binary files.

1. The **text files** are called human readable files which is created by a text editor, such as vi editor, notepad, etc.

and further processed by different programs. A text file contains printable characters, such as letters, numbers, space, punctuation, etc. These files are saved either in plain text (.txt) or rich text format (.rtf).

2. The **binary files** are not human readable files as they contain information encoded in numbers ones and zeros. These files contains only non-textual data that make sense only when read by a program. They cannot be edited by any other program. Binary file formats may include multiple types of data in the same file, such as image, video or audio data.

7.4 Streams and Files

The files and their associated streams are automatically opened when the program is executed. A **stream** is a sequence of characters. It is exactly a sequence of bytes of data. The standard streams are standard file input, standard file output and standard error. A sequence of bytes flowing into a program is an **input stream**, a sequence of bytes flowing from the program is an **output stream**. Hence, the standard file input stream is used to read data from a file and the standard output stream is used to write data onto a file. Opening a file will return pointer to a file structure that contains information used to process the file. The advantage of streams is that input/output programming is device independent. Programmers do not need to create input/output functions for each device. Every stream is connected to a file. The details of interaction between streams, files and devices are performed automatically by the C library functions and the operating systems. There are two types of stream mode called text stream and binary stream. The text stream consists of characters which are organized into lines that is upto 255 characters long and terminated by end of line. Binary stream can handle many data, including, but not limited to, text data. Bytes of data in binary stream are not translated in any special way. There are predefined stream also called standard input/output files. These are automatically opened when a C program starts and automatically closed when it is terminated.

7.5 File System Structures

A file is a logical collection of files on a partition or disk. A partition is a container which has information and can span an entire hard drive if desired. The file system structures are different in different operating systems.

1. In UNIX, the file system are in hierarchical fashion which is upside-down tree, with root (/) at the base of the file system. Everything in UNIX considered as a file, including physical devices such as devices, DVD-ROM's, USB and so on. There are two major forms of UNIX available: AT&T UNIX System V and Berkeley Software Distribution (BSD). The most popular UNIX file system is BSD Fast File System (or FFS).
2. In Windows OS the file system is a method of organizing files on physical media, such as hard disks, CD's and flash drive. It has different choices of file systems when formatting media. The two types of files system in Windows OS are, NTFS (New Technology File System) and FAT (file allocation table) file system.

   - The NTFS is a well formed file system that is most commonly used in Windows2000, XP and vista. NTFS partition can extended upto 16 million TB, it performs read from and write to operations.
   - The FAT file system is a general purpose file system which is compatible with all operating systems. FAT partition cannot extend beyond 2TB, and is used for the device which has small capacity.

7.6 Various Types of File Access Methods

There various types of file access methods are Sequential, Indexed Sequential, Random and Binary.

1. **Sequential access method:** An important advantage of sequential files is that different records can have different lengths, from zero to and higher depending upon the system. In these files, a pointer known as **file pointer** always indicates the next record to be transferred. The files can be read in strict sequential manner on printers, etc. , however, for files stored on disk, the pointer can be reset at the beginning of the file, so that it can be read again or re-written. Sometimes, it is possible to move the pointer back by one record, so that the last record can be read again or over-written.
2. **Indexed sequential access method:** This method of file access is available in many variations on microcomputers, minicomputers and mainframes, and the operating system preferred is DOS. It initially stores records sequentially and then allows both sequential and random access. There are four approaches to indexed sequential access processing: load or extend records, adding records, random retrieval and sequential processing of records.
3. **Random access method:** In a random-access data file, we can read or write information from anywhere in the file. It is also called direct-access method. Most systems allow random access for files stored on random-access devices, such as disks and tapes. C maintains a file pointer to enable read, write or seek any arbitrary structure in the file. When the file is opened, the pointer points to the first record in the file. A read operation then reads the file from the current position of the pointer, and moves it to the next record or structure. A write operation is performed on current position of the pointer, and moves the pointer down one structure. Seek operation moves the pointer to the specified record.
4. **Binary access method:** Binary access gives complete control over a file, as the bytes in the file can represent anything. For example, we can conserve disk space by building variable-length records. This access is used

when it is important to keep the size of file small. To write binary data onto a file, an array variable of the Byte data type is used instead of a string variable.

7.7 Input and Output Operations on Files and Standard Devices

In a computer, data are represented in bits. The several bits are composed together to form bytes. The bytes collectively form a character. The characters are composed together to form fields. Many fields are collectively called records. A file consists of many fields. There are many ways of organizing files, one of which is sequential file in which records are typically stored in order. C language generally takes inputs and displays the output to the user or gets inputs and writes output onto a file.

The C language views files as sequential streams of bytes. Every file ends with either end of file or specified byte number recorded in a system. Stream provides communication between files and programs. For example, file input stream enables a program to read input from a file and file output stream enables a program to write output to a file. To read or write characters into the file first we should open a file and finally we have to close a file after performs all operations. C has a general mechanism for opening, reading, writing and closing files.

The standard library provides many functions for reading data from files and writing data to the files. It also provides the standard input and output operations. These functions are having the prototype in the header file called <stdio.h>.

The C programming language provides some standard inputs and outputs. There are two types of streams called standard input/output streams and file streams. Standard I/O streams are used to read or write the information from the user and the file I/O streams are used to read or write the data into the files.

7.7.1 | Sequential Access I/O Operations

7.7.1.1 Standard Input Functions

The standard input functions getchar(), getch(), getche() and gets() are used to get the data from the user through the input devices.

1. **getchar():** This function is used to read a character that is input during the runtime. It returns the character which reads from the keyboard. Enter key needs to be pressed after each character.

   Syntax

   ```
   int getchar(void);
   ```

   For example,

   ```
   #include<stdio.h>
   #include<conio.h>
   void main()
   {
   getchar();
   }
   ```

2. **getche():** This function is used to read alphanumberic data from console and echoes it to the screen. It returns the character reads from the keyboard.

   Syntax

   ```
   int getche(void);
   ```

   For example,

   ```
   #include<stdio.h>
   #include<conio.h>
   void main()
   {
   getche();
   }
   ```

   If the user input is x, then the output is

   x ← input
   x

3. **getch():** This function is used to get one character at a time from console but it does not echo to the screen. It returns the alphanumberic character read from the keyboard.

   Syntax

   ```
   int getch(void);
   ```

   For example,

   ```
   #include<stdio.h>
   #include<conio.h>
   void main()
   {
   getch();
   }
   ```

4. **gets():** This function is used to read a line from stdin and store it into the string pointed by str. It stopped when newline character is read or when end-of-file is reached or when Enter key is pressed. It returns pointer to a string.

   Syntax

   ```
   char *gets(char *str);
   ```

   For example,

   ```
   #include<stdio.h>
   #include<conio.h>
   void main()
   {
   gets();
   }
   ```

7.7.1.2 Standard Output Functions

The standard output functions putchar(), putch(), and puts() are used to write the data into the output devices.

1. **putchar():** This function is used to write the data which is specified in the argument char to standard output device (stdout). It returns the character which is given in the argument.

   Syntax

   ```
   int putchar(int char);
   ```

   For example,

   ```
   #include<stdio.h>
   #include<conio.h>
   void main()
   {
   putchar(b);
   }
   ```

   The output is

   ```
   b
   ```

2. **putch():** This function displays any alphanumeric characters to the standard output device, one character at a time. It returns the character which is given in the arguments.

   Syntax

   ```
   int putch(int char);
   ```

   For example,

   ```
   #include<stdio.h>
   #include<conio.h>
   void main()
   {
   putch(a);
   }
   ```

   The output is

   ```
   a
   ```

3. **puts():** This function displays a string to the output device. It does not include the null character and also append the newline character.

   Syntax

   ```
   int puts(const char *str);
   ```

   For example,

   ```
   #include<stdio.h>
   #include<conio.h>
   void main()
   {
   puts("Hello");
   }
   ```

   The output is

   ```
   Hello
   ```

7.7.1.3 Formatted Input and Output

The standard C library functions used for input from the input device. It scans input according to the format as described. It also contains conversion specification.

The formatted input functions are scanf() and sscanf().

1. **scanf():** This function is used to scan the standard input from the user.

   Syntax

   ```
   int scanf(const char *format_string, &arg_1,
   &arg_2,...);
   ```

2. **sscanf():** This function is used to scan a string passed as the first parameter. The standard C library functions used for writing to the output device. It writes into the screen according to the format as described. It also contains conversion specification.

   Syntax

   ```
   int sscanf(const char *str, const char
   *format_string, &arg_1, &arg_2,...);
   ```

The formatted output functions are printf(), sprintf().

1. **printf():** This function is used to display the data into the standard output.

   Syntax

   ```
   int printf(const char *format_string,
   arg_1, arg_2, ....);
   ```

2. **sprintf():** This function is used to write a formatted text into an array of characters.

   Syntax

   ```
   int sprintf(const char *str, const char
   *format_string, arg_1, arg_2,...);
   ```

7.7.1.4 Functions for File Operations

There are several functions which are used to perform many operations on the files. To access the files we have the following functions

1. **fopen():** This function opens an existing file.
2. **fflush():** This function synchronizes the output file with the actual file.
3. **fclose():** This function closes the opened file after perform all the operations.

We have another set of input and output operations, which we can call as formatted and unformatted input and output operations performed on the files.

The following are the unformatted file input and output functions:

1. **fgetc():** This function reads a character from the file.
2. **fgets():** This function reads strings from the file.
3. **fputc():** This function writes a character into the file
4. **fputs():** This function writes strings into the file.

Other unformatted file input/output functions like getc(), putc(), getw() and putw() were discussed in Chapter 3.

The formatted file input and output functions are as follows:

1. **fscanf():** This function reads a formatted input from a file stream.
2. **fprintf():** This function prints a formatted output on the file.

7.7.2 Random Access I/O Operations

All the file input/output operations will work to read and write files sequentially, unless the user takes explicit steps to change the position of file pointer. When a read operation is followed by a write operation, which is further followed by a read operation, this will cause the second read to start immediately after the end of the data just written. To avoid this, the random access input/output operations are used to control the implied read/write position in the file. The position of the file pointer is moved without using read or write operations.

The records entered using formatted output function fprintf() in sequential access are not necessarily of the same length. However, in a randomly accessed file, the individual records are normally fixed in length and may be accessed directly without searching through other records. For example, records maintained by airline reservation system, banking system, etc.

Three types of functions exist which allow the position of the file pointer to be examined or changed.

1. **ftell() and fgetpos()** are used to find the position of the file pointer.
2. **rewind()** is used to set the file pointer to zero.
3. **fseek() and fsetpos()** are used to set the position of the file pointer.

7.8 File Operations

The efficiency of a file system depends on how efficiently these operations can be performed on the file.

1. **Creation:** First the file structure is created before feeding the data into the records. Creation of the file determines the name of the file; the position of the file where the I/O operation is performed; the file structure defined, whether it is a text file or binary file and the access method defined.
2. **Open:** This operation prepares the file for read and write operations. One opening a file, we can use the file pointer to let the compiler perform input and output operations on the files. The function used is fopen().

   Syntax

   ```
   FILE *fopen(const char *filename,const char *mode);
   ```

   This function opens the file which is mentioned in the argument. It allows different modes for opening a file. The allowing modes are "r" is to open a file for reading, "w" is to open a file for writing, "a" is for opening a file for appending, "r+" is to open a for reading and writing where it starts from the beginning, "w+" is to opening a file for reading and writing where it overwrites the existing file, "a+" is to open for reading and writing and append if necessary (Table 1).

TABLE 1

Constant strings in mode argument of fopen()

Mode	Explanation
r	To read text mode
w	To write text mode (truncates file to zero length or creates new file)
a	To append text mode for writing (opens or creates file and sets file pointer to the end-of-file)
rb	To read binary mode
wb	To write binary mode (truncates file to zero length or creates new file)
ab	To append binary mode for writing (opens or creates file and sets file pointer to the end-of-file)
r+	To read and write text mode
w+	To read and write text mode (truncates file to zero length or creates new file)
a+	To read and write text mode (opens or creates file and sets file pointer to the end-of-file)
r+b or rb+	To read and write binary mode
w+b or wb+	To read and write binary mode (truncates file to zero length or creates new file)
a+b or ab+	To read and write binary mode (opens or creates file and sets file pointer to the end-of-file)

3. **Read:** To read any information from a file it should be opened in a read mode. The function used is fread().

   Syntax:

   ```
   size_t fread(void *ptr, size_t size, size_t nmemb, FILE *stream);
   ```

It reads data from the given stream into the array pointed to by `ptr`. It reads `nmemb` number of elements of size `size`. The total number of bytes read is (`size*nmemb`). The number of elements read is returned. On error or in case end of file is reached, the total number of elements successfully read (which may be zero) is returned.

4. **Write:** To write any information into the file it should be opened in write mode. The function used is fwrite().

   Syntax

   ```
   size_t fwrite(const void *ptr, size_t size, size_t nmemb, FILE *stream);
   ```

   It writes data from the array pointed to by `ptr` to the given stream. It writes `nmemb` number of elements of size `size`. The total number of bytes written is (`size*nmemb`). The number of elements written is returned. On error, the total number of elements successfully written (which may be zero) is returned.

5. **Append:** To append any information present in two files, we can open the first file in the append mode. Then append the information present in the second file.
6. **Flush the output buffer:** The fflush() synchronizes an output file with the actual file.

   Syntax

   ```
   int fflush(FILE *stream);
   ```

   It flushes the output buffer of a stream. If stream is a null pointer, then all output buffers are flushed. If successful, it returns zero. On error it returns end of file.
7. **Retrieve or search:** This operation is performed to search for a record or a set of records having a particular value in a particular field or where the field value satisfies certain conditions.
8. **Insert:** This operation deals with the insertion of a new record or set of records at a specific location.
9. **Update:** The existing records of the file may be updated by changing the values of the fields or a new record may be inserted. For example, rename() is used to to rename the file.

   Syntax

   ```
   int rename(const char *old_filename,
   const char *new_filename);
   ```

   It causes the filename referred to by old_filename to be changed to new_filename. If the filename pointed to by new_filename exists, the result is implementation-defined. On success, zero is returned. On error, a non-zero value is returned and the file is still accessible by its old filename.
10. **Delete:** Any record or a set of records may be deleted from the file.
11. **Remove:** The remove() is used to remove the file.

    Syntax:

    ```
    int remove(const char *filename);
    ```

    It deletes the given filename so that it is no longer accessible (unlinks the file). If the file is currently open, then the result is implementation-defined. On success, zero is returned. On failure, a non-zero value is returned.
12. **Close:** After performing all operations on the file we have to close the file. The function used is fclose().

    Syntax

    ```
    int fclose(FILE *stream);
    ```

    It closes the stream. All buffers are flushed. If successful, it returns zero. On error it returns end of file.

Program 1: To demonstrate the various file operations.

```
#include<stdio.h>
void main()
{
FILE *fr,*fw; char ch;
fw=fopen("Sample.txt","w");
fr=fopen("Out.txt","r");
if(fw==NULL)
{
printf("Some problem in opening the
file");
}
else
{
while((ch=fgetc(fr))!=EOF)
{
printf("%c",ch);
}
}
fclose(fw);
fclose(fr);
}
```

Program 2: To open a file and count the number of characters in the file

```
#include<stdio.h>
#include<conio.h>
void main()
{
FILE *fp;
char ch;
int p=-1;
clrscr();
fp=fopen("d:\sampl.txt","w");
printf("\nPress q to quit");
while(1)
{
if(ch=='q'||ch=='Q')
break;
ch=getchar();
if((ch>=65& &ch<=90)||(ch>=97&&ch<=122))
p++;
putc(ch,fp);
}
printf("\nThe total number of characters
in the file is: %d\n",p);
fclose(fp);
getch();
}
```

Solved Problem

1. *Write a program in C to*

   (a) *enter characters in the file from the keyboard.*

   (b) *copy the contents of the above file into another file.*

Solution:

```
#include<stdio.h>
#include<conio.h>
void main()
{
FILE *p, *q;
```

```
char ch;
char file1[20], file1[20];
printf("\nEnter the file name to enter
characters:");
gets(file1);
p = fopen(file1,"w");
if(p==NULL){
printf("cannot open %s",file1);
return 0;
}
else{
printf("\nEnter the text and hit Enter to
Terminate\n");
while( (ch = getche()) != '\r' ){
fputc( ch, p );
}
}
fclose(p);
printf("\nEnter the source file name to be
copied:");
p=fopen(file1,"r");
if(p==NULL){
printf("cannot open %s",file1);
return 0;
}
else
{
printf("\nEnter the destination file
name:");
gets(file2);
q=fopen(file2,"w");
if(q==NULL){
printf("cannot open %s",file2);
return 0;
}
while((ch=getc(p))!=EOF)
putc(ch,q);
}
printf("\nCOMPLETED");
fclose(p);
fclose(q);
getch();
}
```

2. *Write a program to sort of a list of numbers entered from the keyboard such that the odd numbers are copied into one while, while the even numbers are copied into another file.*

Solution:

```
#include<stdio.h>
#include<conio.h>
void main()
{
FILE *p, *q;
int n, i, a[20];
char file1[20], file1[20];
printf("Enter the name of file with odd
numbers");
scanf("%s",&file1);
printf("Enter the name of file with even
numbers");
scanf("%s",&file2);
p=fopen(file1,"w");
q=fopen(file2,"w");
if((p==NULL)&&(q==NULL))
{
printf("The files cannot be opened");
}
printf("Enter the numbers in the list\n");
scanf("%d",&n);
for(i=1;i<=n;i++)
{
scanf("%d",&a[i]);
if(a[i]%2===0)
fprintf(p,"%d\n",a[i]);
else
fprintf(q,"%d\n",a[i]);
}
fclose(p);
fclose(q);
}
```

7.9 Error Handling in Files

While performing read and write operations, sometimes we do not get result successfully because the read or write operation used may not be correct. The standard I/O functions maintain two indicators with each open stream to show end-of-file or error status of the stream. Some functions used to handle the errors are as follows:

1. **ferror:** This function checks the file error, returns non-zero if stream's error indicator is set, zero otherwise.

   ```
   int ferror(FILE *stream);
   ```

2. **feof:** This function checks the end of the file, returns non-zero if the stream EOF indicator is set, zero otherwise.

   ```
   int feof(FILE *stream);
   ```

3. **clearer():** This function clears the error and EOF indicators for the stream.

   ```
   void clearerr(FILE *stream);
   ```

4. **perror():** This function prints the single line error message on the program's standard output.

   ```
   void perror(const char *s);
   ```

To know about the current file status, two useful functions are used. These two functions are prototyped in <sys/stat.h> header file.

1. **stat():** This function obtains information about the file named by path irrespective of the read, write or execute permission of the file, however, all directories listed in the pathname leading to the file must be searchable.

Syntax:

```
int stat(char *path, struct stat *buf),
```

2. **fstat():** It obtains the same information about an open file referenced by the argument descriptor, such as would be obtained by an open call (low level I/O).

Syntax:

```
int fstat(int fd, struct stat *buf)
```

Both stat() and fstat() return 0 on success, –1 on failure and set errno to indicate the error. The errors are again defined in #include <sys/stat.h>.

7.10 Command Line Arguments

We can pass some values to the C program during execution. These values are called **command line arguments**, and are the values are passed as the arguments for the main function. The format for the main() function is

```
main(int argc,char *argv[])
```

Here `argc` is the argument counter which represents the number of arguments in the command line and the second argument is an array of characters type pointers that points to the command line argument.

Program 3: To demonstrate command line arguments.

```
#include<stdio.h>
void main(int argc, char *argv[])
{
FILE *fr;
char ch;
if(argc != 2)
{
printf("usage: %s filename", argv[0]);
}
else
{
fr = fopen(argv[1], "r");
if (fr==0)
{
printf("Could not open file\n");
}
else
{
while((ch=fgetc(fr))!=EOF)
{
printf("%c",ch);
}
}
}
fclose(fr);
}
```

POINTS TO REMEMBER

1. A **file** is a collection of records where each record (of same or variable sizes) may contain different fields.
2. The files are classify into **text (ASCII) files** and **binary files**. The text files are readable by humans, whereas the binary files are not.
3. The standard streams are **standard file input**, **standard file output** and **standard error**.
4. The standard library provides many functions for reading data from files and writing data to the files.
5. The **file I/O routines** all work in the same way; unless the user takes explicit steps to change the file position indicator, files will be read and written sequentially.
6. The C language provides standard library function **ferror()**, which is used for detecting, any errors that might occur during reading/writing a file.
7. There are various types of file access methods **sequential, indexed sequential, random, binary**.
8. **Command line arguments** let the user pass values to the main() at the time of execution.

REVIEW QUESTIONS

1. What is meant by files? What are the types of files?
2. How the files are accessed? What are the file access modes?
3. List out the standard library function that are used to access and manipulate the files.
4. What are the difference between random access I/O and sequential I/O functions?
5. Explain the various error handling functions.
6. Differentiate between text and binary files.
7. Explain the following types of file: (a) Serial file, (b) sequential file, (c) indexed sequential file and (d) direct/random access file.

PROGRAMMING ASSIGNMENTS

1. Write a program to read the data from the file and write it to the another file.
2. Write a program to append two files by using command line arguments.
3. Write a program in C to read and write students' information into the file using data members.
4. Write a program in C to read specific records from a file.
5. Write a program to read data from keyboard, write it to a file A, read the same data from file A and display it on the screen.

MS Office Application Software

8

LEARNING OBJECTIVES

After completing this chapter, you will be able to understand the following:

- Introduction to MS Office packages.
- Working with MS Word, understanding its components and features for creation, editing, saving and printing documents.
- Working with MS PowerPoint, understanding its components and features for creation, editing, saving and printing presentations.
- Working with MS Excel, understanding its components and features for creation, editing, saving and printing of worksheets.

8.1 Introduction

There are two kinds of software: System software and Application software. MS Office is a very useful Application software package to handle effectively office activities like data typing, processing, editing, manipulating and formatting various kinds of documents and communication. It is a collection of several application programs such as MS Word, MS PowerPoint, MS Excel, MS Outlook, MS Access, etc. All the Microsoft Office programs share a common design and work in a similar manner. Getting familiar with one program makes it easier to interact with and learn other programs.

1. **MS Word:** It is the most popular word processing software that is used to create, edit, save and print a document on the Windows operating system environment. It also has functionalities available for working with images to be placed on documents. This tool can even be used to create web pages. It provides a graphical user interface (GUI) which makes word processing very simple and efficient through availability of various commands. Other word processing software available in the market are WordStar and Easy Word (for DOS environment), Notepad (for Windows environment), Applix Words (for Linux environment) OpenOffice Writer, Google Docs, etc.
2. **MS PowerPoint:** It is an effective and extremely useful tool for creating effective presentations in seminars, lectures, etc., using tools to create slide shows with lots of preview design templates, color schemes and animation effects, multimedia effects.
3. **MS Excel:** It is the spreadsheet program that gives us the features that make it easier to organize and analyze the information. It allows one to enter numerical values or data into the rows/columns of a spreadsheet, and perform calculations on them, prepare graphs and do statistical analysis of the entered data.
4. **MS Outlook:** It is the personal information manager andcommunication program that provides tools and resources to manage e-mails, calendars, contacts, and other related information.
5. **MS Access:** It is a relational database management system (RDBMS) which provides tools and resources to facilitate effective storage and retrieval of data. Other popular RDMS are Oracle, MS SQL Server, IMB DB2, MS FoxPro, etc.

Solved Problem

1. *List any four office packages.* **(AU 2009)**

or What are the main software in office package. **(AU 2010)**

Solution: MS Office is a very useful application software package consisting of several application programs such as MS Word, MS Excel, MS PowerPoint, MS Access.

8.2 MS Word

In this section, we will discuss various features of MS Word 2010/2013 software and methods to create or open, save, print and close the word document. Before starting work on it, the MS Office 2010/2013 needs to be installed on the computer system. After installing the MS Office, the following steps are required to access the MS Word.

Note: The commands of **MS Office 2007** and **MS Office 2010/2013** are similar with new additional features in 2010/2013 version.

8.2.1 Starting MS Word

There are two ways to start MS Word:

1. If a shortcut is available on the desktop then double click on the shortcut icon.
2. Follow the sequence of clicking as mentioned below:

Start button of the Taskbar → Programs →

Microsoft Office → Microsoft Word option

After clicking on the Microsoft Word, a new GUI window called Word window appears which contains a blank Word document. This blank document can be used to create a letter, notice, note, memo or report. After creating it, save it with a new name.

8.2.2 Components of MS Word

The major components are described as follows. The Microsoft Word window and the blank document appear similar to the one shown in Fig. 1.

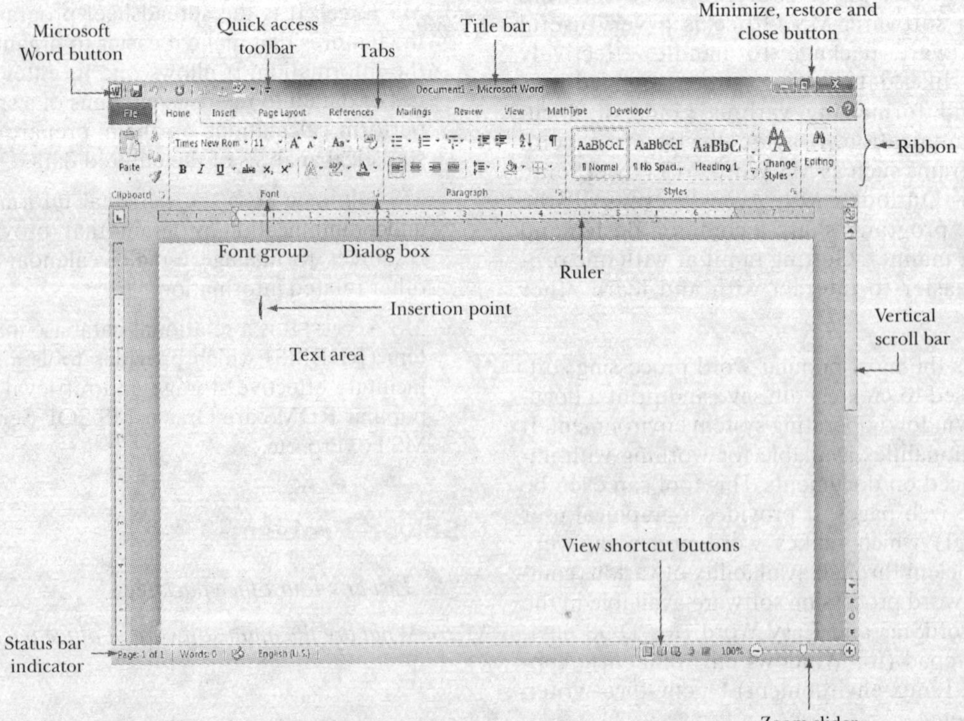

Figure 1 Components of MS Word.

8.2.2.1 File Tab

The **Microsoft Office button** ( ) located at the upper left most corner in MS office 2007 has been replaced with **File tab** in 2010/2013 version. It contains a drop-down list of various commands such as New, Open, Convert, Save, Save As, Print, Prepare, Send, Publish and Close. It also shows the list of recently visited documents, Word options and Exit Word in the submenu. The Esc key is used to move out of the activated drop-down list. An option of the list can be activated when a user clicks on this tab.

8.2.2.2 Title Bar

The Title bar is a horizontal bar located at the very top of the word window and it displays the name of the active document which is being currently used (Fig. 2). When a new document is created the Microsoft Word assigns a default name as Document1 which can be changed by using the Save As option in the File tab. In the right most corner of the Title bar, we can see the button for minimizing/maximizing ( ), restoring ( ) and closing the document ( ). On the left most corner of the Title bar we can see the Microsoft Word button ( ) and next to it is the Quick Access Toolbar ( ).

Figure 2 Title bar.

8.2.2.3 Quick Access Toolbar

Quick Access Toolbar is used to quickly access the different options such as New, Save, Undo, Redo, etc. The user can customize the Quick Access Toolbar by clicking on it and marking the options he/she wants to see on the Quick Access Toolbar. From Fig. 2, we can see that the New ( ), Save ( ), Undo ( ) and Redo ( ) options are selected; therefore their shortcut appears at the left-hand side of Quick Access Toolbar. This toolbar is used to display the frequently used commands so that they can be accessed quickly.

8.2.2.4 Ribbon

The Ribbon is located just below the Quick Access Toolbar and it contains various tabs such as File (discussed earlier) Home, Insert, Page Layout, References, Mailing, Review and View. Each tab consists of several groups of related commands. Clicking on the tab displays the several groups, and each group consists of several commands that are used to perform specific tasks. Each group elements have certain icons which are used to quickly issue the command by just clicking on them. The shortcut keys corresponding to the icons can also be used and these keys are visible when the mouse pointer is left on the icon for a short period of time. Each group also contains the dialog box launcher in the bottom right corner of the group, which contains more commands related to the group.

The Ribbon cannot be repositioned but the user can minimize it by clicking the right mouse button at the Ribbon and then clicking on minimize the ribbon option so that only the Ribbon tabs appear. The Ribbon, Quick Access Toolbar and other tab commands can also be accessed using the Alt key on the keyboard. Pressing the Alt key will display the screen as shown in Fig. 3.

The user can access the ribbon or other tab commands quickly by pressing the shortcut alphabets or number from the keyboard as shown. The various tabs on the Ribbon are as follows:

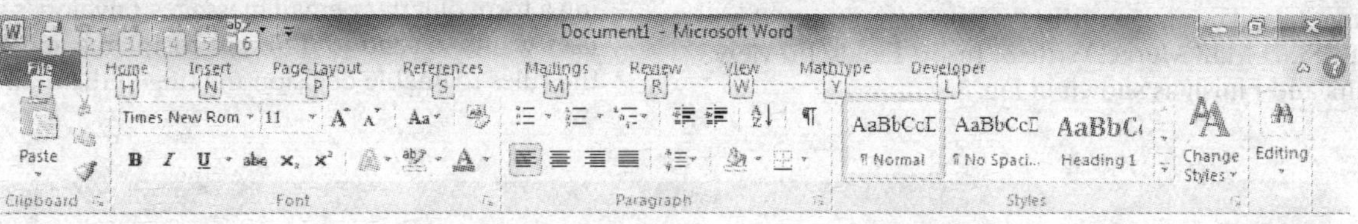

Figure 3 Using Alt key to access commands.

1. **Home tab:** This tab consists of several groups such as Clipboard, Font, Paragraph, Style and Editing as shown in Fig. 4. These groups are used for copying/pasting text; changing font/font size, line spacing; finding/replacing text.

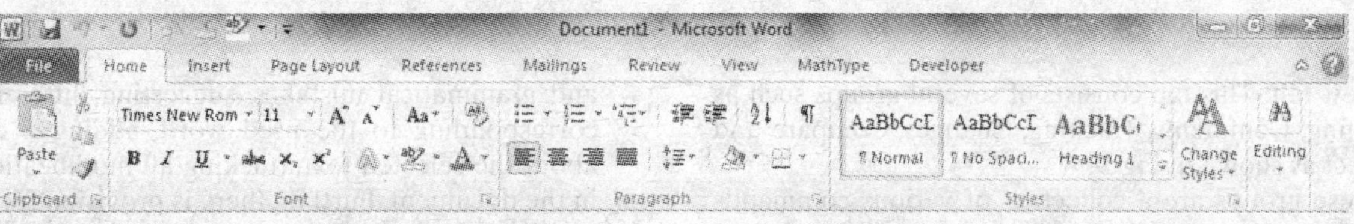

Figure 4 Home tab of the Ribbon.

2. **Insert tab:** The Insert tab consists of several groups such as Pages, Tables, Illustrations, Links, Header and footer, Text and Symbols as shown in Fig. 5.

   These groups are a collection of various commands that basically deal with inserting the various symbols, tables, arts, pictures, etc., into the document, apart from adding header/footer and page numbers to the document.

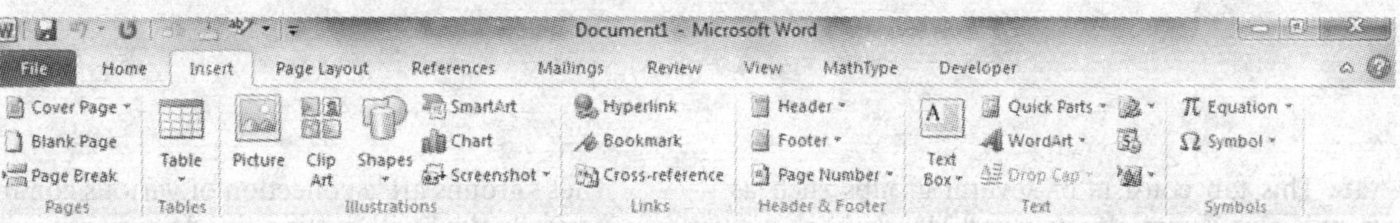

Figure 5 Insert tab.

3. **Page Layout tab:** This tab consists of several groups such as Themes, Page Setup, Page Background, Paragraph and Arrange as shown in Fig. 6. These groups are a collection of various commands that basically deal with the formatting of the text in the selected paragraph or the document, such as selecting

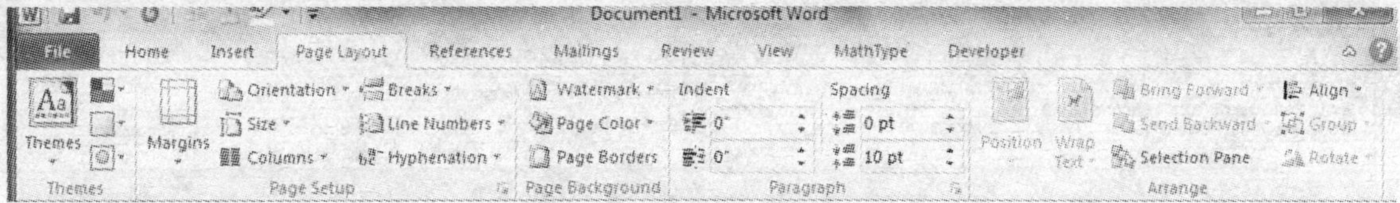

Figure 6 Page Layout tab.

the page orientation, background color, watermark page border, etc.

4. **References tab:** This tab consists of several groups such as Table of Contents, Footnotes, Citation & Bibliography, Captions, Index and Table of Authorities as shown in Fig. 7.

These groups are the collection of various commands that basically deal with inserting a table of predefined format, footnotes, citation and bibliography of a book, journal article or periodicals.

Figure 7 References tab.

5. **Mailing tab:** This tab consists of several groups like Create, Start Mail Merge, Write & Insert Fields, Preview Results and Finish as shown in Fig. 8.

These groups are a collection of various commands that basically deal with creating, printing the envelope, creating a form of letters, email messages, envelopes which the user wants to send to different recipients and specifying the rules to enable decision-making in the mail merge.

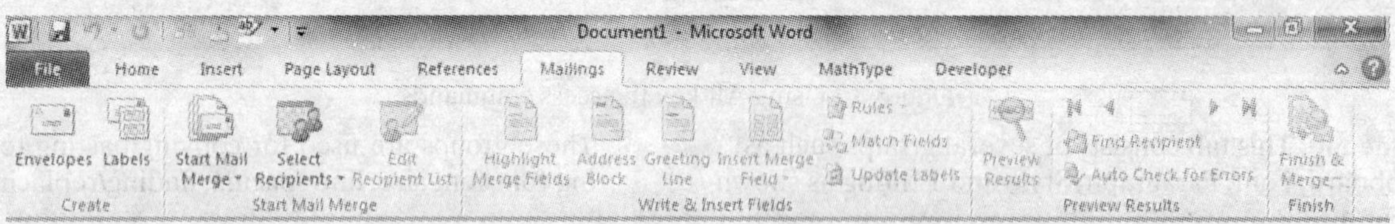

Figure 8 Mailing tab.

6. **Review tab:** This tab consists of several groups such as Proofing, Comments, Tracking, Changes, Compare and Protect as shown in Fig. 9.

These groups are a collection of various commands that deal with setting the language, checking the spelling and grammatical mistakes, suggesting different words corresponding to the used word, adding a comment about the selected text, tracking all modifications done in the document. Further, there is provision for comparing the current word file with another .doc file.

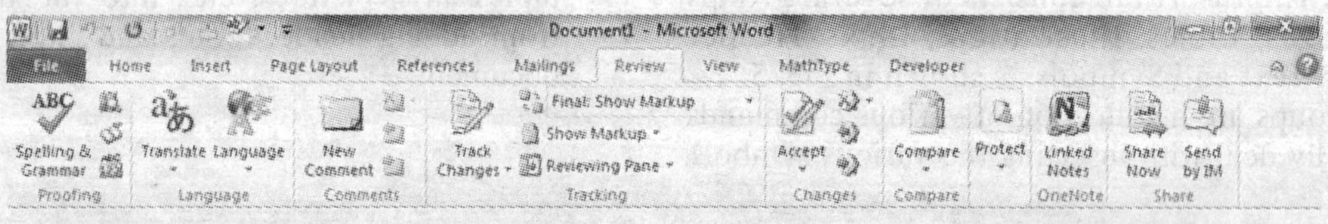

Figure 9 Review tab.

7. **View tab:** This tab consists of several groups such as Document Views, Zoom, Window and Macros as shown in Fig. 10.

These groups are a collection of various commands that basically deal with setting the document view; showing or hiding the ruler bar, document map, gridlines; creating new macros or accessing other existing options, etc.

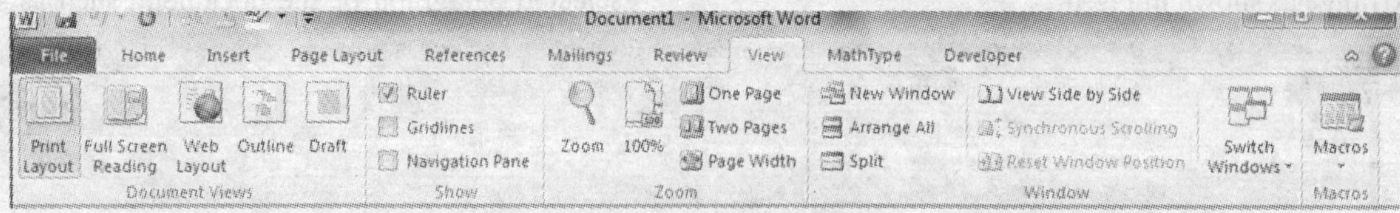

Figure 10 View tab.

8.2.2.5 Ruler

It is located below the Ribbon and is used to change the vertical alignment of the word document quickly. If the ruler bar is not visible then the user can make it visible by clicking the tab view on the Ribbon and then clicking on the ruler option (Fig. 11).

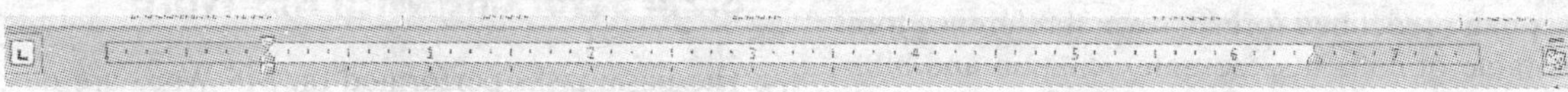

Figure 11 Ruler bar.

8.2.2.6 Scroll Bars

The Microsoft Word window consists of scroll bars which are used to view the contents of the document that do not fit in the word window. The scroll bars are used by clicking and dragging (holding the left button of the mouse) them. There are two scroll bars, namely vertical scroll bar and horizontal scroll bar:

1. The vertical scroll bar is positioned at the right side of the word window and is used to move the document up or down. It can be used to scroll the document one line up and down or one page up and down. It is always visible.
2. The horizontal scroll bar is positioned just above the status bar at the bottom of the Word window and is used to move the document left or right to view the contents of the document. It is only visible when the document does not fit in the window screen size. (Fig. 12).

Figure 12 Horizontal scroll bar.

8.2.2.7 Text Area

It is the actual workplace in word window which is located just below the ruler bar. The user can insert an image or start typing the text right from the blinking insertion point. This insertion point is always positioned after the last typed character.

8.2.2.8 Status Bar

The status bar is positioned at the bottom of the word window and it displays significant information about the active document on which the user is currently working. The status bar shows the current active page number, total page number, line number, word count, column number, zoom percentage, zoom slider, spelling and grammar check indicator, view shortcut buttons, etc. The status bar can be customized by right clicking on the status bar and marking the options which we want to see on the status bar.

8.2.3 | Features of MS Word

1. **Editing tools:** Editing involves modification in the text of the active document. The selected text can be cut/copied to the clipboard from which it can be pasted at the required position in the document. Also selected text can be searched and replaced in the active document. Word processors are not only check spelling mistakes, but also check and suggest alternatives for grammatical errors in the text document. Other tools include tracking changes in text, inserting comments, comparing and protecting documents.
2. **Formatting tools:** Formatting involves changing the style/presentation of the text in a document. These tools can be used to change the color of the text font; change the font face, bold face, italicize or underline the selected text; change the size of the selected text or document; highlight the selected text; clear the formatting of a formatted text; draw a line through the middle of the selected text; draw the shadow behind the selected text and adjust the spacing between the characters. Also, the formatting of one place can be set in another place using format painter. Page layout plays very important role in formatting the document. The user may select the Page Setup group and set the margin size for the entire document, the orientation of the page, the page background color, page border color, etc. Further, Change Case option is present to change the case of a word/sentence to lower case, upper case, sentence case, toggle case, etc.
3. **Paragraph adjustment tools:** Paragraph adjustment involves adjustment of text in a certain manner on the document. These tools are used to arrange the text in the form of bulleted list, numbered list, to align the text to left, center, right or justified (left and right both), specify the line spacing, decrease or increase the indent level of paragraphs, split the text into two or more columns, align the text within the text box (wrap text), etc.
4. **Inserting elements:** Several graphical, multimedia and other elements can be inserted to expand the usability and enhance the presentation of the document, such as cover page, tables through conversion of text into table, illustrations (pictures, clipart, shapes, chart), hyperlinks, header, footer, page numbers for easy tracking, textboxes, decorative text (WordArt), date, time, symbols, equations, etc.

5. **Effective storage:** Documents in a word processor can be autosaved and autorecovered in emergency cases to retrieve documents. Also, a feature can be built for storage and retrieval of several blocks of text.
6. **Creating reference tools:** Based on the text in the document set in a predefined format, several reference tools such as table of contents, footnotes, citation and bibliography, captions and index can be created. These are useful while dealing with books, journal articles and periodicals.
7. **Mail merge:** This facility helps in creating, printing envelopes, creating a form of letters, email messages, which the user wants to send to different recipients and in specifying the rules to enable decision-making in the mail merge.
8. **Viewing options and setting macros:** This facility helps in setting the document view, viewing more than one document simultaneously; showing or hiding the ruler bar, document map, gridlines; zooming in and zooming out for particular portions of the document requiring more focus. Creating macros (setting shortcuts to perform frequent tasks) or accessing other existing macro options, etc. promotes flexible and efficient use.

8.2.4 | Working with MS Word

The basic tasks performed on MS Word are described as follows:

8.2.4.1 *Creating a Document*

The document can easily be created in the MS Word by simply clicking on MS Office button for 2007 or File tab for 2010/2013 version and then clicking on the New command or pressing shortcut key Ctrl + N. This would display the New Document box asking to create a blank document or a new blog post. Double clicking on the blank document displays the word window with Document1 as the title on the Title bar. The user can start typing the text from the insertion point shown in the text area. The sequence of selection and the screens displayed are shown in Fig. 13.

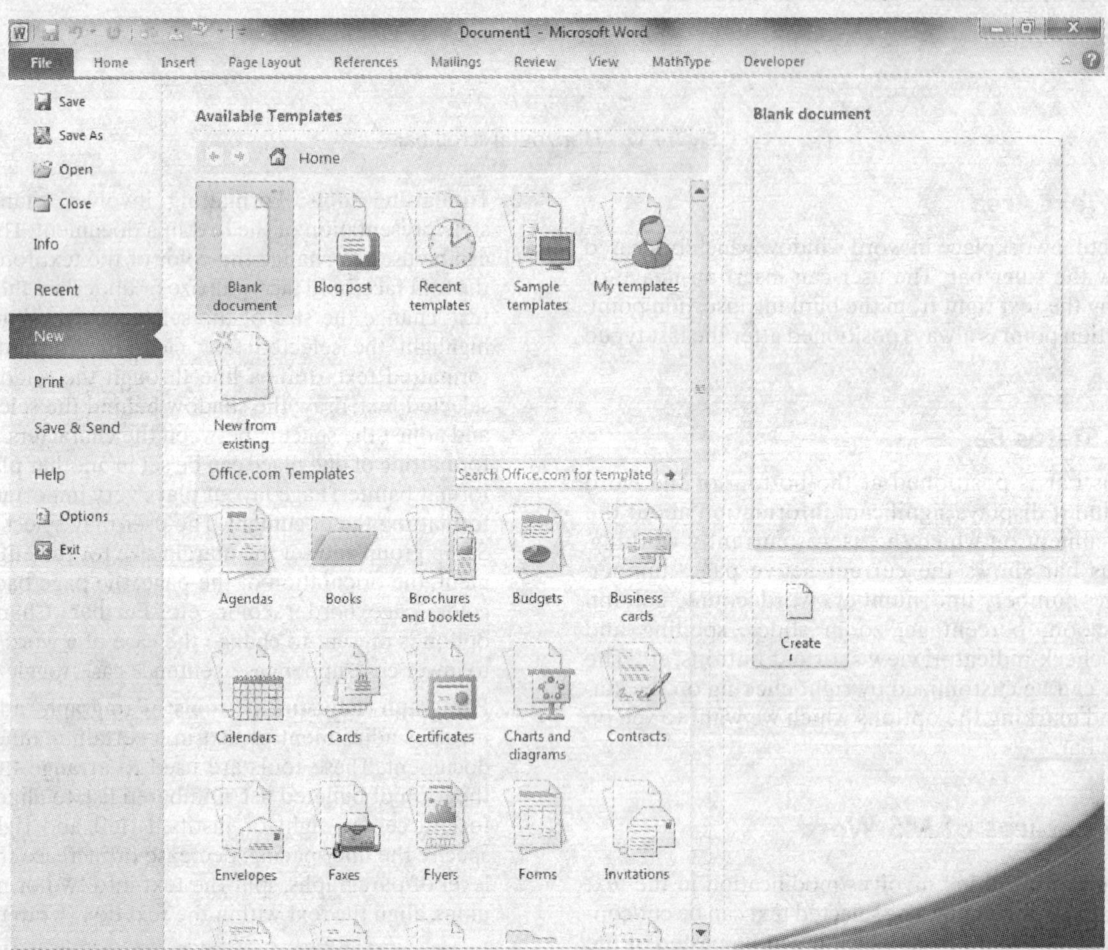

Figure 13 Creating a document in MS Word.

8.2.4.2 *Opening an Existing Document*

An existing document can be opened by performing the following steps:

1. Click on the MS Office button and then click on Open command or press the short key Ctrl + O.
2. The Open dialog box appears asking for the name of the file, the type of file and the location where it is saved.
3. After providing the necessary information (the location, name and type of the file to open), click on the Open button.

8.2.4.3 Saving a Document

Once the typing of the text in the document is finished, the document needs to be saved for future reference. This saving is done in two ways depending on whether the document is a new or an already existing document:

1. **First time saving the document:** The document is saved by performing the following steps:
   - Click on the MS Office button for 2007 or File tab for 2010/2013 version.
   - Click on *Save As* command, the Save As dialog box appears.
   - Select the location and type the filename in the Filename box
   - Click on the Save button.
2. **Saving the existing document:** The existing document is saved directly by clicking on the Save button ( ) in the Quick Access Toolbar, pressing the shortcut Ctrl + S or by performing the following steps:
   - Click on the MS Office button for 2007 or File tab for 2010/2013 version.
   - Click on the Save command, the document is saved with the existing name.

An existing document can also be saved with a different name or at a different location by using the Save As command.

8.2.4.4 Editing a Document

Editing of the documents comprises operations like moving the selected text from one place to another, copying the selected text to a specified position, changing or selecting the font face/color of the text, highlighting the selected text, formatting the paragraphs, changing the style of the document, etc.

In order to perform any editing operation on the text in a document, the required text needs to be selected. This can be done by placing a cursor to the starting position of the text, and then clicking the left mouse button, holding the button and dragging it in the direction of selection. After reaching the end of the selection of text, the left mouse button is released. The Home tab of the Ribbon provides various tools/commands for editing the active document. We can issue any command of the Home tab by just clicking on the command. Editing can also be performed quickly by clicking the right mouse button after selecting the text using the shortcut keys by selecting the appropriate option of the sub-menu as shown in Fig. 14.

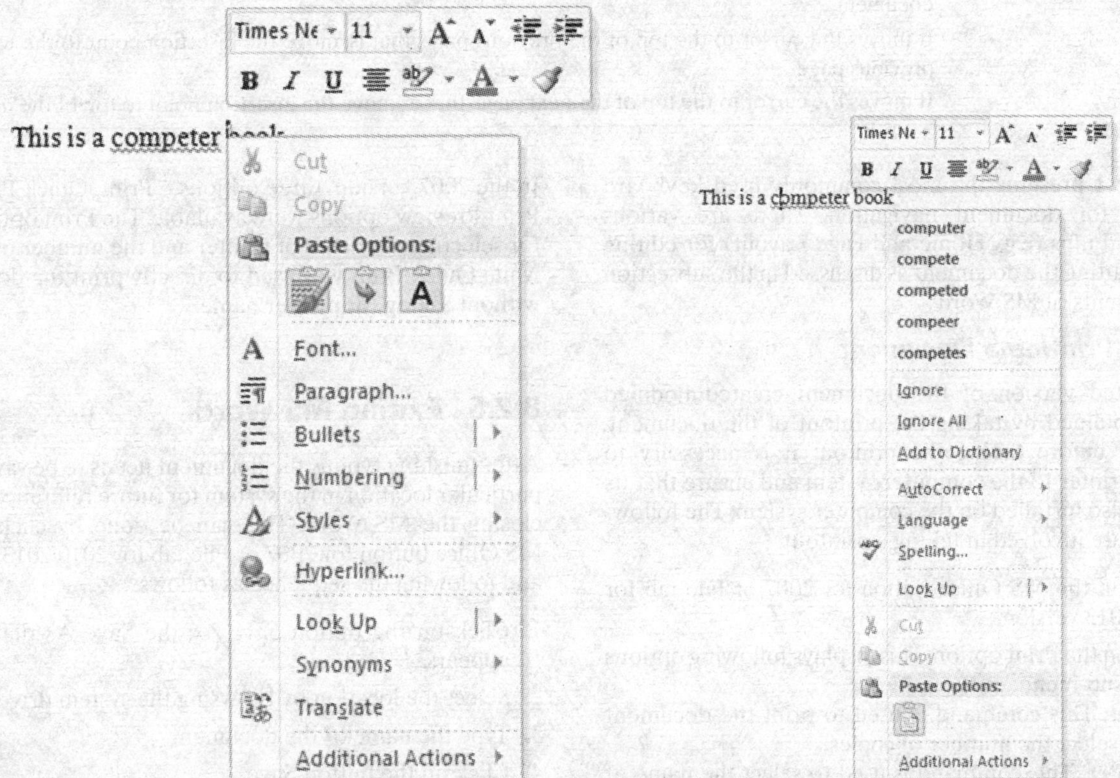

Figure 14 Editing a document in MS Word.

Figure 14(a) shows various editing options. In the 2010/2013 version inside paste option, there are several paste special options such as for keeping the source formatting, merge formatting or keep the text only, etc. Fig. 14(b) suggests the corrected word options for the red underlined word. Various shortcut keys are used to move or place the cursor at the specified position in the document. These keys are listed along with the description in Table 1.

TABLE 1

Various Shortcut Keys with their Descriptions

Shortcut Key	Move the Cursor to
Up arrow (↑)	Up arrow key is used to move the cursor one character up on the line that is just above the line in which the cursor is presently blinking
Down arrow(↓)	Down arrow key is used to move the cursor one character down on the line that is just below the line in which the cursor is presently blinking
Left arrow (←)	Left arrow key is used to move the cursor one character left on the same line in which the cursor is presently blinking
Right arrow (→)	Right arrow key is used to move the cursor one character right on the same line in which the cursor is presently blinking
Ctrl + Right arrow key	This combination is used to move the cursor to the next word on the same line in which the cursor is presently blinking
Ctrl + left arrow key	This combination is used to move the cursor to the previous word on the same line in which cursor is presently blinking
Home	This key is used to move the cursor to the beginning of the same line in which the cursor is presently blinking
End	This key is used to move the cursor to the end of the same line in which the cursor is presently blinking
Ctrl + Home	This combination is used to move the cursor to the left of the first character of the first word of the active document in which the user is presently working, that is, move the insertion point to the beginning of the document
Ctrl + End	This combination is used to move the cursor to the right of last character of the last word of the active document in which the user is presently working, that is, move the insertion point to the end of the document
Page Up	It moves the cursor to the top of the previous page, that is, move the insertion point to the top of the previous page
Page Down	It moves the cursor to the top of the next page, that is, move the insertion point to top of the next page

Table 1 presents the most commonly used keyboard shortcuts for document navigation. There are various groups and tabs (e.g., Home and Page Layout) for editing and formatting the document as discussed in the subsection "Components of MS Word".

8.2.4.5 Printing a Document

The printed version of the document created/modified can be obtained by taking the printout of the document. However, before taking the printout it is necessary to attach a printer to the computer system and ensure that its driver is also installed on the computer system. The following steps are involved in taking a printout:

1. Click on the MS Office button for 2007 or File tab for 2010/2013 version.
2. Click on the Print option. This displays following options in the sub-menu:
   - **Print:** This command is used to print the document and select the number of copies.
   - **Printer:** This command is used to select the name of the printer.
   - **Settings:** This command is used to change the margin, orientation, size, etc., of the document as shown in Fig. 15.
   - **Print Preview:** This window appears on the right. It enables the user to preview the document before printing and check how it will appear on paper after printing, so that the user can make necessary changes before taking the final printout.

In the 2007 version, three options – Print, Quick Print and Print Preview options were available. The Print option uses for selecting the name of printer and the number of copies, while Quick Print was used to directly print the document without asking for printer name.

8.2.5 | Exiting MS Word

After finishing typing, the document needs to be saved at a particular location in the system for future reference before closing the MS Word. This can be done by clicking the MS Office button for 2007 or File tab for 2010/2013 version and following the sequence as follows:

1. Click on the option *Save As*; the Save As dialog box appears.
2. Select the location by browsing the system drives.
3. Type the name of the document.
4. Click on the button Save.

After saving the document the user can either again click on the MS Office button for 2007 or File tab for 2010/2013 version and then click on Exit button to close MS Word or the user can directly click on the close button (X) positioned at the upper right corner of the word window. Before closing the document, a dialog box appears which will ask the user whether he/she wants to save the document or not.

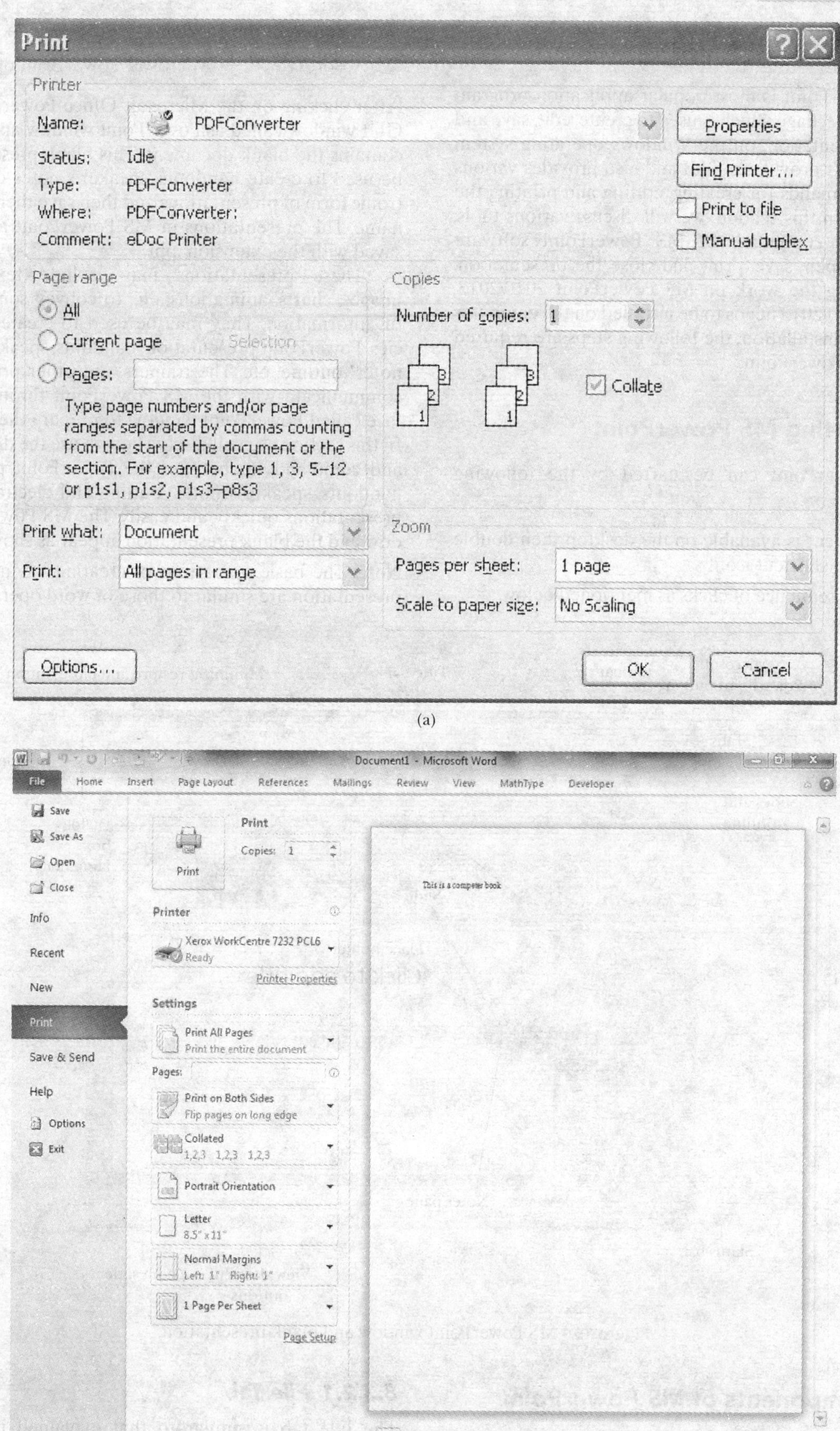

Figure 15 Printing a document in (a) MS Word 2007 and (b) MS Word 2010/2013.

8.3 MS PowerPoint

The MS PowerPoint is most popular application program of MS Office package which is used to create, edit, save and print the presentation, on the Windows operating system environment. It provides a GUI and also provides various tools and commands for creating, editing and printing the presentation. In this section, we will discuss various tools, functions and commands of MS PowerPoint software to create or open, save, print and close the presentation. Before starting the work on MS PowerPoint 2010/2013, MS Office 2010/2013 needs to be installed on the computer system. After installation, the following steps are required to access MS PowerPoint.

8.3.1 | Starting MS PowerPoint

The MS PowerPoint can be started by the following ways:

1. If the shortcut is available on the desktop then double click on the shortcut icon.
2. Follow the sequence of clicks as mentioned below.

Start button of the Taskbar → Programs → Microsoft Office → Microsoft PowerPoint option

After clicking on the Microsoft Office PowerPoint, a new GUI window called as PowerPoint window appears, which contains the blank document. This blank presentation can be used to create handouts, speaker's notes outline, electronic form of presentations and then save them with a new name. The presentations in MS PowerPoint are generally saved with the extension .ppt.

These presentations may include text, graphics, images, charts, animations, etc. to convey some meaningful information. They may be used to create transparencies, PowerPoint presentation, handouts, speaker's detailed notes' outline, etc. The trainers and other presenters can communicate with the MS PowerPoint through an interface called PowerPoint window to prepare their slideshow. In this section, we will discuss how to use the different tools and commands to prepare the PowerPoint presentation, handouts, speaker's notes' outline and electronic form of presentations quickly and easily. The MS PowerPoint window and the blank presentation appear as shown in Fig. 16.

Note: The basic operations of creating, saving, printing a presentation are similar to those of word operations.

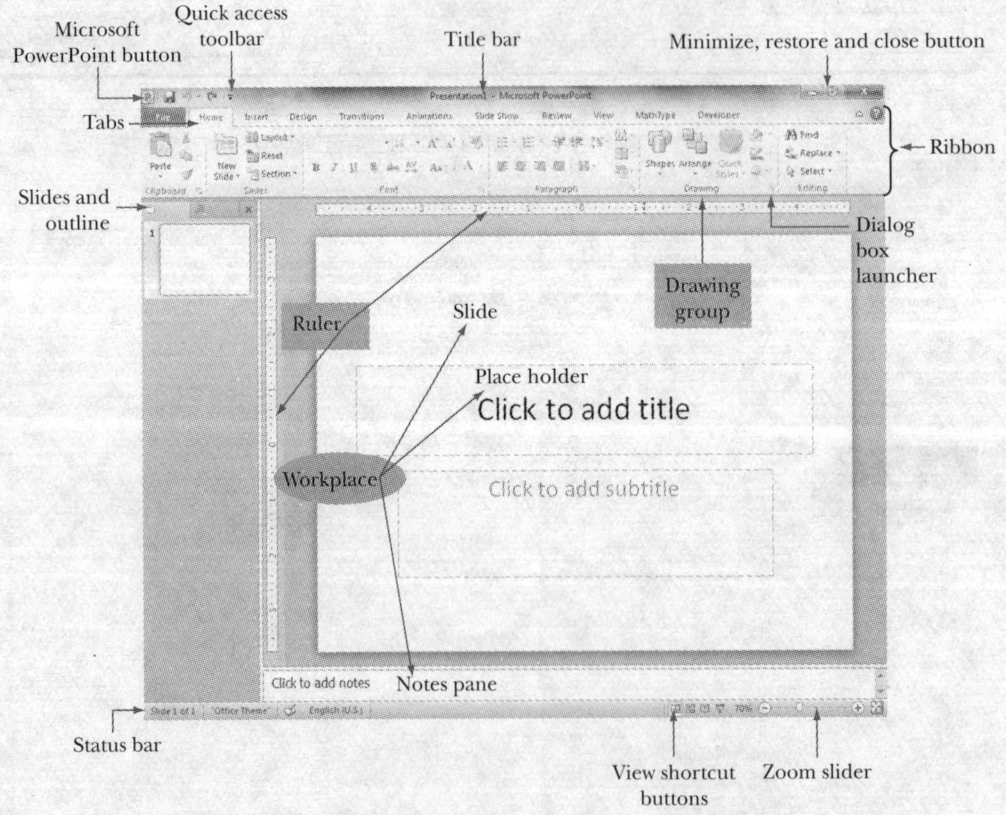

Figure 16 MS PowerPoint window and blank presentation.

8.3.2 | Components of MS PowerPoint

The major components of the MS PowerPoint are described as follows:

8.3.2.1 *File Tab*

The File tab is similar to that explained in MS Word section, except that it shows PowerPoint options and in the sub-menu instead of Word options. The Esc key is used to move out of the activated File tab drop-down list. This is similar to **MS Office button** of MS Power Point 2007. The options of the list can be activated when a user clicks on specific options.

8.3.2.2 Title Bar

Title bar is a horizontal bar located at center of the very top of the PowerPoint window and it displays the name of the active presentation currently being worked upon. If the new presentation is being created, then the Microsoft Office PowerPoint assigns a default name as Presentation1, which can be changed by using the Save As option in the File tab drop-down list. In the rightmost corner of the Title bar, we can see the buttons for minimizing/maximizing ( ), restoring ( ) and closing the presentation ( ). On the leftmost corner of the Title bar we can see the Microsoft Power Point button ( ) and next to it is the Quick Access Toolbar ( ).

8.3.2.3 Quick Access Toolbar

This is similar to that explained in MS Word section, except that some of the options are modified. The Quick Access Toolbar is used to display the frequently used commands to access them quickly. The user can customize the Quick Access Toolbar by clicking on it and marking the options the user wants to see on the Quick Access Toolbar.

8.3.2.4 Ribbon

The Ribbon is located just below the Quick Access Toolbar and it contains various tabs such as File (as discussed earlier), Home, Insert, Design, Animations and Slide show, Review, View and Add-Ins as shown in Fig. 18.

Each tab consists of several groups of related commands. Clicking on the tab displays several groups, and each group consists of several commands that are used to perform specific tasks. These elements are used to quickly issue the command by just clicking on them. The major components of the Ribbon are Tab, Command Group, Command Buttons and Dialog Box Launcher.

The Ribbon cannot be repositioned, but the user can minimize it by clicking the right mouse button at the Ribbon and then clicking on minimize option so that only the Ribbon tabs appear. The Ribbon, Quick Access Toolbar and other tab commands can also be accessed using the Alt key on the keyboard. This will result in displaying the screen as shown in Fig. 17.

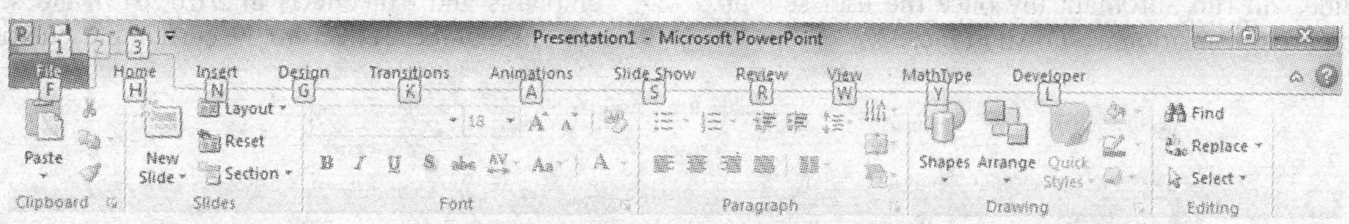

Figure 17 Using Alt key to access commands.

It allows the user to access the Ribbon or other tab commands quickly by pressing the shortcut alphabets or numbers from the keyboard as shown. The details of various tabs on the Ribbon are as follows:

1. **Home tab:** This tab consists of several groups such as Clipboard, Slides, Font, Paragraph, Drawing and Editing as shown in Fig. 18.

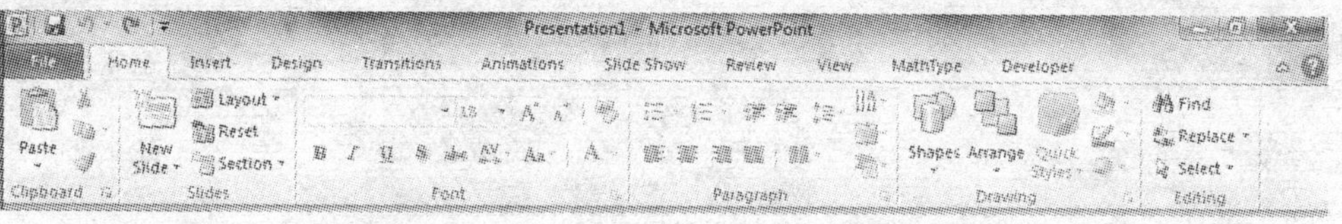

Figure 18 Home tab.

These groups are the collection of various commands that basically deal with formatting of the presentation.

2. **Insert tab:** This tab consists of several groups such as Tables, Illustrations, Links, Text and Media clips as shown in Fig. 19.

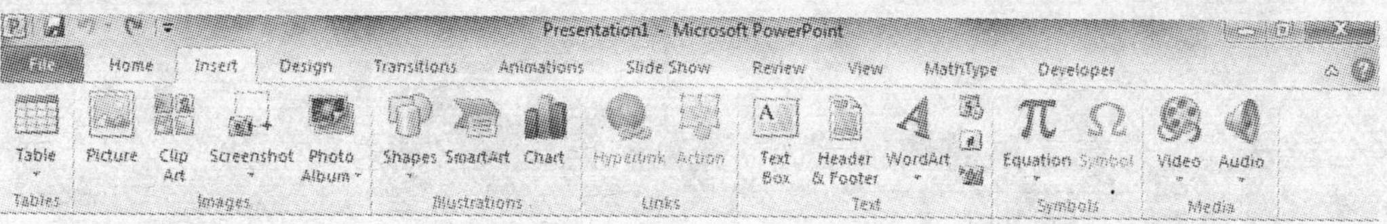

Figure 19 Insert tab.

These groups are a collection of various commands that basically deal with inserting the links, tables, clip arts, pictures, shapes, photo album, etc., in the presentation.

3. **Design tab:** This tab consists of several groups such as Page Setup, Themes and Background as shown in Fig. 20.

Figure 20 Design tab.

These groups are collections of various commands that deal with the formatting of the selected text, selecting the page orientation, background color, font color, etc.

4. **Transition tab:** This tab consists of several groups such as preview, transition to this slide and timing as shown in Fig. 21. These commands are used to apply text appearance, sound settings and duration of transition to a slide. In the 2007 version, transitions could be set in Animation tab itself.

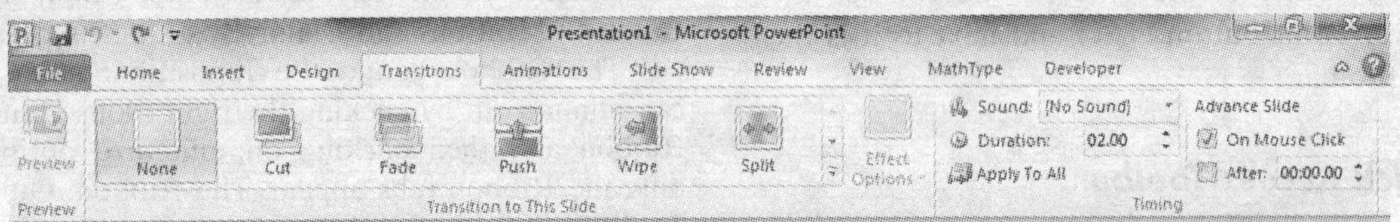

Figure 21 Design tab.

5. **Animation tab:** This tab consists of several groups such as preview, animation, advanced animation and timing. The slide will run automatically once the user sets up the timer and transition as shown in Fig. 22.

These groups are the collection of various commands which deal with inserting some predefined animations (entrance, emphasis and exit effects in 2010/2013) and setting the sequence of these effects to the current presentation.

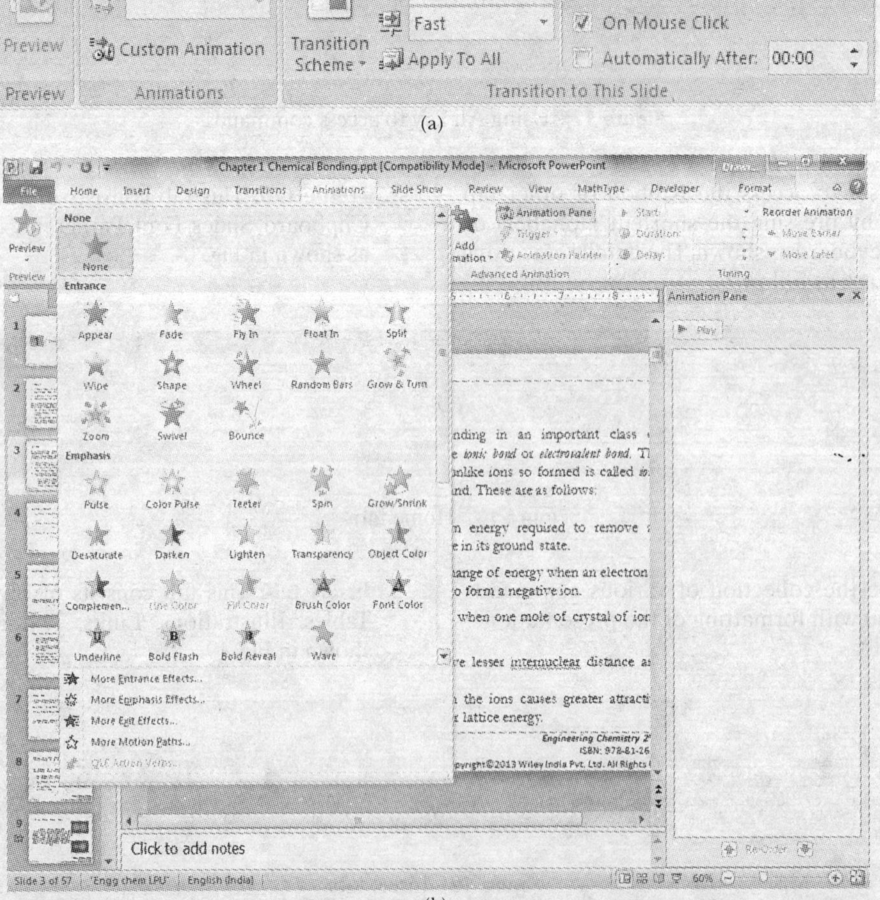

Figure 22 Animation tab in (a) MS PowerPoint 2007 and (b) MS PowerPoint 2010/2013.

6. **Slide Show tab:** This tab consists of several groups like start slide show, set up and monitors (resolution) as shown in Fig. 23.
   These groups are the collection of various commands that basically deal with starting the slide show, narrating the slide show using the microphone attached to the system, choosing the screen resolution for the slide show, etc.

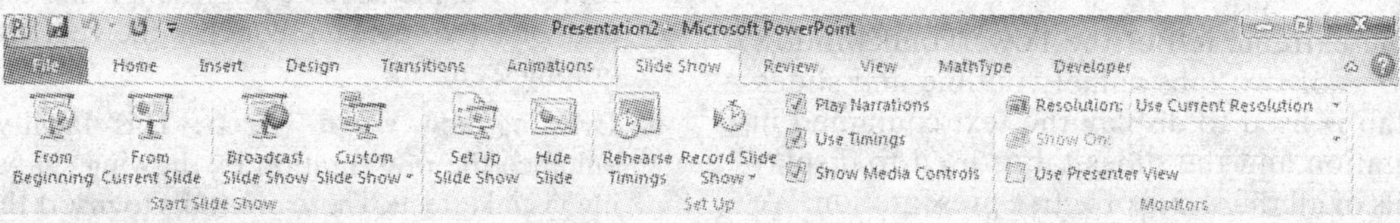

Figure 23 Slide show tab.

7. **Review tab:** This tab consists of several groups such as proofing, language, comments, compare as shown in Fig. 24.
   These groups are collection of various commands that deal with setting the language and checking the spelling and grammatical mistakes, suggesting different words corresponding to the used word, adding comments about the selected text and comparing the cuurent presentation with another .ppt file.

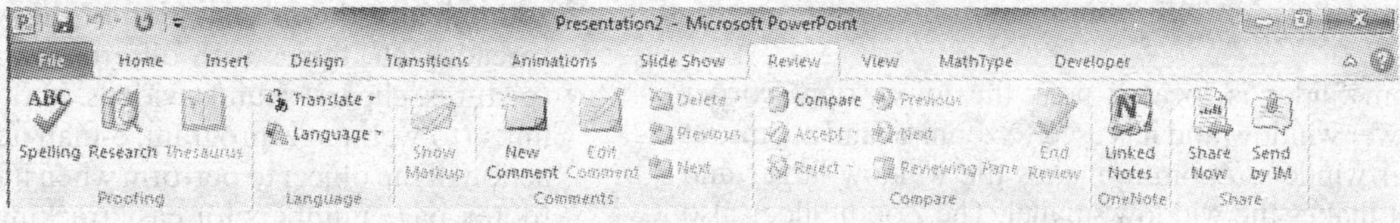

Figure 24 Review tab.

8. **View tab:** This tab consists of several groups such as Presentation Views, Master Views (2010/2013), Show, Zoom, Color/Grayscale (2010/2013), Window and Macros as shown in Fig. 25.
   These groups are collection of various commands that basically deal with setting the presentation view, showing or hiding the ruler bar, gridlines, specifying the zoom level, arranging all open windows side by side or splitting the current window into two parts, creating new macros or accessing other existing options, etc. In 2010/2013 versions, the Slide Master option in Master View helps in setting the formatting of all slides in a presentation in one go.

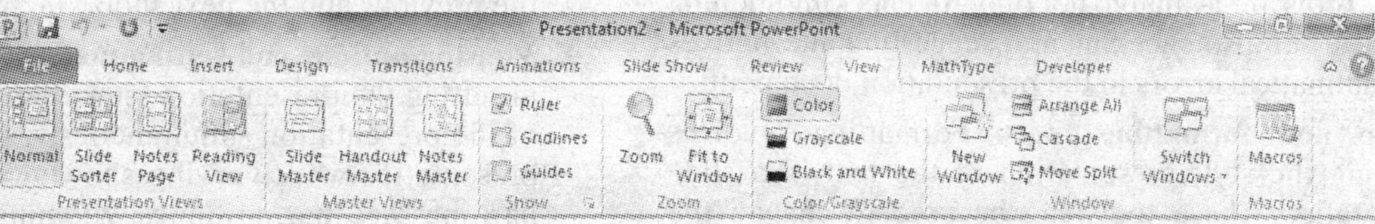

Figure 25 View tab.

8.3.2.5 Ruler

There are two rulers in MS PowerPoint.

1. A ruler located below the Ribbon and it is used to change the vertical alignment of the PowerPoint presentation quickly.
2. A ruler located vertically to the right side of outline and Slide tab, which is used to change the horizontal alignment of the power point presentation quickly.

If the ruler bar is not visible, then the user can enable it by clicking the view tab on the ribbon and then selecting the ruler option.

8.3.2.6 Workplace Area

The actual workplace in power window is divided into three parts: slide, placeholder and the notes area.

1. The slide area is located just below the ruler bar and in the center of the power window. The presentation is created on the slides.
2. The placeholder is used to hold objects such as text, image graphics, charts and animation, etc., within the slides of the presentation.
3. The notes area is used to create the notes which can be referred to at the time of presentation.

8.3.2.7 Status Bar

The status bar is positioned at the bottom of the power window and it displays significant information about the active presentation on which the user is currently working on. The status bar shows the current active slide number, total number of slides, theme, zoom percentage, zoom slider, view shortcut buttons, zoom to fit, signature, spell check, etc. It can be customized by right clicking and marking the options to be displayed on the status bar.

8.10.2.8 *Outline and Slide Tab*

This tab on the extreme left of the PowerPoint window is a combination of two tabs namely outline and slides. The outline tab is used to display the text contained in active presentation and the slides tab is used to display the thumbnails of all the slides of active presentation. We can click the thumbnail to view the slide in the slide pane.

8.3.2.9 *View Shortcut Buttons*

The view shortcut buttons appearing near the lower right corner of power window can be used to change the view between normal, slide sorter and slide show views.

8.3.2.10 *Zoom Slider*

The Zoom Slider is located near the lower right corner of the power window, and it is used to zoom-in and zoom-out the power window. Zoom-in makes the window larger and zoom-out makes the window smaller. The Zoom Slider also shows the percentage of zoom to its left side.

8.3.3 | Features of MS PowerPoint

1. **Editing tools:** Editing involves modification in the text of the active presentation. The selected text can be cut/copied to the clipboard from which it can be pasted at the required position in the presentation. Also selected text can be searched and replaced in the active presentation. Tools are available not only for checking spelling mistakes, but also checking and suggesting alternatives for grammatical errors in the presentation document.
2. **Design and formatting tools:** Formatting involves changing the style/presentation of the text in a slide presentation. These tools can be used to change the color, change the font face, bold face, italicize or underline the selected text, change the size of the selected text of slide, highlight the selected text, clear the formatting of a formatted text, draw a line through the middle of the selected text, draw shadow behind the selected text and adjust the spacing between the characters. Also, the formatting of one place can be set in another place using format painter. The user may select the Page Setup group under Design tab and set the margin size and orientation for the entire presentation. Furthermore, the theme of the presentation and the background of the slide can be selected.
3. **Slide navigation tools:** There are tools to insert a new slide, change the layout of the slide, reset the position, size or formatting of the placeholder to its default setting or to remove the selected slide from the presentation.
4. **Paragraph adjustment tools:** Paragraph adjustment involves adjustment of text in a certain manner on the presentation. These tools are used to arrange the text in the form of bulleted list, numbered list, to align the text to left, center, right or justified (left and right both), specify the line spacing, decrease or increase the indent level of paragraphs, split the text into two or more columns, change the orientation of the text to horizontal, rotate by some specific angle, align the text within the text box (wrap text), convert the text into smart art graphics, etc.
5. **Drawing and visual effects:** This facility enables to enhance the presentation by drawing shapes and applying visual effects. There are tools to insert the readymade shapes such as rectangles, circle, flowchart elements, arrows, line and select colors to fill them or color the outline; make a group of objects to be created as a single object or arrange the order of the objects according to their size, position or rotation; apply a visual effect to the selected shape such as shadows, reflection, rotation, etc.
6. **Inserting elements:** Several graphical, multimedia and other elements can be inserted to expand the usability and enhance the presentation of the worksheet, such as spreadsheets, tables with different borders, illustrations (pictures, clipart, sounds, videos, photos, shapes, chart), links (to web page, program, e-mail address and specify action of the object to perform when it is clicked), header, footer, page numbers for easy tracking, textboxes, decorative text (WordArt), date, time, symbols, equations, etc.
7. **Effective storage:** Worksheets/workbook can be auto-saved and autorecovered in emergency cases to retrieve documents.
8. **Animation and slide transition:** Some predefined animations and slide transitions can be applied to the presentations. There are several tools to custom animation for animating individual objects present on the slide and to select the speed and type of transition between the previous and the next slide.
9. **Viewing options and setting macros:** This facility helps in setting the presentation view; viewing different parts of the presentation simultaneously; setting the color of presentation while viewing; showing or hiding the ruler bar, message bar, gridlines; zooming in and zooming out for particular portions of the presentation requiring more focus. The entire presentation with the animations, transitions and other settings can be visualized by the slideshow option. Creating macros (setting shortcuts to perform frequent tasks) or accessing other existing macro options, etc., promotes flexible and efficient use.

8.3.4 | Exiting MS PowerPoint

After finishing the presentation preparation in the MS PowerPoint, it needs to be saved at a particular location in the system for future reference before closing. This can be done by clicking the MS Office button and following the steps as follows:

1. Click on the option *Save As*; the Save As dialog box appears.
2. Select the location by browsing the system drives.
3. Type the name of the presentation.
4. Click on the button Save.

After saving the presentation document, the user can either again click on the MS Office button in 2007 and File tab in 2010/2013 version and then click on Exit option to close MS PowerPoint, or he/she can directly click on the close button (X) positioned at the upper right corner of the power window. Before closing the presentation, it will ask whether he/she wants to save the document or not.

8.4 MS Excel

MS Excel is the most popular application program of MS Office package, which is used to create, edit, save and print spreadsheets on the Windows operating system environment. The MS Excel sheets are also known as worksheets organized in the form of tables containing rows and columns. The columns are lettered from A onwards and the rows are numbered from 1 to 1,048,576.

Each row has a number to the side of the sheet, and it is called as row header. Similarly, each column has a letter or number that appears above the column and it is called as column header. The intersection of row and column is called a cell and the combination of a column and row headers make up a cell address. For example, cell B12 is located under column header B on row header 12. The user can enter data into the cell and perform various operations on these cells, rows and columns.

MS Excel also provides various tools and commands to enter, examine, view, modify, correct, create, display and print the spreadsheets. The spreadsheets are very useful because the user can quickly analyze the data. In this section, we will discuss the various tools, functions and commands of MS Excel 2007 software to enter, examine, view, modify, correct, create, open, save, display and print and close the excel spreadsheets. Before starting work on it, MS Office 2007 needs to be installed on the computer system. After installation, the following steps are required to access MS Excel.

8.4.1 | Starting MS Excel

The MS Excel can be started using the following ways:

1. If the shortcut is available on the desktop then double click on the shortcut icon.
2. Follow the sequence of clicking as mentioned below:

   Start button of the Taskbar → Programs →

   Microsoft Office → Microsoft Office Excel option

After clicking on the Microsoft Office Excel, a new GUI window called excel window appears, which contains a blank electronic sheet or table. The excel sheets in MS Excel are generally saved with the extension .xlsx. They may be used to accomplish complex data analysis of the business world accurately and quickly.

Note: The basic operations such as creating a worksheet, saving, printing, deleting, editing, etc. are similar to those of word operations.

8.4.2 | Components of MS Excel

The major components of the MS Excel are described in Fig. 26.

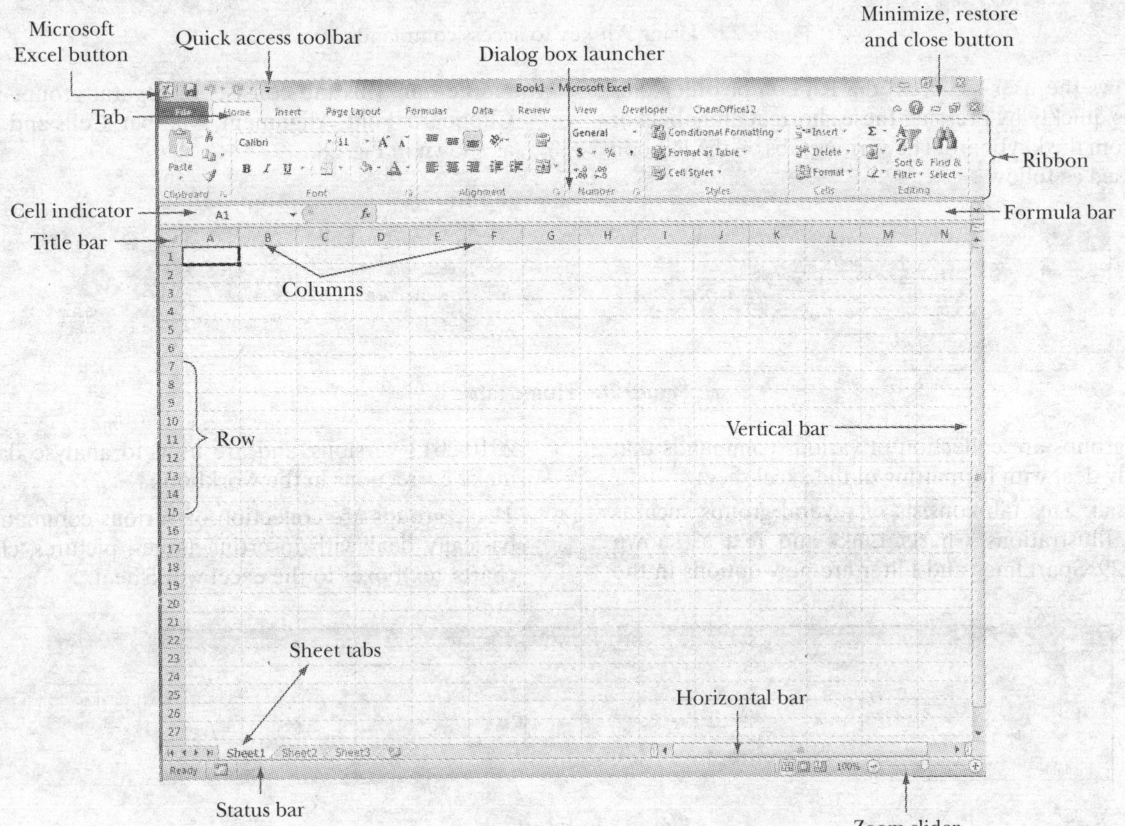

Figure 26 Major components of MS Excel.

8.4.2.1 File Tab

File contains a drop-down list of various commands such as New, Open, Convert, Save, Save As, Print, Prepare, Send, Publish and Close as already explained in MS Word and MS PowerPoint sections, except that it shows Excel options and in the sub-menu instead of Word options/PowerPoint options.

The MS Office button in 2007 version has the functionality as the File tab in 2010/2013 version.

8.4.2.2 Title Bar

Title bar is a horizontal bar located at center, of the very top of the power window and it displays the name of the active worksheet currently being worked on. If the new worksheet is being created then Microsoft Office Excel assigns a default name Book1, which can be changed by using the Save As option in the Microsoft Office button drop-down list. In the right most corner of the Title bar, we can see the button for minimizing/maximizing ( ), restoring ( ) and closing the worksheet ( ). On the leftmost corner of the Title bar, we can see the Microsoft Excel button( ) and next to it is the Quick Access Toolbar ( ).

8.4.2.3 Quick Access Toolbar

This is used to quickly access the different options such as new, save, undo, redo, e-mail, etc. as already explained in MS Word and MS PowerPoint sections, except some of the options are changed. The user can customize the Quick Access Toolbar by clicking on it, and selecting the options he/she wants to see on it.

8.4.2.4 Ribbon

The Ribbon is located just below the Quick Access Toolbar, and it contains various tabs such as Home, Insert, Page Layout, Formulas, Data, Review, View and Add-Ins. Each tab consists of several groups of related commands. Clicking on the tab displays several groups, and each group consists of several commands that are used to perform specific tasks. These are used to quickly issue the command by just clicking on them. Each group also contains the Dialog Box launcher in the bottom right corner of the group, which contains more commands related to the group. The Ribbon cannot be repositioned, but the user can minimize it by clicking the right mouse button, and then clicking on minimize option so that only the Ribbon tabs appear. The Ribbon, Quick Access Toolbar and other tab commands can also be accessed using the Alt key on the keyboard. This will result in displaying the screen as shown in Fig. 27.

Figure 27 Using Alt key to access commands.

It allows the user to access the Ribbon or other tabs commands quickly by pressing these shortcut alphabets or number from the keyboard. The various tabs on the Ribbon are discussed as follows.

1. **Home tab:** This tab consists of several groups such as Clipboard, Font, Alignment, Number, Cells and Editing as shown in Fig. 28.

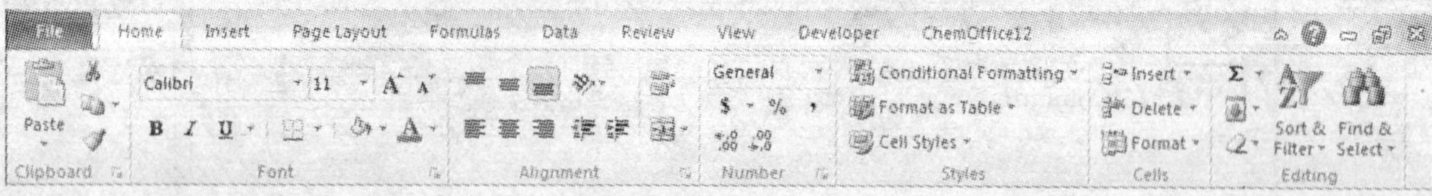

Figure 28 Home tab.

These groups are collection of various commands that basically deal with formatting of the excel sheet.

2. **Insert tab:** This tab consists of several groups such as Tables, Illustrations, Charts, Links and Text as shown in Fig. 29. Sparklines and Filter are new options in the 2010/2013 versions, and are used to analyse data and make corrections in the workbook.

These groups are collection of various commands that basically deal with inserting tables, pictures, clip arts, charts, textboxes to the excel worksheet.

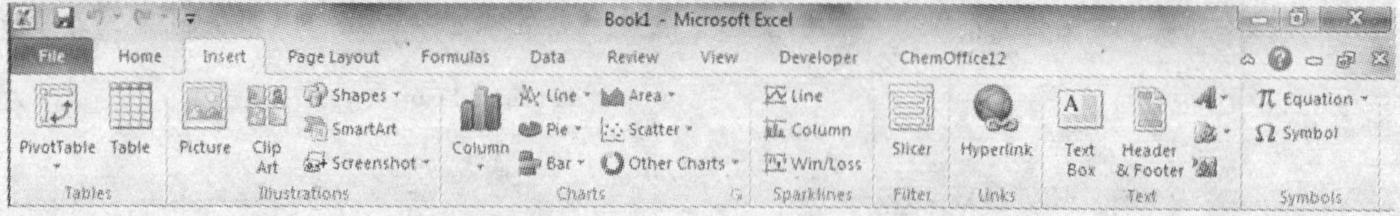

Figure 29 Insert tab.

3. **Page Layout tab:** This tab consists of several groups such as Themes, Page Setup, Scale to Fit and Sheet Options as shown in Fig. 30.

These groups are collection of various commands that basically deal with formatting of text in the selected paragraph or the document such as selecting the page orientation, background color, print area, viewing the lines between the rows and columns, etc.

Figure 30 Page Layout tab.

4. **Formulas tab:** This tab consists of several groups such as function library, defined names, formula auditing and calculation as shown in Fig. 31.

These groups are collection of various commands that basically deal with applying different kinds of formula to the selected cell, defining the names to the cells instead of cell address, etc. Financial data, computations, date, time, mathematical operations, etc. can be carried out using this tab.

Figure 31 Formulas tab.

5. **Data tab:** This tab consists of several groups such as Get External Data, Connections, Sort and Filter, Data Tools and Outline as shown in Fig. 32.

These groups are collection of various commands that deal with getting the data from external sources such as MS Access, Web, sorting the selected cells on different defined criteria, removing the duplicate entries, etc., from the worksheet.

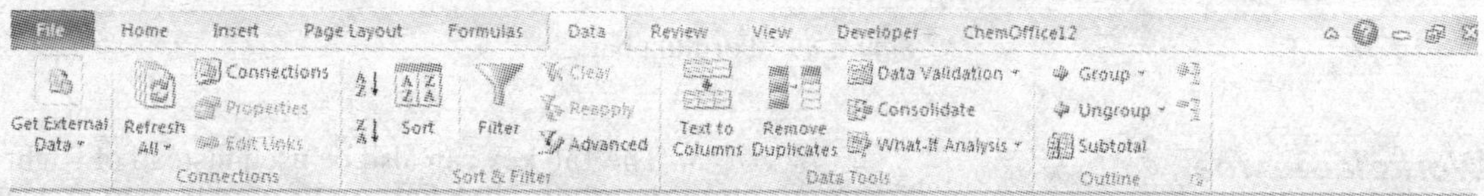

Figure 32 Data tab.

6. **Review tab:** This tab consists of several groups such as Proofing, Comments and Changes as shown in Fig. 33.

These groups are collections of various commands that deal with setting the language and checking the spelling and grammatical mistakes, suggesting different word options corresponding to the used word, adding a comment about the selected text and tracking all the modification to the document.

Figure 33 Review tab.

7. **View tab:** This tab consists of several groups such as Workbook Views, Zoom, Window and Macros as shown in Fig. 34.

These groups are collection of various commands that deal with setting the workbook views, specifying the zoom level of the document, creating new macros or accessing other existing options, etc.

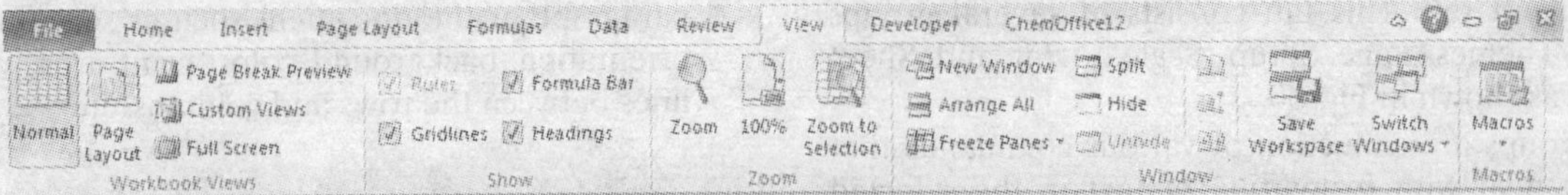

Figure 34 View tab.

8.4.2.5 *Formula Bar*

The formula bar is located just below the Ribbon and is divided into two parts as shown in Fig. 35.

The first part located on the left side is called as name box and it contains the cell address of the cell, and second part may contain the formula. The formula can be inserted by clicking on (fx), which asks the user to select a function to be applied on the selected cell. The formula bar may also be used to edit the information at a particular cell by first placing the cursor in the specified cell. If it is not visible, then click on the View tab on the Ribbon and select Show/Hide group, click it to make the formula bar visible.

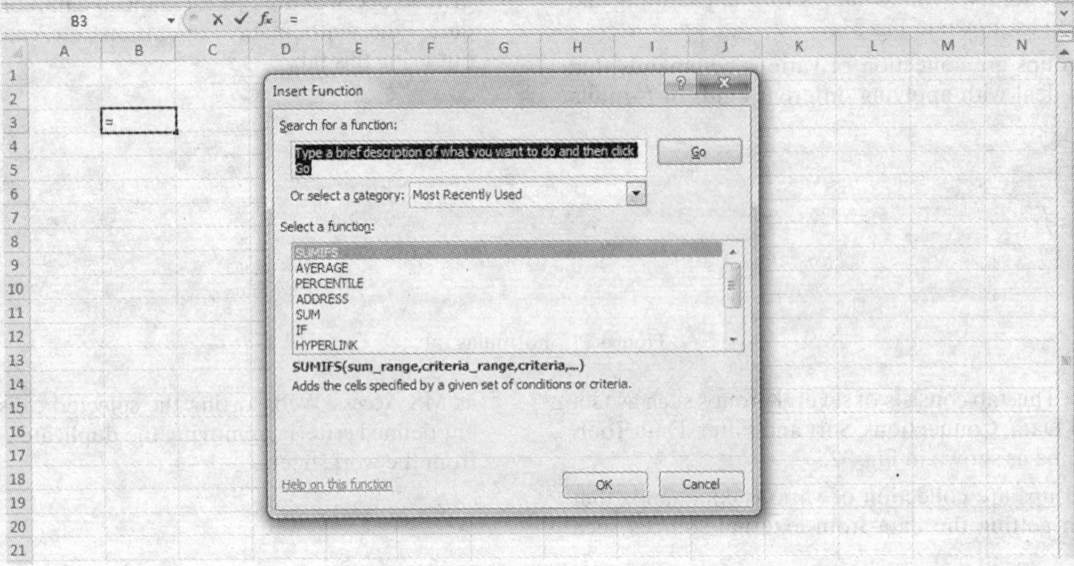

Figure 35 Formula bar.

8.4.2.6 *Workplace Area*

Microsoft Excel consists of worksheets; the actual workplace in excel window consisting of rows and columns.

1. The user can move around the worksheet by using arrow keys. For example, Up arrow key is used to move one cell upward (upper row), Down arrow key is used to move one cell downward (lower row) in the same column, Left arrow key to move one cell left and Right arrow key to move one cell right in the same row, the Page Up and Page Down keys are used to move up and down one page at a time.
2. The user can move to the first cell of the worksheet by using Ctrl + Home key together. Multiple cells can be selected using the Shift key along with the usual arrow keys in the direction of the arrow key. The range of the cells is represented by mentioning the address of the first cell followed by colon, then followed by the address of the last cell. For example, B4:B8 represents the range starting from row heading 4 and up to row heading 8 under column heading B.
3. The Tab key can also be used instead of Right arrow key and Shift + Tab key can be used instead of the Left arrow key for movement to the right cell or left cell at a time.
4. The user can move to the specific cell using the F5 or Ctrl + G key, which will ask the user to enter the cell number to move to.
5. Data can be entered into the cells of the worksheet by placing the cursor at the specified position, entering the data and using the arrow keys to move to a different cell.
6. Data in the specified cell can be edited by placing the cursor at that cell and then using Del or Backspace key to delete one character at a time. The complete data can also be deleted.
7. If the text entered in the cell is too long to fit into the cell then text wrapping is done by performing the following steps:
   - Select the text.
   - Go to the Home tab of Ribbon.
   - Click on ( ) under the Alignment group.

8.4.2.7 Status Bar

The Status bar is positioned at the bottom of the excel window and it displays significant information about the active worksheet on which the user is currently working on. It shows the cell mode, fixed decimal, average, count, minimum, maximum, sum, zoom percentage, zoom slider, view shortcut buttons, signature, etc. It can be customized by right clicking and selecting the options to be displayed on the status bar as discussed in earlier sections.

8.4.2.8 View Shortcut Buttons

These buttons appear near the lower right corner of excel window which can be used to change the view between normal, page layout and page break views.

8.4.2.9 Zoom Slider

The Zoom Slider is located at the lower right corner of the excel window, and is used to zoom-in and zoom-out as discussed in previous sections.

8.4.3 | Features of MS Excel

1. **Editing tools:** Editing involves modification in the text of the active worksheet. The selected cell/text can be cut/copied to the clipboard from which it can be pasted at the required position in the worksheet. Also, the selected text can be searched and replaced in the active worksheet. Tools are available not only for checking spelling mistakes, but also checking and suggesting alternatives for grammatical errors in the worksheet. Other features include inserting comments, protecting the worksheet, tracking all the changes made to the workbook; applying mathematical formula to the selected cell, following a pattern to more than one cell, deleting everything from the cells and arranging worksheet data in a particular order (sorting, filtering).
2. **Formatting tools:** Formatting involves changing the style/presentation of the text in a worksheet. These tools can be used to change the color, change the font face, bold face, italicize or underline the selected text (also choose the color of underline), change the size of the selected text, page formatting, highlight the selected text/cell, clear the formatting of a formatted text and select the border for the selected cells. Also, the formatting of one place can be set in another place using format painter. The user may select the Style group for conditional formatting of the cells.
3. **Inserting elements:** Several graphical, multimedia and other elements can be inserted to expand the usability and enhance the presentation of the worksheet, such as data using pivot table, other tables, illustrations (pictures, clipart, sounds, videos, photos, shapes), charts (column charts, line, pie, bar, area, scatter, etc.) links (to web page, program, e-mail address), header, footer, page numbers for easy tracking, textboxes, decorative text (WordArt), date, time, symbols, equations, etc.
4. **Cell alignment tools:** Cell alignment involves adjustment in a certain manner of text in a cell and cells in worksheet. These tools are used to align text to the top, middle, bottom, left, right and center of the cell; decrease or increase the margin between the text and the border; wrap the text within the cell; merge two or more selected cells; rotate the text to diagonal angle; insert row, column in the sheet; change the row height, column height and protect the cell.
5. **Sheet adjustment tools:** This involves adjusting the sheet as per requirement before printing or sending to external resource. The tools are used to specify page setup and orientation; select the print area; put an image at the background of the sheet; specify the rows and columns to repeat on each printed page; shrink or stretch the area of printed output as per the number of printed pages required; show/hide lines between rows and columns; bring the selected object one level forward/backward to the front/back of all objects, or for the alignment of edges of multiple objects; make a group of multiple objects; rotate the selected object.
6. **Data arrangement tools:** This facility enables importing data from external resources (such as MS Access, Web, etc.); updating data by establishing connections within the workbook; sorting and filtering data by specifying some custom criteria; combining, rearranging and grouping/ungrouping data according to selected criteria; and checking for duplicate and invalid data entries.
7. **Calculation and formula tools:** This facility enables to represent numeric data in a particular format and perform calculations using predefined/user-defined formula. There are tools to choose the general currency (with currency format as $, Euro, etc.), data, time, percentage, etc.; display many values in the cell with separators; set the precision value for the decimal number. The calculations on the entered data can be performed by selecting any of the pre-defined functions in the function library (financial, logical, textual, statistical, etc.). Using design name tool, a name may be used in the formula instead of the cell address to create, edit, delete and find all the names used in the worksheet. Using formula auditing tools, arrows can be used to indicate which cell affects the values of other cells and vice versa (relative reference); to insert formula instead of the value, check the common errors and evaluate the formula; monitor the changes in the cells and display the changes in a separate window. The calculations can be performed now or later based on the user selection.
8. **Effective storage:** Worksheets and the entire workbook can be autosaved and autorecovered in emergency cases to retrieve documents.
9. **Viewing options and setting macros:** This facility helps in setting the worksheet view; viewing different parts of the worksheet simultaneously; viewing and comparing different worksheets simultaneously; showing or hiding the ruler bar, message bar, gridlines, formula bar, row/column headings; zooming in and zooming out for particular portions of the worksheet requiring more focus. Creating macros (setting shortcuts to perform frequent tasks) or accessing other existing macro options, etc. promotes flexible and efficient use.

8.4.4 | Exiting MS Excel

After finishing the worksheet preparation in the MS Excel, it needs to be saved at a particular location in the system for future reference before closing. This can be done by clicking the MS Office button 2007 version or File tab of 2010/2013 version and following the steps as follows:

1. Click on the option *Save As*; the Save As dialog box appears.
2. Select the location by browsing the system drives.
3. Type the name of the worksheet.
4. Click on the button Save.

After saving the excel sheet, the user can either again click on the MS Office button 2007 version or File tab of 2010/2013 version and then click on Exit Excel button to close MS Excel. Or the user can direct click on the close button (×) positioned at the upper right corner of the excel window. Before closing the worksheet, it will ask whether he/she wants to save the worksheet or not.

POINTS TO REMEMBER

1. **MS Office package:** It is a very useful application software package to handle effectively office activities,such as data typing, processing, editing, manipulating and formatting various kinds of documents and communication. It is a collection of several application programs such as MS Word (for managing documents), MS PowerPoint (for managing slide presentations), MS Excel (for managing spreadsheets), MS Outlook (for managing personal information), MS Access (for managing databases), etc.
2. **MS Word:** It is the most popular word processing software that is used to create, edit, save and print a document on the Windows operating system environment. It also has functionalities available such as placing images on documents, etc. This software can even be used to create web pages. It provides a graphical user interface (GUI) which makes word processing very simple and efficient through availability of various commands. Other word processing software available in the market are WordStar and Easy Word (for DOS environment), Notepad (for Windows environment), Applix Words (for Linux environment), OpenOffice Writer, Google Docs, etc.
3. **MS PowerPoint:** It is an effective and extremely useful tool for creating effective presentations in seminars, lectures, etc., using tools to create slide shows with lots of predefined design templates, color schemes and animation effects, multimedia effects.
4. **MS Excel:** It is the spreadsheet program that gives us features that make it easier to organize and analyze the data. It allows users to enter numerical values or data into the rows/columns of a spreadsheet, perform calculations, prepare graphs and do statistical analysis of the entered data.
5. **MS Outlook:** It is a personal information manager and communication program that provides tools and resources to manage e-mails, calendars, contacts and other related information.
6. **MS Access:** It is a relational database management system (RDBMS) which provides tools and resources to facilitate effective storage and retrieval of data. Other popular RDBMSs are Oracle, MS SQL Server, IMB DB2, MS FoxPro, etc.

REVIEW QUESTIONS

1. Briefly describe the usage of word processor and spreadsheet application.
2. What are the features of word processor software packages? (AU 2011, 2013)
3. What are the different methods for accessing the MS Word, MS Excel and MS PowerPoint?
4. How is table inserted into the word document? Describe the procedure.
5. What is sequence of operations to insert the clip arts in MS Excel sheet?
6. How can the new slide be added to the existing presentation before the current slide?
7. Explain the formatting in MS Excel and MS PowerPoint.
8. How do you think that MS PowerPoint is useful? Justify.
9. What are the major components of MS Word? Describe them.
10. Explain the salient features of Office packages. (AU 2013)
11. What do understand by a cell, worksheet and workbook in MS Excel?
12. Explain creation of tables and operations that can be performed on table using word processor. (AU 2009 Suppl.)
13. Briefly explain the use of spreadsheet as all accounting software. (AU 2009 Suppl.)
14. What do you mean by GUI? What are the significant features of GUI based operating system?
15. What is the utility of Mail Merge in MS-Word?
16. Discuss the features of Microsoft Excel. (AU 2013)

PROGRAMMING ASSIGNMENTS

1. Prepare your Resume using various tools and properties of MS Word.
2. Design a Birthday invitation card using the MS PowerPoint.
3. Calculate HRA, DA, TA, PF, GPF, LIC, gross salary, deductions and net salary from the following worksheet data:

	A	B	C	D	E	F	G	H	I	J	K	L
1	Emp. No.	Emp. Name	Basic	HRA	TA	DA	LIC	PF	GPF	Gross sal	Deductions	Net sal
2	51	D	15000									
3	52	A	10000									
4	69	B	20000									
5	60	E	20000									
6	63	C	25000									

where HRA is 18%, DA is 15%, TA is 12%, PF is 10%, GPF is 5%, LIC is 7% of Basic. The computations of gross salary, deductions and net salary are as follows:

Gross sal = Basic + HRA + TA + DA

Deductions = PF + GPF + LIC

Net sal = Gross sal – Deductions.

Also, sort the employee names in alphabetical order.

4. Construct different types of graphs for the following data showing sales figures of different products over the years for a particular company.

	A	B	C	D
1	Year	Product 1	Product 2	Product 3
2	1970	500	1000	1200
3	1980	700	1500	1500
4	1990	600	1200	1600
5	2000	400	1000	1800
6	2010	300	900	2000

5. Create an invitation letter for a seminar and send it to various recipients through e-mail using mail merge.

Solutions to End of Chapter Anna University Questions

Appendix A

Chapter 1 Introduction to Computers

Review Questions

2. *What are the basic operations of the computer?* **(AU 2013)**

Solution

A computer performs basically the following major operations through its components:

(a) **Input:** It accepts data and instruction through the input devices such as keyboard, mouse, scanner, etc., from the user to process it.

(b) **Process and control:** It performs the actions as per the instruction issued and processes the given input data. The processing may include arithmetic and logical operations. It also controls the overall operations like arithmetic and logical operations inside the computer.

(c) **Storage:** It stores the data and the instructions for future execution.

(d) **Output:** It generates the desired output after executing the instructions and processing the input data.

3. *List out the characteristics of computer?* **(AU 2009, 2010, 2011, 2013)**

Solution:

The various characteristics of a computer are:

(a) It can perform complex calculations with speed and generate accurate results.

(b) It has high processing speed and can execute millions of instructions in one second.

(c) It can store large amounts of data and information which can be easily retrieved whenever required.

(d) It can interact with users through its user interface, and provide required information within a fraction of a second.

(e) It can be used for many hours, days and months continuously, without compromising on the work satisfaction.

(f) Its role is versatile, that is, it can be used for commercial use (data processing), scientific use (computing numerical data), office and educational use (word processing), communicating messages (e-mail, messenger), animation and industrial use (image processing) and multimedia pur-poses (voice recognition).

8. *Explain about the block diagram of the computer in detail.* **(AU 2008–2014)**

Solution:

The block diagram of the general-purpose computer is shown in the following figure. The input/output (I/O) devices or peripherals are used so that the computer system can interact with the external environment. The input devices are used to feed data and the instruction by the user; the central processing units convert the given input into a computer-understandable form; and the output devices convert the processed result into a user-understandable form.

(a) **Input Devices:** The function of an input device is to take the data from the user in the raw form for further processing. The input devices commonly used are keyboards, mouse, scanner, joysticks, microphones, digital cameras, scanners, etc.

(b) **Output Devices:** The output generated by the computer after processing the raw data is sent to the output devices, which are basically the hardware components used to store the softcopy (in electronic form) or hardcopy (in printed form) of the output. These devices are connected to the computer system using cables or wireless network. Some of them come in-built with the com-puter system. The various output devices are monitors, printers, plotters, etc.

(c) **Central Processing Unit:** This unit (CPU) is used to execute program instructions and process data fed inside the computer system with input devices. Since CPU is the central unit of the computer, it is responsible for processing of the input data, controlling and managing the operations of the computer and generating the desired output. Therefore, it is also known as the brain of the computer and is the main component of any computer. It consists of registers, control unit (CU) and arithmetic logic unit (ALU).

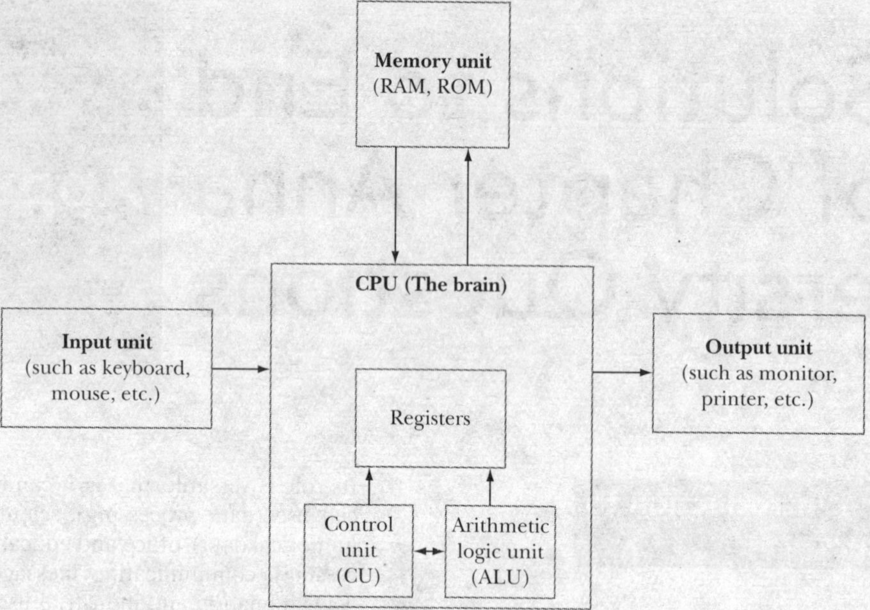

- **Registers:** These are special-purpose high-speed temporary storage areas for holding data, addresses and instructions during processing of the instructions. There are several registers used by the CPU, each for serving specific purposes. The registers work under the control unit of the CPU and they are not referenced by their addresses; rather they are directly accessed, therefore they operate at a higher speed.
- **Control Unit:** It is one of the important components of the CPU, and it is responsible for the proper execution of the instructions. It uses registers for temporary storage of data and instructions, and also uses the ALU to perform the arithmetic and logical operations. Therefore, the control unit controls and coordinates the overall operations of the computer. It also coordinates with the input and output devices to control the flow of data and information.
- **Arithmetic and Logical Unit:** It is a combination of arithmetic and logical unit. The arithmetic unit (AU) is used to perform fundamental arithmetic operations, such as addition, subtraction, mul-tiplication, division. The logical unit (LU) is used to perform logical operations such as equality comparison, less than, less than or equal to, greater than, greater than or equal to, logical AND, logical OR, logical NOT on the input data. The logical operations are performed by using combination of various logic gates such as AND, OR and NOT.

  The ALU coordinates with the control unit for the instruction to be executed, and with the registers for temporary storage and retrieval of data. The result of operation can be temporarily sent to the registers, or it can be sent to the output device by the CPU.

(d) Memory or Storage Unit: CPU receives input data and instructions from the input devices and the program. It performs the arithmetic and logical operations on the received data as per the instructions and produces the output. The processing of input data and instructions requires storage area because some of the intermediate results have to be stored somewhere; and later this result is retrieved for subsequent operations. The storage area for instructions and data to be processed is called the memory. Therefore, the memory is the internal storage area in the computer.

Each memory location has a unique address and the smallest unit of data is called a bit (0 and 1). The collection of 8 bits is called a byte, and collection of 4 bits is called a nibble. The CPU can retrieve these stored data in the form of byte and instruction quickly. The memory can be broadly categorized into two categories, primary memory and secondary memory.

- **Primary Memory:** It is also called as the main memory is of two types:
  - **(i) Random Access Memory (RAM):** From this memory, data and instructions can be retrieved in a random manner using a unique memory address. Hence, the name is random access memory (RAM). It is a volatile memory in which the contents are lost once the power is turned off. This kind of memory is used to store the data temporarily during the computer operations.
  - **(ii) Read Only Memory (ROM):** This is the memory on which data has been recorded on an integrated circuit by the manufacturer. Once the data has been recorded, it cannot be changed. The content can be read but it cannot be modified; hence the name is read only memory. It is designed to perform a specific function that is not changed, and generally instructions are required for initializing the devices stored in ROM. For example, ROM is used in most computers to hold the basic input and output system (BIOS) so that the computer's hardware such as hard disks, RAM, I/O ports and peripherals are

recognized when the computer is switched on; and then the operating system is loaded. If the ROM is damaged, the computer system simply cannot function. This is a non-volatile memory, that is, the contents are not lost even when the power is turned off.

- **Secondary Memory:** It consists of storage devices in which the data can be stored for longer duration, and it is not lost even when the power is turned off. This memory has greater storage capacity than the primary memory. Also, it is inexpensive, but slow. There are two types of access to stored data in secondary storage devices:
  - **(i) Sequential access:** through which data can be retrieved or accessed in the order it was stored. It is useful when there is need to process timesheets or salary slips based on records entered at scheduled intervals. The storage device used for sequential access is magnetic tape.
  - **(ii) Direct access:** through which we can randomly access any particular record at any time without worrying about the sequence in which it was stored. It is useful when we need to access any particular information from a person's record, such as date of birth, or account balance, etc. The various storage devices used for direct access are grouped into three: Magnetic disks (floppy disks and hard disks); optical disks (CD, DVD, etc.), memory storage devices (flash drive and memory cards).
- **Cache Memory:** The cache memory is faster than the CPU registers and slower than the main or primary memory. It is a SRAM placed between the CPU and the main memory, and when CPU needs any data or instruction for processing, it first searches the cache memory. If the required data or instruction is found in the cache memory, it is retrieved by the CPU for processing. Otherwise, the main memory is searched for the same information. The most frequently used instructions and data are placed in the cache memory; therefore, the overall speed of the computer is increased. De-pending upon the type of data that cache memory holds, it is classified as instructor, data or unified cache. The three levels of cache based on the size and speed are L, L2 and L3. If all the three levels of cache are present in the system, then data is fetched in the order: L1 → L2 → L3 → RAM. This means if data is not present in L1, L2 would be checked followed by L3 and then RAM.

10. *List out the features of all generations of computer with their advantages and disadvantages.*

(AU 2010, 2013, 2014)

Solution:

The classification of computers into various generations is based on major developments in technology used for building these machines. The five generations of computers are discussed as follows:

(a) First generation computers: These computers were used in the period 1945–1955. In these computers, thousands of vacuum tubes were used as switching devices for internal circuits and magnetic drums for memory. These vacuum tubes are large in size and generate a lot of heat. The best example of the first generation of computers is ENIAC as was discussed in the previous section. These computers could understand only machine language (binary code of 0's and 1's) and could solve only one problem at a time. The machine language was translated into assembly language (mnemonic codes or symbols) using a compiler; while the assembly language was converted back to machine language using an assembler. This translation and re-translation was time-consuming, and hence the processing speed of these computers was low. Moreover, these computers were bulky, produced a lot of heat and had limited storage capacity.

(b) Second generation computers: These computers were used in the period 1956–1963. In these computers, instead of vacuum tubes, transistors were used. This reduced the amount of heat produced, and the computers became smaller in size. With the use of transistors, use of electricity was reduced, the calculations became faster and more accurate. Moreover, these included primary memory and secondary memory for storing data and programs. These computers were programmed using assembly language instead of machine language.

(c) Third generation computers: The computers were developed in the period 1964–1970. In these computers, integrated circuits (ICs) were used to replace transistors. An IC consisted of various components used in the internal circuitry, such as diodes, transistors, resistors, capacitors, etc., which are fabricated and integrated onto a silicon-composed material known as a chip. The use of ICs reduces the amount of heat generated further as the heat produced could destroy the internal circuitry. In these computers, the user interaction with the computer was through keyboards and monitors interfaced with an operating system which allowed different applications to run at the same time. These computers were smaller, cheaper and thus more accessible to a mass audience. Initially, this technology enabled integration of about 10 components onto a single chip and was referred to as small-scale integration (SSI) technology. Further, hundreds and thousands of components could be integrated on a single chip which were referred to as medium-scale integration (MSI) and large-scale integration (LSI) technologies, respectively.

Integrated circuits are further classified based on the way in which they are mounted on top of printed circuit boards (PCBs).

- **Through-hole mounted:** In this technique, the pins (leads) are inserted through the holes of the PCB on one side and soldered to conductors on the other side. Example, dual-in-package (DIP). Points on the chip are connected to the package pins to establish I/O connections with the other devices. Transformers and heat-sinked power semiconductors can be mounted by this technique.

- **Surface-mounted:** In this technique, the components are mounted directly onto the surface of the PCB. The components using this technology have smaller pins or no pins at all and are smaller in size as compared to components used in through-hole technology. For example, capacitors and resistors are surface-mounted on USB flash drive's circuit board.

(d) Fourth generation computers: These computers were developed in the period 1971–1995. In these computers, very-large scale integration (VLSI) technology, developed by Intel chip manufacturer by which millions of components could be integrated on a single chip, was used in form of 4004 chip. These computers had such a user-friendly interface that even non-technical users could run applications such as word processing and spreadsheets. As these computers used microprocessor chip, they were very small in size, more powerful, faster and cheaper.

(e) Fifth generation computers: These computers belong to the period 1995 and beyond. In these computers, extremely large scale integration would be used. Various scientists and researchers are working on this model in which computers have some knowledge of the real world, understand the spoken language, translate different foreign languages, use the concept of artificial intelligence to assist human beings in various ways; for example, assisting doctors in making a diagnosis and applying steps for treatment of the disease.

11. *Write a note on classification of computers.* **(AU 2009)**

Solution:

Computers can be classified based on their data-processing capacity, memory and application areas. They can be further classified as analog or digital based on the signals received by the computer. Analog and digital computers differ based on the type of data processed by them. Analog computers accept linear combinations of voltage amplitude (or pressure, temperature, currents, etc.) as inputs, process these inputs and give outputs also in the same analogous form. For example, speedometer in the car. Digital computers accept inputs in the form of higher (i.e., 1) or lower (i.e., 0) voltage state, process these and give a digital output sequence. For example, personal computers, Mac computers.

The size of a computer may vary from palm-size handheld device to room-size supercomputers. Based on their size and computing speed, computers can broadly be classified into four main categories:

(a) Microcomputers: These are the smallest in the category of computers, and are generally used by individuals for their personal use. Their processing speed and storage capacity is quite low as compared to other types of computers.

The microcomputers have their own processor; input, output and storage devices. The processor is used to carry out the arithmetic and logical operations, input device is used to provide data or in-struction, output device is used to display the output generated by the computer and storage device is used to keep the data and instructions for future use. Apart from these, a power cable and other cables are required to connect the system.

These are also known as personal computers because they are developed and designed for personal use. A personal computer may also be connected to a network, so that many users can share their data and resources. One of the first and most popular personal computers was the Apple II, introduced in 1977 by Apple Computers. IBM's first microcomputer was designed in 1981 and was named as IBM-PC. Nowadays, these computers are inexpensive, use very little power, do not require special wiring, are easy to use, stable and reliable; hence they have become a necessity of modern lifestyle. These computers are widely used by individuals for programming, gaming, watching movies, listening to songs or maintaining database and accounts of small business units. The most popular types of personal computers are IBM-PC and Apple PC. The IBM-PC and other compatible PCs use the Windows operating system; whereas Apple PCs use the Macintosh operating system (MacOS).

The personal computers or microcomputers are classified as follows:

- **Desktop computer:** This is the most common type of microcomputers or personal computers. It is a standalone personal computer that can be placed on top of a desk. It consists of three primary components: an input device like keyboard and mouse; an output device like monitor and printer and a system unit consisting of central processing unit (CPU), memory, hard disk, etc. These computers are small and inexpensive, so they are very popular for personal use. They can be used to manage small databases, play games, learn programming, communicate using internet, watch movies, etc. There are many manufacturers of desktop computers such as HP Compaq, IBM, HCL, ACER, DELL, APPLE, LENOVO, etc.
- **Laptop:** It can also be used for similar purposes as the desktop computers, because it has all the features of a desktop computer. The advantages of the laptop are that it can be carried anywhere; does not require direct power supply; can work and operate on the battery backup; and due to small size, it can be put into the briefcase just like a notebook. Therefore, the laptops are also known as the notebook. However, one disadvantage of laptops is that the batteries need to be recharged every few hours. The flexibility of carrying the laptop anywhere, working anytime and the portability increases its cost, so the laptop is costlier than the desktop computer. The notebook has gained significant popularity in recent times. There are many manufacturers of laptop computers who are also manufacturers of desktop computers such as HP Compaq, IBM, HCL, ACER, DELL, APPLE, LENOVO, etc.
- **Handheld computers:** These are small computers which can be fit into the palm of the hand, and are also known as palmtop computers or pocket computers. The personal digital assistant (PDA) is a

popular handheld computer. This is a portable computer not much bigger than an appointment book, which can be operated using a digital pen or stylus instead of keyboard or mouse. It has a small monitor to view the output; but it has limited storage capacity. However, external cards can be used to increase storage capacity to store data and programs.

The handheld computers can be connected to larger computers for exchanging data or to the printer for taking hardcopies of the output. A PDA can function as a cellular phone, fax sender and personal organizer. Casio and Apple are some of the manufacturers of PDA. The Newton MessagePad introduced in 1993 was the first PDA. Some other examples of PDAs include Franklin eBookMan and Casio Cassiopeia.

(b) **Mainframe computers:** They are the second largest and expensive computers. The mainframe computers can handle processing of many users at a time; therefore, they are defined as multiuser, multiprogramming, high-storage and fast-processing computers generally used in centralized and extensive database manipulations. They have large capacity of data storage and very high processing speed. These computers can communicate with multiple users at the same time through the terminals connected to a central computer or a server through satellite link. These terminals may be dumb terminals consisting of I/O devices only, or intelligent terminals consisting of I/O devices as well as the processor. The terminals do not have storage facility; they use the large disk of the mainframe computer for data storage. Further, these terminals need not be in the same room in which the mainframe computer is located, but can be operated remotely also, that is, from a different room, building, city or even country. They are very expensive, of large size and require a very large clean room with air-conditioner. The mainframe computers are used in organization such as big hospitals; government agencies; insurance companies; universities; banks etc., to manage high volume of applications; and where many people require frequent access to the same data. Some examples of mainframe computers include CDC 6600, MEDHA, Sperry, DEC, S/390, VAX 8000, HP, HCL and IBM ES000 series.

(c) **Minicomputers:** These computers came into existence in mid-1960s, when it was observed that many tasks do not require such high-end computing facility as possible with mainframe computers. Minicomputers are as powerful as mainframe computers, but limited number of terminals (ranging from 4 to 200) can be connected to them. The minicomputers support multiprocessing, where multiple users can be connected through their terminals. They also have the high processing speed and storage capacity, but comparatively lower than the mainframe computers. They are much less expensive and also smaller than mainframe computers. These generally are used as servers in medium and small sized businesses, colleges, government departments, real-time applications, etc. Minicomputers do not require air conditioning, and can be operated at room temperature. Some examples of minicomputers include PDP 11, IBM 8000 series, VAX 7500 and AS/400. The storage and processing capabilities of a minicomputer lies between mainframe and microcomputer, which is discussed next.

(d) **Supercomputers:** These are most powerful computers which can carry out trillions of instructions per second. These computers were specifically designed and developed to be more powerful than the computers of 1980s to solve problems that require intensive numerical computations. These machines have the highest processing speed because many processors are used in parallel. The speed of supercomputers is generally measured in FLOPS (floating point operations per second). These are the biggest and most expensive computers; even bigger than mainframe computers, so they are used in large organizations, research laboratories, aerospace centers, nuclear research centers, etc. Examples of supercomputers include Cray-1, Cray-2, Cyber 205, CDC, ETA 10, ETA 20, IBM 3090, Intel ASCI Red. India has also developed its supercomputer named as PARAM. It was assembled by C-DAC (Centre for Development of Advanced Computing) in Pune. The latest supercomputer of PARAM series is PARAM Padma in India-China's Tianhe is also one of the recent supercomputers to be developed.

17. *Define binary, decimal, octal and hexadecimal number systems.* **(AU 2009)**

or

Write a note on the various types of number systems. **(AU 2010)**

Solution:

Number systems are of two types: Positional and non-positional. In ancient times, an additive approach was used for counting the number items; this additive approach is also called *non-positional number system*. In this system, we have symbols representing numbers, for instance, I for 1, II for 2, III for 3, and so on; thus we find that each symbol is representing the same value regardless of its position. Arithmetic operations are difficult to perform on these number systems; hence new number systems called positional number systems came into existence.

In *positional number systems*, only a few symbols called digits are used to represent numbers. Depending upon the position these digits occupy, different numbers are represented. The number rep-resented by each digit is determined based on three considerations – the digit itself, the position occupied by it and the base (or radix) of the number system. Numbers have arbitrary bases. The base of a number system defines the range of values a digit may have. Some of the base systems used in computing are as follows:

(a) **Binary:** This number system has base 2. A binary digit (or bit) can have only one of the two possible values (0 and 1).

(b) **Decimal:** This number system has base 10. in the decimal system the digit may have one of the 10 possible values (0, 1, 2, 3, 4, 5, 6, 7, 8 and 9).

(c) **Octal:** This number system has base 8. This base value indicates that the octal number system has 8 possible values (0, 1, 2, 3, 4, 5, 6, 7).

(d) **Hexadecimal:** This number system has bas value 16. This indicates that a hexadecimal digit has 16 possible values (0, 1, 2, 3, 4, 5, 6, 7, 8, 9, A, B, C, D, E, F).

All binary, decimal, octal and hexadecimal number systems belong to positional number systems.

Chapter 2 Problem Solving through Algorithms, Flowcharts and Pseudocodes

Review Questions

6. *(b) Describe pseudocode with its advantages and disadvantages.* **(AU 2009 Suppl.)**

Solution:

The sequence of instructions to solve a computational problem can be expressed in a code which is written in the form of English-like statements resembling the programming languages. This code is known as pseudocode and is designed by using basic programs constructs, such as sequence, branching and looping. The pseudocode contains a logical sequence of statements which cannot be compiled or executed.

The advantages of pseudocode are as follows:

(i) A pseudocode is language independent and hence can be used by programmers of diverse backgrounds.

(ii) Since it is logic-driven and no set style elements or symbols are used to express instructions, it can be updated or modified whenever the need arises.

(iii) It is not cumbersome to design pseudocodes for complex problems unlike in the case of flowcharts.

(iv) Since the keywords used in pseudocode are in line with the basic computer operations, it is easy to translate them into programming languages.

The disadvantages of pseudocode are as follows:

(i) It does not provide the visual representation of the solution that aids easy comprehension.

(ii) Since it cannot be compiled or executed, the final code needs to be structured based on syntax rules of the programming language selected.

6. *(c) Enlist the advantages of algorithm.* **(AU 2012)**

Solution:

The advantages are as follows:

(i) Any input (raw value) can be supplied to the algorithm externally to solve the computational problem.

(ii) The data is processed by applying some operations on them, and then the desired output is generated.

(iii) Each and every instruction step in an algorithm is precise and unambiguous and written in sequence.

(iv) The language used in the instructions is English, and hence can be easily translated into programming language.

(v) The desired result is obtained from the algorithm as soon as it terminates.

7. *Write down steps involved in writing a program to solve a problem.* **(AU 2010 Suppl.)**

Solution:

A program is defined as the set of instructions written in a proper syntax and in a certain order to perform some specific task. The various steps involved in writing a program to solve a problem are:

(a) **Defining the problem:** It is important to be first define the problem or set of problems and define clear objectives to solve the problem(s).

(b) **Requirement analysis:** After defining the problem, it is split into several small problems and the possible solutions to these problems are analyzed. The solution that is feasible practically and economically is chosen.

(c) **Designing algorithms:** The solution is outlined in form of tasks to be performed and steps to be carried out in sequential order.

(d) **Algorithm testing:** Some sample data is run though the steps of the algorithm to check its correctness. Any logical errors found are rectified. This step is very important before converting the algorithm into program code. Usual data as well as data with certain exceptions are tested to check variance in both the cases.

(e) **Coding:** In this phase, the actual program coding is done. Once the initial code is written, it is checked against design and specification requirements and updated accordingly to maintain consistency.

(f) **Testing:** The developed program is tested on the grounds of functionality, performance, business logic and data accuracy. A program compiler is used to compile the program and a list of errors is generated. These errors are checked and rectified one by one. The required changes are incorporated in the coding and the testing process is repeated to ensure that all changes have been incorporated and that no inadvertent discrepancy is introduced during updation. More complex the program, more rounds of testing are required. After testing, the work is started on the functional environment or user interface.

(g) **Documentation:** This documentation is done throughout the various phases. It contains the internal design structure of the program and other details required for running the program by any user. During its lifetime, the program can be implemented by many programmers; therefore, it is better to document the changes and understand the logic behind the changes.

(h) **Implementation:** The program is installed on the end user's machine and user is briefed about the proper working of the program. The feedback from various users is collected and the changes are incorporated to enhance the program's functionality.

(i) **Maintenance, enhancement and evolution:** The program is updated periodically for it to be reliable and long-lasting. Also, the existing program is relooked upon in view of emerging and evolving technologies. The new technical and functional requirements are implemented accordingly and new versions of the existing program are developed.

8. *List the general characteristics of writing pseudocode.* **(AU 2009)**

Solution:

The characteristics of a pseudocode are listed as follows:

(a) A pseudocode is language independent and hence can be used by programmers of diverse backgrounds.

(b) Since it is logic-driven and no set style elements or symbols are used to express instructions, it can be updated or modified whenever the need arises.

(c) It is not cumbersome to design pseudocodes for complex problems unlike in the case of flowcharts.

(d) Since the keywords used in pseudocode are in line with the basic computer operations, it is easy to translate them into programming languages.

(e) It does not provide the visual representation of the solution that aids easy comprehension.

(f) Since it cannot be compiled or executed, the final code needs to be structured based on syntax rules of the programming language selected.

Programming Assignments

1. *Write an algorithm to compute the factorial of a number n.* **(AU 2012)**

Solution:

The algorithm is as follows:

1. Start
2. Read a number n
3. Initialize a variable i = n – 1
4. Compute fact = n * i
5. If n = 1 goto step 6 else goto step 3
6. Print fact
7. Stop

2. *Draw a flowchart to find the highest marks in a set of marks.* **(AU 2012)**

Solution:

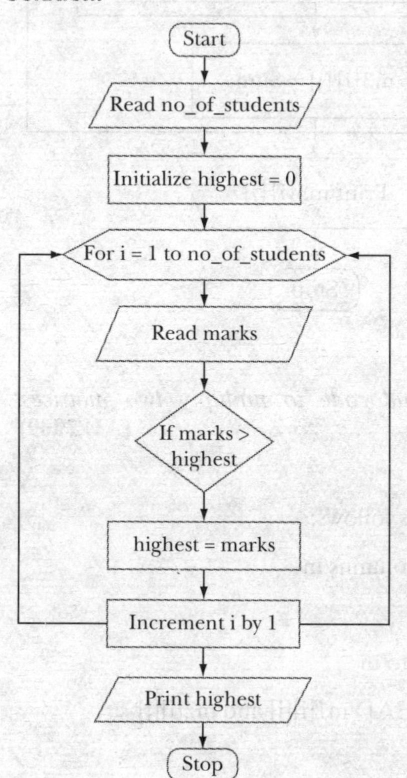

3. *What are the essential properties of an algorithm? Develop an algorithm for printing Fibonacci series upto 100.* **(AU 2007 Suppl.)**

Solution:

The properties of a good algorithm are as follows:

(a) Each instruction in an algorithm should be unambiguous.

(b) The steps of an algorithm should be written in sequence, and there should not be any uncertainty about which step should be followed next.

(c) The steps should not be repeated infinitely, they must reach their concluding state; that is, they must terminate after executing certain number of instructions.

(d) The algorithm must not be open-ended, and its description must be finite.

(e) The algorithm should be general enough to deal with any contingency.

The algorithm for displaying Fibonacci series up to 100 is as follows:

1. Start
2. Set i = 1, prev_number = 0, number = 1
3. Print prev_number, number
4. Compute fibo = prev_number + number
5. Set prev_number = number
6. Set number = fibo
7. Increment i by 1
8. If(i < 100) then print fibo else goto step 4
9. Stop

4. *Draw a flowchart to find the sum of first n natural numbers.* **(AU 2008 Suppl.)**

Solution:

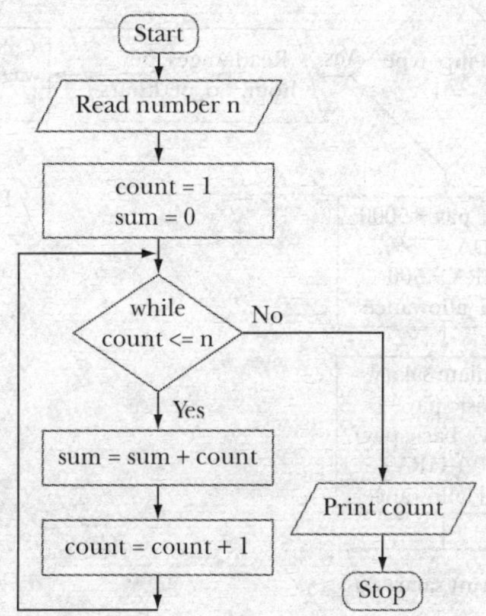

5. *Draw a flowchart to find a factorial of a given number.* **(AU 2008 Suppl.)**

Solution:

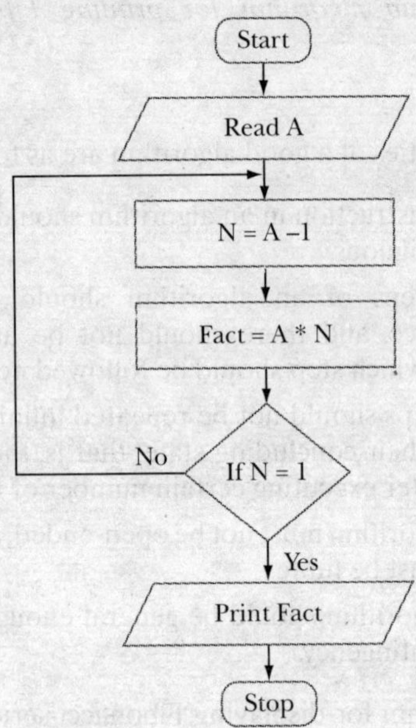

6. *Draw a flowchart to compute the salary of an employee in a company. Assume that there are two types of employees in the company: daily wages and regular. Salary is calculated as (the number of hours worked * wages per hour) for daily wagers and as (basic pay+ (%DA + basic pay)/100 + HRA + medical allowance) for regular employees. Sketch the flow of your design for a regular employee with basic pay = 5000, % of DA = 75% and HRA = 500.* **(AU 2010)**

Solution:

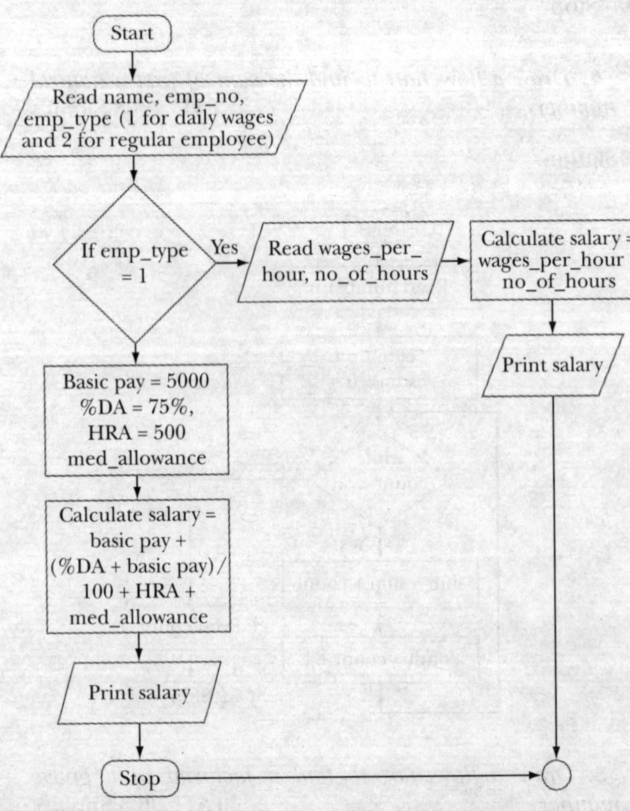

7. *Draw a flowchart to multiply two matrices.* **(AU 2009)**

Solution:

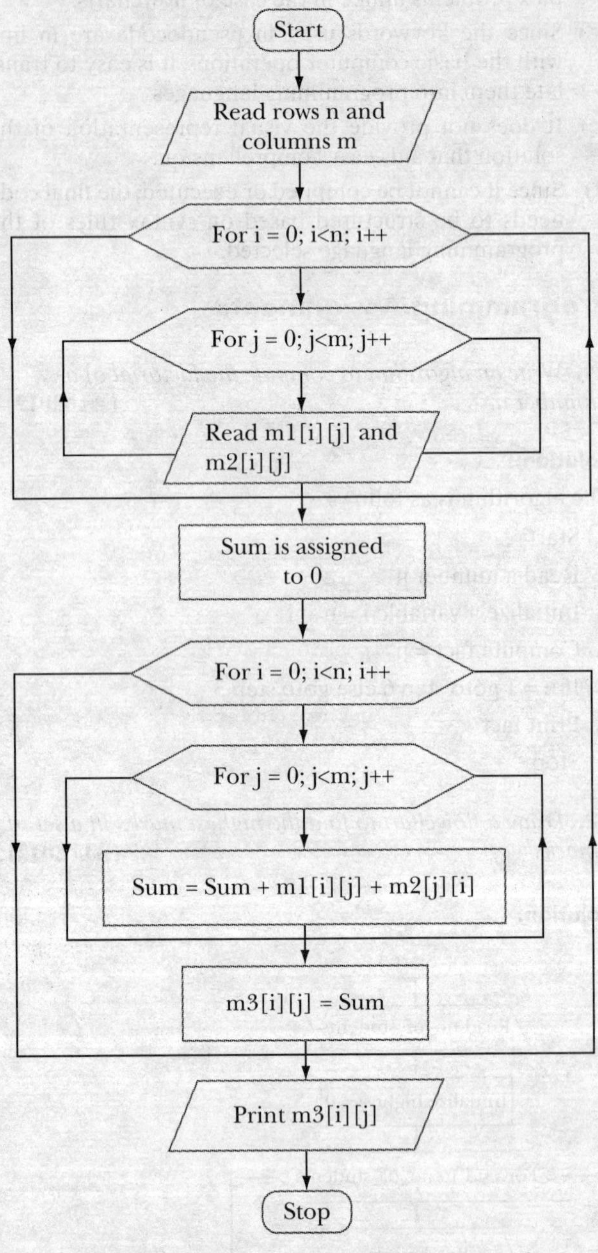

8. *Write the pseudocode to multiply two matrices.* **(AU 2009)**

Solution:

The pseudocode is as follows:

```
READ rows n and columns m
FOR i = 0 to n
    ||FOR j = 0 to m
        READ m1[i][j] and m2[i][j]
```

```
            INCREMENT j by 1
    UNTIL j < m
    INCREMENT i by 1
UNTIL i < n
INITIALIZE sum = 0
FOR i = 0 to n
        FOR j = 0 to m
                sum = sum + m1[i][j] + m2[j][i]
                INCREMENT j by 1
        UNTIL j < m
                m3[i][j] = sum
        INCREMENT i by 1
UNTIL i < n
PRINT m3[i][j]
```

9. *What is an algorithm? Write an algorithm to print even numbers from 2 to 100.* **(AU 2009)**

Solution:

An algorithm is defined as a sequence of instructions to solve a computational problem. These instructions are applied on some raw data called the input, and the solution of the problem produced is called the output.

1. Start
2. Set count = 2
3. Print count
4. Increment count by 1 till count <= 100
5. If count%2 = 0 then goto step 3 else goto step 4
6. Stop

10. *Write an algorithm to find the maximum among the given three numbers. Draw a flowchart for your algorithm.* **(AU 2009 Suppl.)**

Solution:

The algorithm is as follows:

1. Start
2. Read three numbers x, y and z
3. If x> y and y > z goto step 6 else goto step 4
4. If y > z goto step 7 else goto step 5
5. Print z is the maximum among the three numbers and goto step 8
6. Print x is the maximum among the three numbers and goto step 8
7. Print y is the maximum among the three numbers and goto step 8
8. Stop

The flowchart is as follows

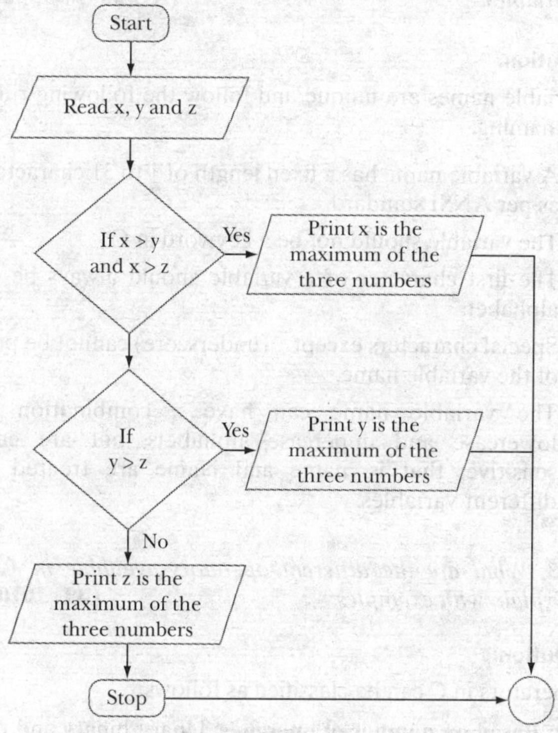

Chapter 3: C Programming Basics

Review Questions

1. *State and explain the various data types supported by "C" languages.* **(AU 2007 Suppl., 2009 Suppl.)**

Solution:

The various data types supported by C are built-in (int, char, float, double, void), us-er-defined data types (structure, union, enumerated) and derived data types (array, function and pointer). Refer section 3.2.5 for detailed explanation.

2. *List the rules that are to be followed while declaring variables.* **(AU 2007 Suppl.)**

Solution:

Variable names are unique and follow the following rules for naming:

1. A variable name has a fixed length of 1 to 31 characters as per ANSI standard.
2. The variable should not be a keyword in C.
3. The first character of a variable should always be an alphabet.
4. Special characters except _ (underscore) cannot be part of the variable name.
5. The variable name can have a combination of lowercase and uppercase alphabets, but are case sensitive; that is, name and Name are treated as different variables.

3. *What are the different operators available in C? Explain with examples.* **(AU 2010)**

Solution:

Operators in C can be classified as follows:

(a) **Based on number of operands:** Unary, binary and ternary operators.

(b) **Based on the nature of operation:** Arithmetic, relational, logical, assignment, incre-ment/decrement, conditional, bitwise and special operators.

- **Arithmetic operators:** These are basic binary operators requiring two variables to be evaluated. The list of arithmetic operators includes =; + and +=;– and –=; * and *=; / and /=;% and %=; and –(unary). For example, a+=b means a = a + b.
- **Relational operators:** These are used to compare the value between two variables and give the result as true or false. The list of relational operators includes <; <=; >; >=; ==; and != For example, a < b means Is a less than b or not?
- **Logical operators:** These operators are used to combine two or more conditional ex-pressions in a statement. These are also called Boolean operators. The list of logical operators includes &&; ||; and !! For example, a && b means a and b.
- **Bitwise operators:** These operators are used to perform operations on the bits of the binary pattern of the numbers. The list of bitwise operators includes & and &=; | and |=; ^ and ^=; >> and >>=; << and <<=; and ~ (bitwise complement). For example, a &= b means a = a & b.
- **Special operators:** These operators include the increment (++) and decrement (– –) operators, which can precede or follow the operand; *(Value at address); & (Address of); sizeof()(Size of); ?:(Ternary operator); ,(Comma); [](Array element reference); ()(Function call); . (Dot operator); and ->(Pointer to structure).

4. *List the bitwise operators supported by C.* **(AU 2007 Suppl.)**

Solution:

The bitwise operators are used to perform operations on the bits of the binary pattern of the numbers. The list of bitwise operators in C includes & and &= (bitwise AND); | and |= (bitwise OR); ^ and ^= (bitwise XOR); >> and >>= (bitwise right shift); << and <<= (bitwise left shift); and ~ (bitwise complement).

5. *Explain the various looping constructs. Give an example for each and explain the working of the construct.* **(AU 2009, 2014)**

Solution:

The iterative or looping statements are used when we want to repeat a set of state-ments for certain number of times. The number of iterations depends on the test condition. A set of statements are repeated again and again till the condition is true. As soon as the condition becomes false, the repetition stops. The set of statements that are repeated is called the body of the loop. C offers various kinds of looping statements, such as for loop; nested for; while loop; do-while loop.

Syntax (for)

```
for (Initialization;
Condition; Updation)
{
(Body of the loop)
Statements;
}
```

Syntax (while)

```
initialization;
while(condition)
{
statements;
updation;
}
```

Syntax (do-while)

```
initialization;
do
{
statements;
updation;
} while(condition);
```

Working: First, the expression or the variable is initialized and then the condition is checked. If the condition is false, the loop terminates. Program skips the body of the loop and comes to the next statement just after the loop. If the condition is true then body of the loop is executed. After execution of the body the variable is updated and again the condition is checked. If it is false then the loop is terminated, otherwise again the body of the loop is executed. In this way the loop is executed again and again till the condition is true. We know that the condition can be any valid C expression including the value of a variable, a unary or binary expression, or the value returned by a function. The body of the loop may contain a single or a compound statement.

(a) In **for loop**, the body of the loop is executed for the fixed number of iterations as long as the condition is true.

(b) In the **while loop**, the condition is evaluated at the entry level of the loop. If the condition evaluates to true then only the statements of the loop body are executed otherwise the loop is not executed at all. So, the while loop is called an entry controlled loop.

(c) In **do-while loop**, the body of the loop is executed first and then the condition is checked. So, the do-while loop is also called an exit controlled loop. In do-while loop the body of the loop is executed at least once even if the condition is false. As long as the condition is true, the loop statements will be repeated again and again.

Examples:

(a) for loop construct to find factorial of number n:

```
long double factorial=1;
for(i=1;i<=n;i++)
{
factorial=factorial*i;
}
```

(b) while loop construct to print n terms of the Fibonacci series:

```
int first=0,second=1,next;
while(i<=n)
{
next=first+second;
printf("%d\t",next);
first=second;
second=next;
i++;
}
```

(c) do-while loop construct to check whether the number is palindrome or not:

```
int ori-num,chnum,rev=0,digit;
chnum=orinum;
do
{
digit=chnum%10;
rev=rev*10+digit;
chnum=chnum/10;
}while(chnum!=0);
```

6. *Compare in terms of their functions, while and do-while. Give examples.*
(AU 2005 Suppl., 2008 Suppl., 2010 Suppl., 2013)

Solution:

In while statement, the condition is checked at the entry level. If it is true then the body of the loop is executed. So, the while loop is called an entry controlled loop. Whereas, in do-while statement at least once the body of the loop is executed even if condition is not true because condition is evaluated at the exit level. So, the do-while loop is also called an exit controlled loop. The do-while loop is terminated by semicolon, whereas the while loop is not terminated by semicolon. For example,

```
int i=5;
do
{
printf("i = %d", i);
i=i-1;
}while(i>5);
```

In the above loop construct, the output is

```
5
4
3
2
1
```

whereas using the while loop, the loop is terminated as i = 5 and not less than 5.

8. *What are the input and output functions in C?*
(AU 2007 Suppl., 2013)

Solution:

The input/output operations in C are carried out by standard library functions. These functions are of two types: Formatted functions [scanf(), printf(), etc.] and unformatted functions [getch(), getche(), getchar(), gets(), putch(), putchar(), put(), etc.].

11. *Illustrate the use of getc(), putc(), fprintf(), fscanf() with suitable examples.* **(AU 2008 Suppl.)**

Solution:

These functions are used to read and write characters/strings into files. Out of these, getc() and putc() are unformatted functions and fprintf() and fscanf() are formatted functions.

(a) getc(): To read a character from the file. For example, c=getc(fp2); where fp2 is the file pointer pointing the file opened in reading mode. It returns EOF as soon as end of file is reached.

(b) putc(): To write a character onto the file. For example, `putc(c,fp1);`); where fp1 is the file pointer pointing the file opened in writing mode. It returns EOF as soon as end of file is reached.

(c) fprintf(): To write a set of data values onto the file. For example, `fprintf(f1, "%d %f\n",i,f);` where f1 is the file pointer pointing the file opened in reading mode.

(d) fscanf(): To read a set of data values from the file. For example, `fscanf(f2, "%d %f", &i, &f);` where f2 is the file pointer pointing the file opened in reading mode.

12. *Explain the data types, operators with precedence and expressions in C language.* **(AU 2009 Suppl.)**

Solution:

Refer to solutions to Review Questions 1 and 3 for data types and operators. The precedence of operators is as follows:

Operator	Precedence
++, --	Highest
++, --, sizeof, !, -, +	↑
*, /, %	
+,-	
<,<=,>,>=	
==,!=	
&&	
||	
?:	
= and other assignment operator	
Comma operator	Lowest

13. *With examples, explain the statements used for selection, and iteration in C.* **(AU 2009 Suppl.)**

Solution:

Refer to solution to Review Question 5 for statements used for iteration.

For selection, the statements are also called decision-making or conditional statements. In these statements, the execution of body (statements) depends on the test condition. If the condition evaluates to true, one set of statements are executed otherwise another set of statements are executed. The various types of conditional statements used in C are as follows:

(a) if Statement: In this statement, if the expression evaluates to true, the statements following if statement are executed, otherwise body of if statement is skipped and execution continues with the next statement. The syntax is as follows:

```
if(expression)
{
Statements; (Body of if)
}
```

For example, the following if construct is used to display whether the number entered is even or not

```
printf("Enter number");
scanf("%d", number);
if(number%2==0)
{printf("%d is even", number);
}
```

(b) if–else statement: In the if–else statement, if the expression evaluates to true, the statements or the body of if statement is executed, otherwise body of if statement is skipped and the body of else statement is executed. Thereafter the next statement is executed. The syntax for if–else statement is as follows:

```
if(expression)
{
 (Body of if)
Statements 1;
}
else
{
 (Body of else)
Statements 2;
}
```

For example, the following if construct is used to determine whether the entered number is even or odd:

```
int number;
printf("Enter number");
scanf("%d", number);
if(number%2==0){
printf("%d is even", number);}
else{
printf("%d" is odd", number);}
```

(c) Ladder if–else statement: In the ladder if–else statement, if the expression evaluates to true, the statements or the body of if statement is executed, otherwise the body of if statement is skipped and the body of else if statement is executed only if the expression in else if statement evaluates to true, otherwise the statements are skipped and body of else statement is executed. The syntax is as follows:

```
if(expression)
{
 (Body of if)
Statements 1;
}
else if
{
 (Body of else)
Statements 2;
}
else
{
 (Body of else)
Statements 3;
}
```

For example, the following ladder if–else construct is used to determine the smallest out of three numbers:

```
int a, b, c;
printf("Enter three numbers");
scanf("%d %d %d", a,b,c);
if(a <b&& a>c){
printf("%d is the smallest", a);}
elseif(b <c){
printf("%d" is the smallest", b);}
else
printf("%d" is the smallest", c);}
```

(d) Nested if–else statement: In the nested if–else statement, if the expression evaluates to true, the statements or the body of if statement is executed. Again in the if statement inside the if construct, the statement after if is executed when it evaluated to true, otherwise the statement after else is executed. If the expression in the parent if statement evaluates to false, then the entire if construct is skipped and body of else statement is executed.The syntax for nested if–else statement is as follows:

```
if(expression)
{
Statements 1;/*Body of if statement*/
   if(expression)
       statement 2;
   else
       statement 3;
}
else
{
Statements 4;
}
```

For example, the following nested if–else construct is used to check whether the entered number is even or odd and whether it is divisible by 4 or not.

```
int number;
printf("Enter any number: ")
scanf("%d", &number);
if(number%2==0)
  printf ("The number is even");
    if(number%4==0)
      printf("It is di-visible by 4");
    else
      printf("It is not divisible by 4");
else
  printf("The  number  is  odd  and  not
divisible by 4");
```

(e) switch Statement: The switch statement is used to test multiple conditions for the same var-iable or expression in a program and execute statements accordingly. It takes a variable or expression of integer data type as its argument. The argument is evaluated and matched with the conditions in the case statement. If none of the case conditions match, then the statements in the default section is executed. The syntax for the switch case construct is as follows:

```
switch (variable or expression)
{
case constant A:
statement;
break;
case constant B:
statement;
break;
default:
statement;
}
```

For example, the following switch construct performs addition or subtraction on the numbers x and y depending upon the user's choice.

```
int x, y, choice, sum, difference;
printf("Enter numbers x and y");
scanf("%d%d",x,y);
A: printf("Enter choice: 1 for addition
and 2 for subtraction");
scanf("%d",choice);
switch (choice)
{
case 1:
sum=x+y;
printf("Addition of %d and %d gives sum
as %d", x, y, sum);
break;
case 2:
difference=x-y;
printf("Subtraction of %d from %d gives
difference as %d", x, y, differ-ence);
break;
default:
goto A;
}
```

(f) Nested switch–case: An inner switch construct can be contained as part of the outer switch statement. The same variables and constants can be used in the two switch const ructs. For example, the following nested switch-case construct determines whether a number is "odd" or "even" and prints the message.

```
int x;
char a,b;
a = "Even";
b = "Odd";
printf("Enter a number: ");
scanf("%d", &x);
switch(x)
{
case 0:
printf ("%c",a);
break;
case 1:
printf("%c",b);
break;
default:
   switch(x%2)
   {
   case 0:
   printf("Even number");
   default:
   printf("Odd number");
   }
}
```

(g) Ternary Operator: The ternary operator can be used to form a conditional decision making statement as shown in the following example to check whether the given year is a leap year or not.

```
int y,leap;
clrscr();
printf("Enter any year:");
scanf("%d", &y);
leap=(y%400==0)?:(y%100!=0)?
(y%4==0)?1:0:0;
```

```
if(leap==1)
printf(" The given year is leap year");
else
printf(" The given year is not leap
year);
```

14. *List out the rules involved in formatting an identifier* **(AU 2010)**

Solution:

The rules to name an identifier are as follows:

(a) Only alphabetic letters, digits and underscores are permitted in an identifier.

(b) An identifier name cannot start with a digit.

(c) A declared keyword or reserve word cannot be used as a variable name.

(d) There is no set length for an identifier.

18. *With example describe the structure of (a) if–else statement, (b) Nested if–else statement, (c) switch statement in C language.* **(AU 2011)**

Solution:

Refer to solution to Review Question 13.

20. *Explain the following conditional statements: (a) nested if-else statement and (b) switch-case statement* **(AU 2010):**

Solution:

Refer to solution to Review Question 13.

21. *Discuss about the bitwise and logical operators in C.* **(AU 2013)**

Solution

For bitwise operators, refer Review Question 4. The logical operators in C are used to combine two or more conditional expressions in a statement. There are three such operators in C.

(a) **Logical AND (&&):** It will produce true when both operands produce true values, and has associativity from left to right.

(b) **Logical OR(||):** It will produce true when when atleast one of the operands produce true values, and has associativity from left to right.

(c) **Logical NOT (!):** It will produce negation value of the operand, and has associativity from right to left.

22. *Write the syntax of "for contruct" in C. Give an example.* **(AU 2013)**

Solution

In **for loop**, the body of the loop is executed for the fixed number of iterations as long as the condition is true. The syntax is

```
for (initialization;condition;updation)
{
/*body of the loop*/
Statements;
}
```

For example, to find factorial of number n the for loop construct is:

```
long double factori-al=1;
for(i=1;i<=n;i++)
{
factorial=factorial*i;
}
```

23. *What are constants? Explain the various types of constants in C.* **(AU 2013)**

Constants in C are the fixed data values that never change their values during the execution of a program. These are also called literals; these include the following types: integer constants, floating point constants, character and string constants, and symbolic constants. Refer section 3.2.3 for details.

24. *Explain any four format strings with examples.* **(AU 2013)**

Solution

The first input to `printf()` or `scanf()` should be a format string. A format string consists of format specifiers. A format specifier specifies the format according to which the printing will be done. There is a different format specifier for each data type. For example, %c for single character, %d for integer, %f for float, %s for string.

Example	Output
`printf("%d",4567);`	4567
`printf("%6d",4567)`	␣␣4567
`printf("%2d",4567);`	4567
`printf("%7.4f",98.7654)`	98.7654
`printf("%7.2f",98.7654)`	␣␣98.76
`printf("%c",a);`	
`printf("%20s",name);`	

Programming Assignments

6. *The numbers in sequence 1, 1, 2, 3, 5, 8, 13, 21 are called Fibonacci numbers. Write a C program to print the first n Fibonacci numbers.* **(AU 2008 Suppl.)**

Solution:

```
#include<stdio.h>
#include<conio.h>
#include<stdlib.h>
int main(){
long int temp=1,i,n;
printf(" \n Enter how many numbers in
se-ries:");
scanf("%lu",&n);
printf("\n Series ");
printf("\n ------ ");
printf("\n");
printf("\n%lu,",temp);
for(i=1;i<=n;i++)
```

```
{
temp = 3 * temp;
printf("\t%lu,",temp);
}
getch();
}
```

8. *Write a program to find the number of and the sum of all integers greater than 200 and less than 400 that are divisible by 6.* **(AU 2005 Suppl.)**

Solution:

```
#include<stdio.h>
#include<conio.h>
int main()
{
int i,n=0,sum=0;
for(i=200;i<400;i++)
{
if(i%6==0)
{
n++;
sum +i;
}
}
printf("\n The number of numbers greater
than 200 \n and less than 400 which is
divisible by 6 is%d",n);
printf("\n The sum of the numbers greater
than 200 \n and less than 400 which is
divisible by 6 is%d",sum);
getch();
}
```

```
C:\Users\fathimazishan\Desktop\CPrograms\DivisiblebySix.exe

The number of numbers greater than 200
and less than 400 which is divisible by 6 is33
The sum of the numbers greater than 200
and less than 400 which is divisible by 6 is9900_
```

9. *Write a program to count the letters in a sequence of characters.* **(AU 2009, 2013)**

Solution:

```
#include<stdio.h>
#include<conio.h>
#include<string.h>
int main()
{
int counter = 0;
char string;
int i;
printf("\n    Enter    a    sequence    of
charac-ters:");
gets(string);
for(i=0;i<string[i]!=0;i++)
{
if(string[i]!= ' ')
{
counter++;
}
}
printf("\n The number of characters is %d",
counter);
getch();
}
```

```
C:\Users\Zishan khan\Desktop\CPrograms\CountingCharacters

Enter a sequence of characters:I am a girl

The number of characters is 8
```

10. *Write a C program to generate Fibonacci series upto 200.* **(AU 2012)**

Solution:

```
#include<stdio.h>
#include<conio.h>
int fibonacci (int prev_number, int number,
int limit)
{
int fibo;
fibo=prev_number+number;
prev_number = number;
number = fibo;
if(number<limit){
printf ("\n%d", fibo);
fibonacci (prev_number, number, limit); //
recursion
}
}
int main()
{
static int limit, prev_number=0, num-ber=1;
// static: so value is not lost
printf("\n  Enter  limit  upto  which  the
Fibonacci series must be generated:");
scanf("%d",&limit);
fibonacci (prev_number,number,limit);
getch();
}
```

11. *Write a C program to compute and print a table of factorials for a given integer.* **(AU 2010 Suppl.)**

Solution:

```
#include<stdio.h>
#include<conio.h>
void main()
int num, f;
printf("\nEnter a number:");
scanf("%d", &num);
f=fact(num);
printf("\nFactorial of %d is: %d", num, f);
}
int fact(int n)
{
if (n==1)
return (1);
else
factorial=n*fact(n-1);
return (factorial);
}
```

Chapter 4: Arrays and Strings

Review Questions

4. *Explain the need for array variables. Describe the following with respect to arrays: Declaration of array, two-dimensional array and accessing an array element.* **(AU 2005 Suppl.)**

Solution:

In programming, a need may arise wherein operations on multiple variables or similar data items need to be carried out. In such cases, instead of declaring and initializing each variable, it is beneficial to store variables of similar data type under a single reference name called array. The array elements are stored in consecutive memory locations; and hence are linear data structures. There are two types of arrays: one-dimensional (a list of similar data items) and multidimensional array (collection of similar data items, with each data item is an array of fixed size. The two-dimensional array is a collection of one-dimensional arrays.

Declaration of array

(a) One-dimensional: The one-dimensional array is defined by specifying its name, size and data types of the items. The elements of a one-dimensional array can be accessed using a single subscript. The general format in C for defining one-dimensional array is
`storage_classdata_typearray_name[size];`
where the storage class (external, auto or static) specifies the scope of the array variable and is op-tional; takes default value auto if not specified. The array name follows the same naming conventions as variable. The size must be an integer value or integer constant (without any sign) and not a variable specifying the number of elements to be stored into the array. The array must be declared before using it in the program, like other variables. For example, `int arr[5];`

(b) Two-dimensional arrays: These are the simplest form of the multidimensional arrays and are a collection of one-dimensional arrays. The syntax to define two dimensional arrays is
`storage_class data_type array_ name [row][col];`
where only two dimensions are required, with the first dimension referring to the number of rows and the second referring to the number of columns. It is just like a matrix in mathematics. For example,
`char student[10][5];`

Accessing/modifying array elements:

(a) One-dimensional array: The array elements are accessed by using their index or subscript and are initialized just like variables. The general format for initialization of array elements is as follows:
`storage_class data_type array_name [size] = {value1, value2 ...... valuesize};`
The initial values are enclosed in the {} curly braces separated by comma. For example,
`int X[5]={9, 5, 6};`
The elements of array X are initialized as follows

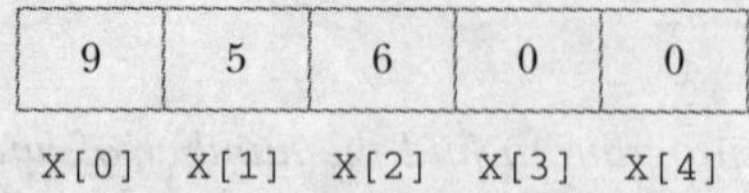

Although only three elements of the array are initialized, the memory is allocated to five elements; thus, the remaining two elements are initialized to 0.

(b) Two-dimensional array: These are accessed/initialized in the same manner as one-dimensional array. The assignment is always done in row major order; that is, initially the first row is initialized, then second row is initialized, then third and so on. To change the order of initialization then we can use the extra {} braces. For example, `int X[3][4]={{2,3,4},{6,8,10,2},{4}};` or `X[3][4]={{1,2,4,5},{9,6,7,9},{10,13,14,15}};` which is a matrix X having 3 rows and 4 columns. The first three elements of the first row are initialized; the last element, that is, in the fourth column is initialized to 0 by default. In the second row, all the four elements are initialized. In the third row, the first element is initialized and the rest are initialized to 0 by default.

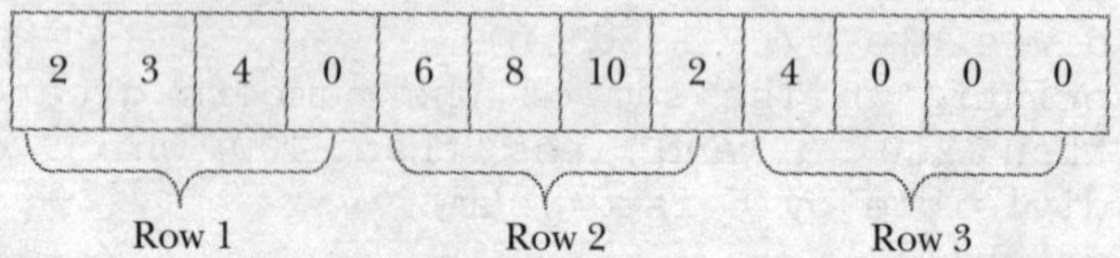

12. *Name any two library functions used for string handling.* **(AU 2014)**

Solution:

Two string functions are strlen(string) to determine the length of a string not including null character; and strcpy(dest,source) to copy the source string into destination string, where source and destination both must be character array.

Programming Assignments

1. *Write a program in C to find the first and second biggest element from the given array of integers.* **(AU 2009 Suppl.)**

Solution:

```
#include<stdio.h>
#include<conio.h>
int main()
{
int i,n=0,sum=0;
for(i=200;i<400;i++)
{
if(i%6==0)
{
n++;
```

```
sum +i;
}
}
printf("\n The number of numbers greater than 200 \n and less than 400 which is divisible by 6 is%d",n);
printf("\n The sum of the numbers greater than 200 \n and less than 400 which is divisible by 6 is%d",sum);
getch();
}
```

```
C:\Users\fathimazishan\Desktop\CPrograms\Higes
Enter how many numbers in array:10
Enter distinct numbers:1
9
6
3
2
11
18
5
4
8

Second largest element is 11
First largest element is 18
```

2 *Write a C program to sort the elements of an n × n matrix and to display the elements in the following pattern:*

5 4 3
6 1 2
7 8 9

(AU 2007 Suppl.)

Solution:

```
#include<stdio.h>
#include<conio.h>
int main()
{
int mat[20][20],n,i,j;
printf("\n Input dimensions of an n*n matrix \n\n");
scanf("%d",&n);
printf(" \n\n");
for(i=0;i<n;i++)
{
for(j=0;j<n;j++)
{
scanf("%d", &mat[i][j]);
}
}
printf("\n\n Matrix : \n\n");
for(i=0;i<n; ++i)
{
for(j=0;j<n; ++j)
{
printf("%d\t", mat[i][j]);
}
printf("\n\n");
}
getch();
}
```

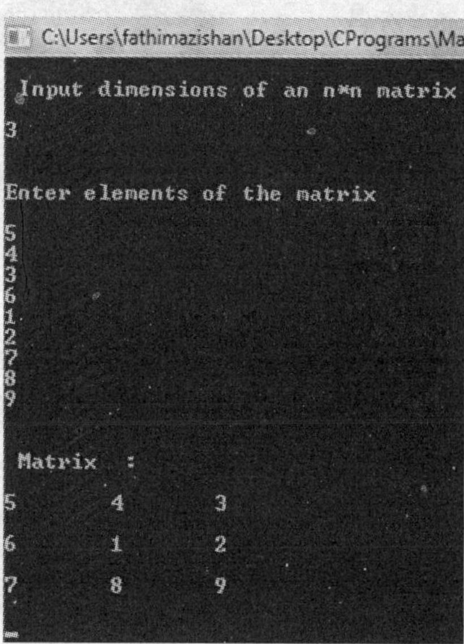

3 *Write a C program to read m × n matrix and to check whether the element of the last column of each row is the sum of the elements of the other columns in that row.* **(AU 2007 Suppl.)**

Solution:

```
#include<stdio.h>
#include<conio.h>
#include<stdlib.h>
int main()
{
int mat[20][20],row,col,i,j,sum,flag=1;
printf("\n Input row and column of the matrix \n\n");
scanf("%d%d",&row,&col);
int * flags = (int *) calloc(row, sizeof(int));
printf("\n\n Enter elements of the matrix \n\n");
for(i=0;i<row;i++)
{
for(j=0;j<col;j++)
{
scanf("%d", &mat[i][j]);
}
}
printf("\n\n Matrix : \n\n");
for(i=0;i<row; ++i)
{
for(j=0;j<col; ++j)
{
printf("%d\t", mat[i][j]);
}
printf("\n\n");
}
for(i=0;i<row;i++)
{
sum =0;
for(j=0;j<col-1;j++)
{
sum = sum + mat[i][j];
}
flags[i]=0;
```

```
if(sum==mat[i][col-1])
{
flags[i]++;
}
}
for(i=0;i<row;i++)
{
if(flags[i]!=1)
{
printf("\n All the elements of the last
column of all rows \n is not the sum of the
elements of the other columns in that row.
\n ");
system("pause");
exit(0);
}
}
if(flag =1)
{
printf("\n All the elements of the last
column of all rows \n is the sum of the
elements of the other columns in that
row.");
}
getch();
}
```

```
C:\Users\fathimazishan\Desktop\CPrograms\MatrixSumOfElements.exe
 Input row and column of the matrix
2
3

Enter elements of the matrix
1
2
3
2
4
6

 Matrix  :
1       2       3
2       4       6

 All the elements of the last column of all rows
 is the sum of the elements of the other columns in that row_
```

Chapter 5: Functions and Pointers

Review Questions

1. *What is the need for functions?*

Solution:

A complex program has large number of instructions that need to be executed. For better management in terms of convenient testing, easier identification and rectification of errors, reduced size of programs and their modular functionality, these complex programs are split into a number of modules with each module having some specific set of instructions to be executed. Such modules are called functions and are the building blocks of C programming.

2. *Write notes on pointers.* **(AU 2009)**

Solution:

Pointer is a variable that holds the address of other variables or address of a value. Therefore, using pointers we can access the memory locations and the data stored in those memory locations by indirect reference. Thus, pointers not only provide the access to the memory location, but also provide a method for dynamic memory allocation. They are the most useful and strongest feature of C. In fact, a pointer can point to any type of data item or a function.

Operators associated with pointers:

(a) A pointer is also a variable, therefore, the declaration of a pointer variable is similar to that of a normal variable except for the addition of the unary `*` character. This symbol informs the compiler that the variable is a pointer variable. The `*` (asterisk) means "pointer to". For example, `int *ptr;`

(b) "Address of operator" is a unary operator that returns the address of the variable following it. Since it is a unary operator, it requires only one operand and so it is represented by using the ampersand sign (&) followed by the variable name. For example, `ptr=&sample;`

(c) "Indirection operator" is a unary operator that returns the contents stored at the memory location (address). It is also called "value at operator" or "dereference operator". This operator can be represented by a combination of `*` with a variable. For example, `ptr=&sample;`

Pointers can be implemented in the following ways:

(a) **Pointers and arrays:** In C, arrays and pointers are closely related. In fact the versatility of pointers is established due to their ability to handle arrays. In C the array name acts as a pointer be-cause the array name always refers to the address of first element of the array. So we can say that array name is a pointer which holds the address of its first element.

(b) **Pointers and strings:** Pointers are very useful for the string manipulations as they make the manipulation of strings much easier. Pointers are used to perform various string operations such as string copy, string length, string concatenate, string compare, etc. In fact we can easily exchange the position of strings in the array using pointers.

(c) **Pointers and functions:** Just like the normal arguments, functions can also have pointers as arguments. When we call a function we have to pass the address of the variable which can be stored in the corresponding pointer variables. In this mode of parameter passing, we pass the addresses to the function. It is similar to the call by reference in the sense that in this method also the changes in formal parameters are reflected in actual parameters.

- **Function returning a pointer:** Functions can return any data type; they can also return a pointer variable.
- **Pointer to a function:** A pointer to function is just like a normal pointer. It contains the address of the function, that is, the value of pointer to function is the address of the function name. Since the name itself is a pointer, therefore it is a constant pointer. A pointer to a function is declared as a pointer to the data type by the function, like `void`, `int`, `float`, etc. By using the pointer to function technique, we can pass the function as argument to another function.

(d) **Pointer to void:** The pointer is a variable which can hold the address of some another variable of same type. In other words if `ptr` is an `int` pointer then it can hold the value of `int` type. So the address we put into the pointer must be the same type as the pointer. We cannot assign the address of a `float` variable to an `int` pointer. `void` pointer is a special type of pointer which can point to any data type.

(e) **Pointer to a structure:** Pointer to a structure is useful in accessing all the members of the structure using arrow (->) op-erator.

5. *Explain about the different parameter passing methods with examples.* **(AU 2009)**

Solution:

The parameters can be passed to the function in two ways:

(a) **Call by value:** In this mode of parameter passing the values of actual parameters are copied into formal parameters (temporary variable). The function does not have access to the actual param-eters (original values) and can work only on the copies of the values created as formal parameters. In this method, changes made in the formal parameter do not get reflected in the actual parameter even if the names of actual and formal parameters are same. So this method is useful when we want to keep the values of actual parameters intact.

(b) **Call by reference:** In this mode of parameter passing, instead of passing the value to a function, a reference or the alias to the actual parameter is passed. Therefore, the actual parameters can be accessed by two names, the original name and the alias or reference name. When a function is called then the formal parameter becomes a reference to the actual parameter. In this method of pa-rameter passing, actual parameters are referred by another name (formal parameter), therefore the changes made in the formal parameters are reflected in the actual parameters. This implies that call by reference is useful when we want to change the values of the actual parameter in case formal pa-rameters change their values.

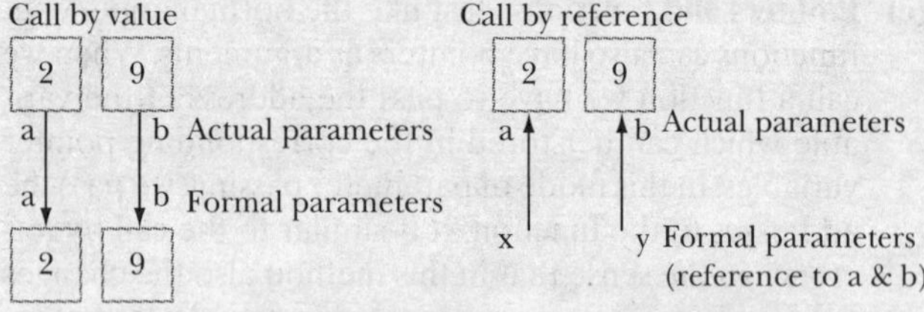

13. *How is a pointer variable initialized?*

Solution:

The pointer variable needs to be initialized and if the address of base data type variable is not assigned to the pointer variable, it may be initialized with null. It is important that the variable whose address is assigned to a pointer variable is declared first. The general rules for assigning value to the pointer variable are the same as that of any other variable data type. For example,

```
char X;
char *ptr1,*ptr2;
```

Here we can assign address of char variable to ptr1 and ptr2 so

(a) `ptr1=&X;` the memory address of X is assigned to ptr1.

(b) `ptr2=&X;` the memory address X is assigned to ptr2.

(c) `*ptr1='Y';` the character Y is assigned to the location pointed by ptr1.

14. *Explain call by reference with suitable examples.*

Solution:

C uses call by reference by passing an alias to an argument, instead of argument itself. In this mode of parameter passing instead of passing the value to a function, a reference or the alias to the actual parameter is passed. Therefore, the actual parameters can be accessed by two names, the original name and the alias or reference name. When a function is called then the formal parameter becomes a reference to the actual parameter. In this method of parameter passing, actual parameters are referred by another name (formal parameter); therefore the changes made in the formal parameters are reflected in the actual parameters. This implies that call by reference is useful when we want to change the values of the actual parameters in case formal parameters change their values.

This can be easily understood considering the following program to calculate swap to number using call by reference method.

```
#include<stdio.h>
#include<conio.h>
void swap (int &, int &);
void main()
{
clrscr();
int a=2,b=9;
printf("\nThe a value before swap is\t
%d",a);
printf("\nThe b value after swap is\t
%d",b);
swap(i,j);
printf("\nThe a value before swap is\t
%d",a);
printf("\nThe b value after swap is\t
%d",b);
}
void swap (int &x, int &y)/*&x and &y are
reference variables */
{
int temp;
temp=x;
x=y;
y=temp;
}
Output
The a value before swap is 2
The b value before swap is 9
The a value after swap is  2
The b value after swap is  9
```

Programming Assignments

3. *Write a program in C that reads a list of student records and counts the number of male students in the list.* **(AU 2009 Suppl.)**

Solution:

```
#include<stdio.h>
#include<conio.h>
#include<string.h>
#include<stdlib.h>
struct student{
int rollno;
char name[15];
char gender[5];
};
int findAllMales(int number, struct student
stud[])
{
int i,j=0;
for(i=1;i<=number;i++)
{
if(strcmp(stud[i].gender,"M")==0)
{
j++;
}
}
return j;
}
void getData(int number, struct student
stud[]){
int i;
printf("\nEnter student data\n");
for(i=1; i<=number; i++)
{
// storing the data
printf("\n Enter roll number for student
%d:", i);
scanf("%d",&stud[i].rollno);
printf("\n Enter name of student %d:", i);
```

```
scanf(" %[^\n]s",stud[i].name);
printf("\n Enter gender(M/F) of student
%d:",i);
scanf(" %s",stud[i].gender);
}
}
void displayData(int number, struct stu-
dent stud[]){
int i,j;
// Displaying data
printf("\n Rollno\tName\tGender\n");
for(i=1; i<=number; i++)
{
printf("\n ");
printf("%d\t",stud[i].rollno);
printf("%s\t",stud[i].name);
printf("%s\t",stud[i].gender);
}
printf("\n--------------------------\n");
}
main() /* program which introduces keyboard
input */
{
int number,numberOfMales;
printf("Keying in student data and then
display-ing\n");
printf("----------------------------\n");
printf("\n Enter number of students:");
scanf("%d",&number);
struct student *stud = (struct student*)
malloc(sizeof(struct student) * number);
getData(number,stud);
numberOfMales = findAllMales(number,stud);
printf("Displaying data\n");
printf("----------------------------\n");
displayData(number,stud);
printf("\n There are %d male students",
numberOfMales);
getch();
}
```

```
C:\Users\fathimazishan\Desktop\CPrograms\FileHandling5.exe
Keying in student data and then displaying

 Enter number of students:4
Enter student data
Enter roll number for student1:1299
Enter name of student1:Mary
Enter gender(M/F) of student1:F
Enter roll number for student2:1233
Enter name of student2:Tony
Enter gender(M/F) of student2:M
Enter roll number for student3:1234
Enter name of student3:Sam
Enter gender(M/F) of student3:M
Enter roll number for student4:1235
Enter name of student4:Bill
Enter gender(M/F) of student4:M
Displaying data

 Rollno Name    Gender

 1299   Mary    F
 1233   Tony    M
 1234   Sam     M
 1235   Bill    M

 There are 3 male students
```

9. *Write a C program To evaluate the following series.* **(AU 2009, 2010, 2012)**

$$e = 1 + \frac{1}{1!} + \frac{1}{2!} + \frac{1}{3!} + \frac{1}{4!} + \ldots\ldots\ldots\ldots + \frac{1}{n!}.$$

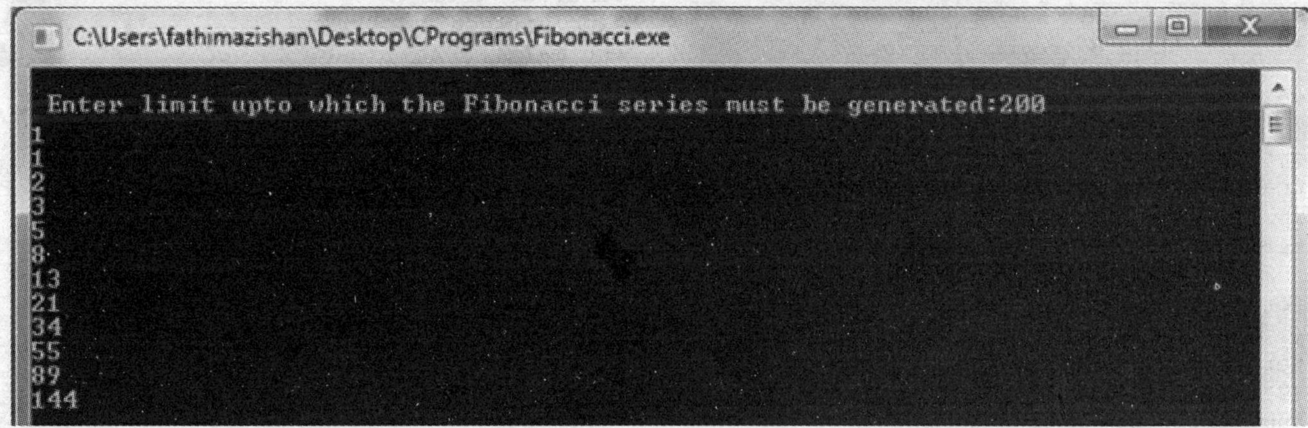

Solution:

```
# include <stdio.h>
#include<conio.h>
int factorial(int number)
{
int fact;
if (num-ber==1){
return (1);
}
else{
fact=number*factorial(number-1);
}
return (fact);
}
double calculateSeries(int n)
{
double e = 0.0;
int i;
e = e + 1;
for(i=1;i<=n;i++)
{
e = e + (1.0/factorial(i));
}
return e;
}
int main(){
int n;
float e;
```

```
printf("\n Upto how many terms do you want
to calcu-late:");
scanf("%d",&n);
e = calculateSeries(n);
printf("\n Value of e = %.15lf",e);
getch();
}
```

C:\Users\fathimazishan\Desktop\CPrograms\Seriesfactoriale.exe

```
Upto how many terms do you want to calculate:4
Value of e = 2.708333253860474_
```

10. *Write a program to evaluate the following series*

$$\sin x = x - \frac{x^3}{3!} + \frac{x^5}{5!} - \frac{x^7}{7!} + \ldots + \frac{x^n}{n!}$$ **(AU 2013)**

Solution:

```
#include<stdio.h>
#include<conio.h>
#include<math.h>
floatsum_sineseries(float x, int n);
void main()
{
int n;
float x, val, sum;
printf("Enter the value of x in degrees");
scanf("%f",&x);
printf("Enter the number of terms for which
sum of the series is to be calculated);
scanf("%d",&n);
val=x;
sum=sum_sineseries(x,n);
printf("The sum of the sine series for %f
is %f",val,sum);
}
void sum_sineseries(float x, int n);
{
int i;
float term,sum_series;
x=x*3.14159/180;
term=x;
sum_series=x;
for(i=1;i<n+1;i++)
{
term=(term*pow((double)(-1),(double)
(2*i-1))*x*x)/(2*i*(2*i+1));
sum_series=sum_series+term;
}
return sum_series;
}
```

11. *Write a C program to find the sum of the series:*

$$S = 1 + \frac{x}{1!} + \frac{x^2}{2!} + \frac{x^3}{3!} + \ldots \frac{x^n}{n!}$$ **(AU 2009)**

Solution:

```
#include<stdio.h>
#include<conio.h>
int main()
{
int i, x, n, f;
float sum = 1.0;
printf("Enter the number of terms of the
se-ries");
scanf("%d", n);
for(i=1;i<n;i++)
{
f=fact(i);
x=pow(x, i);
sum=sum+(x/f);
}
printf("The sum of the series is =%f", sum);
getch()
}
int fact(int x)
{
int f;
if(x==1)
return (1)
else
f=x*fact(x-1);
return (f)
}
```

12. *Write a C program to compute the following function:* $S = (x^2 + x^4 + \ldots + x^{2n}) = Sqrt(x) * (1\text{-}power(x,n))/(1\text{-}x)$. *Trace the program for the values x = 2 and n = 5.* **(AU 2010 Suppl.)**

Solution:

(Result is approximate not accurate)

```
#include<stdio.h>
#include <math.h>
#include<conio.h>
int main(){
int n,i,x;
double total = 0.0,result;
printf("\n Enter number of terms n:");
scanf("%d",&n);
printf("\n Enter value of x:");
scanf("%d",&x);
for(i=2; i<=n;i++){
if(i%2 == 0){
total = total + pow(x,i);
}
}
printf("\n LHS = %f",total);
result = sqrt(x) * (1-pow(x,n))/(1-x);
printf("\n RHS = %f",result);
getch();
}
```

C:\Users\fathimazishan\Desktop\CPrograms\SeriesCheckExpression.exe

```
Enter number of terms n:5
Enter value of x:2
LHS = 20.000000
RHS = 43.840620_
```

13. *Write a C program to perform string operations without using string library functions and using pointers.* **(AU 2007 Suppl.)**

(a) *Find the length of a given string.*

(b) *String copy.*

(c) *String concatenate.*

Solution

(a) To find length of string without using strlen() using pointers.

```
#include<stdio.h>
#include<conio.h>
int length(char*);
void main()
{
char str[100];
int len;
printf("\nEnter a string:");
gets(str);
len=length(str);
printf("\nThe length of the entered string
%s is %d",str,len);
}
int length(char *pt)
{
int l=0;
while(*pt!='\0')
{
l++;
s1++;
}
return l;
}
```

Output
Enter a string: AFTERNOON
The length of the entered string AFTERNOON is 10

(b) To copy a string to another without using strcpy() using pointers.

```
#include<stdio.h>
#include<conio.h>
char* cpy(char*dest,char* scr);
void main()
{
char src[100],dest[100];
printf("\nEnter the source string:");
gets(src);
cpy(dest,src);
printf("\nThe copied string is:");
puts(src);
}
char* cpy(char *dest,char *src)
{
int i=0;
while(src[i]!='\0')
{
dest[i]=src[i];
i++;
}
dest[i]='\0';
return dest;
}
```

Output
Enter the source string: AFTERNOON
The copied string is: AFTERNOON

(c) To concatenate a string to another without using strcat() using pointers.

```
#include<stdio.h>
#include<stdlib.h>
#include<conio.h>
char* concatenateStrings(char *str1, char
*str2)
{
int i=0;
while(str1[i])
i++;
int j=i;
while(str2[j])
j++;
char *str=(char*)malloc(j*sizeof(char));
i= 0;
while(str1[i])
{
str[i]=str1[i];
i++;
}
j=0;
while(str2[j])
{
str[i+j]=str2[j];
j++;
}
str[i+j]='\0';
return str;
}
int main()
{
char *str1;
char *str2;
char *str3;
str1=(char *)malloc(100*sizeof(char));
str2=(char *)malloc(100*sizeof(char));
printf("Enter the first String\n");
scanf("%s",str1);
printf("Enter the second String\n");
scanf("%s",str2);
str3=concatenateStrings(str1,str2);
printf("the final string is : %s\n", str3);
getch();
}
```

```
C:\Users\fathimazishan\Desktop\CPrograms\stringconcatenation.exe
Enter the first String
Love
Enter the second String
India
the final string is : LoveIndia
```

Chapter 6: Structures and Unions

Review Questions

2. *Explain about structures and unions with suitable examples.* **(AU 2009)**

Solution:

(a) Structure: It is a collection of different types of data elements which are related together. The data items in a structure are called the members of the structure. In other words we can say that the similar or different data types can be grouped to form a structure to represent the single entity. For example, suppose we want to represent the complex number. We know that each complex number will have the two components: Real and Imag. If both components may be of integer type then should we represent complex number as an array? The answer is No. This is because although complex number is a collection of two integer numbers (Real and Imag), these two integer numbers together make a single unit which is the complex number.

The structure variable cannot read or write the values in the single command. For example, if X is a structure variable,

```
scanf(%d,&X);
```

This statement produces error since a single statement cannot read the values for all members of X.

Each member of a structure is accessed by using three components: a variable name followed by a dot, and then the member name. Once the structure variable is defined, its members can be accessed by using **dot operator**. For example,

```
bdate.month=10;
X.price=340.5;
X.pubyear=2012;
```

The structure variable `bdate` is followed by a dot and the field name or member name (month). Similarly, the structure variable name `X` is followed by dot, then the member name (`price` or `pubyear`). The format for the dot operator is as follows:

```
structure variable.member name;
```

The structure variable can be initialized in the same way as variables of other data types are initialized. The only thing that we must keep in mind when structure variable is initialized; the values assigned to the members must be in the same order in which they are declared in the structure. For example

```
book X = {"Computers","ABC", "WILEY",
2012, 250.95};
```

Here `X` is a variable of `book` type whose members are initialized as

```
X.title="Computers"
X.author="ABC"
X.publication="WILEY"
X.pubyear=2012
X.price=250.95
```

Hence, the compiler not only allocates the memory but also stores values into the structure members.

Structures can be implemented in various ways:

- **Array within structure:** Like the simple data type, an array can also be a member of a structure. When a structure consists of array elements, they are treated in the same way as normal arrays are treated. The array elements of a structure are also accessed by using the dot operator.
- **Array of structures:** As we already know that an array is a collection of similar data items. The collection of same structure type of variables is called array of structure. To declare an array of structure, we have to first define the structure and then we can define the array of that structure type.
- **Nested structures:** When a structure is declared as a member of another structure, then it is called a nested structure. Structures can be nested to any depth.
- **Function and structure:** The structure variables can also be passed to the function in two ways (call by value and call by reference) just like other variables. When the structure variable is passed by using call by value, the actual parameters are not changed if formal parameters are changed. When the structure variables are passed by using call by reference, then the changes made in the formal parameters are also reflected in the actual parameters. The function can return a structure also. The structures are generally defined as global declaration, so that structure tag can be used in any function. Apart from passing the whole structure variable, we can also pass the individual structure elements in two ways: call by value and call by reference.

(b) Union: It is similar to structure in the sense that it is also a collection of different types of data. The difference between the two is that union stores values of different types in a single location and each member of the structure has its own storage location.In union, space is reserved for the largest data type only. Therefore, union provides a way to manipulate different kinds of data in a single area of storage. If a new assignment is made, the previous value is automatically erased. Like nested struc-tures, we can have one **union within** another **union**, or a **union within** a **structure**.

For example, the following program is used to find the size of union and the number of bytes reserved for it.

```
#include<stdio.h>
#include<conio.h>
union techno
{
    int id; //4 bytes for int
    char nm[50]; //50 bytes for char and
    2 bytes for padding
}tch;
int main()
{
    printf("\n  Size  of  Union  and
    the  number  of  bytes  reserved:%d
    bytes",sizeof(union techno));
    getch();
}
```

```
C:\Users\fathimazishan\Desktop\CPrograms\unionsample.exe
Size of Union and the number of bytes reserved:52 bytes
```

3. *Describe with example: (a) Declaring a structure, (b) pointer to multidimensional array and (c) union.* **(AU 2011)**

Solution:

(a) Structure declaration: Structure is a collection of different types of data elements which are related together. The data items in a structure are called the members of the structure. The general format for structure declaration in C is as follows:

Syntax

```
struct structure_name
{
data type field 1;
data type field 2;
:
:
:
data type field n;
} variable name;
```

Example:

```
struct book//structure tag
{
char title[20];//first member,a char array
char  author[10];//second  member,a  char
array
char publication [20]; //third member, a
char array
int pubyear; //fourth member, an int
float price //fifth member, float
}var; //end of definition and declaration of
structure variable var
```

(b) Pointer to multidimensional array: If we have an array `A[2][2][3]={{{1,2,4},{5,6,8}},{{11,7,3}, {0,9,12}}};`

then we can represent the allocation of memory for array A as follows:

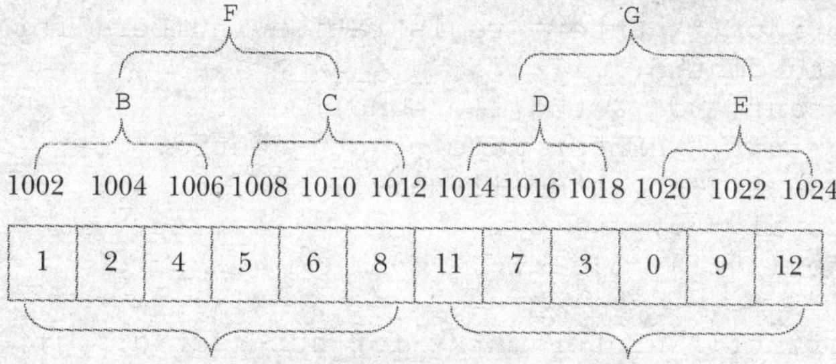

We can say that the three-dimensional array A is a collection of two-dimensional arrays. Here in this example array A is a collection of two-dimensional arrays, F and G, of dimensions 2 × 3 where each element of the two-dimensional arrays is a collection of 2 single-dimensional arrays of 3 elements. So F is a collection of B(1, 2, 4) and C(5, 6, 8)and G is a collection of D(11, 7,3) and E(0, 9, 12). Now

`printf("%d",A);` will produce the base address, that is 1002.

`printf("%d",A+1);` will produce the address of the next element of A that is a two-dimensional array (G). So it will give you the base address of G, that is, 1014.

`printf("%d",*(A+1));` will produce the content at 1014, that is, a two-dimensional array (G). So it will give you the base address of G again that is 1014.

`printf("%d",*(A+1)+1);` will produce the address of the next element of G (at 1014), that is a single-dimensional array (E). So it will give you the base address of E, that is, 1020.

`printf("%d",*(*(A+1)+1));` will produce the content at 1020, that is, a single-dimensional array (E). So it wl give you the base address of E again, that is 1020.

`printf("%d",*(*(A+1)+1)+1));` will produce the address of the next element of E (at 1020), that is 9. So it will give you the base address of 9 which is 1022.

`printf("%d",*(*(*(A+1)+1)+1));` will produce the content at 1022 that is an individual value 9.

`printf("%d",A[1][1][1]);` will also give us 9.

So for three-dimensional arrays we can give the following formula to access the contents:

`A[i][j][k]=*(*(*(A+i)+j)+k)`

Similarly we can formulate the formula for arrays with dimensions more than three.

(c) Refer to part (b) of Review Question 1.

8. *Explain the purpose of storage classes auto, extern, static and register with suitable examples.* **(AU 2008 Suppl.)**

Solution:

The storage class of a variable gives the following information to the compiler: (a) storage size of the variable, the initial value of the variable in case it is not initialized and (b) the scope of the variable and the duration of the variable in which it will be actively used throughout the program. There are four storage classes in C used to define variables:

(a) auto: All local variables that are defined inside a function are auto variables. The keyword auto is optional as by default all variables are treated as auto variables. The scope of the variable is localized to the function in which it is declared. For example,

```
void main()
{int a; /*local variable*/
}
```

(b) extern: All global variables that are defined outside all function blocks to be used throughout the program are external variables. The compiler does not allocate memory while compiling the pro-gram as the memory is allocated in another module when they are declared. For example,

```
int a; /*global variable*/
void main()
{/*function body*/
}
```

In case both auto and extern variables have the same name, then priority is given to the auto variable first.

(c) static: These can be global or local depending upon where the variable is declared. The keyword static is mandatory. Once the variable is declared static, its garbage value is set to null; it is initialized only once in the program, and the last change made to the static variable is retained the next time the program is executed. This helps in finding out how many times the function modifying the static variable has been called. For example,

```
void display();
void main()
{int static a;
a++;
display(a);
)
void display()
printf("\na=%d",a);
}
```

(d) **register:** The keyword register implies that the values of the variables are stored in the reg-isters in the central processing unit (CPU) instead of the memory. Register access is faster than the memory access; however, there are only limited registers in the CPU. If the limit is exceeded, the compiler automatically treats the rest of the variables as automatic variables. For example, the float and double variables cannot be stored in the register as they require more than 16 bits for storage.

```
void main()
{
register int a=10
a--;
while(a!=null)
{printf("a=%d",a);
}
}
```

10. *Write the syntax of structure declaration and give an example.* **(AU 2013)**

Solution:

The general format for structure declaration in C is as follows.

Syntax

```
structure_name
{
data_type field 1;
data_type field 2;
.
.
.
.
data_type field n;
}structure var_name;
```

For example,

```
structure book//structure tag
{
char title[20];//first member, a char array
char author[10];//second member, a char
array
char publication[20];//third member, a char
array
int pubyear;//fourth member, an int
float price//fifth member, an float
}var_name;//end of definition and declara-
tion structure variable var_name
```

The structure variable var_name can also be declared as follows: struct book var_name;

11. *What is storage class? List and explain with example.* **(AU 2014)**

Solution:

A storage class is used to specify the scope of a variable. Further, it also specifies the initial value of the variable in case it is not initialized.The storage class can be external, register, static or auto. Examples are given in the solution to Review Question 8.

Programming Assignments

5. *Define a structure called student that would contain name, reg-no and marks of five subjects and percentage. Write a program to read the details of name, reg-no and marks of five subjects for 30 students, calculate the percentage and display the name, reg-no, marks of 30 subjects and percentage of each student.*

```
#include<stdio.h>
#include<conio.h>
#include<string.h>
#include<stdlib.h>
struct student
{
int regno;
char name[15];
float marks[5];
float percentage;
};
void getData(int number, struct student
stud[]){
int i,j;
float total;
printf("\nEnter student data\n");
for(i=1; i<=number; i++)
{
// storing the data
printf("\nEnter registration number for
stu-dent%d:",i);
scanf("%d",&stud[i].regno);
printf("\nEnter name of stu-dent%d:",i);
scanf("%s",&stud[i].name);
total = 0;
for(j=1;j<=5;j++)
{
printf("\nEnter marks for sub-ject%d:",j);
scanf("%f",&stud[i].marks[j]);
total = total + stud[i].marks[j];
}
stud[i].percentage = (total/500)*100;
}
}
void displayData(int number, struct stu-
dent stud[]){
int i,j;
// Displaying data
printf("\n     Reg-no\tName\tMark1\tMark2\
tMark3\tMark4\tMark5\tPercentage");
for(i=1; i<=number; i++)
{
```

```
printf("\n ");
printf("%d\t",stud[i].regno);
printf("%s\t",stud[i].name);
for(j=1;j<=5;j++)
{
printf("%.2f\t",stud[i].marks[j]);
}
printf("%.2f\t",stud[i].percentage);
}
printf("\n -------------------------------
--------\n");
}
Int main() /* program which introduces key-
board input */
```

```
{
int number = 30;
struct student stud[30];
printf("Keying in student data and then
display-ing\n");
printf("-----------------------------------
-----\n");
getData(number,stud);
printf("Displaying data\n");
printf("-----------------------------------
-----\n");
displayData(number,stud);
getch();
}
```

Output

```
Enter registration number for student29:129

Enter name of student29:Jeff

Enter marks for subject1:75

Enter marks for subject2:83

Enter marks for subject3:89.25

Enter marks for subject4:86

Enter marks for subject5:82

Enter registration number for student30:130

Enter name of student30:Steve

Enter marks for subject1:76

Enter marks for subject2:72

Enter marks for subject3:75

Enter marks for subject4:92

Enter marks for subject5:82
Displaying data
----------------------------------------------

Regno  Name     Mark1   Mark2  Mark3  Mark4   Mark5  Percentage
101    Aisha    100.00  91.50  92.75  89.00   93.65  93.65
102    Arna     92.00   93.50  89.25  75.00   89.95  89.95
103    Mary     97.00   81.50  82.50  89.00   85.40  85.40
104    Sam      87.00   76.50  73.00  85.00   81.80  81.80
104    Victori:83.75    85.00  92.00  77.00   89.50  83.75
106    Evan     86.00   92.00  91.50  77.00   89.10  89.10
107    Mark     77.00   75.50  79.00  82.00   79.70  79.70
108    Alex     76.00   65.00  79.50  82.00   74.50  74.50
109    Monica   93.00   92.00  86.00  70.00   83.30  83.30
110    Isha     75.00   65.00  78.00  72.50   74.07  74.07
111    Stanley  76.00   77.00  82.50  83.75   80.75  80.75
112    Meera    73.00   65.00  62.50  67.50   69.70  69.70
113    Preeti   89.00   92.50  93.45  68.50   82.79  82.79
114    David    72.00   83.00  82.50  99.00   86.30  86.30
115    Tara     85.00   82.50  87.00  79.50   82.80  82.80
116    George   82.00   67.00  68.00  57.00   73.80  73.80
117    Fred     75.00   77.00  85.00  100.00  84.80  84.80
118    Anna     80.00   82.50  82.50  77.00   81.40  81.40
119    Bill     82.50   83.75  87.00  87.50   85.35  85.35
120    Michelle79.25    80.00  84.50  79.50   75.25  79.25
121    Mathew   76.25   89.00  80.00  99.00   84.05  84.05
122    John     73.50   92.50  82.00  85.00   85.20  85.20
123    Leela    65.00   93.45  67.00  70.00   74.09  74.09
124    Sanjay   77.00   68.50  68.00  75.50   73.00  73.00
125    Kadija   95.00   70.50  59.00  77.00   74.90  74.90
126    Mariam   100.00  95.00  95.00  91.50   94.10  94.10
127    Kelly    92.00   99.00  92.00  79.00   86.80  86.80
128    Ryan     72.00   82.50  93.50  79.50   82.50  82.50
129    Jeff     75.00   83.00  89.25  86.00   83.05  83.05
130    Steve    76.00   72.00  75.00  92.00   79.40  79.40
----------------------------------------------
```

Chapter 8: Office Application Software

Review Questions

2 *What are the features of word processor software packages?* (AU 2011, 2013)

Solution:

The various features of MS Word are as follows:

(a) **Editing tools:** Editing involves modification in the text of the active document. The selected text can be cut/copied to the clipboard from which it can be pasted at the required position in the document. Also selected text can be searched and replaced in the active document. Word processors are not only capable of checking spelling mistakes, but also check and suggest alternatives for grammatical errors in the text document. Other tools include tracking changes in text, inserting comments, comparing and protecting documents.

(b) **Formatting tools:** Formatting involves changing the style/presentation of the text in a docu-ment. These tools can be used to change the color of the text font, change the font face, bold face, italicize or underline the selected text, change the size of the selected text or document, highlight the selected text, clear the formatting of a formatted text, draw a line through the middle of the selected text, draw the shadow behind the selected text and adjust the spacing between the characters. Also, the formatting of one place can be set in another place using format painter. Page layout plays very important role in formatting the document. The user may select the Page Setup group and set the margin size for the entire document, the orientation of the page, the page background color, page border color, etc.

(c) **Paragraph adjustment tools:** Paragraph adjustment involves adjustment of text in a certain manner on the document. These tools are used to arrange the text in the form of bulleted list, numbered list, to align the text to left, center, right or justified (left and right both), specify the line spacing, decrease or increase the indent level of paragraphs, split the text into two or more columns, align the text within the text box (wrap text), etc.

(d) **Inserting elements:** Several graphical, multimedia and other elements can be inserted to expand the usability and enhance the presentation of the document, such as cover page, tables through conversion of text into table, illustrations (pictures, clipart, shapes, chart), hyperlinks, header, footer, page numbers for east tracking, textboxes, decorative text (WordArt), date, time, symbols, equations, etc.

(e) **Effective storage:** Documents in a word processor can be autosaved and autorecovered in emergency cases to retrieve documents. Also, a feature can be built for storage and retrieval of several blocks of text.

(f) **Creating reference tools:** Based on the text in the document set in a predefined format, several reference tools such as table of content, footnotes, citation and bibliography, captions and index can be created. These are useful while dealing with books, journal articles and periodicals.

(g) **Mail merge:** This facility helps in creating, printing the envelope, creating a form of letters, email messages, envelopes which the user wants to send to different recipients and specifying the rules to enable decision-making ability in the mail merge.

(h) **Viewing options and setting macros:** This facility helps in setting the document view, viewing more than one document simultaneously; showing or hiding the ruler bar, document map, gridlines; zooming in and zooming out for particular portions of the document requiring more focus. Creating macro (setting shortcuts to perform frequent tasks) or accessing other existing macros options, etc. promotes flexible and efficient use.

10. *Explain the salient features of Office packages.* (AU 2013)

Solution:

Refer sections 8.2.3, 8.3.3 and 8.4.3 for details.

12 *Explain creation of tables and operations that can be performed on table using word processor.* (AU 2009 Suppl.)

Solution:

In MS Word, tables are created using the Table group () from the Insert tab. This group consists of a drop-down list containing various options such as create table, draw table, convert text to table, Excel spreadsheet and quick tables in the active document. When the table is created, it asks for the number of rows and columns to be created for the table.

Step 1: For creating a table, select Insert from the menu, and click on Table.

Step 2: Some pre-defined tables will appear, which can be chosen or a customized table with user-defined rows and columns can be created.

Step 3: The table is created on the main document at the position in which the cursor was positioned. Details can be filled accordingly.

Step 4: In case any row/column of the table needs to be deleted, then right-click on the table and select the appropriate option of inserting/deleting row above or below.

Once the table is created, it can be modified/formatted using the Table Tools option containing design and layout tabs as shown:

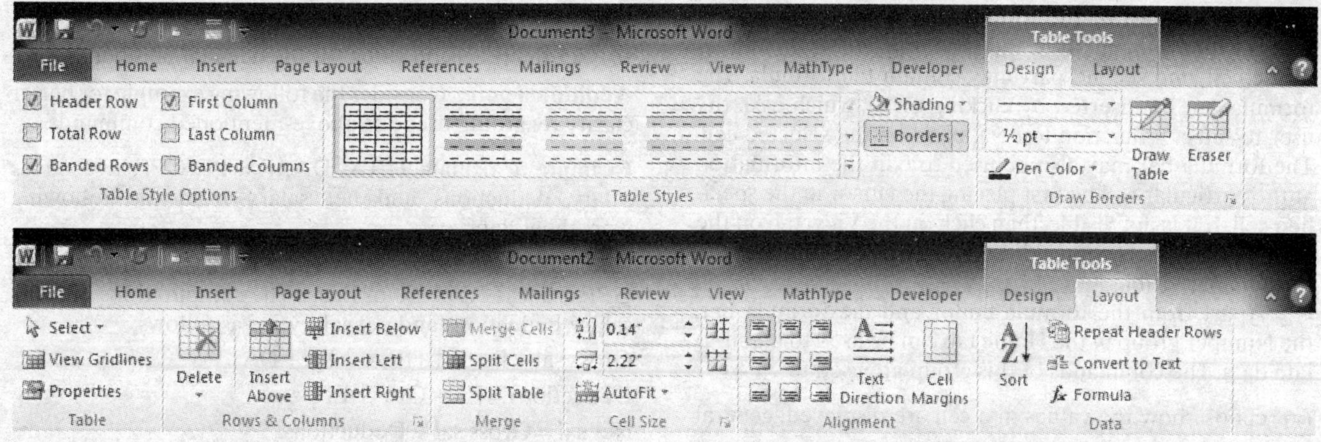

13 *Briefly explain the use of spreadsheet as all accounting software.* **(AU 2009 Suppl.)**

Solution:

Formula Editor feature of MS Excel is useful for calculations involved in accounting. The formulas tab consists of several groups such as function library, defined names, formula auditing and calculation as shown:

These groups are collection of various commands that basically deal with applying different kinds of formula to

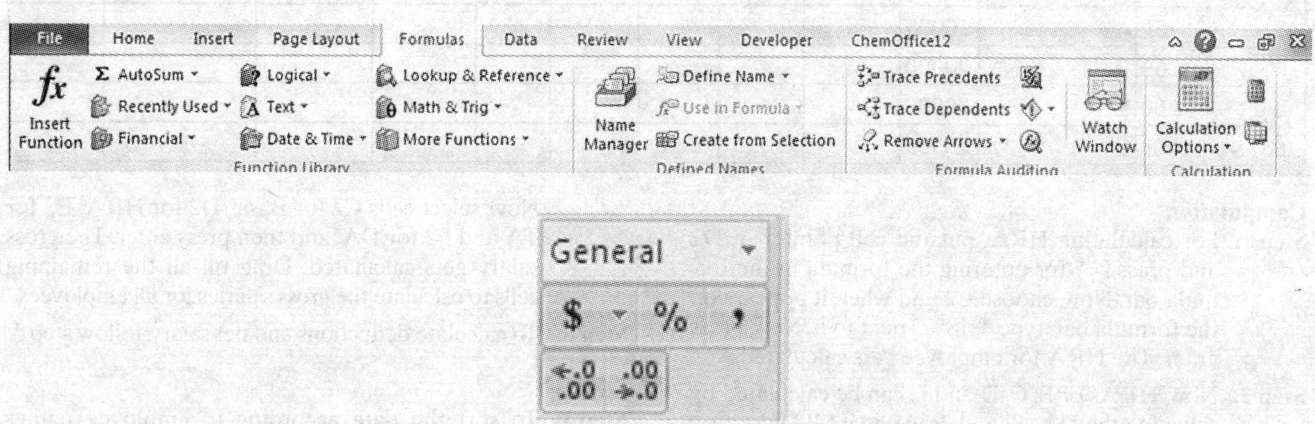

the selected cell, defining the names to the cells instead of cell address, etc. The descriptions of the commands of various groups are summarized as follows:

(a) Function Library: The commands of this group are used to calculate the sum of the selected cells and display it just after the selected cell; browse and select from the recently used functions or financial functions, logical functions, etc.

(b) Defined Names: The commands of this group are used to name a particular cell. So the name may be used in the formula instead of the cell address. This is also used to create, edit, delete and find all the names used in the worksheet.

(c) Formula Auditing: The commands of this group are used to show the arrows to indicate what cells affect the value of the current selected cell; indicate what cells are affected by the value of the currently selected cell; remove the arrows shown by above two selection; show the formula instead of the value, check the common errors and evaluate the formula; monitor the changes in the cells and display the changes in the separate window.

(d) Calculation: This command is used to specify when the formulas are to be calculated, either calculate the complete workbook now or calculate the current sheet now.

The formula bar is located just below the Ribbon and is divided into two parts as shown:

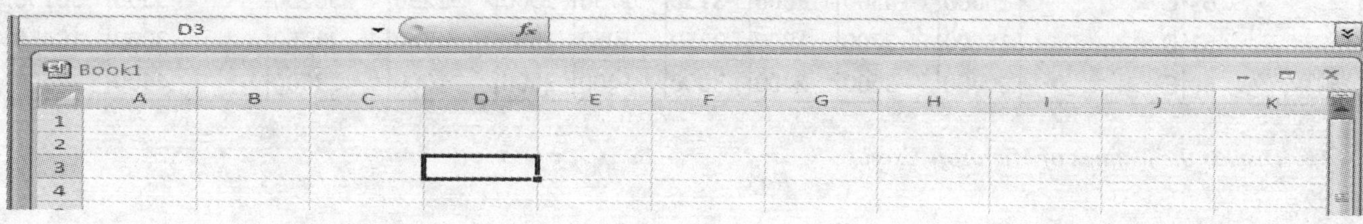

The first part of the formula bar located on the left side is called as name box and it contains the cell address of the cell, and second part may contain the formula. The formula can be inserted by clicking on (), which asks the user to select a function to be applied on the selected cell. The formula bar may also be used to edit the information at the particular cell by first placing the cursor in the specified cell. If it is not visible, then click on the View tab on the Ribbon and select Show/Hide group, click it to make the formula bar visible.

Apart from the formula editor and the formula bar, the Number group in the Home tab can be used to manipulate data. The commands of this group are used to

(a) choose how the values in a cell are displayed, general currency, data, time, percentage, etc.

(b) choose the currency format (dollar, euro, etc.) for the currency value in the cell.

(c) display many values in the cell with separators.

(d) set the precision value for the decimal number.

Additional note: Consider the following example for better clarity regarding usage of above-mentioned commands.

Example: Calculate HRA, DA, TA, PF, GPF, LIC, gross salary, deductions and net salary from the following worksheet data:

where HRA is 18%, DA is 15%, TA is 12%, PF is 10%, GPF is 5%, LIC is 7% of Basic. The computations of gross salary, deductions and net salary are as follows:

Gross sal = Basic + HRA + TA + DA

Deductions = PF + GPF + LIC

Net sal = Gross sal – Deductions.

Also, sort the employee names in alphabetical order.

	A	B	C	D	E	F	G	H	I	J	K	L
1	Emp. No.	Emp. Name	Basic	HRA	TA	DA	LIC	PF	GPF	Gross sal	Deductions	Net sal
2	51	D	15000									
3	52	A	10000									
4	69	B	20000									
5	60	E	20000									
6	63	C	25000									

Computation

Step 1: For calculating HRA, put the cell pointer in D2 and press "=" for entering the formula in the formula bar. Now, choose C2 and when it appears on the formula bar, type "*18%" next to it. Now, press enter. The HRA for employee A is calculated.

Step 2: Now, HRAs of B, C, D and E can be calculated by selecting the D2 cell and dragging it till D6.

Step 3: For calculating TA, similar procedure as in step 1 is followed, except that E2 cell is selected and "*15%" is typed on the formula bar next to C2. To calculate TA's for all the employees, select E2 and drag it till E6.

Step 4: Similar steps can be followed for calculation of DA, PF, GPF and LIC.

Step 5: For calculation of gross salary, place the cell pointer at J2 and press "=" to enter into the formula bar. Now, select cells C2 for Basic, D2 for HRA, E2 for TA and F2 for DA, and then press enter. The gross salary gets calculated. Drag till all the remaining cells to calculate the gross salaries for all employees.

Step 6: To calculate deductions and net salary, follow step 5.

Sorting

Step 1: To sort the data according to employee names in alphabetical order, select all the data in the worksheet, and click Data tab on the menu. Now, choose Sort from the Sort & Filter group.

Step 2: The Sort dialog box appears, choose Sort by as name, and order as A to Z.

Step 3: Click OK. The worksheet now gets sorted in alphabetic order of employee names.

	A	B	C	D	E	F	G	H	I	J	K	L
1	Emp. No.	Emp. Name	Basic	HRA	TA	DA	LIC	PF	GPF	Gross sal	Deductions	Net sal
2	52	A	10000	1800	1200	1500	700	1000	500	14500	2200	12300
3	69	B	20000	3600	2400	3000	1400	2000	1000	29000	4400	24600
4	63	C	25000	4500	3000	3750	1750	2500	1250	36250	5500	30750
5	51	D	15000	2700	1800	2250	1050	1500	750	21750	3300	18450
6	60	E	20000	3600	2400	3000	1400	2000	1000	29000	4400	24600

16. *Discuss the features of Microsoft Excel.*

(AU 2013)

Solution:

Refer section 8.4.3 for details.

ASCII Set

Appendix B

Non-Printable Characters

Abbreviation	Name	Decimal	Hexadecimal
NUL	Null character (\0)	0	00
SOH	Start of Header	1	01
STX	Start of Text	2	02
ETX	End of Text	3	03
EOT	End of Transmission	4	04
ENQ	Enquiry	5	05
ACK	Acknowledgment	6	06
BEL	Bell (\a)	7	07
BS	Backspace (\b)	8	08
HT	Horizontal Tab (\t)	9	09
LF	Line feed (\n)	10	0A
VT	Vertical Tab (\v)	11	0B
FF	Form feed (\f)	12	0C
CR	Carriage return (\r)	13	0D
SO	Shift Out	14	0E
SI	Shift In	15	0F
DLE	Data Link Escape	16	10
DC1	Device Control 1 (oft. XON)	17	11
DC2	Device Control 2	18	12
DC3	Device Control 3 (oft. XOFF)	19	13
DC4	Device Control 4	20	14
NAK	Negative Acknowledgement	21	15
SYN	Synchronous idle	22	16
ETB	End of Transmission Block	23	17
CAN	Cancel	24	18
EM	End of Medium	25	19
SUB	Substitute	26	1A
ESC	Escape (\e)	27	1B
FS	File Separator	28	1C
GS	Group Separator	29	1D
RS	Record Separator	30	1E
US	Unit Separator	31	1F
DEL	Delete[k][e]	127	7F

Printable Characters

Character	Dec	Hex	Character	Dec	Hex	Character	Dec	Hex
sp	32	20	@	64	40	`	96	60
!	33	21	A	65	41	a	97	61
“	34	22	B	66	42	b	98	62
#	35	23	C	67	43	c	99	63
$	36	24	D	68	44	d	100	64
%	37	25	E	69	45	e	101	65
&	38	26	F	70	46	f	102	66
‘	39	27	G	71	47	g	103	67
(	40	28	H	72	48	h	104	68
)	41	29	I	73	49	i	105	69
*	42	2A	J	74	4A	j	106	6A
+	43	2B	K	75	4B	k	107	6B
,	44	2C	L	76	4C	l	108	6C
-	45	2D	M	77	4D	m	109	6D
.	46	2E	N	78	4E	n	110	6E
/	47	2F	O	79	4F	o	111	6F
0	48	30	P	80	50	p	112	70
1	49	31	Q	81	51	q	113	71
2	50	32	R	82	52	r	114	72
3	51	33	S	83	53	s	115	73
4	52	34	T	84	54	t	116	74
5	53	35	U	85	55	u	117	75
6	54	36	V	86	56	v	118	76
7	55	37	W	87	57	w	119	77
8	56	38	X	88	58	x	120	78
9	57	39	Y	89	59	y	121	79
:	58	3A	Z	90	5A	z	122	7A
;	59	3B	[	91	5B	{	123	7B
<	60	3C	\	92	5C	|	124	7C
=	61	3D	]	93	5D	}	125	7D
>	62	3E	^	94	5E	~	126	7E
?	63	3F	_	95	5F			

Appendix C

Header Files and Standard Library Functions

Type	Function	Description
		stdio.h
	`fclose (f)`	To close a file and return **0** if file is successfully closed.
File I/O operations	`feof(f)`	To determine whether end of the file has been reached, and return a nonzero value, otherwise return 0.
	`ferror(f)`	To check for a file error on the given stream, and return 0 if nor error is found.
	`*fopen(f1,f2)`	To open a file named **f1** of type **f2**, return a pointer to the file.
	`clearerr(f)`	To reset the error flag associated with the stream to zero.
	`remove(c,f)`	To check whether the file was deleted or not, and return zero for successful deletion.
	`rename(f1,f2)`	To change the name of the file, and return zero if successful.
	`fread(s,x1,x2,f)`	To enter **x2** number of data items, each of size **x1** bytes, from file.
	`fwrite(s,x1,x2,f)`	To send **x2** number of data items, each of size **x1** bytes from string **s** to file.
	`fseek(f,1,i)`	To move the pointer for file a distance **1** bytes from the location **i**.
	`ftell(f)`	To return the current pointer position within file.
	`rewind(f)`	To move the pointer to the beginning of the file.
	`*tmpfile(void)`	To open a temporary binary file for read/write operations, and returns pointer to the stream.
	`*tempname(c,*name)`	To generate a unique filename and stores it in the array pointed to by name.
Formatted I/O functions	`scanf()`	To read input from the standard input device.
	`printf()`	To send output to the standard output device.
	`scanf()`	To read input from the standard input device.
	`sscanf()`	To return value equal to the number of variables that were actually assigned values.
	`sprint()`	To return value equal to the number of characters actually placed into the array.
	`fprintf()`	To send output to a file.
	`fscanf()`	To read data from a file.
Character I/O functions	`fgetc(f)`	To read a single character from a file.
	`fputc(c,f)`	To write a single character to a file.
	`getc(f)`	To read a single character from a file where f is the file pointer pointing the file opened in writing mode. It returns EOF as soon as end of file is reached.
	`getchar(void)`	To read a single character from the standard input device.
	`getch(ch)`	To read alphanumeric data one character at a time from the keyboard.
	`getche(void)`	To read alphanumeric data from the keyboard and display it onto the screen.

(*Continued*)

(Continued)

Type	Function	Description
	`putc(c,f)`	To write a single character to a file where f is the file pointer pointing the file opened in writing mode. It returns EOF as soon as end of file is reached.
	`putchar(c)`	To send a single character to the standard output device.
	`putch(ch)`	To display any alphanumeric data one character at a time from the keyboard input onto the screen.
	`ungetc(ch,f)`	To return the character specified by the low-order byte of **ch** to the input stream.
Integer I/O functions	`getw(fp1)`	To read an integer from the file.
	`putw(i,fp1)`	To write an integer onto the file.
String I/O functions	`gets(s)`	To enter string from the standard input device.
	`puts(s)`	To send string to the standard output device.
	`fgets(s,i,f)`	To read string containing **i** characters, from file.
	`fputs(s,f)`	To write string onto file.
	`cgets(char *p)`	To read string from the keyboard input. It requires character pointer as an argument.
	`cputs(char *p)`	To display string onto the screen. It requires character pointer as an argument.
		stdlib.h
String functions	`atof(s)`	To convert string into double precision.
	`atoi(s)`	To convert string into integer.
	`atol(s)`	To convert string into long integer.
	`strtod(...)`	To convert the string representation of a number stored in the string pointed to by start into double.
	`strtol(...)`	To convert the string representation of a number stored in the string pointed to by start into long int.
	`strtoul(...)`	To convert the string representation long of a number stored in the string pointed to by start into unsigned long int.
Environment control functions	`exit(u)`	To close all files and buffers, and terminate the program.
	`abort(void)`	To cause immediate abnormal termination of a program.
	`atexit(void)`	To check if the function is successfully registered as a termination function, and return zero.
	`system(s)`	To pass command string to the operating system, and return zero it is successfully executed.
	`getenv()`	To search for the environment string pointed to by *name*, and return the associated value to the string.
Memory functions	`*calloc(x1,x2)`	To allocate memory for an array having x1 elements, each of length x2 bytes. It returns a pointer to the beginning.
	`free(p)`	To free a block of allocated memory whose beginning is indicated by p.
	`*malloc(x)`	To allocate x bytes of memory, and return a pointer to the beginning of the allocated space.
	`*realloc(p,x)`	To allocate x bytes of new memory to the pointer variable p, and return a pointer to the beginning of the new memory space.
Math functions	`abs(i)`	To return the absolute value of i.
	`div(d1,d2)`	To return the quotient and the remainder of the operation numerator/denominator in a structure of type div_t.
	`labs(l)`	To return the absolute value of 1.
	`ldiv(d1,d2)`	To return the quotient and remainder of the operation numerator/denominator in an **idiv_t** structure.
	`rand(void)`	To return a random positive integer.
	`srand(u)`	To initialize the random number generator.

(*Continued*)

(Continued)

Type	Function	Description
Multibyte functions	mblen(*str, n)	To return the length of a multibyte character pointed to by the argument *str*. It examines at the most *n* bytes.
	mbstowcs(*pwcs, *str, n)	To convert the string of multibyte characters pointed to by the argument *str* to the array pointed to by *pwcs*. It stores no more than *n* values into the array.
	mbtowc(*pwc, *str, n)	To examine the multibyte character pointed to by the argument *str*, convert the value and store it in the argument *pwc* if *pwc* is not null. It scans at the most *n* bytes.
	wcstombs(*str, *pwcs, n)	To convert the codes stored in the array *pwcs* into multibyte characters and store them in the string *str*. It copies at the most *n* bytes to the string.
	wctomb(*str, wchar)	To examine the code corresponding to multibyte character represented by the argument *wchar*. The code is converted to multibyte character and stored into the string pointed to by the argument *str* if *str* is not null.
		string.h
String functions	*memchr(...)	To search the array pointed to by buffer for the first occurrence of the character in the first count characters.
	memcmp (...)	To compare the first count characters of the arrays pointed to by two pointers, say, f1 and f2.
	*memcopy(...)	To copy characters from the array pointed to by, say, f1 into the array pointed to by, say, f2.
	*memmove(...)	To copy count characters from the array pointed to by, say, f1 into the array pointed to by, say, f2.
	*strchr(...)	To return a pointer to the first occurrence of the low-order byte of ch in the string pointed to by str.
	*strrchr(...)	To return a pointer to the last occurrence of the low- order byte of ch in the string pointed to by str.
	strcmp(s1,s2)	To return a negative value if s1 < s2; 0 if s1 and s2 are identical; and positive value if s1 > s2.
	strncmp(...)	To lexicographically compare not more than count characters from the two null-terminated strings and return integer based on the outcome.
	*strcpy(s1,s2)	To copy string s2 to string s1.
	*strncpy(...)	To copy upto count characters from the string pointed to by converting the string representation of a number stored in the string pointed to by start into a double and returns the result.f2 into the array pointed to by f1.
	*strcat(...)	To concatenate a copy of f2 to f1 and terminate with a null.
	*strncat(...)	To concatenate not more than count characters of the string, pointed to by f2 to the string pointed to by f1 and terminates str1 with a null.
	*strpbrk(...)	To return a pointer to the first character in the string pointed to by f1 matching with any character in the string pointed to by f2.
	*strstr(...)	To return a pointer to the first occurrence in the string pointed to by f1 in the string pointed to by f2.
	strlen(s)	To return the number of characters in string.
	strspn(...)	To return the length of the initial substring of the string pointed to by f1 composed of only those characters contained in the string pointed to by f2.
	strcspn(...)	To return the length of the initial substring of the string pointed to by f1composed of only those characters contained in the string pointed to by f2.
		math.h
Trigonometric functions	acos(x)	To return the arc cosine of x.
	asin(x)	To return the arc sine of x.
	atan(x)	To return the arc tangent of x.
	atan2(x1,x2)	To return the arc tangent of x1/x2.
	cos(x)	To return the cosine of x.
	cosh(x)	To return the are hyperbolic cosine of x.

(*Continued*)

(Continued)

Type	Function	Description
	`sin(x)`	To return the sine of x.
	`sinh(x)`	To return the hyperbolic sine of x.
	`tan(x)`	To return the tangent of x.
	`tanh(x)`	To return the hyperbolic tangent of x.
Exponential functions	`exp(x)`	To raise e to the power x.
	`frexp(...)`	Consists of family of functions that decomposes the number num into a mantissa in the range 0.5 to less than 1.
	`ldexp(...)`	Consists of family of functions that return the value of num*2^{exp}.
Logarithmic functions	`log(x)`	To return the natural logarithm of x.
	`log10(x)`	To return the logarithm (base 10) of x.
Power functions	`pow(x1,x2)`	To return x1 raised to the x2 power.
	`sqrt(x)`	To return square root of x.
Other functions	`ceil(x)`	To return a value rounded up to the next higher integer.
	`fabs(x)`	To return the absolute value of x.
	`floor(x)`	To return a value rounded down to the next lower integer.
	`fmod(x1,x2)`	To return the remainder of x1/x2 (with same sign as x1)
	`modf(...)`	To decompose num into its integer and fractional parts.
		ctype.h
is...functions	`isalnum(c)`	To determine if argument is alphanumeric, and return non-zero value if true.
	`isalpha(c)`	To determine if argument is alphabetic, and return non-zero value if true.
	`isascii(c)`	To determine if argument is an ASCII character, and return non-zero value if true.
	`iscntrl(c)`	To determine if argument is an ASCII control character, and return non-zero value if true.
	`isdigit(c)`	To determine if argument is a decimal digit, and return non-zero value if true.
	`isgraph(c)`	To determine if argument is a graphic printing ASCII character, and return non-zero value if true.
	`isspace(c)`	To determine if argument is in lower case or not, and return non-zero value if true.
	`isupper(c)`	To determine if the argument is an octal digit, and return non-zero value if true.
	`isxdigit(c)`	To determine if the argument is a printing ASCII character, and return non-zero value if true.
	`islower(c)`	To determine if the argument is a punctuation character, and return non-zero value if true.
	`isodigit(c)`	To determine if the argument is a whitespace character, and return non-zero value if true.
	`isprint(c)`	To determine if the argument is in upper case, and return non-zero value if true.
	`ispunct(c)`	To determine if the argument is a hexadecimal digit, and return non-zero value if true.
to...functions	`toascii(c)`	To convert value of the argument to ASCII.
	`tolower(c)`	To convert letter to lowercase.
	`toupper(c)`	To convert letter to uppercase.
		time.h
	`*asctime(...)`	To return a pointer to a string that contains the information stored in the structure pointed to by ptr.
	`clock(void)`	To return a value that approximates the amount of time the calling program has been running.

(Continued)

(Continued)

Type	Function	Description
	`mktime(...)`	To return the calendar-time equivalent of the broken-down time found in the structure pointed to by time.
	`*gtime(...)`	To return a pointer to the broken-down form of time in the form of a **tm** structure.
	`*ctime(...)`	To return a pointer to a string of the form.
	`*localtime(...)`	To return a pointer to the broken down form of time in the form of a **tm** structure. The time is represented in local time.
	`time(t)`	To return the number of seconds elapsed beyond a designated base time.
	`difftime(t1,t2)`	To return the time difference t1 – t2, where t1 and t2 represent the elapsed time beyond a designated base time.

Syntax Statements Appendix D

1. *Declaration and initialization of variables*

Syntax

```
Specifiers data_type variable_name;
```

2. *enumerated data type*

Syntax

```
enum tag{enumeration list} variable list;
or
enum tag{enumeration list}
tag variable name;
```

3. *typedef data type*

Syntax

```
typedef data_type newname;
```

4. *Type conversion*

Syntax

```
(desired data_type) old data_type;
```

5. *Structure of C program*

Syntax

```
Preprocessor directives
Global variable declaration if any
Global constant declaration if any
void main()
{
/*comments*/
local variable declaration;
statements;
function call (parameters);
}
User-defined function (arguments)
{
Function body
}
```

6. *if statement*

Syntax

```
if(expression)
{
  statements;/*body of if*/
}
```

7. *if–else statement*

Syntax

```
if(expression)
{
/*body of if*/
statement 1;
    }
else
{
/*body of else*/
statement 2;
}
```

8. *Ladder if–else statement*

Syntax

```
if(expression)
{
/*body of if*/
statement 1;
  }
else if
{
/*Body of else*/
statement 2;
}
else
{
/*Body of else*/
statement 3;
}
```

9. *Nested if–else statement*

Syntax

```
if(expression)
{
Statement 1;/*body of if statement*/
  if(expression)
       statement 2;
  else
       statement 3;
}
else
{
Statements 4;
}
```

10. *goto statement*

Syntax

```
goto label;
```

11. *switch statement*

Syntax

```
switch (variable or expression)
{
case constant A:
statement;
break;
case constant B:
statement;
break;
default:
statement;
}
```

12. *Nested switch-case*

Syntax

```
switch (variable or expression)
{
case constant A:
statement;
break;
case constant B:
statement;
break;
default:
  switch (variable or expression)
  {
  case constant C:
  statement;
  break;
  case constant D:
  statement;
  break;
  default:
  statement;
  }
}
```

13. *Ternary operator*

Syntax

```
z?a:b
```

If z is true (not zero), then a is returned otherwise b is returned.

14. *for loop*

Syntax

```
for (Initialization; Condition; Updation)
{
/*body of the loop*/
Statements;
}
```

15. *while loop*

Syntax

```
initialization;
while(condition)
{
statements;
updation;
}
```

16. *do-while loop*

Syntax

```
initialization;
do
{
statements;
updation;
} while(condition);
```

17. *Nested for loop*

Syntax

```
for(Initialization; Condition; Updation)
{
/*body of the loop*/
  for(Initialization; Condition; Updation)
  {
  /*body of the loop*/
  Statements;
  }
Statements;
}
```

18. *break statement*

Syntax

```
{
/*body of decision making statement/looping
statement*/
break;
}
```

19. *continue statement*

Syntax

```
{
/*body of decision making statement/loop-
ing statement*/
continue;
}
```

20. *exit statement*

Syntax

```
exit(int)
```

21. *Declaration of one-dimension array*

Syntax

```
storage_class data_type array_name[size];
```

22. *Initialization of one-dimensional array*

Syntax

```
storage_class data_type
array_name[size]={value1,value2.valuesize};
```

23. *Declaration of multidimensional array*

Syntax

Storage_class data_type array_name $[Dim_1]$ $[Dim_2]...[Dim_n]$;

where Dim_1, Dim_2,..., Dim_n are the dimensions of the array.

24. *Declaration of two-dimensional array*

Syntax

```
storage class data_type array name [row]
[col];
```

25. *Function declaration/prototype*

Syntax

```
return_type function_name (individually
declared parameters);
```

26. *Function definition*

Syntax

```
return_type function_name (para 1, para 2,...
para n)
{
body of the function;
}
```

27. *Function call*

Syntax

with no return value

```
function_name (actual parameters);
```

with return value

```
variable/expression = function_name (actual
parameters);
```

28. *Recursive function*

Syntax

```
return type function1 (parameter list)
{
body of the function;
function1()/*function1 directly being
called*/
}
```

or

```
return type function1 (parameter list)
{
body of the function;
function2()/*function2 indirectly being
called*/
}
```

29. *Inline function*

Syntax

```
inline return_type function_name
(parameters);
```

30. *Passing one-dimensional array to function*

Syntax

```
data_type function_name(array_
name[],size);/*function declaration*/
functionname (array_name,size);/*function
call*/
data_type function_name (array_
name[],size)/*function definition*/
{
function body;
}
```

31. *Passing two-dimensional array to function*

Syntax

```
data_type function_name(int array_name[]
[col],int size);/*function declaration*/
function_name(array_name);/*function
call*/
data_type function_name(arrayname[])
/*function definition*/
{
function body;
}
```

32. *Declaring character array*

Syntax

```
storage_class char array_name[size];
```

33. *Initialization of character array*

Syntax

```
char array_name[size]={'element1',' ele-
ment1',..., '\0'};
```

or

```
char array_name[]={'element1',
'element1',…, '\0'};
or
char array_name[]="String";
```

34. *String functions*

Function	Syntax
strlen	strlen(string)
strcpy and strncpy	strcpy (dest,source)
strncpy (dest, source, length)	
strcmp and stricmp	strcmp(S1,S2);
stricmp(S1, S2);	
strlwr and strupr	strlwr(string);
strupr(string);	
strdup	strdup(string);
strchr and strrchr	strchr(string, ch);
strrchr (string, ch);	
strstr	strstr(S1, S2);
strcat	
strncat	strcat(dest, source);
strncat(dest, source, length)	
strrev	strrev(string);
strpbrk	strpbrk(S1, ch);

35. *Macro substitution directive*

Syntax

```
#define identifier substitute_value
```

36. *File inclusion directive*

Syntax

```
#include<filename>
```

37. *Compiler control directive*

Syntax

```
#define identifier substitute_value
#ifdef identifier
{
Statement 1;/*Body of ifdef*/
}
#else
{
Statement 2/*Body of else*/
}
#endif
```

38. *Structure declaration*

```
struct structure_name
{
data_type field1;
data_type field2;
…
data_type fieldn;
}structure_name structure_
varname;/*declaring structure variable*/
```

39. *Accessing members of a structure using dot operator*

Syntax

```
structure variable.member name;
```

40. *Union declaration*

Syntax

```
storage class union union_name
{
datatype member 1;
datatype member 2;
:::
datatype member n;
};
```

41. *Accessing members of a union using dot operator*

Syntax

```
union_name.member_name;
```

42. *Pointer declaration*

Syntax

```
data_type * pointer_variable;
```

43. *Address of operator*

Syntax

```
pointer_variable=&variable_name;
```

44. *Value at operator*

Example

```
printf("%d",*ptr);
```

The (`*ptr`) is read as "the value at the address contained in `ptr`" or the "value at `ptr`".

45. *Pointer Arithmetic*

Pointer arithmetic syntax	Equivalent to
ptr++	ptr=ptr+sizeof(data type)
++ptr	ptr=ptr+sizeof(data type)
ptr--	ptr=ptr-sizeof(data type)
--ptr	ptr=ptr-sizeof(data type)
(*ptr)++	*ptr then *ptr=*ptr+1
*ptr++	*ptr then ptr=ptr+1
* ++ptr	ptr=ptr+1 then *ptr
++ *ptr	*ptr then *ptr=*ptr+1

46. *Arrays of pointers*

Syntax

```
data_type *array name [size];
```

47. *Pointers and strings*

Syntax

```
char *ptr= "Sample string";
```

48. *Pointer and functions*

Syntax

```
return_type function_name(data_type
*variable1,data_type *variable2);
```

49. *Function returning a pointer*

Syntax

```
return_type *function_name(parameters)
```

50. *Pointer to function*

Syntax

```
return_type  (*pointer  variable)(list  of
parameters);
```

51. *Passing a function to another function*

Syntax

```
return_type function_name((*pointer_to_
function),other parameters));
```

52. *Pointer to a pointer*

Syntax

```
data_type *(*pointer variable);
```

53. *Pointer to void*

Syntax

```
void *pointer variable;
```

54. *Pointer to structures and unions*

Syntax

```
structure pointer ->member_name;
union pointer ->member_name;
```

Predicting Outputs and Identifying Errors

Appendix E

Predict the output

1.
```
void main()
{
int y=15,z=25;
function(&y,&z);
printf("%d\t%d",z,y);
getch();
}
function(int *p, int *q)
{
return(*p=(*p+*q)-(*q=*p));
}
```

Output: 1525
This is because the values of y and z get passed to pointer variables *p and *q, respectively. In function(), the operation `*p=(*p+*q)-(*q=*p)` means that *p=(15+25) – (*q = 15) or *p=40 – 15 = 25. Hence *p = 25 and *q = 15 are returned to the main().

2.
```
int main()
{
short int si=16453;
printf("%c", si);
return 0;
}
```
Assume that short int reserves 2 bytes of memory

Output: E
This is because short int si occupying 2 bytes of memory is typecasted to char data type which occupies 1 byte of memory. Thus, only lower order bits from si will be stored in 1 byte, this equals to 69, whose ASCII value is E.

3.
```
int main()
{
float f=0.8;
if(f==0.8)
printf("Good");
else printf("Bad");
return 0;
}
```

Output: Bad
This is because the float f value is compared with double constant in the expression of if statement. The binary equivalent of 0.8 float is not eual to that of 0.8 double, hence the condition in if expression is false.

4.
```
int main()
{
int x=10,y;
y=++x + --x + x++ + x--;
printf("%d",y);
return 0;
}
```

Output: 40
This is because the expression of y is read as y = (++x) + (––x) + (x++) + (x––) = (11)+(9) + (10) + (10) = 20 + 10 + 10 = 40

5.
```
void main()
{
int a=1,b=2,c=3,d;
d=a>b?b>c?5:1:0?a:b++;
printf("%d",d);
}
```

Output: 2
This is because the ternary operator has associativity from right to left and the evaluation of the expression is as follows:
d=a<b?b>c?5:1:0?a:b++ = a<b?b>c?5:1:(0?a:b++)
= a<b?b>c?5:1:b++ = a<b?(b>c?5:1:b++)
= a<b?5:b++ = b++ = 2

6.
```
void main()
{
int x;
char str[80];
scanf("%s", str);
x=strlen(str);
printf("%d",x);
}
```
Assume 123.82 is entered.

Output: 6
This is because the input will be treated as string. The strlen function will find the number of characters in the entered string which is 6 including the decimal point.

7.
```
#define D 20-10
#define A 40-30
void main()
{
```

```
double ratio=D/A;
printf("ratio=%lf\n",ratio);
}
```

Output: `-10.000000`
This is because the evaluation is done as follows:
Ratio=D/A=20 – (10/40) – 30= 20 – 0 – 30 = –10
In double format, –10 becomes –10.000000

8.
```
void main()
{
char *str1= "abcd"
char str2[]= "abcd";
printf("%d %d %d", sizeof(str1),sizeof(s
tr2),sizeof("abcd"));
}
```

Output: 2 5 5
The str1 is a character pointer, so the size of the pointer variable is obtained as 2. In the second and the third sizeof statements, the array size (including the null character) gets displayed.

9.
```
void main()
{
int i=4, j=3, k =5;
printf("%d\t%d\t%d");
}
```

Output: Some garbage value is printed. Since a printf takes values of the first two assignments of the program. In case assignments more than two are made, then a garbage value is taken by printf statement.

10.
```
void main()
{
char str[]="abc";
int i;
for (i=0;str[i]!='\0';i++)
{
printf("\t%c%c%c%c", str[i], *(str+i),
*(i+str),i[str]);
}
}
```

Output: `aaaa   bbbb   cccc`
This is because the expressions str[i], *(str+i), *(i+str),i[str] all mean the same thing, hence in the first iteration all the four expressions are equal to a, so a gets displayed four times.

11.
```
void main()
{
static int var=5;
printf("%d",var--);
if(var);
main();
}
```

Output: 5 4 3 2 1
This is because the static storage class is initialized once, and the value of the static variable is retained even between function calls.

12.
```
void main()
{int i=0;
while(+(+i--!=0)
i-=i++
printf("%d",i);
}
```

Output: `-1`
This is because the unary operator has no effect on the expression, and the expression in the while loop can be read as while(i--!=0) which is false, and the loop is not executed. The output is –1 due to post-decrement operation on i.

13.
```
void main()
{
int a[5]={1};
int b=0, k=0;
for(b=0;b<=4;b++);
{printf("%d",++a[k])
}
}
```

Output: 2 3 4 5 6
This is because the ++a[k] operation can be read as ++a[0] as k = 0. Now, a[0] = 1 so each time the loop is run, the value of a[0] that is 1 is incremented by 1.

14.
```
void main()
int c[]={2.8, 3.4, 4, 6.7, 5};
int i, *p=c,*q=c;
for(i=0;i<5;i++)
{
printf("%d",*c);
++q;
}
for(i=0;i<5;i++)
{
printf("%d",*p);
++p;
}
```

Output: 2 2 2 2 2 2 3 4 6 5
This is because in the first loop, only pointer q is incremented, not c. Hence the value of c, that is, c[0] will be displayed 5 times. In the second loop, *p is included in the printf statement and not *c, so the integer values 2, 3, 4, 6 and 5 are displayed.

15.
```
int i;
void main()
{
int t;
for(t=4;scanf("%d",&i)-t;printf("%d\n",i))
{
printf("%d--", t--);
}
```

Assume inputs are 0, 1, 2, 3.

Output:
```
4--0
3--1
2--2
```
The dry run table is as follows:

t	i	x
4	0	4
3	1	–2
2	2	0

Identify the Error(s)

1.
```
main{}
{
float x; x=25;
y=exp(x);
/*Printing section*/
print(x,y)
}
```

Error: The "main" function should have () instead of {}
The variable x can be declared and defined in a single sentence, and the given value of x is an integer,hence the correct statement is `int x=25;`
The variable y is not declared, hence it needs to be declared after the declaration of x as `float y;`
The printf statement should be used for printing, the format of the output should be specified and the statement should terminate with a semicolon. The correct statement for displaying the output is `printf("%d %f", x,y);`

2.
```
void main()
{
struct book
{
int pages;
float price;
}*p;
p.pages=200;
p.price=250;
printf("\nPages = %d", p.pages);
printf("\nPrice = %d", p.price);
}
```

Error: Since p is a pointer of book type, to access members of the structure book, → (arrow) operator must be used as `p→pages=200;`

3.
```
void main()
{
int a[5]=[4,3,2,1,0];
int i, result=1;
for(i=0;i>=5;i++)
result=result*a[i];
printf("\nresult of multiplication=%d",
result);
getche();
}
```

Error: The compiler would not show any error; however, the output will be a garbage value, as the for loop should be from 0 to 4.

4.
```
void main()
{
int a[]={1,8,9,0,8};
for(i=0;i<9;i++)
{printf("d", a[i]);
}
}
```

Error: The for loop should be from 0 to 4 instead of 0 to 8 as the attempt to read more elements than declared in an array will result in error.

5.
```
void main()
{
void func1(), func2;
func1();
}
void func1()
{
printf("In func1");
func2();
}
void func2()
{
printf("In func2");
func1();
}
```

Error: There is infinite recursion with the functions func1 and func2 calling each other.

6.
```
void main()
{
void f();
f(5.6);
}
void f(float a)
{
printf("%f", a);
}
```

Error: This results in function prototype error as there is no mention of the float variable a being passed as argument of function f in the prototype.

7.
```
void main()
{
struct a
{
int a=9;
char text[]="hello";
};
struct *p;
printf("%d", p→a);
printf("%s", p→text);
}
```

Error: Initialization of structure variables cannot be done inside the structure.

8.
```
void main()
{
int i=5;
printf("%d", i++i++);
}
```

Error: The combination of operators is wrong.

9.
```
void main()
{
int argc =10;
char argv;
int sum(int num1, int num2);
printf("Enter a character");
getchar();
sum(argv, argc);
printf("%d", sum);
}
int sum(int num1, int num2)
{
return(num1+num2);
}
```

Error: The variable argv is of char type and needs to be converted into integer type before passing it to the sum function.

10.
```
void main()
{
char c= 'a';
get(c);
putchar("a");
}
```

Error: The format of getc() is wrong, and putchar() cannot be used to display string.

11.
```
void main()
{
if(0)
printf("false");
else
printf("true");
}
```

Error: The statement if(0) is always false statement.

12.
```
void main()
{
main();
}
```

Error: The main function keeps calling itself. As there is no condition to terminate the function call, this results in stack overflow causing runtime error.

13.
```
void main()
{
printf("%d", 5/2);
printf("%f", 5.0/2);
printf("%f", float5/2);
}
```

Error: In the last statement, placing float in parenthesis will display the float value of the division of 5/2. The output after correction will be

```
2
2.5
2.5
```

14.
```
#define a = 8;
void main()
{
int a1=10;
int prod;
prod=a1*a;
printf("%d",prod);
}
```

Error: The syntax of #define statement is wrong. It should be #define a 8

15.
```
void main()
{
char *c;
float a=2;
c=a;
printf("%d",*c);
}
```

Error: Since the value 2 is of integer type, the variable a should be of integer type. For c to point to variable a, both the pointer and the variable should be of the same data type. Instead of c=a; the assignment statement should be c=&a as c is the pointer variable pointing to address of a.

16.
```
void main()
{
register int x;
scanf("%d",&x);
printf("%d",x);
}
```

Assume 10 is entered.

Error: This will result in compilation error, as the address of the register variable is not known to the user. This is because the memory for a register variable is allocated from the CPU registers and not from the main memory. Hence, pointers and the operator & cannot be used for register variables.

17.
```
struct S
{
int x;
float f;
};
void main()
{
struct S s1,s2;
s1.x=s2.x=10;
s1.f=s2.f=100.95;
if(s1==s2)
printf("Both are the same");
else
printf("Both are not the same");
}
```

Error: This will result in compilation error, as the two structure variables cannot be compared. It should be either if(s1.x==s2.x) or if(s1.y==s2.y)

Model Question Paper 1

Time: Three Hours **Maximum: 100 Marks**

Answer All Questions

Part A – (10 × 2 = 20)

1. Find the equivalent octal number for AF6.
2. What are the guidelines for writing a pseudocode.
3. Differentiate between ladder if statement and nested if statement.
4. Compare while and do-while loops.
5. What is meant by index of an array?
6. Differentiate between array and character array.
7. What are the various methods of parameter passing?
8. How can a function return a pointer?
9. Can there be a union within a structure? Give an example.
10. Give four built-in functions in stdlib.h header file.

Part B – (5 × 16 = 80)

11. (a) (i) Write the pseudocode for finding the product of N integers using pointers? (8)

(ii) Find the binary, hexadecimal and octal equivalent of $(850)_{10}$. (8)

Or

(b) What are the various types of memory and storage devices in the computer? (16)

12. (a) What is meant by planning of a computer program? Write a basic structure of C program and describe each of its elements. Write a program to check whether a given number is prime or not. (16)

Or

(b) With example describe the structure of (a) if–else statement, (b) nested if–else statement, (c) switch case statement in C language. (16)

13. (a) What do you understand by array? Give declaration of onc-dimensional, two-dimensional and three-dimensional array. Write a program to sort a list in ascending order. (16)

Or

(b) Write a program to find the smallest and largest element of an array using dynamic memory management technique. (16)

14. (a) Write a program to convert a decimal number into hexadecimal number using functions. (16)

Or

(b) (i) Differentiate between recursion and iteration using examples. (8)

(ii) What is dynamic memory management technique? Explain the different functions using examples. (8)

15. (a) Write a menu-driven program to read distances in meter and centimeter, add and subtract two distances using structure and functions. (16)

Or

(b) (i) List and explain the types of storage classes. (8)

(ii) Write a program to find the size of union and the number of bytes reserved for it. (8)

Model Question Paper 2

Time: Three Hours **Maximum: 100 Marks**

Answer All Questions

Part A – (10 × 2 = 20)

1. What are the characteristics of computers?
2. What are the properties of a good algorithm?
3. What are the various data types in C? Explain the enumerated data type with examples.
4. What is meant by entry controlled and exit controlled loops?
5. Matrix is a form of two-dimensional array. Explain.
6. How are strings stored in C? Differentiate between strcmp() and stricmp().
7. Differentiate between actual and formal parameters.
8. What are the differences between array of pointers and pointer to the array?
9. Differentiate between structure and array.
10. What are the various types of preprocessor directives in C.

Part B – (5 × 16 = 80)

11. (a) (i) Draw a flowchart and write an algorithm to calculate compound interest. (8)

    (ii) Draw and explain the various symbols of flowchart and also draw the flowchart to multiply all elements of an array of N elements (8)

    Or

    (b) Explain the evolution of computers and its various generations. (16)

12. (a) What are the types of branching statements and why are they required? (16)

    Or

    (b) Explain the types of formatted and unformatted input/output functions in C? (16)

13. (a) Write a C program to

    (i) find the sum of each row in an array

    (ii) find the sum of each column in an array

    (iii) check if a number is present in the array (16)

    Or

    (b) (i) Write a C program to swap two variables without using a third variable. (8)

    (ii) Write a C program to copy String1 to String2 and count the number of copies (8)

14. (a) What is recursion? Write a recursive procedure to print *n* terms of Fibonacci series. (16)

    Or

    (b) (i) What is the call by pointers method of passing parameters to a function? Write a code explaining the same. (8)

    (ii) What are the different arithmetic operations possible on pointers. Give examples. (8)

15. (a) Write a C program that gets and displays the report of *n* students with their personal and academic details using structures. (16)

    Or

    (b) Write short notes on (i) storage classes and (ii) preprocessor directives. (16)

Model Question Paper 3

Time: Three Hours **Maximum: 100 Marks**

Answer All Questions

Part A – (10 × 2 = 20)

1. What are microcomputers? Name three types of microcomputers.
2. What are the different types of control structures?
3. How can ternary operator be used as a decision making statement? Give an example.
4. Compare for, while and do-while statements.
5. What are arrays? Write the syntax for their declaration and initialization.
6. Which string library function is used to (a) copy a string to another, (b) duplicate a string.
7. What is recursion? What the different types of recursion?
8. What is the difference between & and * operator in pointers?
9. Differentiate between array of structures and array within structure.
10. What is a union? What is its purpose?

Part B – (5 × 16 = 80)

11. (a) Discuss the evolution of computers and the various computer generations. (16)

Or

(b) (i) Convert binary number 11110.11011 to hexadecimal number. (4)

(ii) Draw a flowchart to multiple two matrices. (8)

(iii) Differentiate between RAM and ROM. (4)

12. (a) What is the structure of a C program? Explain the compilation, linking and execution of a C program. (16)

Or

(b) (i) What are the different types of tokens in C? Explain with examples. (16)

13. (a) (i) Write a program to simulate a simple calculator using switch and if–else statement. (8)

(ii) Write a program to find whether the entered string is a palindrome or not. (8)

Or

(b) Write a menu-driven program to add, subtract and multiply two matrices. (16)

14. (a) Write a program to accept student data name, roll numbers and marks of 5 subjects. Calculate the total and arrange these records in descending order of marks using pointers and functions. (16)

Or

(b) Explain the following with examples: call by reference, call by value and call by pointers. (16)

15. (a) Declare a structure for an employee payroll slip containing (i) eno, (ii) ename, (iii) basic pay, (iv) hra, (v) da, (vi) gross, (vii) income tax, (viii) professional tax. (16)

Or

(b) Write a program to print the bill details of 10 customers with the following data: Meter number, customer name, number of units consumed, bill date, last date to deposit and the city name. The bill is to be calculated according to the following condition: (16)

No. of units	Charge
For first 100 units	₹0.75 per unit
For the next 200 units	₹1.80
For the next 300 units	₹2.75

COMPUTER PRACTICE LABORATORY

- MS Office
- Problem Formulation, Problem Solving (Flowcharts, Algorithms and Pseudocodes)
- C Programming

Exercise 1 | MS Office

Introduction

MS Office is a very useful application software package to handle effectively office activities like data typing, processing, editing, manipulating and formatting various kinds of documents and communication. It is a collection of several application programs such as MS Word, MS PowerPoint, MS Excel, MS Outlook, MS Access, etc. All the Microsoft Office programs share a common design and work in a similar manner. Getting familiar with one program makes it easier to interact with and learn other programs. Since the commands of MS Office 2007 and 2010/2013 are similar only with some modifications in 2010/2013, we have used screenshots predominantly from 2010/2013 and few from the 2007 version.

1. **MS Word:** It is the most popular word processing software that is used to create, edit, save and print a document on the Windows operating system environment. It also has functionalities available such as placing images on documents, etc. This software can even be used to create web pages. It provides a graphical user interface (GUI) which makes word processing very simple and efficient through availability of various commands. Other word processing software available in the market are WordStar and Easy Word (for DOS environment), Notepad (for Windows environment), Applix Words (for Linux environment), OpenOffice Writer, Google Docs, etc.
2. **MS PowerPoint:** It is an effective and extremely useful tool for creating effective presentations in seminars, lectures, etc., using tools to create slide shows with lots of predefined design templates, color schemes and animation effects, multimedia effects.
3. **MS Excel:** It is the spreadsheet program that gives us features that make it easier to organize and analyze the data. It allows users to enter numerical values or data into the rows/columns of a spreadsheet, perform calculations, prepare graphs and do statistical analysis of the entered data.
4. **MS Outlook:** It is a personal information manager and communication program that provides tools and resources to manage e-mails, calendars, contacts and other related information.
5. **MS Access:** It is a relational database management system (RDBMS) which provides tools and resources to facilitate effective storage and retrieval of data. Other popular RDBMSs are Oracle, MS SQL Server, IMB DB2, MS FoxPro, etc.

Search, Generate, Manipulate Data

Document Creation

A document can easily be created in the MS Word by simply clicking on Microsoft Office button and then clicking on the New command or pressing shortcut key Ctrl + N. This would display the New Document box asking the user to create a blank document or a new blog post. Double clicking on the blank document displays the word window with Document1 as the title on the Title bar. The user can start typing text from the insertion point shown in the text area. The sequence of selection and the screens displayed are shown as follows. Following similar steps, a presentation can be created in MS PowerPoint and a worksheet can be created in MS Excel.

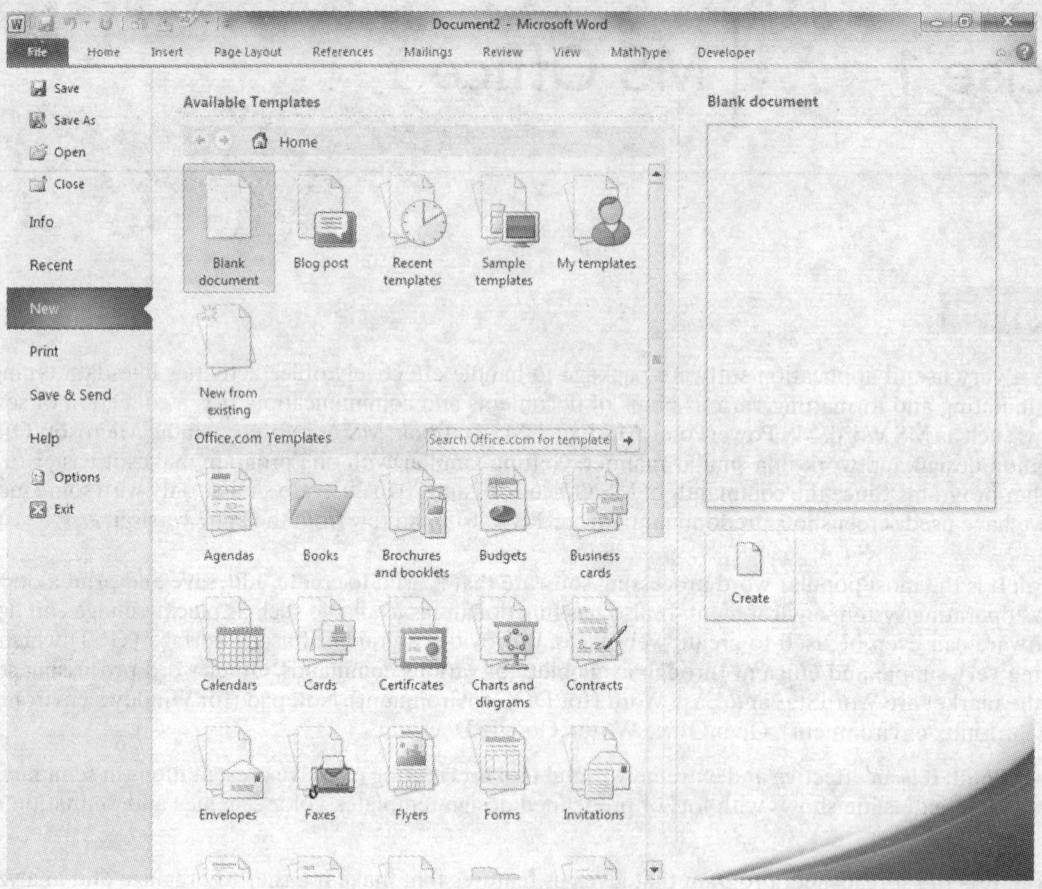

Problem 1: Prepare your Resume using various tools and properties of MS Word.

Solution

Step 1: Open MS Word. Click on the File menu and choose New.

Step 2: From the Templates list, select Resumes/CVs.

Step 3: Thumbnails of various resume documents appear on the screen. Choose the most appropriate resume.

Step 4: In the resume document selected, details can be modified accordingly.

Step 5: In case predefined resume templates are not good enough, then the page layout and size of the document can be set by the user. To do this, Page Layout is selected from the menu, and then the orientation (portrait/landscape), size (A4, letter, executive, etc.) and margin (normal, moderate, narrow, wide, etc.) are selected.

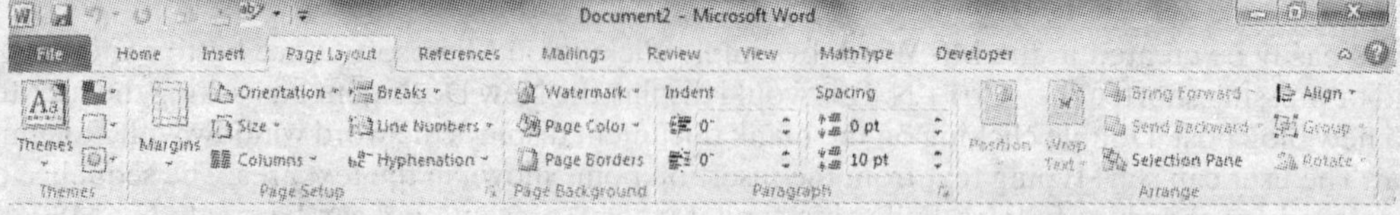

Step 6: In case a table needs to be inserted, say to enter educational qualification, then select Insert from the menu, and click on Table.

Step 7: Some pre-defined tables will appear, which can be chosen or a customized table with user-defined rows and columns can be created.

Step 8: The table is created on the main document at the point where the cursor was positioned. Data can be entered accordingly.

Step 9: In case any row/column of the table needs to be deleted, then right-click on the table and select the appropriate option of inserting/deleting row above or below.

Step 10: Header and footer can be inserted in the document by selecting the Insert tab from the menu, and selecting Header. This gives a drop down list of various header styles that can be chosen. Similarly, Footer can be selected and footer styles can be chosen.

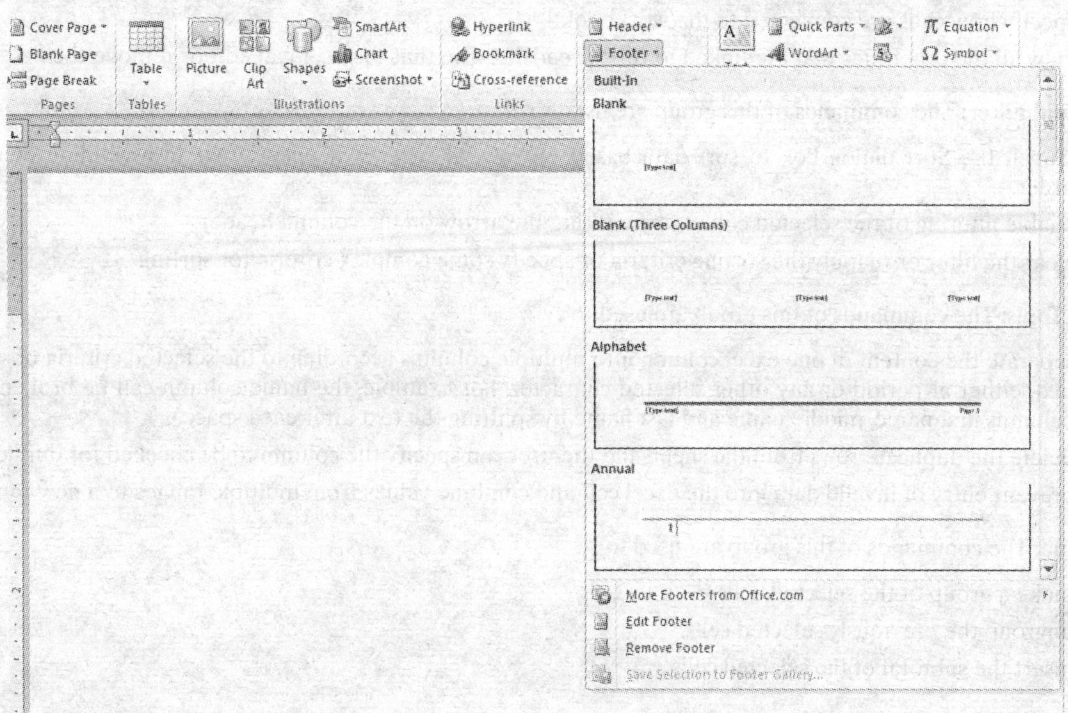

Step 11: After selecting the header/footer, type the required text, and click anywhere on the rest of the document. The text in the header and footer would appear on every page of the document.

Step 12: Once all the data have been entered, the document can be sent to print through the File tab, by selecting the print option.

Sorting and Import/Export Features

The sorting and import/export features are present in MS Word and MS Excel as follows:

1. **MS Word:** A given list can be sorted by clicking on Home tab and selecting the Sort tool (A Z ↓). It is used to arrange the text alphabetically or sort numerical data. To import or add an object (text/graphics) from another file, the object tool (Object) is used.

2. **MS Excel:** The Data tab in MS Excel consists of several groups such as Get External Data, Connections, Sort and Filter, Data Tools and Outline as shown:

These groups are collection of various commands that basically deal with getting the data from external sources such as MS Access, Web, sorting the selected cells on the different defined criteria, removing duplicates entries, etc., from the worksheet. The descriptions of the commands of various groups are summarized as follows:

- **Get External Data:** This group provides the option to the user to select and import the data either from MS Access, Web, text, other sources or from the existing connections.

- **Connections:** The commands of this group are used to
  - **(a)** update all the information in the workbook coming from the data source.
  - **(b)** display all data connections to the workbook.
  - **(c)** specify how cells are connected to the workbook.
  - **(d)** view all the other files that are linked to this spreadsheet, so that the user can edit or remove the links.
- **Sort and Filter:** The commands of this group are used to
  - **(a)** launch the Sort dialog box to sort data based on several criteria at once either in ascending or descending order.
  - **(b)** enable filtering of the selected column by clicking the arrow on the column header.
  - **(c)** clear the filter or reapply the sorting criteria or specify some complex criteria for sorting.
- **Data Tools:** The commands of this group are used to
  - **(a)** separate the content of one excel column into multiple columns according to the selected criteria of splitting the text, either at period or any other selected character. For example, the name column can be broken into three columns first name, middle name and last name by splitting the text after each space.
  - **(b)** delete the duplicate rows from the sheet, and the user can specify the column to be checked for duplicity of data.
  - **(c)** prevent entry of invalid data into the excel cell and combine values from multiple ranges to a new range.
- **Outline:** The commands of this group are used to
  - **(a)** make a group of the selected cells.
  - **(b)** ungroup the previously selected cells.
  - **(c)** insert the subtotal of the selected cells.

Formula Editor

This feature is more associated with MS Excel, though certain features are available in MS Word, such as evaluating data entered in tables. The Formulas tab consists of several groups such as function library, defined names, formula auditing and calculation as shown:

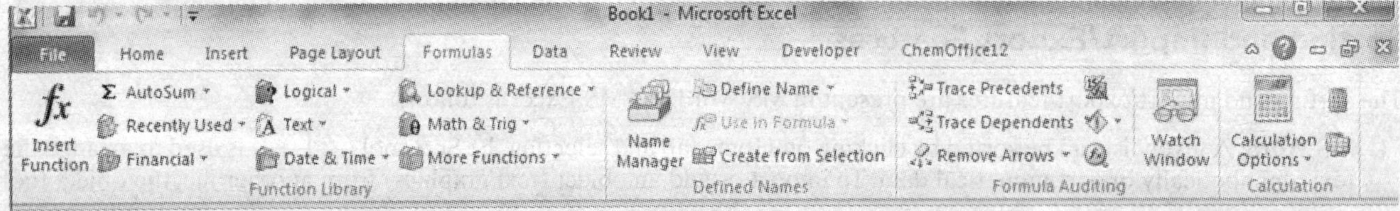

These groups are collection of various commands that basically deal with applying different kinds of formula to the selected cell, defining the names to the cells instead of cell address, etc. The descriptions of the commands of various groups are summarized as follows:

1. **Function Library:** The commands of this group are used to
   - calculate the sum of the selected cells and display it just after the selected cell.
   - browse and select from the recently used functions or financial functions, logical functions (e.g., AND, OR, NOT, etc.), text functions (e.g., CHAR, CLEAN, EXACT, FIND), date and time functions (e.g., DATE, DAY, MONTH, DATEVLAUE, etc.), lookup and reference functions (e.g., ROW, ROWS, COLUMN, COLUMNS, etc.), math and trigonometry functions (e.g., ACOS, ASIN, COS, FACT, etc.) or statistical or engineering and cube functions (e.g., AVERAGE, COUNT, DELTA, BIN2HEX, BIN2OCT, CUBESET, CUBEVALUE, etc.).
2. **Defined Names:** The commands of this group are used to name a particular cell. So the name may be used in the formula instead of the cell address. This is also used to create, edit, delete and find all the names used in the worksheet.
3. **Formula Auditing:** The commands of this group are used to show the arrows to
   - indicate what cells affect the value of the current selected cell.
   - indicate what cells are affected by the value of the currently selected cell.

- remove the arrows shown by above two selections.
- show the formula instead of the value, check the common errors and evaluate the formula.
- monitor the changes in the cells and display the changes in a separate window.

4. **Calculation:** This command is used to specify when the formulas are to be calculated, either to calculate for the complete workbook now or for the current sheet now.

The formula bar is located just below the Ribbon and is divided into two parts as shown:

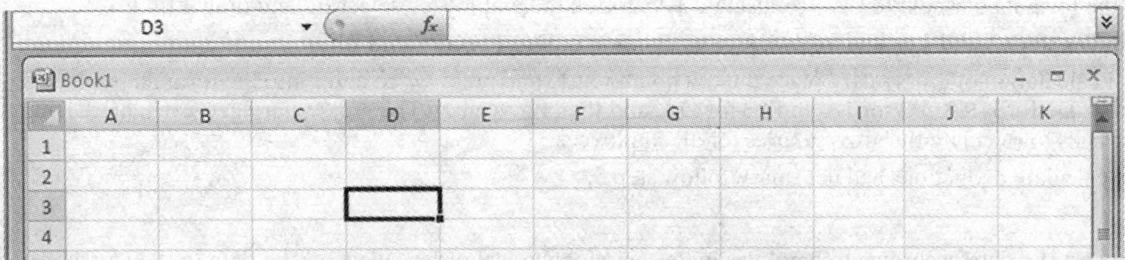

The first part located on the left side is called as name box and it contains the cell address of the cell, and second part may contain the formula. The formula can be inserted by clicking on (*fx*), which asks the user to select a function to be applied on the selected cell. The formula bar may also be used to edit the information at the particular cell by first placing the cursor in the specified cell. If it is not visible, then click on the View tab on the Ribbon and select Show/Hide group, select to make the formula bar visible.

Apart from the formula editor and the formula bar, the Number group in the Home tab can be used to manipulate data. The commands of this group are used to

1. choose how the values in a cell are displayed, general currency, data, time, percentage, etc.
2. choose the currency format (dollar, euro, etc.) for the currency value in the cell.
3. display many values in the cell with separators.
4. set the precision value for the decimal number.

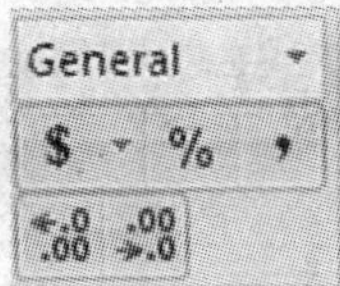

Problem 2: Calculate HRA, DA, TA, PF, GPF, LIC, gross salary, deductions and net salary from the following worksheet data:

	A	B	C	D	E	F	G	H	I	J	K	L
1	Emp. No.	Emp. Name	Basic	HRA	TA	DA	LIC	PF	GPF	Gross sal	Deductions	Net sal
2	51	D	15000									
3	52	A	10000									
4	69	B	20000									
5	60	E	20000									
6	63	C	25000									

where HRA is 18%, DA is 15%, TA is 12%, PF is 10%, GPF is 5%, LIC is 7% of Basic. The computations of gross salary, deductions and net salary are as follows:

Gross sal = Basic + HRA + TA + DA

Deductions = PF + GPF + LIC

Net sal = Gross sal – Deductions.

Also, sort the employee names in alphabetical order.

Solution

Computation

Step 1: For calculating HRA, place the cell pointer in D2 and press "=" for entering the formula in the formula bar. Now, choose C2 and when it appears on the formula bar, type "*18%" next to it. Now, press enter. The HRA for employee A is calculated.

Step 2: The HRAs of B, C, D and E can be calculated by selecting the D2 cell and dragging it till D6.

Step 3: For calculating TA, similar procedure as in step 1 is followed, except that pointer is placed in E2 cell and "*15%" is typed on the formula bar next to C2. To calculate TA's for all the employees, select E2 and drag it till E6.

Step 4: Similar steps 1 and 2 can be followed for calculation of DA, PF, GPF and LIC.

Step 5: For calculation of gross salary, place the cell pointer at J2 and press "=" to enter into the formula bar. Now, select cells C2 for Basic, D2 for HRA, E2 for TA and F2 for DA, and then press enter. The gross salary gets calculated. Drag till all the remaining cells to calculate the gross salaries for all employees.

Step 6: To calculate deductions and net salary, follow step 5.

Sorting

Step 1: To sort the data according to employee names in alphabetical order, select all the data in the worksheet, and click Data tab on the menu. Now, choose Sort from the Sort & Filter group.

Step 2: The Sort dialog box appears, choose Sort by as name, and order as A to Z.

Step 3: Click OK. The worksheet now gets sorted in alphabetic order of employee names.

	A	B	C	D	E	F	G	H	I	J	K	L
1	Emp. No.	Emp. Name	Basic	HRA	TA	DA	LIC	PF	GPF	Gross sal	Deductions	Net sal
2	52	A	10000	1800	1200	1500	700	1000	500	14500	2200	12300
3	69	B	20000	3600	2400	3000	1400	2000	1000	29000	4400	24600
4	63	C	25000	4500	3000	3750	1750	2500	1250	36250	5500	30750
5	51	D	15000	2700	1800	2250	1050	1500	750	21750	3300	18450
6	60	E	20000	3600	2400	3000	1400	2000	1000	29000	4400	24600

Presentation and Visualization – Graphs, Charts, Tables, 2D, 3D

Drawing Flowcharts

In MS Word, MS Excel and MS PowerPoint, the Illustrations group in the Insert tab can be used to create different flowcharts by selecting the Shapes tool and then selecting the required shape in Flowchart section. For organizational and hierarchical flowcharts, the SmartArt tool can be used.

Problem 3: Draw a flowchart to compute the salary of an employee in a company. Assume that there are two types of employees in the company: daily wages and regular. Salary is calculated as the number of hours worked (wages per hour for daily wagers and basic pay + (%DA + basic pay)/100 + HRA + medical allowance for regular employees. Sketch the flow of your design for a regular employee with basic pay = 5000, % of DA = 75% and HRA = 500.

Solution

Step 1: Click on Insert tab of the menu. Now, from the Illustrations group, select Shapes.

Step 2: From the drop down list, select the shape of box in the flowchart section. Drag to required size in the text area.

Step 3: To show the flow of control, select arrow from lines section.

Step 4: For the decision box "If employee type = 1", place a diagonal box with two arrow lines emerging from it. Above one arrow line, type "Yes" by selecting the "Text Box" option from Insert tab. And similarly, place "No" above the other arrow line.

Step 5: After you are through, the flowchart will look like this:

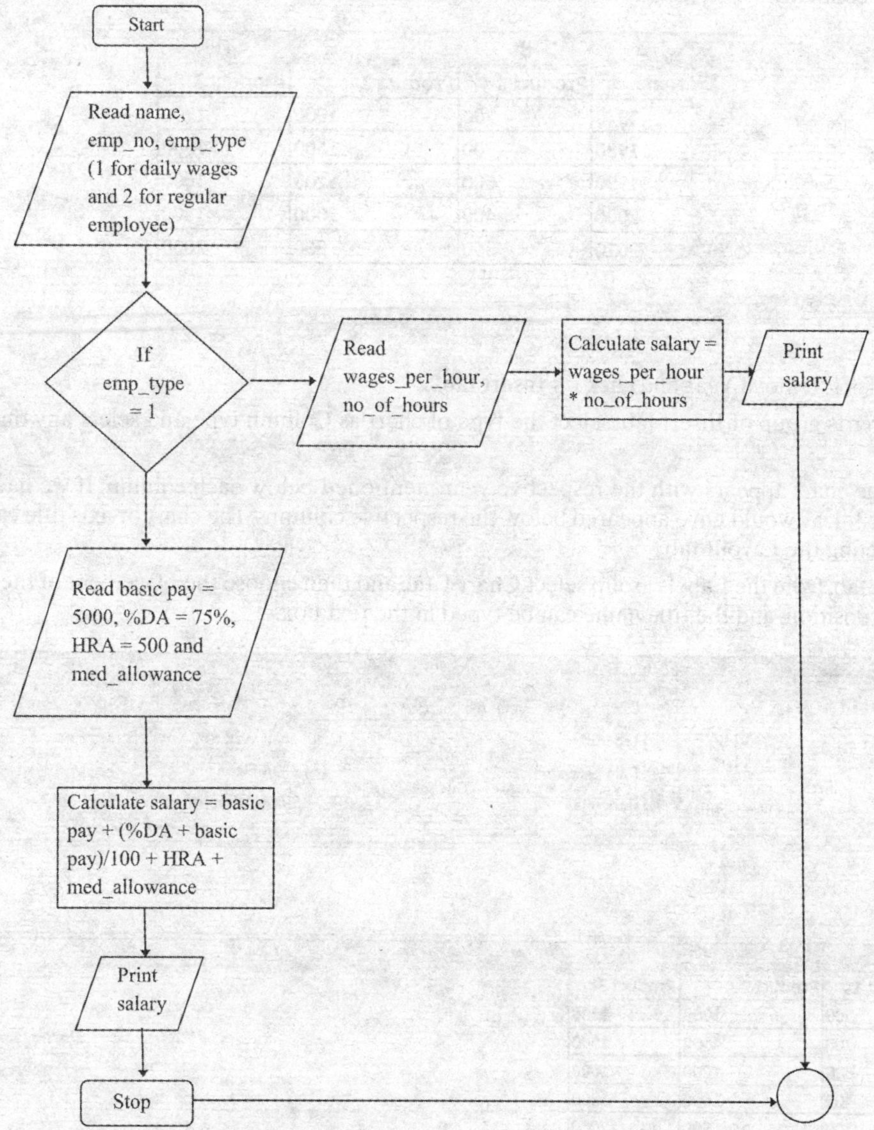

Graphs – Line, XY, Bar and Pie

In MS Word graphs/charts can be constructed using the Charts tool in the Illustrations group of the Insert tab. In MS PowerPoint, they can be constructed using Illustrations group of Insert tab.

(a) In MS PowerPoint 2007 (b) In MS PowerPoint 2010/2013

In MS Excel, a separate group is devoted to chart in the Insert Tab. This group's commands are used to

1. insert column charts used to compare values across categories.
2. insert line, pie, bar, area, scatter or any other chart in the worksheet.

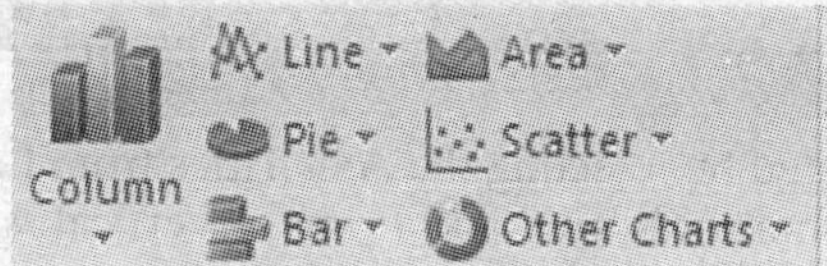

Problem 4: Construct different types of graphs for the following data showing sales figures of different products over the years for a particular company.

	A	B	C	D
1	Year	Product 1	Product 2	Product 3
2	1970	500	1000	1200
3	1980	700	1500	1500
4	1990	600	1200	1600
5	2000	400	1000	1800
6	2010	300	900	2000

Solution

Step 1: Select the cell A1, remove Year and click on Insert tab.

Step 2: Under the Charts group of Insert tab, select the type of chart as Column type and select any one (say 3D) from the drop down list.

Step 3: A column type chart appears with the respective year mentioned below each column. If we had retained "Year" in the A1 cell, then '1, 2, 3, 4, 5" would have appeared below the respective columns. The chart or axis title can be modified using Chart tools, and selecting the Layout tab.

Step 4: In the Layout tab, from the Labels group select Chart Title, and then choose the placement of the title. A textbox gets placed at the chosen position, and the title name can be typed in the text box.

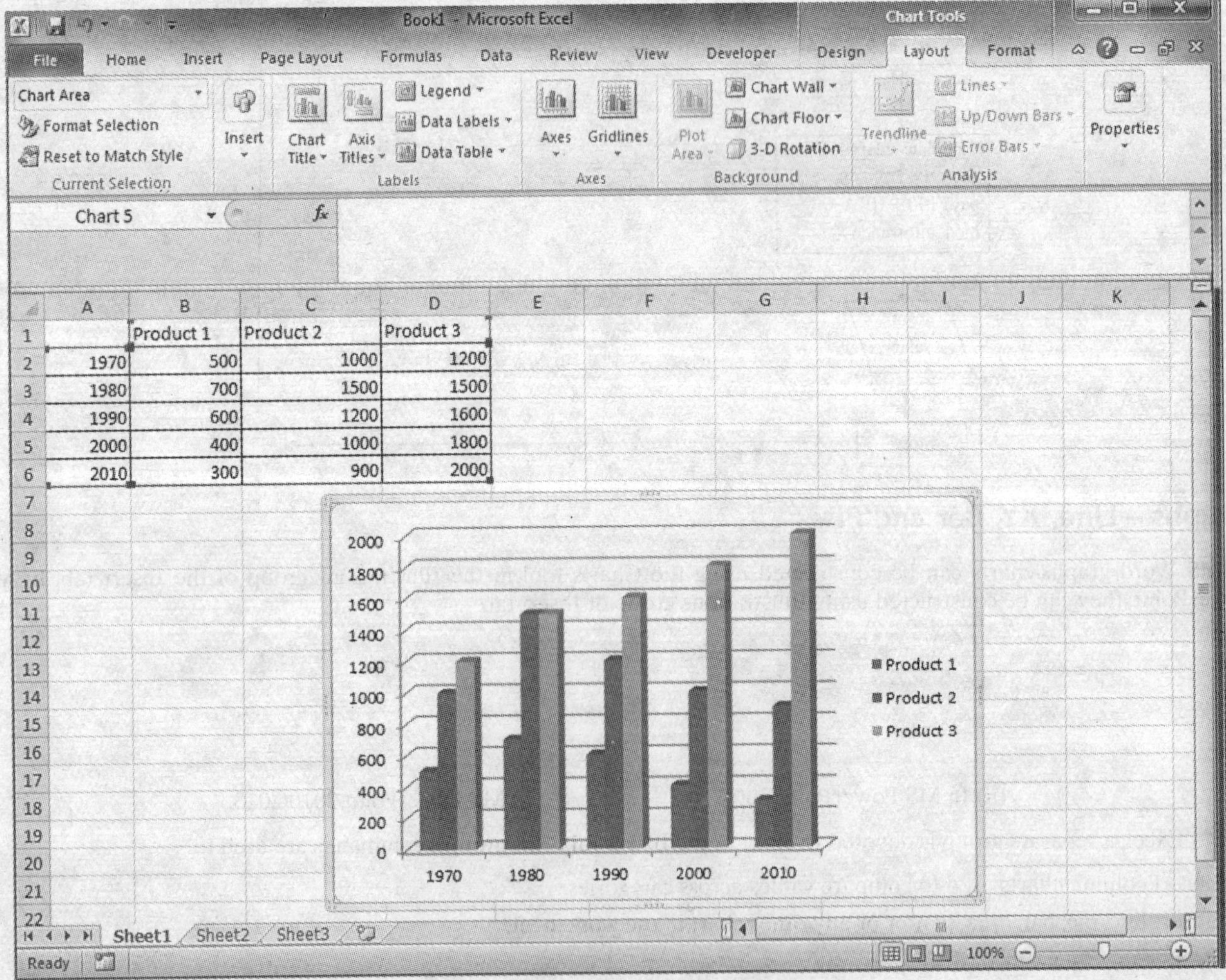

Step 5: Similarly, the axis title can be changed by selecting the Axis Titles from Layout tab of Chart Tools. A drop down list appears with two options Primary Horizontal Axis Title and Primary Vertical Axis Title. On selecting either one, another

drop down list appears containing the option to place the title below the axis. Select that option, and type in the required title names in the text boxes that appear near the axes.

Step 6: To change the position of legends and values, display data table, etc., Legend, Data Labels and Data Table options can be used, respectively, from the Layout tab.

Step 7: To change the chart type, in the Design tab of Chart Tools, Change Chart Type option can be selected, and the required chart type can be selected from the Change Chart Type dialog box.

Table Creation, Table Formatting and Conversion

In MS Word and MS PowerPoint, tables are created using the Table group ( ) from the Insert tab. This group consists of a drop-down list containing various options such as create table, draw table, convert text to table, Excel spreadsheet and quick tables in the active document. When the table is created, it asks for the number of rows and columns to be created for the table. We can quickly create the table by selecting any of the various predefined tables in the quick table option. Once the table is created, it can be modified/formatted using the Table Tools option containing Design and Layout tabs as shown.

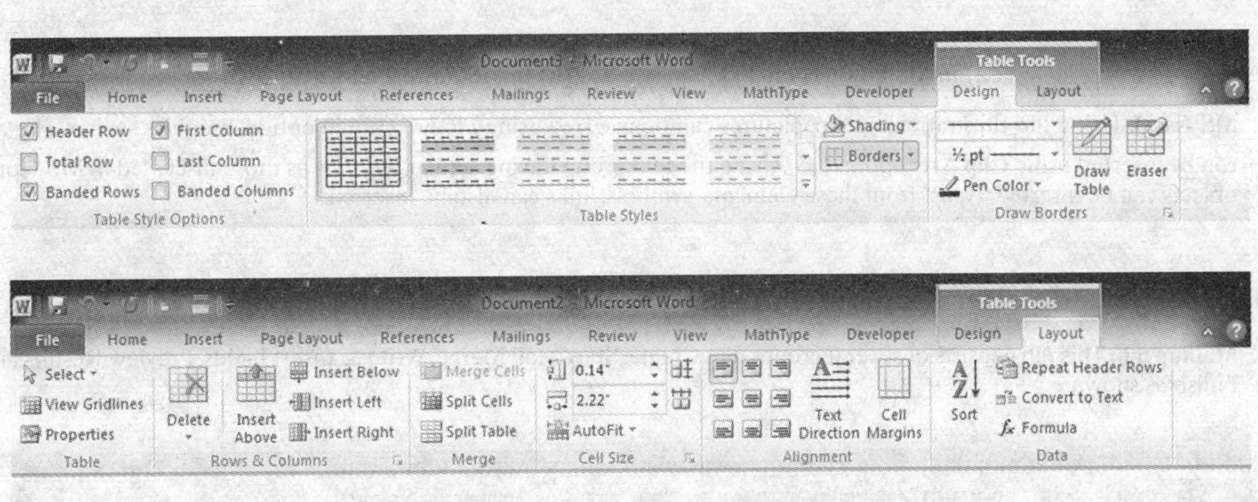

In MS Excel, tables can be created using the Tables group (

) from the Insert tab. This group consists of the commands for summarizing the data using pivot table or inserting the table in the cells. Once the table is created, it can be modified/formatted using Table Tools group containing only the Design tab.

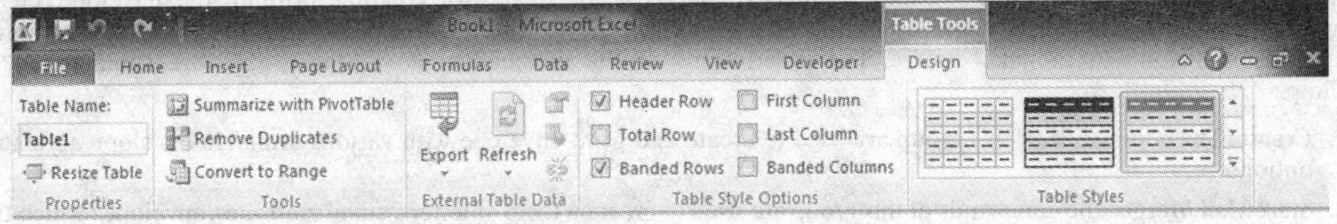

Inclusion of Object, Picture and Graphics

1. **MS Word:** Using the Illustrations group, pictures can be inserted using Picture ( ) option, graphics such as clip art can be inserted using Clip Arts option ( ) and objects can be inserted using the Text group from the Insert tab.

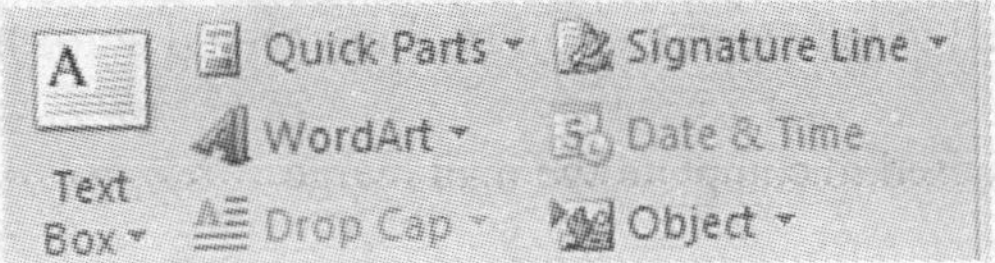

The text group consists of various commands to insert the following in the active documents: preformatted text box, reusable pieces of content, decorative text (WordArt), signature line containing the name of the signatory, date and time and objects from other files or formats. Apart from these elements, equations, symbols, links, header, footer and page numbers can also be inserted.

2. **MS PowerPoint:** Using the Illustrations group, pictures, graphics and photographs ( ) can be inserted. Using the text group, having similar features as those discussed above, objects can be inserted. Apart from these elements, equations, symbols, links, header, footer and slide numbers can also be inserted. Another important feature of MS PowerPoint is that it enables videos and sounds to be embedded as well. These multimedia objects can be inserted using Media Clips group in 2007 version or Media group in 2010/2013 version.

(a) In MS PowerPoint 2007 (b) In MS PowerPoint 2010/2013

3. **MS Excel:** Using the Illustrations group, pictures can be inserted using Picture ( ) option, graphics such as clip art can be inserted using Clip Arts option ( ).Using the text group having similar features as those discussed in MS Word, objects can be inserted. Apart from these elements, symbols, links can also be inserted.

Mail Merge and Letter Preparation Using MS Word

1. **Mailing tab:** This tab consists of several groups like Create, Start Mail Merge, Write & Insert Fields, Preview Results and Finish as shown:

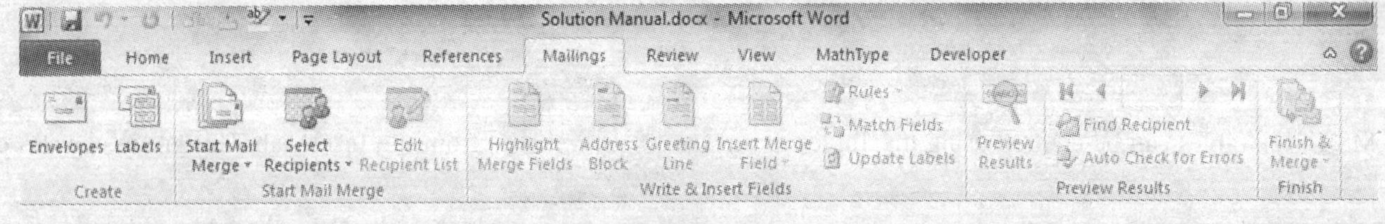

These groups are a collection of various commands that basically deal with creating, printing the envelope, creating a form of letters, email messages which the user wants to send to different recipients and specifying rules to enable decision-making in the mail merge. The descriptions of the commands of various groups are summarized as follows:

1. **Create:** The commands of this group are used to create and print envelope with various available envelope and label options.
2. **Start Mail Merge:** The commands of this group are used to create a form of letters, email messages, envelopes which the user wants to send to different recipients. It asks the user to enter the recipient information.
3. **Write and Insert Fields:** The commands of this group are used to make the mail merge facility more effective by
   - specifying rules to enable decision-making in the mail merge.
   - highlighting the fields inserted into the document.
   - adding an address to the letter.
   - adding a greeting line to the document, etc.
4. **Preview Results:** This group is used to take a preview of mail merge and auto check errors before printing or finishing the mail merge.
5. **Finish & Merge:** This command is used to complete the mail merge.

Problem 5: Create an invitation letter for a birthday party and send it to various recipients through e-mail.

Solution

Creating the Mail Merge Document

Step 1: Choose Mailings → Start Mail Merge

Step 2: In the drop down menu, select Step by Step Mail Merge Wizard. A Mail Merge task pane will appear.

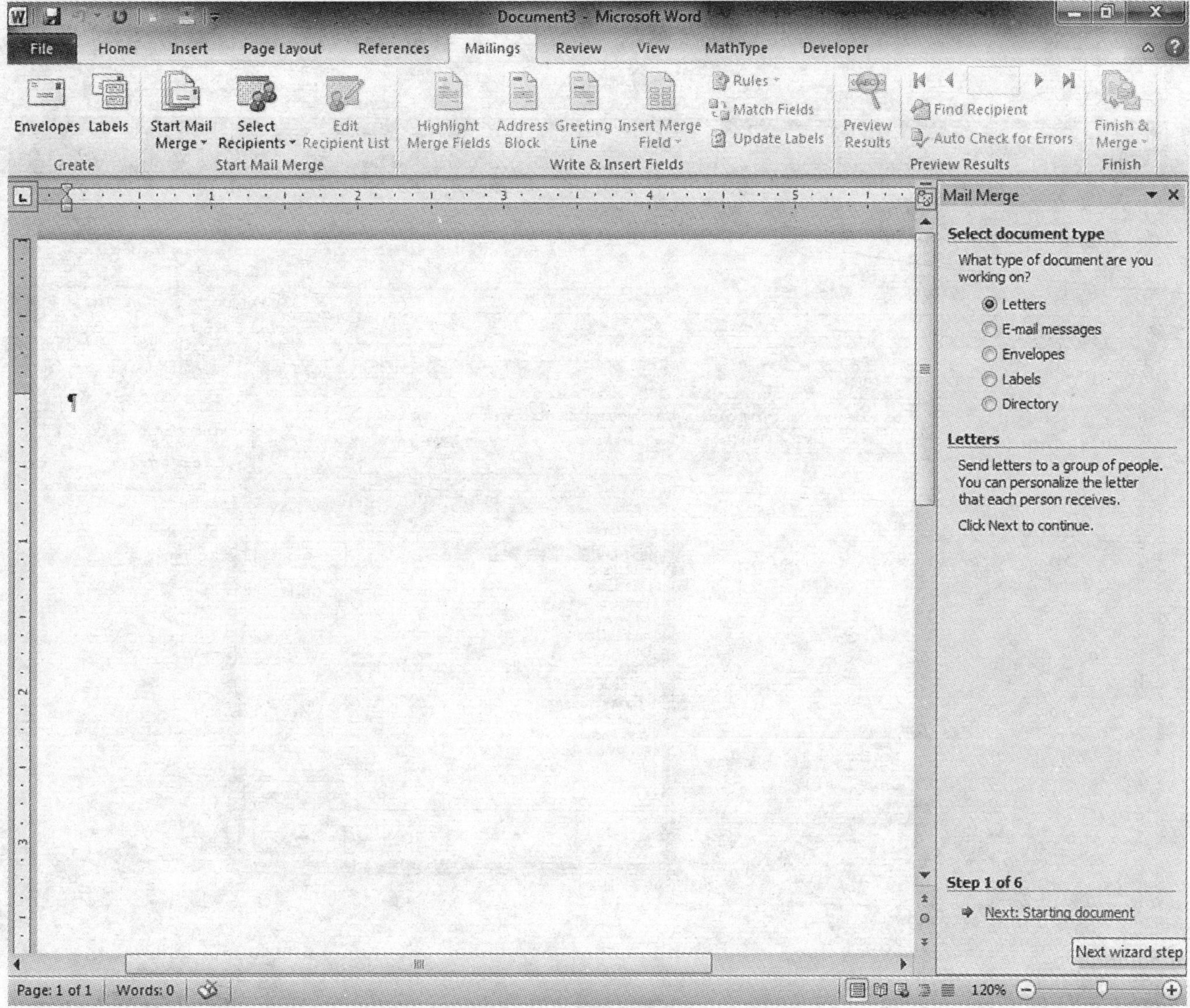

Step 3: From the Mail Merge task pane on the extreme right, select Letter (to create a letter to send to many individuals) from the drop down menu (containing E-mail Messages to personalize a message to send via e-mail; Envelopes to print envelopes with different addresses; Labels to print labels with different addresses; and Directory to gather varied but related information into a list.)

Step 4: Click on Next: Starting Document

Step 5: The existing Mail Merge task pane gets replaced by a new one with a drop down list containing three options on how to set up the letter (current document, from template, existing document). Choose "Current document".

Step 6: Click on Next: Select Recipient

Creating the Data Source

A data source is a list containing the names and addresses of all the invitees. It would contain the following fields: First name, Last name, Address, City, State and Pincode. After inserting the required field in the data source, details of each invitee (known as record, containing name and address of that invitee) would be added.

Step 1: After clicking on Next: Select Recipient, a new Mail Merge task pane appears with three options in the drop down list (use an existing list, select from Outlook contacts or type a new list). Select "Type a new list" option.

Step 2: Click on Create option under Type a new list. A New Address List dialog box appears on the screen. In this dialog box, a number of tabs can be seen with their corresponding fields.

Step 3: Click on Customized Columns which opens a dialog box containing all possible list items such as Title, First Name, Last Name, etc., which can be selected by the user.

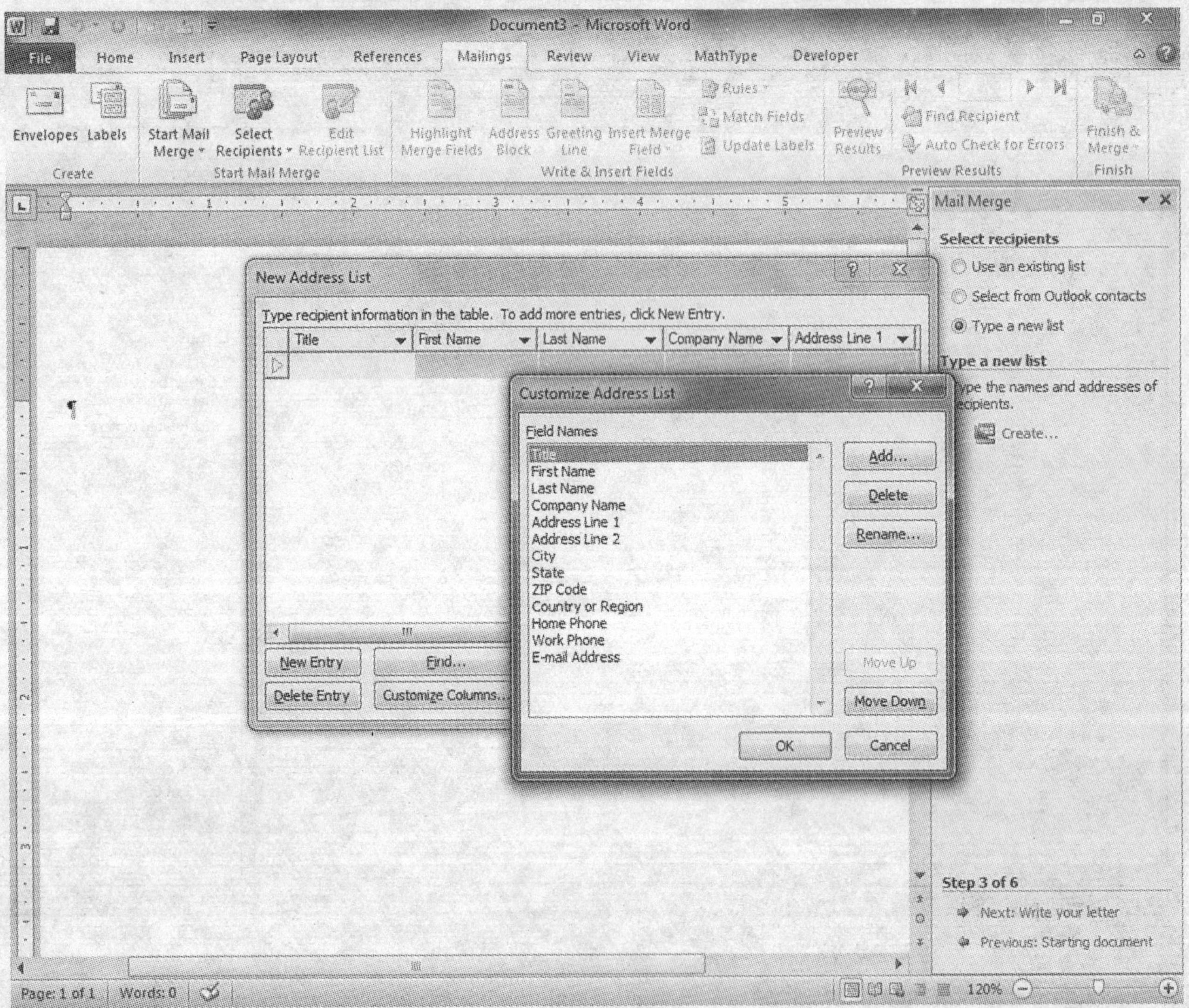

Step 4: To remove a particular field, select that title and click on Delete. Similarly, a new field can be added by Clicking on Add.

Step 5: After finalizing the field list, click on OK. The New Address List dialog box is used to enter the names and addresses of the invitees and create the required Data Source.

Step 6: After entering one complete entry, click on New Entry to enter the next record.

Step 7: After entering all the records, click on OK and save the data source through the Save Address List dialog box by a filename xyz.

Step 8: Once the address list is saved, the Mail Merge Recipients dialog box appears on the screen displaying the information of the invitees.

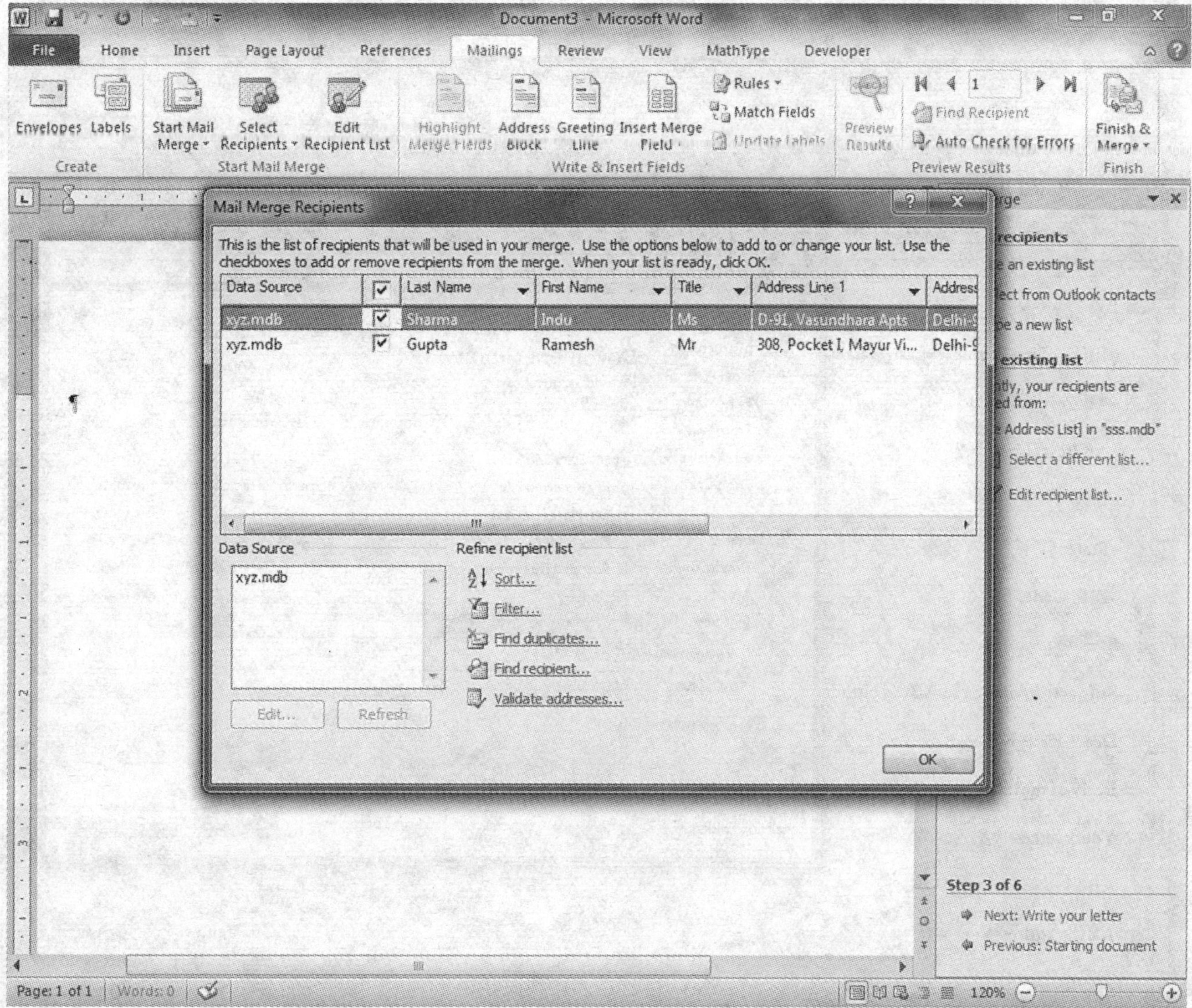

Step 9: Now, click the OK button. The dialog box closes, and a blank document appears on the screen. Now click on Next: Write your letter.

Creating the Main Document

Once the data source has been compiled, we can create the mail document, that is, invitation letter in this case.

Step 1: Type "To" on the main document, then press Enter key. Now, we need to make First Name, Last Name, Address, City, State and Pincode as merge fields. To do this, click on the Mailings tab. In the Write & Insert Fields group, select Insert Merge Field.

Step 2: Select First Name from the drop down list. The first name gets inserted as a merge field in the main document as <<First_Name>>.

Step 3: Similarly, merge fields for Last Name, Address, City, State and Pincode are inserted.

Step 4: Now, we need to place a Subject line stating "Invitation to ABC's birthday party".

Step 5: Now, press Enter and type the salutation "Dear". Insert space and again insert merge field for first name as in step 2. After inserting the merge field for first name, press comma (,).

Step 6: Now, the body of the letter, concluding remarks can be written. Before finishing the letter, the closing of the letter by Yours sincerely, etc. can be written followed by the host's name and address. Since these fields would be fixed in every letter, we do not need insert merge fields for these.

Step 7: Save the letter with filename "Letter".

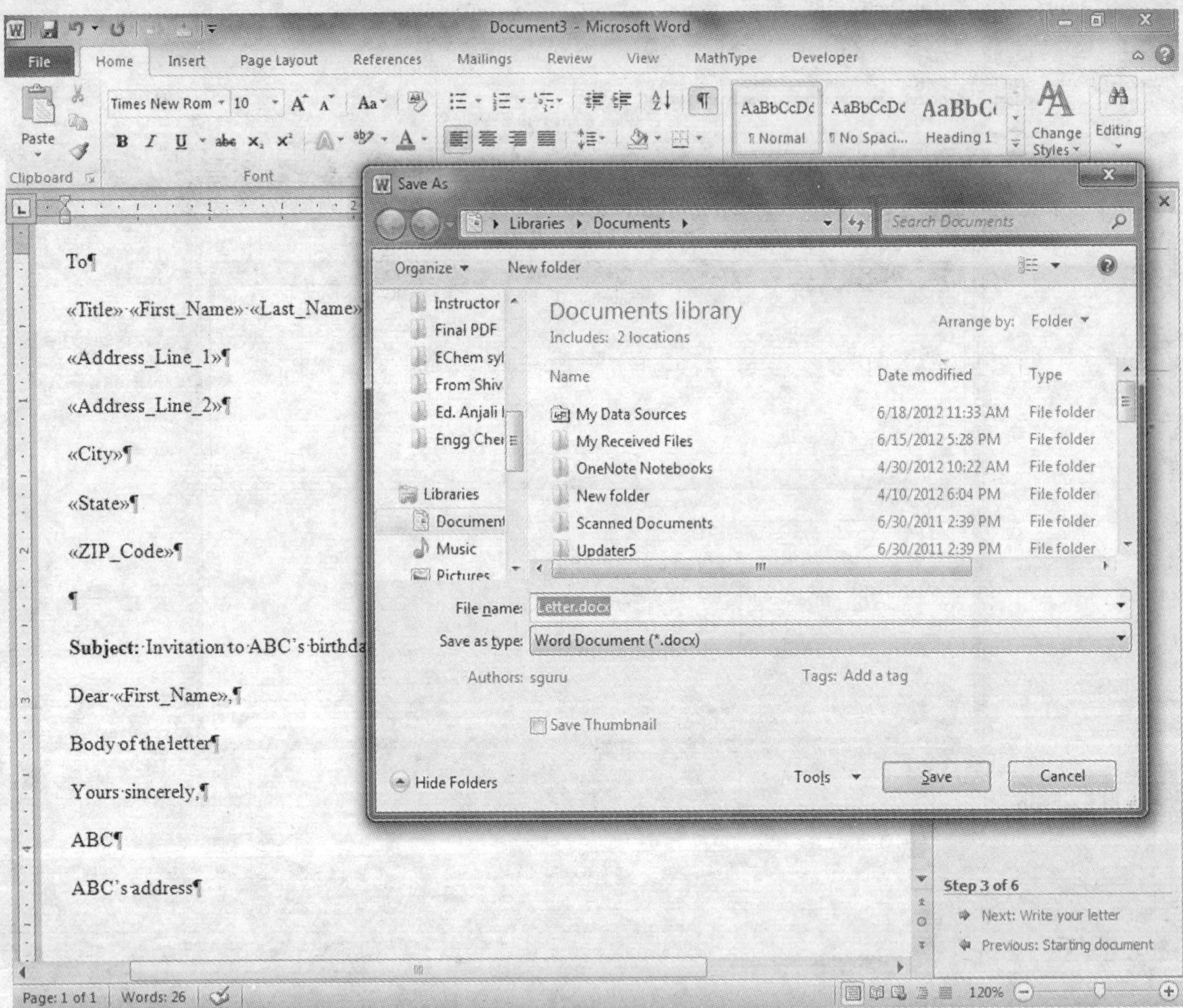

Merging the Main Document with Data Source

To create a personalized letter for each invitee on the mailing list, we need to merge the main document with the data source.

Step 1: Click on the Mailings tab. In the Finish group, select the Finish & Merge option.

Step 2: From the drop down list, select Edit Individual Document option.

Step 3: The Merge to New Document dialog box appears, asking the user which records to merge (all, current or some range of records). Select "All" and click OK.

Step 4: A new document named Letter1 appears on the screen showing all merged letters sequentially arranged in separate pages.

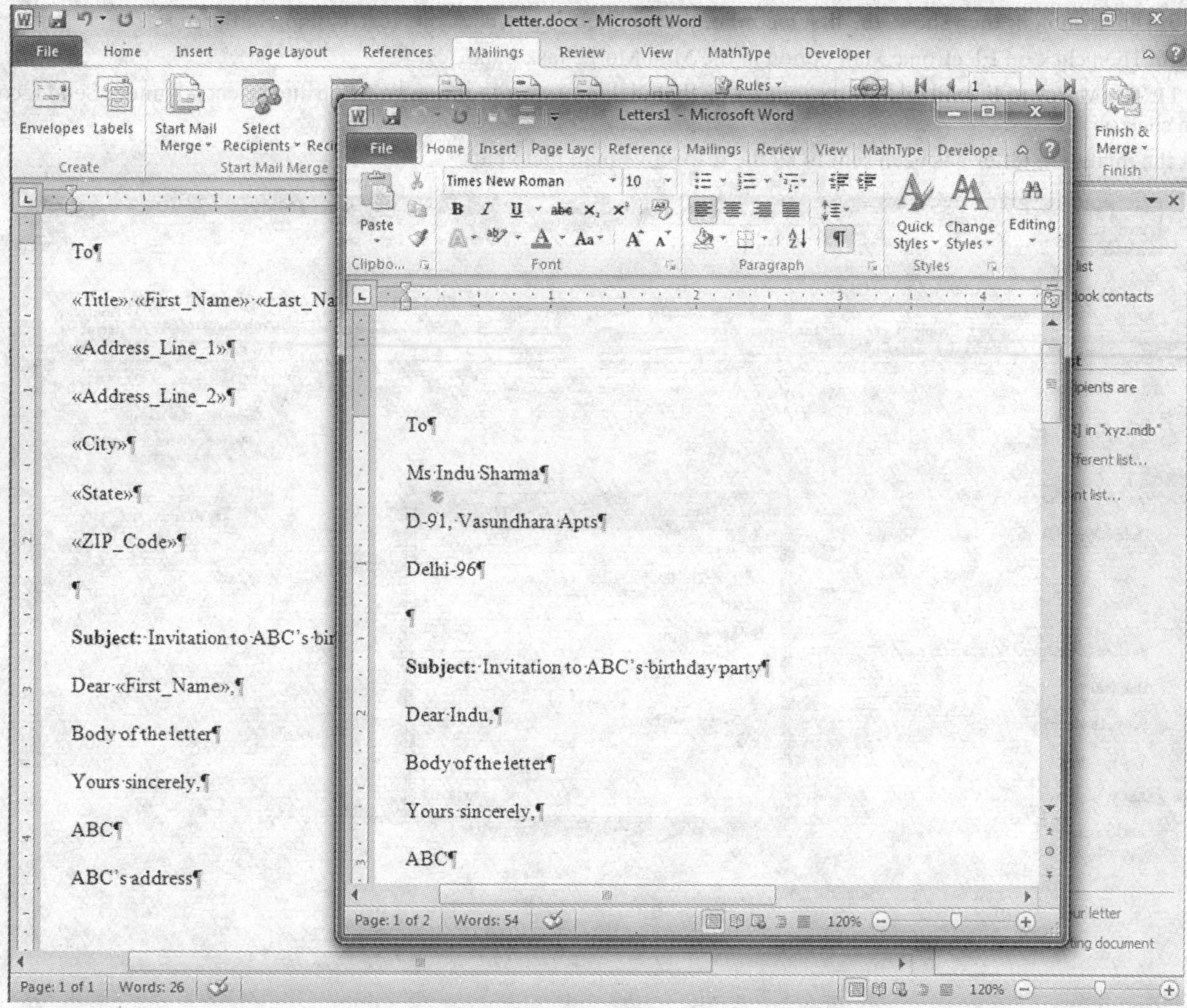

Sending Merged Document to the Printer

We can print letters addressed to all the invitees using the following steps:

Step 1: Click on Mailings tab. In the Finish group, select Finish & Merge button.

Step 2: From the drop down list, select Print Documents option. The Merge to Printer dialog box appears asking the user which records to print (all, current or some range of records). Select "All" and click OK.

Step 3: The Print dialog box appears. Click on OK to print.

Sending Letter through Email to Many Recipients

Step 1: Click on the Mailings tab. In the Start Mail Merge group, click on Start Mail Merge option.

Step 2: From the drop down list, select E-Mail Messages option. Now, the document opens in Web Layout view.

Step 3: Now, again click on Start Mail Merge option and select Start Mail Merge option. In the drop down list, select Step by Step Mail Merge Wizard.

Step 4: A Mail Merge task pane appears. Select the document type as E-mail messages from the drop down list and then click on Next: Select recipients.

Step 5: In the Mail Merge task pane, select the starting document as current document, and then click on Next: Select recipients.

Step 6: In the Mail Merge task pane, select Use an existing list and browse and select the data source file.

Step 7: The Mail Merge Recipients dialog box appears. Check the boxes and select the required recipients, then click on Next: Write your e-mail message.

Step 8: As the message/letter is already written, click on Next: Preview your e-mail message.

Step 9: The document then shows the first record of the recipient. Now, click on Next: Complete the merge.

Step 10: Then click on Electronic Mail option in the Mail Merge task pane.

Step 11: The Merge to E-mail dialog box appears. In that dialog box, write the subject line and select All under Send records. Then click on OK.

Now, the invitation letter has been sent to all the respective mail recipients.

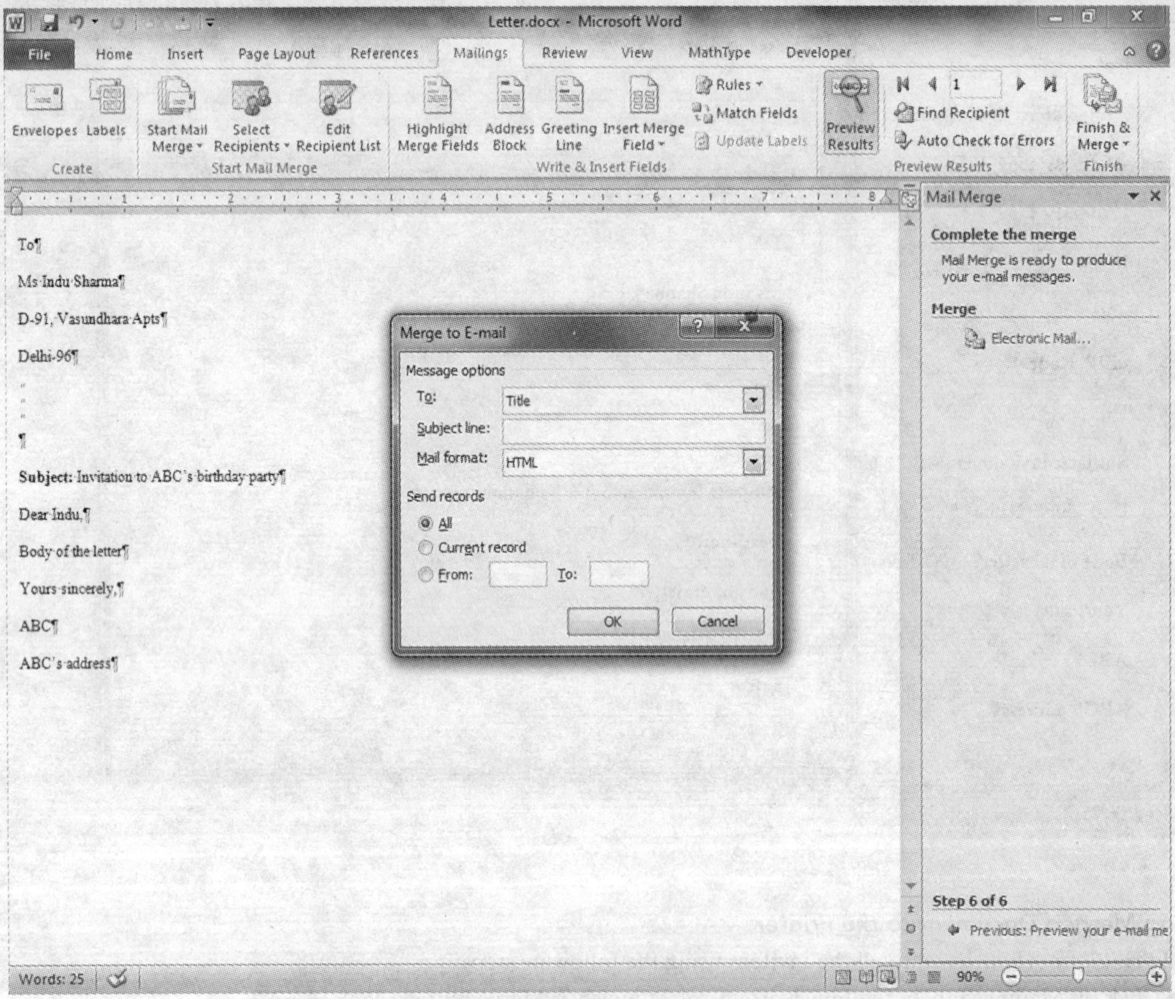

Protecting the Document and Sheet

1. **MS Word and MS PowerPoint:** In 2007 version under the Review tab, Protect Document or Protect Presentation option is used to restrict the users from formatting, editing or accessing the document/presentation. In 2010/2013 version, however, under the File tab, by clicking on the Info option we get the respective options for MS Word and MS PowerPoint, as well as for MS Excel.

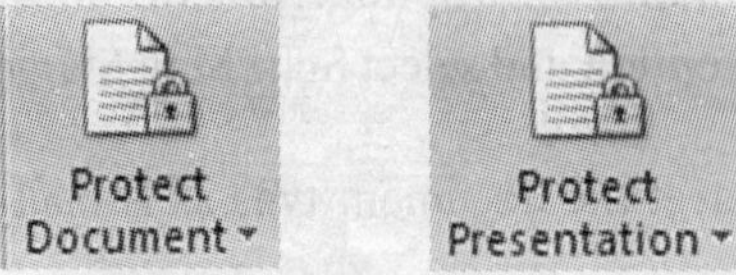

2. **MS Excel:**
   - **Protect cell:** To protect or lock a cell, in the Home tab, from the Cell group, select the Format cell option. In the drop down list, click on Lock cell to protect the cell against any changes.
   - **Protect worksheet/workbook:** In the Review tab, the commands of the Changes group are used to
     - **(a)** prevent unwanted changes, that is, formatting, editing or accessing the data by specifying what information can be changed.
     - **(b)** restrict the users from creating new sheets.

(c) allow multiple users to work simultaneously on the same workbook by sharing the workbook.

(d) protect the workbook by password.

(e) allow the users to make changes only to unrestricted cells.

(f) track all the changes made to the workbook.

Creating Presentation Slides Using PowerPoint

The MS PowerPoint is most popular application program of MS Office package which is used to create, edit, save and print a presentation, on the Windows operating system environment. It provides a GUI and also provides various tools and commands for creating, editing and printing the presentation. We have already discussed how to create presentations, insert illustrations, and multimedia into the current slide. In the problem below, we would be using all these tools to design a birthday card.

Problem 6: Design a Birthday invitation card using MS PowerPoint.

Solution

Step 1: From the file, choose New option and select the template for "Invitations" from the list of templates. In case the template is unavailable, then open a blank presentation.

Step 2: Click on the "Click to add title", and then from the Text group or Insert tab, choose WordArt styles.

Step 3: From the A▾ option, choose the style in which you want the title text to appear. Now click on "Click to add subtitle" again to type the required title name.

Step 4: The text for the subtitle can be the entire invitation body matter citing the venue, time, etc., the appearance of the text can be changed in the same way as in step 3.

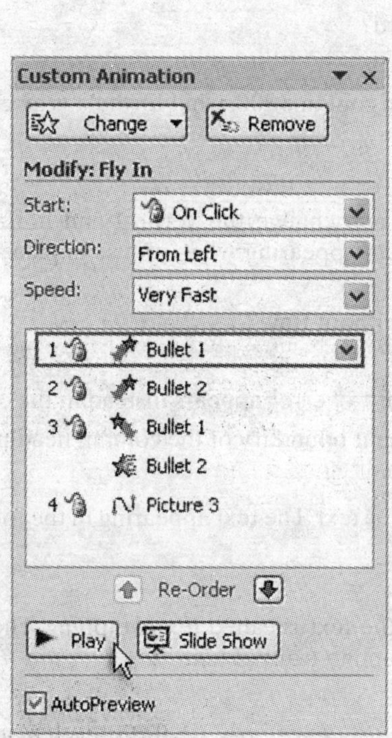

(a) In MS PowerPoint 2007

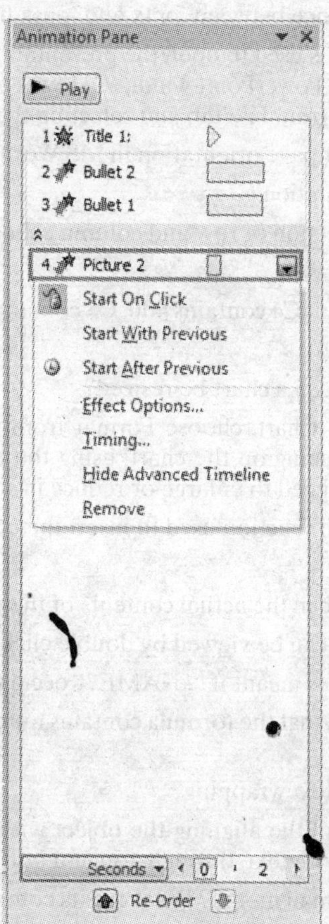

(b) In MS PowerPoint 2010/2013

Step 5: To change the background of the slide and make it more attractive, click on the Design tab, and choose the required theme from the Themes group.

Step 6: To insert a picture/clip art or photograph, go to Insert tab and from the Images group (Illustrations group in 2007 version), select the required illustration to be added. Then by browsing through the illustrations in the file, add the required image.

Step 7: To animate the text and images of the slide, go to Animations tab and open the Animation pane (or Custom Animation pane in 2007 version) to select animation for individual objects present on the presentation slide.

Step 8: The Animation text pane appears on the right of the window. In this pane, every element of the slide can be animated by specifying the Start, Direction and Speed modes (which appear on right-click in 2010/2013 version).

Step 9: By selecting Play, the animations applied to the slide can be tested for that particular slide, and changes can be made accordingly.

Step 10: Transition effects with sound and time settings can be applied to an entire slide by Transitions tab in 2010/2013 version (or Transition to this slide group under Animations tab in 2007 version).

Step 11: Now after including the required text, graphics and animating them, the slide can be viewed by using options under the Slide Show tab.

Step 12: The presentation can then be saved in slide show format, that is, as .ppsx instead of .pptx to be sent to the invitees, since it needs to be modified only by the host, and only read by the invitees.

Viva Voce Questions

1. What is meant by wordprocessing?

   Ans: The process of creating, editing, sorting, saving, printing, transferring and retrieving data in form of files in required format is called wordprocessing.

2. What are the tabs present in the Page Setup dialog box

   Ans: The tabs present are Margins (to set the margin, orientation and pages), Paper (to select the paper size and paper source) and Layout (to change the appearance of start of a section, headers, footers, page and insert line numbers and borders to the pages).

3. What is the difference between .pptx and .ppsx files in MS PowerPoint?

   Ans: The .ppsx file is used to open the presentation in read-only slide show format by clicking on it. Whereas .pptx file is opened in editable PowerPoint window. However, the .ppsx file can be opened and edited in PowerPoint window mode by choosing Open from File tab and selecting the .ppsx file.

4. What is the default page orientation in MS Word?

   Ans: Portrait orientation.

5. What is the intersection of row and column called in MS Word?

   Ans: Cell

6. In MS Excel, if a cell C4 contains 400, C5 contains 100 and C6 contains 200, what formula is given to calculate the sum?

   Ans: = SUM(C4:C6)

7. In MS Excel, how can a chart be resized?

   Ans: Click on the Chart, choose Format from Chart tools and change the vertical and horizontal size accordingly. Alternately, on clicking on the chart, using the arrow pointers appearing when mouse is placed at the corners of the chart, it can be dragged to enlarge or reduce in size.

8. In MS Excel, which function used to insert the current date without time?

   Ans: TODAY()

9. In MS Excel, how can the actual contents of the cell be seen if ### error appears instead in the cell?

   Ans: The contents can be viewed by double clicking on the right boundary of the column heading.

10. In MS Excel, what is meant if "#NAME?" occurs in a cell?

    Ans: This indicates that the formula contains numbers as well as text. The text appearing in the formula is not recognized by MS-Excel.

11. What is meant by text wrapping?

    Ans: The process of the aligning the object with respect to the text is called text wrapping. The various ways to align object are in line with text, through, top and bottom, behind and in front of text.

12. What is meant by mail merge? What are its components?

    Ans: The process of creating personalized letters, e-mail messages, envelopes, labels for each member of the mailing list. The components of mail merge are main document, data source and merged document.

13. What are the databases supported by Excel?

    Ans: Microsoft SQL Server OLAP Services (OLAP provider), MS Access, dBase, MS FoxPro, Oracle, Paradox, SQL Server, Text file databases.

14. In MS Word, how can we calculate the sum of the salaries of five employees A, B, C, D and E entered in the third column of a table?

    Ans: The following steps can be followed to calculate the sum:

    Step 1: Create the last row as total, by right click on the current last row and selecting Insert row option.

    Step 2: Go to Table Tools, and select Layout tab, In the Data group, select formula.

    Step 3: In the formula line, the default formula displayed is = SUM(ABOVE). Click OK.

    The sum of the salaries gets displayed in the last row.

Step 1: Create the table with the salaries entered. Right-click on the cell below the last entry and select Insert Formula.

Exercise 2 | Problem Formulation, Problem Solving (Flowcharts, Algorithms and Pseudocodes)

Introduction

Problem Formulation

This is one of the basic steps in problem solving in which the problem to be solved or the task to be performed is understood thoroughly is clearly understood and the following requirements are analyzed:

1. The instructions to be performed can be ideated by reading the problem statement.
2. The input data required.
3. The output data to be generated.

Setting Up Algorithms or Designing Flowcharts

The logic for solving the problem should be planned by charting the sequence in which instructions should be given. This can be done in two ways:

1. Written stepwise in English-like statements using algorithms.
2. Pictorial representation using flowcharts.

Developing Program

A program is defined as the set of instructions written in a proper syntax and in a certain order to perform some specific task. The coding of programs is done by:

1. Selecting the appropriate programming language for expressing the instruction.
2. Converting the pseudocode or flowchart instructions into the programming language based on a predefined structure called the syntax.

Once the program is coded in the programming language, it is tested to rectify errors, and once all the errors are rectified, it is ready for implementation.

Problem Solving Tools

In order to solve a computational problem, it is necessary to consider the various factors involved in solving the problem.

1. Since the computer has a limited memory, the first requirement is the consideration of memory space and its efficient utilization, called the space complexity of the program.
2. Time required in solving the computational problem is called time complexity of the program.
3. Selection of programming languages in which the problem-solving tool can be implemented.

The computational problem can be solved by using different problem-solving tools; however, the selection of efficient tools is very important so that it reduces the space utilization and time utilization for that problem.

Algorithm	Flowchart	Pseudocode
Definition		
It defined as a sequence of instructions in English-like language used to solve a computational problem.	It is a pictorial and a very structured representation of the algorithm.	It is a sequence of instructions to solve a computational problem expressed in a code which is written in the form of English-like statements resembling the programming languages.
Guidelines		
(a) Precise and unambiguous instructions. (b) Steps in sequence. (c) English-like language. (d) Steps should not be repeated infinitely and the algorithm should terminate to give the desired result. (e) General enough to deal with any kind of contingency.	(a) The flowchart should have a logical start and stop. (b) Standard flowchart symbols should be used for input, output, decision, start, stop operations. (c) Intersection of flow lines should be avoided to obtain a chart with better clarity. (d) Connector symbols should be used in complex flowcharts to reduce the extensive nature of flowcharts.	(a) One statement per line. (b) English-like language. (c) Capitalize initial keywords (d) Steps in sequence. (e) Indent to show loop/structure (f) End structure and then the pseudocode.
Advantages		
(a) Explicit instructions in a form understandable by any person with or without programming knowledge can understand. (b) Basic instructions which can be expressed in various forms such as flowcharts and pseudocodes.	(a) Graphical representations of the code, they are better in communicating the logic of the statements, and easier to convert into a programming code. (b) Symbols and arrows are helpful in reducing the amount of errors, as well as detecting the exact position where errors can take place.	(a) It is language independent, can be used by programmers of diverse backgrounds. (b) Since it is logic-driven and no set style elements or symbols are used to express instructions, it can be updated or modified whenever the need arises. (c) It is not cumbersome to design pseudocodes for complex problems unlike in the case of flowcharts. (d) Since the keywords used in pseudocode are in line with the basic computer operations, it is easy to translate them into programming languages.
Disadvantages		
Algorithms cannot be as such used by programmers, They need to be made more effective by converting them into flowcharts and pseudocodes.	(a) For complex problems, the flowcharts need to be very extensive and it is cumbersome to design such extensive flowcharts. (b) Any update or modification in the statements would result in complete re-designing of the flowchart.	(a) It does not provide the visual representation of the solution that aids easy comprehension. (b) Since it cannot be compiled or executed, the final code needs to be structured based on syntax rules of the programming language selected.

Problem 1: Write an algorithm for finding sum and average of *n* numbers. Also state the properties of a good algorithm.

Solution

The algorithm for finding sum and average of *n* numbers is as follows:

1. `Start`
2. `Read n, a1, a2, …, an`
3. `Set sum = 0`
4. `Set i = 1`
5. `Calculate sum = sum + ai`
6. `Set i = i + 1`
7. `Goto Step 5`
8. `Is i > n else goto Step 5`
9. `Calculate average = sum/n`
10. `Print sum and average`
11. `Stop`

Problem 2: Write a pseudocode to add all the even numbers between 0 and 100 and print the result is as follows:

```
SET i = 2
SET sum = 0
LOOP
  sum += i
  i += 2
UNTIL i <= 100
PRINT sum
```

Problem 3: Write an algorithm to compute the factorial of a number n.

Solution

The algorithm is as follows:

1. Start
2. Read a number n
3. Initialize a variable i = n - 1
4. Compute fact = n * i
5. If n = 1 goto step 6 else goto step 3
6. Print fact
7. Stop

Problem 4: Draw a flowchart to find the highest marks in a set of marks.

Solution

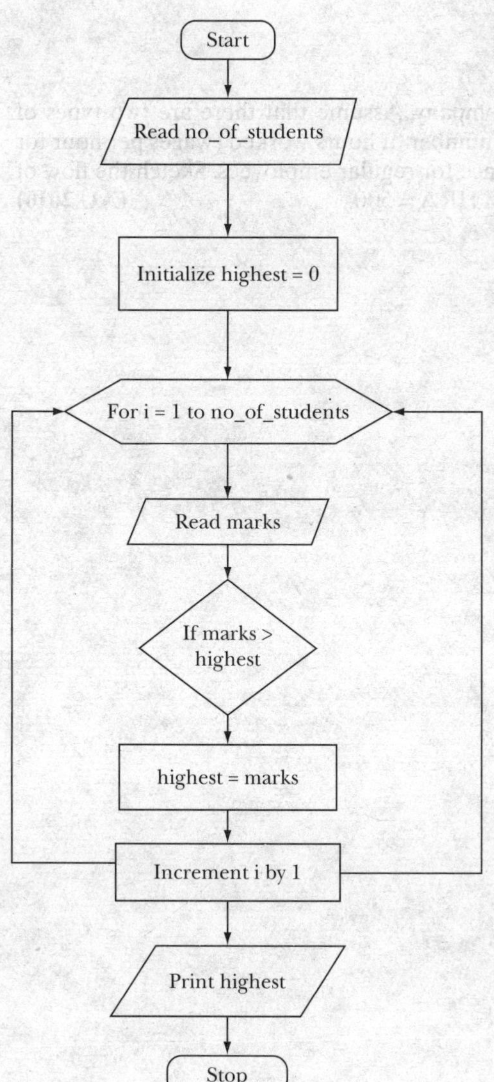

Problem 5: Draw a flowchart to find a factorial of a given number.

Solution

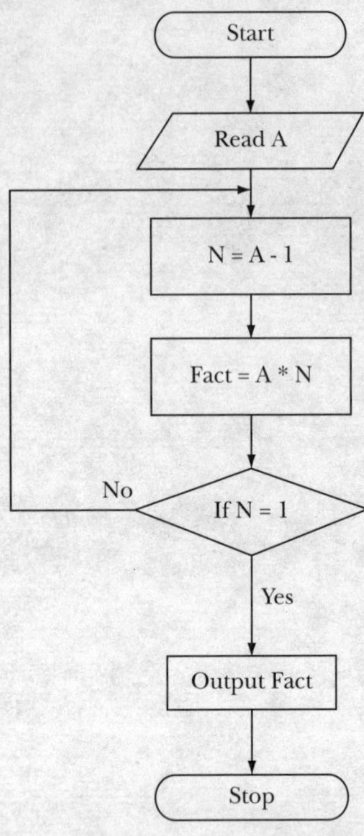

Problem 6: Draw a flowchart to compute the salary of an employee in a company. Assume that there are two types of employees in the company: daily wages and regular. Salary is calculated as the number of hours worked (wages per hour for daily wagers and basic pa + (%DA + basic pay)/100 + HRA + medical allowance for regular employees. Sketch the flow of your design for a regular employee with basic pay = 5000, % of DA = 75% and HRA = 500. **(AU 2010)**

Solution

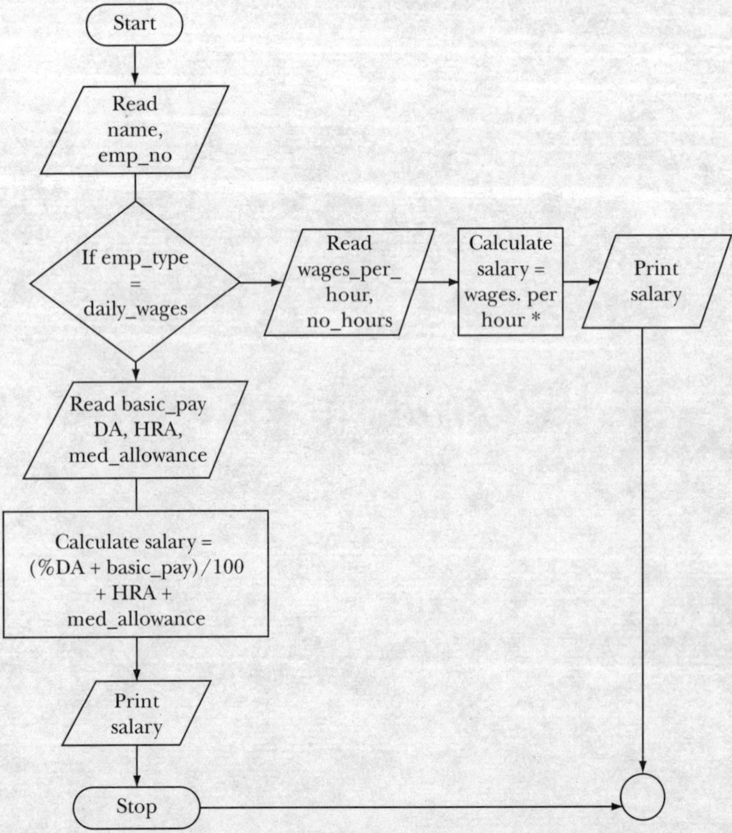

Problem 7: Write an algorithm to print even numbers from 2 to 100.

Solution

1. `Start`
2. `Set count = 2`
3. `Print count`
4. `Increment count by 1 till count <= 100`
5. `If count%2 = 0 then goto step 3 else goto step 4`
6. `Stop`

Problem 8: Write an algorithm to find the maximum among the given three numbers. Draw a flowchart for your algorithm.

Solution
The algorithm is as follows:

1. `Start`
2. `Read three numbers x, y and z`
3. `If x > y and y > z goto step 6 else goto step 4`
4. `If y > z goto step 7 else goto step 5`
5. `Print z is the maximum among the three numbers and goto step 8`
6. `Print x is the maximum among the three numbers and goto step 8`
7. `Print y is the maximum among the three numbers and goto step 8`
8. `Stop`

The flowchart is as follows

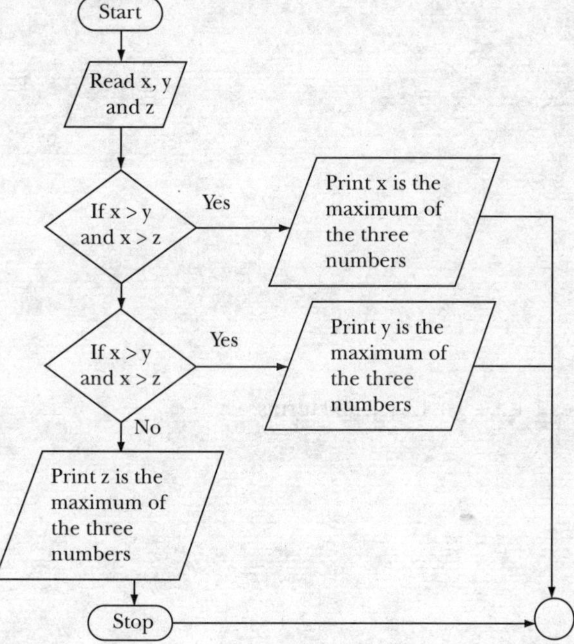

Problem 9: Write an algorithm for displaying Fibonacci series up to 100

Solution

The algorithm is as follows

1. `Start`
2. `Set i = 1, prev_number = 0, number = 1`
3. `Print prev_number, number`
4. `Compute fibo = prev_number + number`
5. `Set prev_number = number`
6. `Set number = fibo`
7. `Increment i by 1`
8. `If(i < 100) then print fibo else goto step 4`
9. Stop

Problem 10: Draw a flowchart to find the sum of first n natural numbers. **(AU 2008 Suppl.)**

Solution

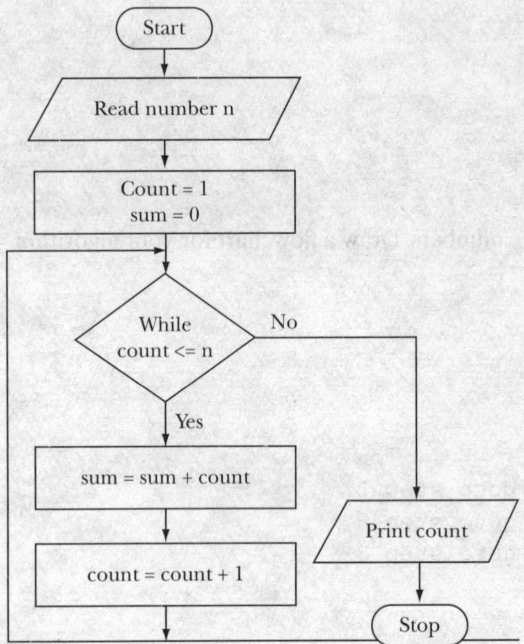

Problem 11: Write the pseudocode to add two matrices.

Solution:

```
READ row, col
SET i = 0, j = 0
LOOP
  READ a[i][j], b[i][j]
  c[i][j]=a[i][j]+b[i][j]
  PRINT c[i][j]
  j = j + 1
UNTIL j < col
  i = i + 1
UNTIL i < row
```

Problem 12: Write an algorithm to find the sum of the following series 1 + 5 + 9 + 13 + … 20 terms.

Solution:

1. Start
2. Set sum = 1 and n = 1.
3. Check if (n <= 20)
4. n = n + 1
5. sum = sum + 4
6. Goto Step 3
7. Print sum
8. Stop

Problem 13: Write an algorithm to find whether a given number is even or odd.

Solution

1. Start
2. Read n
3. Is (n%2 = 0) else goto Step 5
4. Print "Number is even" and goto step 6
5. Print "Number is odd"
6. Stop

Problem 14: Write a pseudocode for calculating compound interest.

Solution

The formula for compound interest is FV = P ∗ $(1 + r/n)^{Y*n}$ where FV is the future value, P is the present value (principal amount), r is the interest rate, n is the number of times the interest is calculated per year and Y is the number of years.

```
READ amount, years, interest_rate, numtimes
CALCULATE compound_interest=amount * pow((1 + (interest_rate/100)/numtimes), numtimes * years)
PRINT compound_interest
EXIT
```

Viva Voce Questions

1. Define algorithm. How is it different from a program?

Ans: Algorithm is defined as a sequence of instructions to solve a computational problem. Algorithm provides the basic plan of the task to be done. It is a (finite) sequence of steps which can be followed to solve a specific problem. Whereas program is a sequence of steps expressed in the syntax of the programming language used, compiled and executed to accomplish a certain task.

2. What is pseudocode?

Ans: The sequence of instructions to solve a computational problem can be expressed in a code which is written in the form of English-like statements resembling the programming languages. This code is known as pseudocode and is designed by using basic programs constructs, such as sequence, branching and looping. The pseudocode contains a logical sequence of statements which cannot be compiled or executed.

3. What are the characteristics of algorithms in computer?

Ans: The characteristics of an algorithm are as follows:

(a) Each instruction in an algorithm should be unambiguous.

(b) The steps of an algorithm should be written in sequence, and there should not be any uncertainty about which step should be followed next.

(c) The steps should not be repeated infinitely, they must reach their concluding state; that is, they must terminate after executing certain number of instructions.

(d) The algorithm must not be open-ended, and its description must be finite.

(e) The algorithm should be general enough to deal with any contingency.

4. Explain guidelines for preparing flowcharts, benefits and limitation of flowcharts.

Ans: The guidelines for preparing flowchart are as follows:

(a) The flowchart should have a logical start and stop.

(b) Standard flowchart symbols should be used for input, output, decision, start, stop operations.

(c) Intersection of flow lines should be avoided to obtain a chart with better clarity.

(d) Connector symbols should be used in complex flowcharts to reduce the extensive nature of flowcharts.

The benefits of flowcharts are as follows:

(a) As these are graphical representations of the code, they are better in communicating the logic of the statements, and are easier to convert into a programming code.

(b) The symbols and arrows are helpful in reducing the amount of errors, as well as detect the exact position where errors can take place.

The limitations are as follows:

(a) For complex problems, the flowcharts need to be very extensive and it is cumbersome to design such extensive flowcharts.

(b) Any update or modification in the statements would result in complete re-designing of the flowchart.

5. What are the properties of a good algorithm?

Ans: The properties of a good algorithm are as follows:

(a) Each and every instruction should be precise and unambiguous.

(b) All steps in the algorithm should be written in sequence.

(c) The language used in the instructions should be like English.

(d) The steps should not be repeated infinitely and the algorithm should terminate at some point.

(e) The desired result should be obtained from the algorithm as soon as it terminates.

6. How does a pseudocode differ from flowchart?

Ans: The advantages of pseudocode over flowcharts are as follows:

(a) As it is logic-driven and no set style elements or symbols are used to express instructions, the pseudocode can be updated or modified whenever the need arises unlike flowcharts.

(b) It is not cumbersome to design pseudocodes for complex problems unlike flowcharts.

Exercise 3 | C Programming

Simple Statements and Expressions, Control Statements (Decision-Making and Looping)

C supports various **types of data** that can be held by variables. These are categorized into three categories:

1. **Built-in:** There are four types of built-in data types, (a) `int` stores the whole numbers, (b) `float` stores the decimal values, (c) `char` stores character values and (d) `void`. Except the `void` data type, all other built-in data types may have several modifiers such as `signed`, `unsigned`, `long` and `short`. The modifier `short` may be applied to integer and character data types and `long` can also be applied to double data type.
2. **Derived:** They are `array`, `function` and `pointer`. These are the data types which are basically derived from the built-in data types.
3. **User-defined:** They are `structure`, `union` and `enumerated` data types. These data types are basically defined by the user and contain the built-in data type as their member.

Operators and expressions are used to denote computations in a program. Operator is a symbol such as +, –, etc. operating upon two variables or constants (called operands); an expression is the combination of operands (variables/constants) and operators written according to the syntax of the programming language. For example, (x – y)*5 = 4 is an expression. Operators can be classified as follows:

1. *Based on number of operands*: Unary, binary or ternary operators.
2. *Based upon the nature of operation*: Arithmetic, relational, logical, assignment, increment/decrement, conditional, bitwise and special operators.

In order to solve a computational problem, we need to have **control statements** written in a particular format called syntax based on the programming language being used. The control statements used in C are of the following types: **decision making**, **looping** and **branching** statements.

1. In **decision-making** or **conditional statements**, the execution of body (statements) depends on the test condition. If the condition evaluates to true, one set of statements are executed otherwise another set of statements are executed. These statements are also called decision construct, because they allow choosing the set of statements for execution depending upon expression's truth value. C provides various types of selection statements, such as `if`, `if-else`, `ladder if-else`, `nested if-else`, `switch-case`, `nested switch-case`.
2. The **iterative** or **looping** statements are used when we want to repeat a set of statements for certain number of times. The number of iterations depends on the test condition. A set of statements are repeated again and again till the condition is true. As soon as the condition becomes false, the repetition stops. The set of statements that are repeated is called the body of the loop. C offers various kinds of looping statements, such as `for` loop, `nested for`, `while` loop, `do-while` loop.
3. The **branching** statements are used to terminate the execution of looping or conditional statements and direct the control to another part of the program. C offers various kinds of looping statements, such as `break`, `continue`, `goto` and `exit`.

Program 1: Write a program to find whether the number is even or odd using nested switch statement.

Solution

```
#include <stdio.h>
#include <conio.h>
#include <stdlib.h>
void main()
{
int number;
int result;
printf("\n Enter any number:");
```

```
scanf("%d",&number);
switch(number)
{
case 0: printf("\n Number is even");
break;
case 1: printf("\n Number is odd");
break;
default: result=number%2;
switch(result)
{
case 0: printf("\n Number is even");
break;
default: printf("\n Number is odd");
}
}
}
```

Output

Flowchart

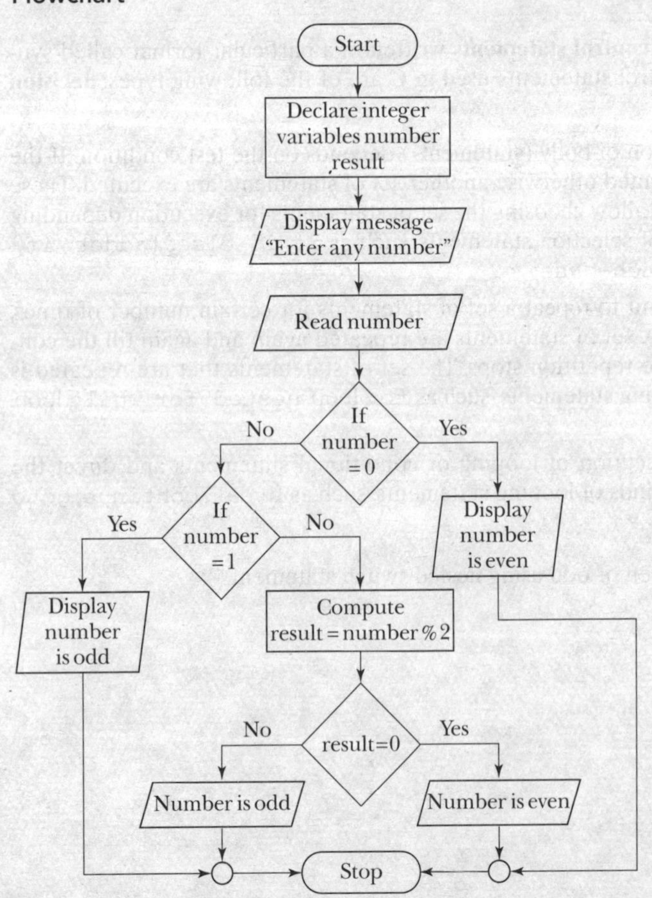

Pseudocode

START
PROMPT to enter number
READ number
IF number = 0 THEN
  PRINT message "The number is even"
ELSE IF number = 1
  PRINT message "The number is odd"
ELSE COMPUTE result = number%2
  IF result = 0
    PRINT message "Number is even"
  ELSE
    PRINT message "Number is odd"
STOP

Program 2: Write a program to show the multiplication table of 12.

Solution

```
#include <stdio.h>
#include <conio.h>
#include <string.h>
#include <stdlib.h>
int main()
{
int i;
printf("\n Multiplication table of 12 ");
printf("\n -------------------------- ");
printf("\n");
for(i=1;i<=10;i++)
{
printf("12x%d=%d\n", i, 12 * i);
printf("\n");
}
getch();
}
```

Output

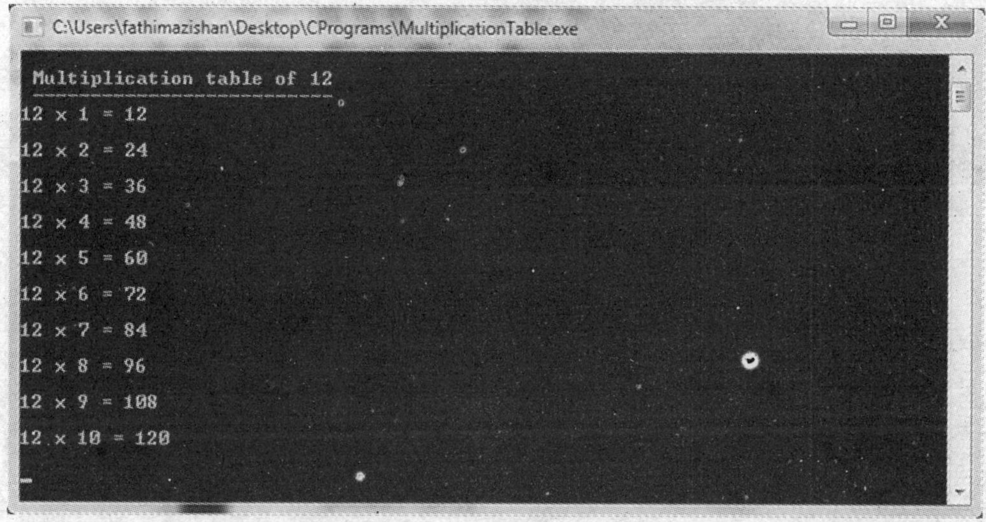

Flowchart

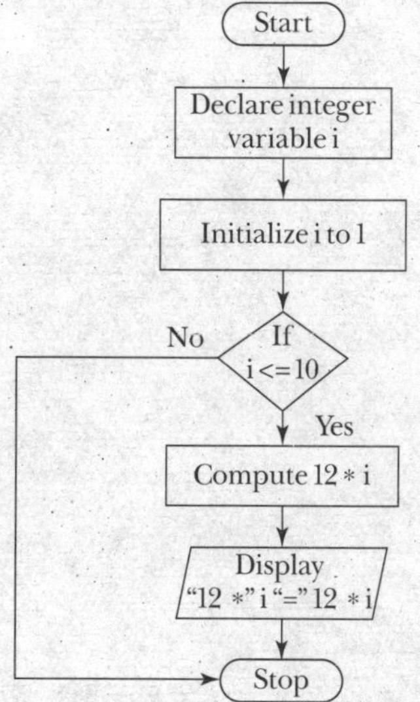

Pseudocode

START
INITIALIZE i to 1
WHILE i < 10
  PRINT 12 * i = (product of 12 and i)
  INCREMENT i by 1
UNTIL i = 10
STOP

Program 3: Write a program to implement the expression ((m + n)/p – m)∗m), where m = 4, n = 6, p = 8.

Solution

```
#include <stdio.h>
#include <conio.h>
int main()
{
float m,n,p,result;
printf("\n Enter value of m:");
scanf("%f",&m);
printf("\n Enter value of n:");
scanf("%f",&n);
printf("\n Enter value of p:");
scanf("%f",&p);
result=(((m+n)/p-m)*m);
printf("\n Result substituting values of m,n and p in the expression ((m+n)/p-m)*m):
  %.2f",result);
getch();
}
```

Output

```
C:\Users\fathimazishan\Desktop\CPrograms\Expression.exe

Enter value of m:4

Enter value of n:6

Enter value of p:8

Result substituting values of m,n and p in the expression ((m + n)/ p - m)* m):
-11.00
```

Flowchart

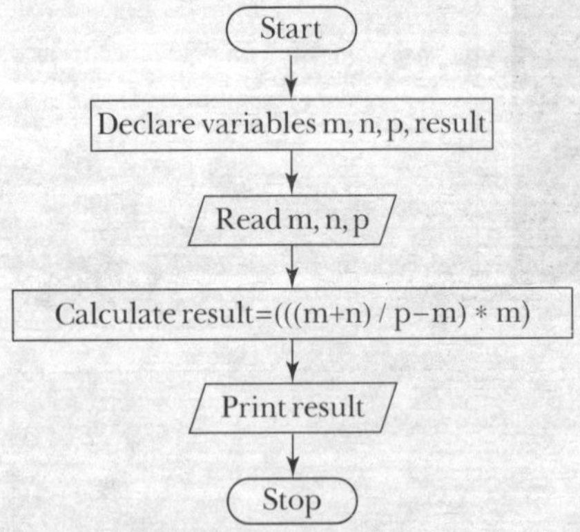

Pseudocode

START
READ m, n, p
CALCULATE result = (((m + n)/ p – m)∗ m)
PRINT result
STOP

Program 4: Write a program for the following expressions:
(a) a = 5 <= 8 && 6! = 5
(b) a = b++ + ++b where b = 50

Solution

```
#include <stdio.h>
#include <conio.h>
int main()
{
int a;
int b;
a=5<=8 && 6!=5;
printf("\n a=%d in the expression a=5<=8 && 6!=5",a);
```

```
b=50;
a=b++ + ++b;
printf("\n Now a=%d when b=50",a);
getch();
}
```

Output

```
C:\Users\fathimazishan\Desktop\CPrograms\Expression1.exe
a = 1 in the expression a = 5<=8 && 6!=5
Now a = 102 when b = 50_
```

Flowchart

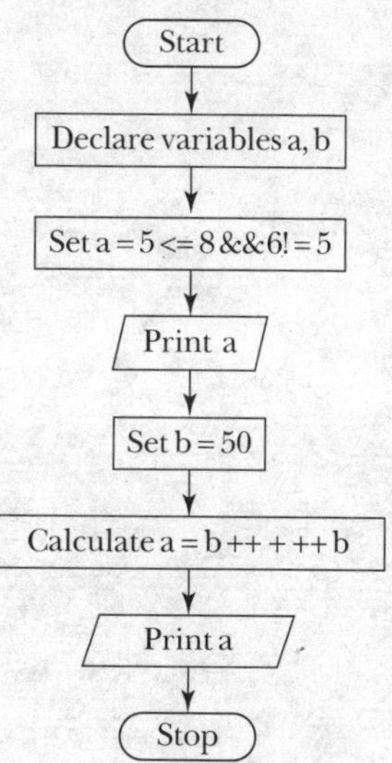

Pseudocode

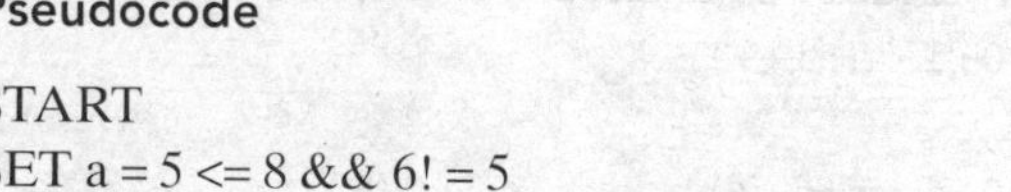

START
SET a = 5 <= 8 && 6! = 5
PRINT a
SET b = 50
CALCULATE a = b++ + ++b
PRINT a
STOP

Simple Programming for One-Dimensional and Two-Dimensional Arrays

An **array** is a collection of similar data items which may be of the same data type. The data type can be int, char, float or any user-defined type such as structure or class. Therefore, arrays are derived data types. The array elements are stored in consecutive memory locations; therefore, they are linear data structures. In other words, an array is a collection of similar items which are referred by a common name, that is, the array name.

There are two types of arrays:

1. **One-dimensional array:** It is a collection of similar data items. It is sometimes called a list and is the simplest form of an array. The one-dimensional array is defined by specifying its name, size and data types of the items.
2. **Multidimensional array:** It is also a collection of similar data items where each data item is also an array of fixed size. The number of square brackets is more (a pair for each subscript is required) in multidimensional arrays. There will be two pairs of square brackets for two-dimensional arrays, three pairs for three-dimensional arrays and so on.
3. **Two-dimensional array:** It is a simple case of multidimensional array where each element of the array is a one-dimensional array itself. So we can say that two-dimensional array is a collection of one-dimensional arrays. In two-dimensional arrays, only two dimensions are required where the first dimension refers to the number of rows and the second dimension refers to the number of columns. It is just like a **matrix** in mathematics.

Program 5: Write a program to add two matrices.

Solution

```
#include <stdio.h>
#include <conio.h>
int main()
```

```
{
int i,j,m1[100][100],m2[100][100],m3[100][100],m,n,sum;
printf("Enter values of n and m to set order mxn of both the matrices");
scanf("%d %d",&n,&m);
printf("Enter elements of 1st matrix");
for(i=0;i<n;i++)
{
for(j=0;j<m;j++)
{
scanf("%d",&m1[i][j]);
}
}
printf("Enter elements of 2nd matrix");
for(i=0;i<n;i++)
{
for(j=0;j<m;j++)
{
scanf("%d",&m2[i][j]);
}
}
printf("Matrix after addition of two matrices is -- \n");
sum=0;
for(i=0;i<n;i++)
{
for(j=0;j<m;j++)
{ sum=m1[i][j]+m2[i][j];
m3[i][j]=sum;
printf("%d\t",m3[i][j]);
}
printf("\n");
}
getch();
}
```

Output

```
C:\Users\Zishan khan\Desktop\CPrograms\AdditionMatrices.exe
Enter values of n and m to set order m x n of both the matrices 2 3
Enter elements of 1st matrix2
2
-1
4
3
7
Enter elements of 2nd matrix-1
3
6
5
-3
4
Matrix after addition of two matrices is --
1       5       5
9       0       11
```

The above output is interpreted as follows:

$$\begin{bmatrix} 2 & 2 & -1 \\ 4 & 3 & 7 \end{bmatrix} + \begin{bmatrix} -1 & 3 & 6 \\ 5 & -3 & 4 \end{bmatrix} = \begin{bmatrix} 1 & 5 & 5 \\ 9 & 0 & 11 \end{bmatrix}$$

Flowchart

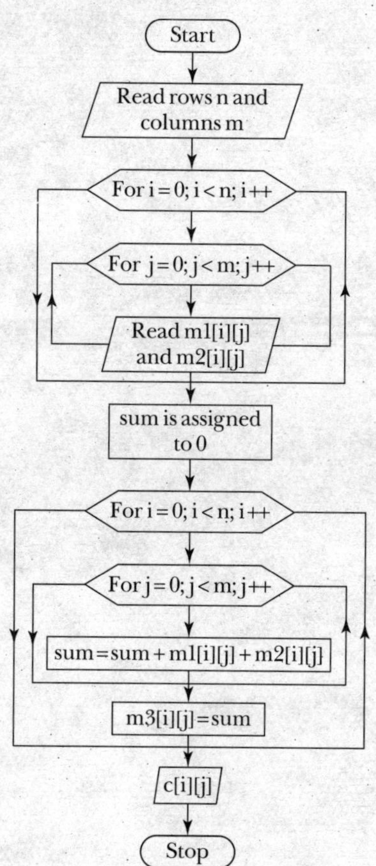

Pseudocode

```
START
READ n, m
READ m1[i][j], m2[i][j]
SET sum = 0
FOR i = 0 to n
  FOR j = 0 to m
    CALCULATE sum = sum + m1[i][j] + m2[i][j]
    m3[i][j] = sum
    INCREMENT j by 1
  UNTIL j < m
  INCREMENT i by 1
UNTIL i < n
PRINT m3[i][j]
STOP
```

Program 6: Write a program to find the sum of diagonal elements, upper triangular elements and lower triangular elements.

Solution

```
#include <stdio.h>
#include <conio.h>
int main()
{
int n,choice,i,j,a[10][10],sum=0,upperCount=0,lowerCount=0;
printf("\n Enter the dimensions of an n*n matrix:");
scanf("%d",&n);
printf("\n Enter the elements of matrix: ");
for(i=0;i<n;i++)
{
for(j=0;j<n;j++)
{
scanf("%d",&a[i][j]);
}
}
printf("\n The matrix is \n");
for(i=0;i<n;i++)
{     printf("\n");
for(j=0;j<n;j++)
{
printf("%d\t",a[i][j]);
}
}
do
{
```

```
printf("\n \n");
printf("\n 1. Sum of diagonal elements");
printf("\n 2. Sum of Upper trianglar elements");
printf("\n 3. Sum of Lower triangular elements");
printf("\n Choose any one option...");
scanf("%d",&choice);
switch(choice)
{
case 1:
for(i=0;i<n;i++)
{
for(j=0;j<n;j++)
{
if(i==j)
sum=sum+a[i][j];
}
}
printf("\n Sum of the diagonal elements of a matrix is: %d",sum);
break;
case 2:
for(i=0;i<n;i++)
{
for(j=0;j<n;j++)
{
if(i>=j)
{
if(a[i][j]==0)
upperCount++;
}
}
}
if(upperCount==n)
{
printf("\n The matrix is upper triangular");
for(i=0;i<n;i++)
{  for(j=0;j<n;j++)
{     if(j>=i)
{
sum+=a[i][j];
}
}
}
printf("\n The sum of upper triangular elements are : %d",sum);
}
else
{
printf("\n The matrix is not upper triangular");
}
break;
case 3:
for(i=0;i<n;i++)
{
for(j=0;j<n;j++)
{
if(i<=j)
{
```

```
if(a[i][j]==0)
lowerCount++;
}
}
}
if(lowerCount==n)
{
printf("\n The matrix is lower triangular");
for(i=0;i<n;i++)
{  for(j=0;j<n;j++)
{       if(j<=i)
{
sum+=a[i][j];
}
}
}
printf("\n The sum of the lower triangular elements are : %d",sum);
}
else{
printf("\n The matrix is not lower triangular");
}
break;
default:
printf("\n Pls choose 1,2 or 3");
main();
break;
}
}while(choice<4);
getch();
}
```

Output

```
C:\Users\fathimazishan\Desktop\CPrograms\SumOfDiagonalsUpperTriLowerTri.exe

Enter the dimensions of an n*n matrix:3

Enter the elements of matrix: 1
4
2
0
3
4
0
0
1

The matrix is

1       4       2
0       3       4
0       0       1

1. Sum of diagonal elements
2. Sum of Upper trianglar elements
3. Sum of Lower triangular elements
Choose any one option...2

The matrix is upper triangular
The sum of upper triangular elements are : 15


1. Sum of diagonal elements
2. Sum of Upper trianglar elements
3. Sum of Lower triangular elements
Choose any one option...3

The matrix is not lower triangular


1. Sum of diagonal elements
2. Sum of Upper trianglar elements
3. Sum of Lower triangular elements
Choose any one option...
```

Programs with User-Defined Functions and Parameter Passing Techniques

A complex program contains a large number of instructions which are not easy to manage. Therefore, such programs are generally decomposed into different modules containing small sets of instructions to perform specific tasks. These modules are called **functions**. There are various types of functions based on the tasks accomplished by them – user defined, standard library and string functions.

Any function defined by the user to carry out operations to solve a particular problem is called a **user defined function**. In C, main() itself is a user-defined function that invokes other functions in the program to perform various tasks. A function can be invoked from other parts of the program. Usually, if some sequence of instructions is repeatedly appearing in a program then a function can be defined for that particular sequence rather than repeating it again. Also the function may or may not return a value to the calling function; therefore there is no difference between a function and a subroutine (procedure) in C.

There are three important features associated with a function:

1. **Function prototype or declaration:** The function prototype is also called the function declaration. A function must be declared before it is used anywhere in the C program. It is a very useful feature in C as the compiler compares the function to its prototype to determine whether the number and data type of parameters are matching or not. If they do not match, it generates an error. A function prototype must have a return type. The *return type* is any C data type which describes that the function will return the value of *return type* from the body of the function to the calling function. But if the function *return type* is void, then it specifies that the function is not returning any value and so there is no need of the return statement.
2. **Function definition:** A function definition is a declaration that contains the function body. Actually, it tells the program what statements are to be executed and how they are executed. It may or may not have any parameters. If it does not contain any parameter then we may write void in the parenthesis. A function definition, just like a function declaration, must have a return type.
3. **Function call:** If a program uses a function then it requires to be called for execution. When a function is called, the control is transferred to the function; the body of the function is executed and then the control returns to the statements following the function call. A function is called in two ways:
   - `function_name (actual parameters);`
   - `variable/expression = function_name (actual parameters);`

   In the first case, function is called by providing the function name, followed by the actual parameters. In this case, function does not return a value. In the second case, the function is called in the same manner as in the first case but the value returned by that function is stored in some variable of the same type as of function return type or it may be used in some expression.

The parameters can be passed to the function in two ways:

1. **Call by value:** In this mode of parameter passing the values of actual parameters are copied into formal parameters (temporary variables). The function does not have access to the actual parameters (original values) and can work only on the copies of the values created as formal parameters. In this method, changes made in the formal parameter do not get reflected in the actual parameter even if the names of actual and formal parameters are same. So this method is useful when we want to keep the values of actual parameters intact.
2. **Call by reference:** In this mode of parameter passing, instead of passing the value to a function, a reference or the alias to the actual parameter is passed. Therefore, the actual parameters can be accessed by two names, the original name and the alias or reference name. When a function is called then the formal parameter becomes a reference to the actual parameter. In this method of parameter passing, actual parameters are referred by another name (formal parameter), therefore the changes made in the formal parameters are reflected in the actual parameters. This implies that call by reference is useful when we want to change the values of the actual parameters in case formal parameters change their values.

   In the following program, x and y are actual parameters and a and b are formal parameters. Changes made in formal parameters a and b are reflected in actual parameters x and y.

Program 7: Write a function to accept values x and y, and return x^y.

Solution

```
#include <stdio.h>
#include <conio.h>
#include <math.h>
float Power(float *,float *);/*Function prototype for call by reference*/
int main()
{
```

```
float x;
float y;
printf("\n Enter any number x:");
scanf("%f",&x);
printf("\n Enter its power y:");
scanf("%f",&y);
printf("\n Calculating x raised to y:%f", result=Power(&x,&y));/*Actual parameters x and y*/
getch();
}
float Power(float *a,float *b)/*Formal parameters a and b*/
{
int i;
float result=1;
for(i=1;i<=b;i++)
{
result=result*a;
}
return result;
}
```

Output

Flowchart

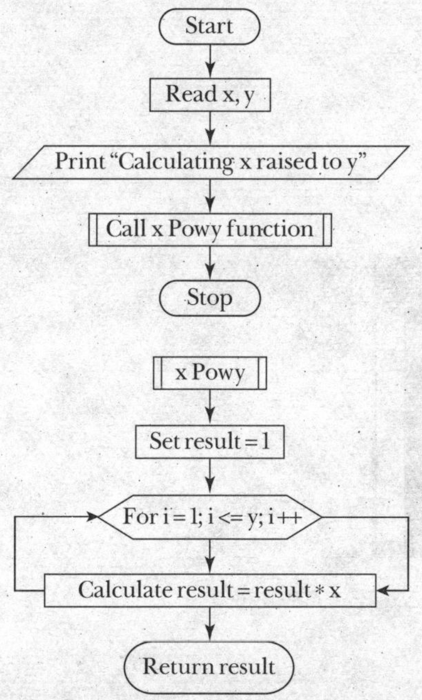

Pseudocode

START
READ x, y
PRINT result ← xPowy(x, y)
STOP

xPowy START
SET result = 1
FOR i = 1 to y
  CALCULATE result = result*y
  INCREMENT i by 1
UNTIL i <= y
RETURN result

Program 8: Write a program to display Pascal's triangle using ^nC_r method.

Solution

```
#include <stdio.h>
#include <conio.h>
```

```
long factorial(int);
void space(int);
int nCr(int,int);
main()
{
int i,j,rows;
printf("\n Enter no of rows: ");
scanf("%d",&rows);
for(i=0;i<rows;i++)
{
space(3*(rows-i));
for(j=0;j<=i;j++)
{
printf("%3d",nCr(i,j));
space(3);
}
printf("\n");
}
getch();
}
int nCr(int n,int r)
{
int i,ncr=1;
for(i=1;i<=n-r;i++)
{
ncr=ncr*(n-i+1)/i;
}
return ncr;
}
void space(int n)
{
int i;
for(i=0;i<n;i++)
printf(" ");
}
```

Output

```
C:\Users\fathimazishan\Desktop\CPrograms\pascaltriangle.exe

Enter no of rows: 10
                                1
                             1     1
                          1     2     1
                       1     3     3     1
                    1     4     6     4     1
                 1     5    10    10     5     1
              1     6    15    20    15     6     1
           1     7    21    35    35    21     7     1
        1     8    28    56    70    56    28     8     1
     1     9    36    84   126   126    84    36     9     1
```

Problems using Recursive Functions

Recursion is an ability of a function or procedure or algorithm to repeatedly call itself until a certain condition is met. Such condition is called the *base condition*. The function which calls itself is called a *recursive function*. The following conditions must be satisfied for using recursion:

1. There must be some base condition for which the function calls itself.
2. Each time, the function calling should lead to the base condition.

Recursion can be classified into two categories: *Direct recursion*, which occurs when the function calls itself directly, and *indirect recursion*, which occurs when the function calls another function that may eventually call the original function.

To find the factorial of 5, the following operations need to be carried out:

$5! = 5 * 4!$

$4 * 3!$

$3 * 2!$

$2 * 1!$

1

$= 5 * 4 * 3 * 2 * 1 = 120$

Hence, we can see that to find the factorial of 5 we are using 5 ∗ 4! which means to calculate the factorial (of 5), we are again using factorial (of 4). This is recursion because function factorial calls itself. But for factorial of 1 it does not have to call itself; rather it uses the value 1 for factorial of 1. This is the base condition for factorial function and we can see here that each time function is called with a lesser (5, 4, 3, 2, 1) value thus moving towards the base condition (factorial of 1 = 1).

Program 9: Write a C program to find the factorial of a given number using recursion.

Solution

```
#include <stdio.h>
#include <conio.h>
int rec(int number);
int main()
{
int number, factorial;
printf("\n Enter the number for which you want to find the factorial : ");
scanf ("%d", &number);
factorial=rec (number);
printf("\n Factorial Value=%d", factorial);
getch();
}
int rec(int number)
{
int factorial;
if (number==1){
return (1);
}
else{
factorial=number*rec(number-1);
}
return (factorial);
}
```

Output

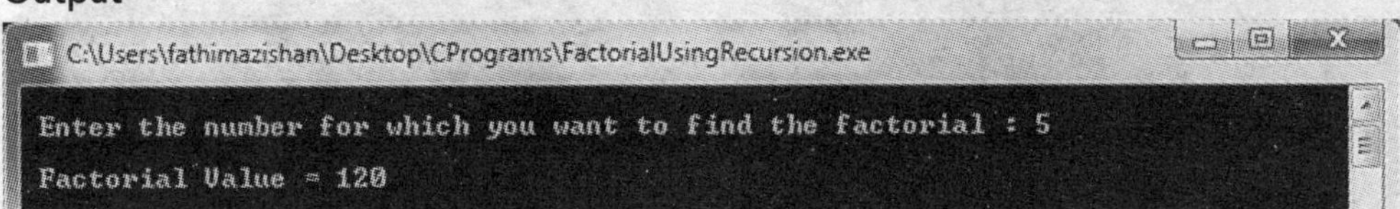
C:\Users\fathimazishan\Desktop\CPrograms\FactorialUsingRecursion.exe

```
Enter the number for which you want to find the factorial : 5
Factorial Value = 120
```

Flowchart

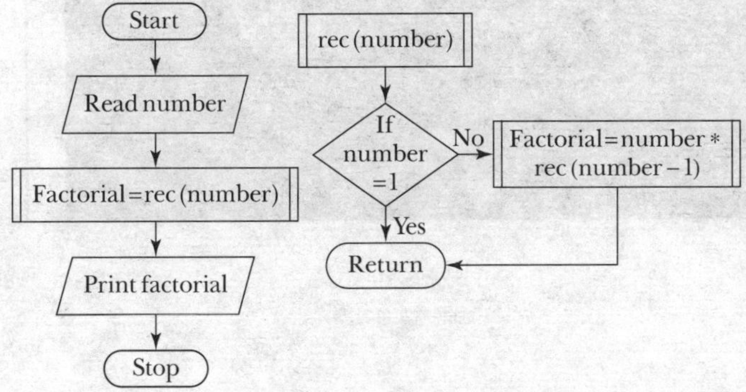

Pseudocode

START
READ number
SET factorial ← rec(number)
PRINT factorial
STOP
rec START
IF number = 1 THEN
  RETURN 1
ELSE
  CALCULATE factorial ← number ∗ rec(number – 1)
RETURN factorial

Program 10: Write a recursive program for the Fibonacci series.

Solution

```
#include <stdio.h>
#include <conio.h>
static int limit;
void fibonacci (int prev_number, int number)
{
static int i=1; /*i is not 0, because 1 is already counted in main*/
int fibo;
while(i!=limit)
{
fibo=prev_number+number;
prev_number=number; /*important steps*/
number=fibo;
printf ("\n%d", fibo);
i++;
fibonacci (prev_number,number);/*recursion*/
}
}
int main()
{
static int prev_number=0, number=1;/*static: so value is not lost*/
printf("\n Enter how many numbers to be displayed of Fibonacci series:");
scanf("%d",&limit);
printf ("1 ");/*to avoid complexity*/
fibonacci (prev_number,number);
getch();
}
```

Output

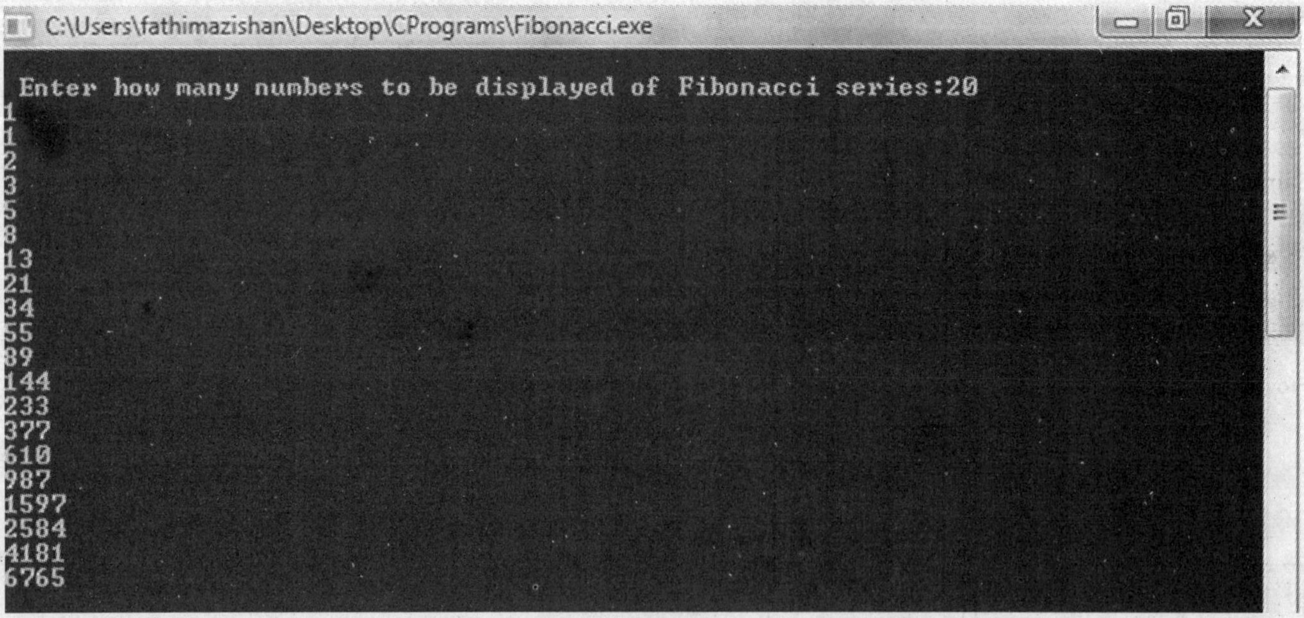

```
C:\Users\fathimazishan\Desktop\CPrograms\Fibonacci.exe

 Enter how many numbers to be displayed of Fibonacci series:20
1
1
2
3
5
8
13
21
34
55
89
144
233
377
610
987
1597
2584
4181
6765
```

Flowchart

Start

Declare two static integer variables prev_number and number

Initialize prev_number to 0 and number to 1

Call fibonacci function recursively passing prev_number and number as arguments

Stop

Fibonacci

Prompt to enter how many numbers to be displayed of Fibonacci series

Read limit

Declare static integer i and initalize to 1 and also integer variable fibo

While i < limit

Yes

Compute fibo = prev_number + number

prev_number = number

number = fibo

Display fibo

Increment i by 1

Stop

Pseudocode

```
START
SET prev_number = 0
SET number = 1
Call fibonacci(prev_number, number)
STOP

Fibonacci START
PROMPT to enter how many numbers to be displayed
of Fibonacci series
READ limit
INITIALIZE i to 1
WHILE i < limit
   CALCULATE fibo = prev_number + number;
   SET prev_number = number
   SET number = fibo;
   PRINT fibo
   INCREMENT i by 1
UNTIL i! = limit
```

Iterative Problems – Trigonometric Series Evaluation

Iteration is generally used for repetitive computation in which each action is defined in terms of the previous result. It looks just like recursion, but this is not true. There are some differences between recursion and iterations as compiled in Table 1.

Table 1 Comparison of recursion and iteration

S. No.	Recursion	Iteration
1.	When a function calls itself, it is called recursion.	In iteration, a set of statements is executed repeatedly until some specified condition is satisfied.
2.	Recursion is based on the base condition; execution of statements moving towards the base condition.	Iteration is based on the initialization, termination condition, updation and execution.
3.	Recursion is a top-down approach.	Iteration is bottom-up approach.
4.	Recursion runs out of memory if base condition is not checked.	Iteration results in infinite loop if termination condition is not met.
5.	Recursion takes more space to store new set of local variables.	Iteration does not take much time as compared to recursion.
6.	Recursion is not efficient.	Iteration is efficient.
7.	Every recursive algorithm can be converted into its iterative version.	Every iterative method cannot be converted into its recursive version.
8.	For proper function recursion saves the return address.	Iterative method does not save the return address.

Program 11: Write a program to find the value for the cos(x) series:

$$\cos(x) = x - \frac{x^2}{2!} + \frac{x^4}{4!} - \frac{x^6}{6!} + \frac{x^8}{8!} - \cdots$$

Solution

```
#include <stdio.h>
#include <conio.h>
float series_sum(float x);
void main()
{
clrscr();
int n;
float x, sum;
printf("Enter the number of terms in the series: %d",n);
scanf("%d",&n);
printf("Enter the value of x in degree: %d",x);
scanf("%d",&x);
float series_sum(x);
printf("cos(x): %f",sum);
getch();
}
float series_sum(float x)
{
int i;
float term=1,sum=1
x=x*3.14/180;
for(i=1;i<=n;i++)
{
term=(-1*term*x*x)/((2*i)*(2*i-1));
sum=sum+term;
}
return (sum)
}
```

Output

```
Enter the number of terms in the series: 25
Enter the value of x in degree: 60
cos(x): 0.50046
```

Program 12: Write a program to find the perfect squares from 1 to 500.

Solution

```
#include <stdio.h>
#include <stdlib.h>
#include <conio.h>
int main()
{
int i,j;
perfsquare(i,j);
getch();
}

for(i=1;i<=500;i++)
{
for(j=1;j<=500;j++)
{
if(i==j)
{
printf ("%d\t ", i*j);
}
}
}
```

Output

```
C:\Users\fathimazishan\Desktop\CPrograms\PerfectSquare.exe
1     , 4     , 9     , 16    , 25    , 36    , 49    , 64    , 81    , 100
, 121 , 144   , 169   , 196   , 225   , 256   , 289   , 324   , 361   , 400
, 441 , 484   , 529   , 576   , 625   , 676   , 729   , 784   , 841   , 900
, 961 , 1024  , 1089  , 1156  , 1225  , 1296  , 1369  , 1444  , 1521  , 1600
, 1681 , 1764 , 1849  , 1936  , 2025  , 2116  , 2209  , 2304  , 2401  , 2500
, 2601 , 2704 , 2809  , 2916  , 3025  , 3136  , 3249  , 3364  , 3481  , 3600
, 3721 , 3844 , 3969  , 4096  , 4225  , 4356  , 4489  , 4624  , 4761  , 4900
, 5041 , 5184 , 5329  , 5476  , 5625  , 5776  , 5929  , 6084  , 6241  , 6400
, 6561 , 6724 , 6889  , 7056  , 7225  , 7396  , 7569  , 7744  , 7921  , 8100
, 8281 , 8464 , 8649  , 8836  , 9025  , 9216  , 9409  , 9604  , 9801  , 10000
, 10201 , 10404 , 10609 , 10816 , 11025 , 11236 , 11449 , 11664 , 11881 , 12100
, 12321 , 12544 , 12769 , 12996 , 13225 , 13456 , 13689 , 13924 , 14161 , 14400
, 14641 , 14884 , 15129 , 15376 , 15625 , 15876 , 16129 , 16384 , 16641 , 16900
, 17161 , 17424 , 17689 , 17956 , 18225 , 18496 , 18769 , 19044 , 19321 , 19600
, 19881 , 20164 , 20449 , 20736 , 21025 , 21316 , 21609 , 21904 , 22201 , 22500
, 22801 , 23104 , 23409 , 23716 , 24025 , 24336 , 24649 , 24964 , 25281 , 25600
, 25921 , 26244 , 26569 , 26896 , 27225 , 27556 , 27889 , 28224 , 28561 , 28900
, 29241 , 29584 , 29929 , 30276 , 30625 , 30976 , 31329 , 31684 , 32041 , 32400
, 32761 , 33124 , 33489 , 33856 , 34225 , 34596 , 34969 , 35344 , 35721 , 36100
, 36481 , 36864 , 37249 , 37636 , 38025 , 38416 , 38809 , 39204 , 39601 , 40000
, 40401 , 40804 , 41209 , 41616 , 42025 , 42436 , 42849 , 43264 , 43681 , 44100
, 44521 , 44944 , 45369 , 45796 , 46225 , 46656 , 47089 , 47524 , 47961 , 48400
, 48841 , 49284 , 49729 , 50176 , 50625 , 51076 , 51529 , 51984 , 52441 , 52900
, 53361 , 53824 , 54289 , 54756 , 55225 , 55696 , 56169 , 56644 , 57121 , 57600
, 58081 , 58564 , 59049 , 59536 , 60025 , 60516 , 61009 , 61504 , 62001 , 62500
```

```
C:\Users\fathimazishan\Desktop\CPrograms\PerfectSquare.exe
, 63001 , 63504 , 64009 , 64516 , 65025 , 65536 , 66049 , 66564 , 67081 , 67600
, 68121 , 68644 , 69169 , 69696 , 70225 , 70756 , 71289 , 71824 , 72361 , 72900
, 73441 , 73984 , 74529 , 75076 , 75625 , 76176 , 76729 , 77284 , 77841 , 78400
, 78961 , 79524 , 80089 , 80656 , 81225 , 81796 , 82369 , 82944 , 83521 , 84100
, 84681 , 85264 , 85849 , 86436 , 87025 , 87616 , 88209 , 88804 , 89401 , 90000
, 90601 , 91204 , 91809 , 92416 , 93025 , 93636 , 94249 , 94864 , 95481 , 96100
, 96721 , 97344 , 97969 , 98596 , 99225 , 99856 , 100489        , 101124
, 101761        , 102400        , 103041        , 103684        , 104329
, 104976        , 105625        , 106276        , 106929        , 107584
, 108241        , 108900        , 109561        , 110224        , 110889
, 111556        , 112225        , 112896        , 113569        , 114244
, 114921        , 115600        , 116281        , 116964        , 117649
, 118336        , 119025        , 119716        , 120409        , 121104
, 121801        , 122500        , 123201        , 123904        , 124609
, 125316        , 126025        , 126736        , 127449        , 128164
, 128881        , 129600        , 130321        , 131044        , 131769
, 132496        , 133225        , 133956        , 134689        , 135424
, 136161        , 136900        , 137641        , 138384        , 139129
, 139876        , 140625        , 141376        , 142129        , 142884
, 143641        , 144400        , 145161        , 145924        , 146689
, 147456        , 148225        , 148996        , 149769        , 150544
, 151321        , 152100        , 152881        , 153664        , 154449
, 155236        , 156025        , 156816        , 157609        , 158404
, 159201        , 160000        , 160801        , 161604        , 162409
, 163216        , 164025        , 164836        , 165649        , 166464
```

Flowchart

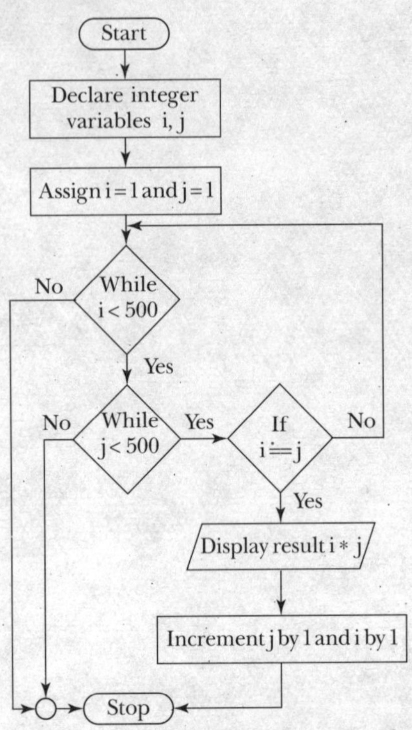

Pseudocode

```
START
SET i = 1 and j = 1.
WHILE i < 500
  WHILE j < 500
    IF i is equal to j
    PRINT result of i*j.
    INCREMENT j by 1
  UNTIL j = 500
  INCREMENT i by 1
UNTIL i = 500
STOP
```

Solving Problems using String Functions

String constants are declared within double quotes. In an extension to arrays, strings can also be expressed in the form of character arrays. Each string is terminated by a **null character** "\0"which takes one byte for its storage. Hence, the string length would be the number of characters (which take one byte each) plus one byte for null character. The null character is very important because it refers to the end of a string. The compiler automatically initializes a null character at the end of each character array by default. Therefore, we must declare the size of the character array one more than the actual number of characters we want to store, leaving room for the null character Otherwise on displaying the string, the output will be the desired string followed by some garbage value. In case of two-dimensional array, the first dimension determines the number of strings and the second dimension determines the number of characters in each string. For example, `char empname[5][10];` Here empname can have 5 elements (name) of length 10 characters.

There are various built-in functions which are frequently used with the character array. These functions are defined in `string.h` so we must include that file whenever we want to use such functions. Some of the functions are given in Table 2.

Table 2 String functions

Function	Syntax	Description	Example
`strlen`	`strlen(string)`	This function determines the length of a string not including null character.	`int len=strlen(justname);`

`strcpy` and `strncpy`	`strcpy (dest,source)` `strncpy (dest, source,length)`	This function copies the source string into destination string, where source and destination both must be character arrays.
		The strncpy function copies one string into another upto a specified length indicated in the argument.
			`char dest;`
			`int length;`
			`char source[ ]="ABC";`
			`strcpy(dest,source);`
			`strncpy(dest,source, length);`

`strcmp` and `stricmp`	`strcmp(S1,S2);` `stricmp(S1,S2);`	The comparison starts with the first character of the string and continues until a corresponding character differs or end of string is reached.
		The stricmp function does not discriminate between two strings if the characters are same, but the case is different.
			`strcmp("Monday", "monday");`
			`Produce 1 if s1!=s2`
			`Produce 0 if s1=s2`
			`strcmp returns 1, whereas stricmp returns 0.`

Function	Syntax	Description	Example
strlwr and strupr	strlwr(string); strupr(string);	It converts all uppercase characters to lowercase. It converts all lowercase characters to uppercase.	strlwr("Monday"); The output is monday. strupr ("Monday"); The output is MONDAY.
strdup	strdup(string);	It duplicates the string	
strchr and strrchr	strchr(string, ch); strrchr(string, ch);	It finds the first occurrence of character ch in the string. It finds the last occurrence of character ch in the string.	strchr ("Monday",'o');
strstr	strstr(S1,S2);	It finds the first occurrence of a given string in another string.	strstr("Monday","on");
strcat strncat	strcat(dest, source); strncat(dest, source,length)	It appends the destination string to the source string. The strncat function appends the strings upto specified length.	strcat("Today is ", "Monday");
strrev	strrev(string);	It reverses the order of characters in the given string.	strrev("Monday");
strpbrk	strpbrk(S1,ch);	It displays the rest of characters of a string after the first occurrence of the specified character.	strpbrk("Monday","d");

Program 13: Write a C program to check whether a string is a palindrome or not.

Solution

```
#include <stdio.h>
#include <string.h>
#include <conio.h>
#include <ctype.h>
int main()
{
char string[100];
int start_ctr, end_ctr;
int i=0, j=0;
int flag;
printf("\n Enter a string to check whether the string is a palindrome or not:");
scanf("%s",&string);
for(i=0;string[i]!='\0';i++)/*To trim spaces*/
{
if(isalpha(string[i]))
{
string[j]=string[i];
j++;
}
}
string[j]='\0';
end_ctr=strlen(string)-1;
start_ctr=0;
flag=1;
while((start_ctr!=end_ctr) && (end_ctr>start_ctr))
{
if(strlwr(string[start_ctr])!=strlwr(string[end_ctr]))
{
flag=0;
break;
}
start_ctr++;
end_ctr--;
}
```

```
if(flag)
{
printf("\n String is a palindrome.");
}
else
{
printf("\n String is not a palindrome.");
}
getch();
}
```

Output

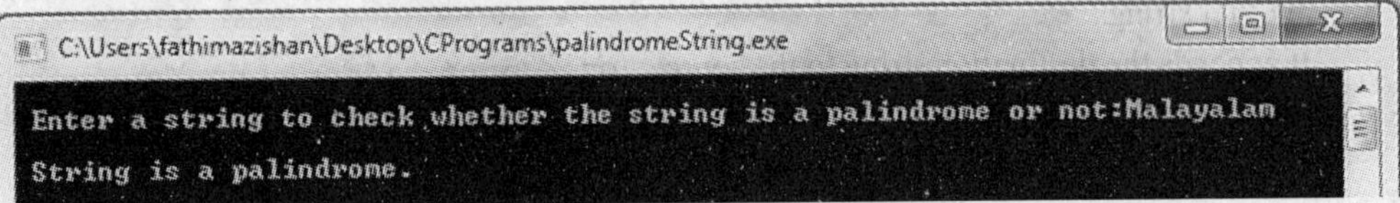

Flowchart

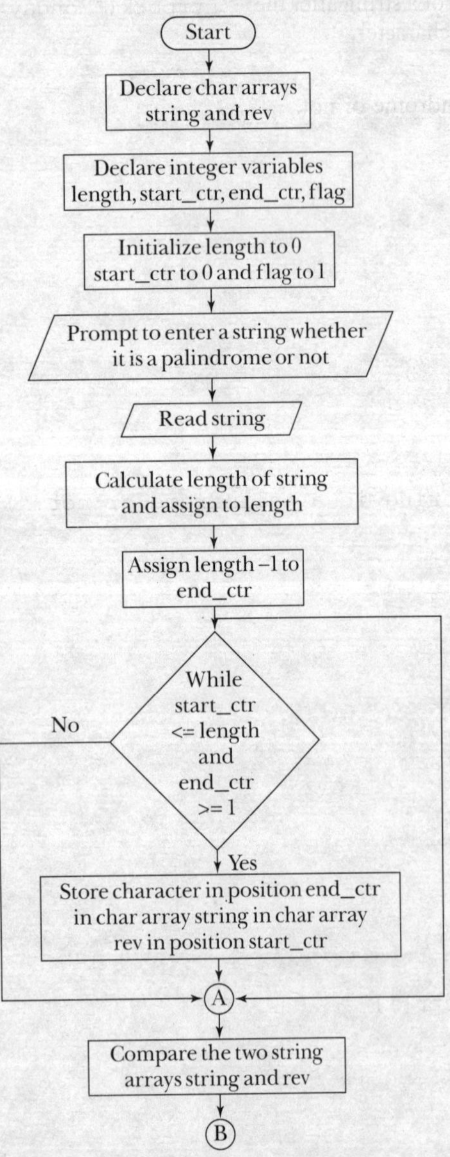

Pseudocode

START
INITIALIZE start_ctr to 0 and flag to 1.
PROMPT to enter a string to check whether it is a palindrome or not.
READ string.
CALCULATE end_ctr = length of string – 1
WHILE start_ctr < length and end_ctr > 1
  IF string[start_ctr] != rev[end_ctr]
    flag = 0
  INCREMENT start_ctr by 1
  DECREMENT end_ctr by 1
UNTIL star_ctr = length and end_ctr = 1
IF flag is true
  PRINT "String is a palindrome"
ELSE
  PRINT "String is not a palindrome"
STOP

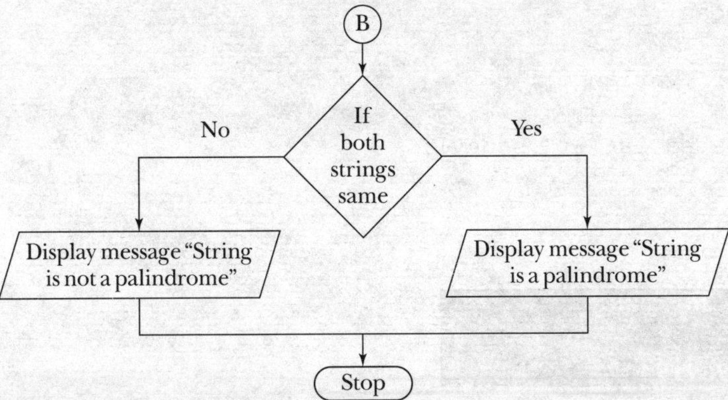

Statistical Problem Solving: Mean, Variance, Mode, Median, Range and Standard Deviation

C language can be used to solve statistical problems such as computing mean, variance, mode, median, range, etc., for a given set of data. The formulas for calculating these are as follows:

1. **Mean:** The average of a given set of values is called mean. Mean = sum of n numbers/n.
2. **Median:** The number present at the middle of a given list of n numbers is called the median. If n is even, then the mean of the two middle numbers is taken as median.
3. **Mode:** The values appearing more than the rest of the data values are called modes.
4. **Range:** The difference of the smallest value from the largest value in a given list is called the range.
5. **Variance:** The sum of squares of all the values divided by the number of data values gives the variance.
6. **Standard deviation:** The square root of variance gives the standard deviation.

Program 14: Write a program using array to calculate the mean, standard deviation and variance of the given elements.

Solution

```
#include <stdio.h>
#include <conio.h>
#include <math.h>
void main()
{
clrscr();
float X[20],mean,variance,stdev;
int i,num;
float sumsquare=0,sum=0;
printf("Enter size of the array: ");
scanf("%d",&num);
printf("** Enter array elements **\n");
for(i=0;i<num;i++)
{
scanf("%f",&X[i]);
sum=sum+X[i];
}
mean=sum/num;
clrscr();
cout<<"Array elements enterd are:\n";
for(i=0;i<num;i++)
{
printf("%f",X[i]);
sumsquare=sumsquare+(mean-X[i])*(mean-X[i]);
}
```

```
printf("\n\nThe mean calculated is: %f",mean);
variance=sumsquare/num;
printf("\n\nThe variance calculated is: %f",variance);
stdev=sqrt(variance);
printf("\n\nThe standard deviation calculated is: %f",stdev);
getch();
}
```

Output

```
Array elements enterd are: 12   22   47   36   28
The mean calculated is: 29
The variance calculated is: 168.199997
The standard deviation calculated is: 12.969194
```

Flowchart

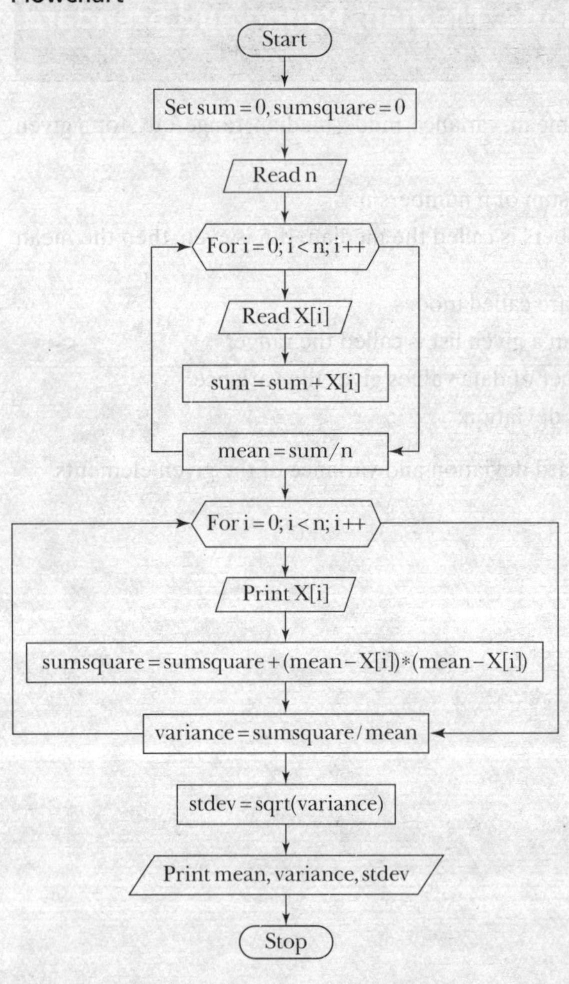

Pseudocode

```
START
SET sum = 0, sumsquare = 0
READ n
FOR i = 1 to n
   READ X[i]
   CALCULATE sum = sum + X[i]
   INCREMENT i by 1
UNTIL i < n
CALCULATE mean = sum/n
FOR i = 1 to n
   PRINT X[i]
   CALCULATE sumsquare = sumsquare + (mean –
   X[i])* (mean – X[i])
   INCREMENT i by 1
UNTIL i < n
CALCULATE variance = sumsquare/mean
CALCULATE stdev = sqrt(variance)
PRINT mean, variance, stdev
STOP
```

Solving Numerical Problems using Decision-Making and Looping

Program 15: Write a program to calculate the electricity bill. Read the starting and ending meter reading. The charges for the units consumed are as follows:

No. of units consumed	300–600	100–300	Less than 100
Rates (Rs.)	3.5	2.50	1.50

Solution

```
#include <stdio.h>
#include <conio.h>
```

```
#include <string.h>
#include <stdlib.h>
float calculateElectricityBill(float difference);

int main()
{
float startingMetreReading,endMetreReading,difference,rate;
printf("\n Enter starting metre reading:");
scanf("%f",&startingMetreReading);
printf("\n Enter end metre reading:");
scanf("%f",&endMetreReading);
difference=endMetreReading-startingMetreReading;
rate=calculateElectricityBill(difference);
printf("\n Charges for the unit consumed : %f",rate);
getch();
}
float calculateElectricityBill(float difference)
{
float rate=0;
if(difference>=300 && difference<600)
{
rate=3.50*difference;
}
else if(difference>=100 && difference<300)
{
rate=2.50*difference;
}
else if(difference<100)
{
rate=1.50*difference;
}
return rate;
}
```

Output

For number of units consumed less than 100

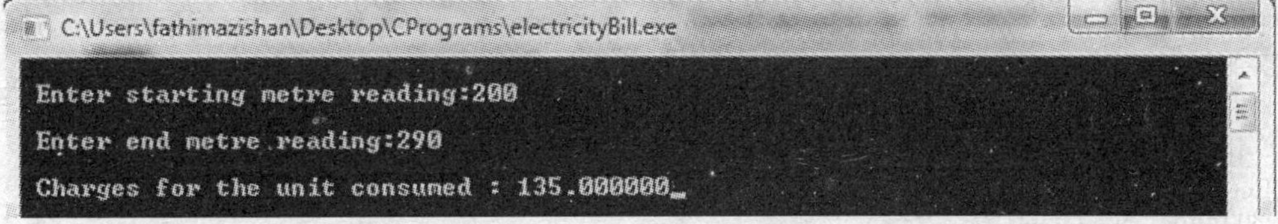

For number of units consumed between 100 and 300

For number of units consumed between 300 and 600

```
C:\Users\fathimazishan\Desktop\CPrograms\electricityBill.exe

Enter starting metre reading:400

Enter end metre reading:800

Charges for the unit consumed : 1400.000000_
```

Flowchart

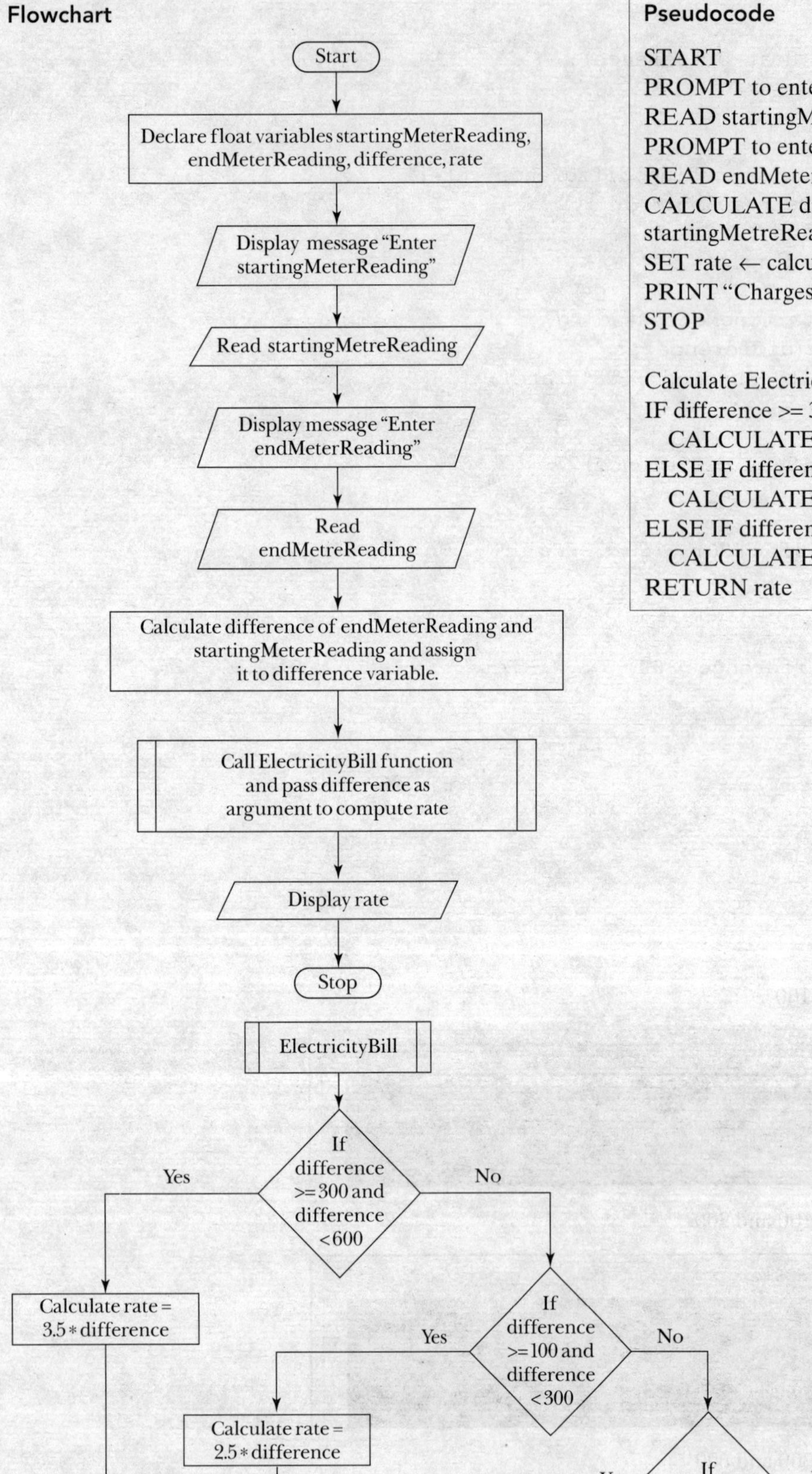

Pseudocode

START
PROMPT to enter startingMeterReading
READ startingMeterReading
PROMPT to enter endMeterReading
READ endMeterReading
CALCULATE difference = endMetreReading – startingMetreReading
SET rate ← calculateElectricityBill(difference)
PRINT "Charges for the unit consumed" is rate
STOP

Calculate ElectricityBill START
IF difference >= 300 and difference < 600
  CALCULATE rate = 3.50 * difference
ELSE IF difference >= 100 and difference < 300
  CALCULATE rate = 2.50 * difference
ELSE IF difference < 100
  CALCULATE rate = 3.50 * difference
RETURN rate

Program 16: Write a program to convert decimal to hexadecimal number.

Solution

```
#include <stdio.h>
#include <conio.h>
#include <string.h>
#include <stdlib.h>
void decimalToHexadecimal(int n);
int main()
{
int decimalNumber;
printf("\n Enter a decimal number:");
scanf("%d",&decimalNumber);
printf("\n The hexadecimal representation of %d is",decimalNumber);
decimalToHexadecimal(decimalNumber);
getch();
}
void decimalToHexadecimal(int n)
{
int b,c=0,a[5],i=0;
b=n;
while(b>15)
{
a[i]=b%16;
b=b/16;
i++;
c++;
}
a[i]=b;
for (i=c;i>=0;--i)
{
if (a[i]==10)
printf("A");
else if (a[i]==11)
printf("B");
else if (a[i]==12)
printf("C");
else if (a[i]==13)
printf("D");
else if (a[i]==14)
printf("E");
else if (a[i]==15)
printf("F");
else
printf("%d",a[i]);
}
}
```

Output

```
C:\Users\fathimazishan\Desktop\CPrograms\ControlStatements6.exe

Enter a decimal number:125

The hexadecimal representation of 125 is 7D
```

Flowchart

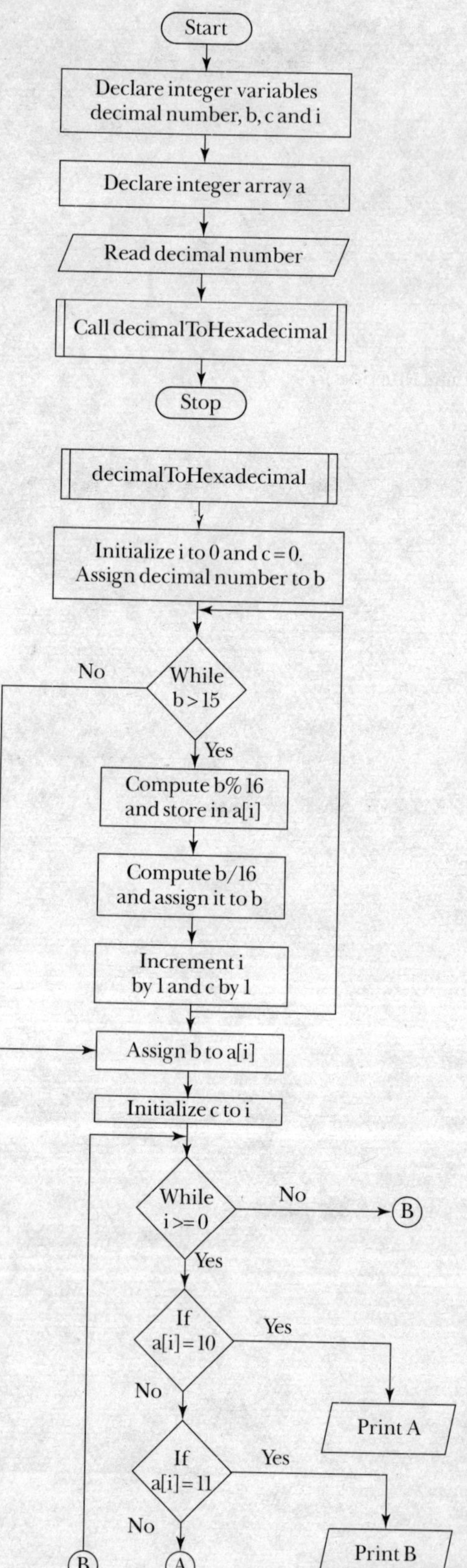

Pseudocode

START
PROMPT to enter decimal number
READ decimal number.
CALL function decimalToHexadecimal
STOP

decimalToHexadecimal START
INITIALIZE i = 0 and c = 0
SET decimalNumber = b
WHILE b > 15
  COMPUTE a[i] = b%16
  COMPUTE b = b/16
  INCREMENT i by 1 and c by 1
UNTIL b > 15
SET b = a[i]
INITIALIZE c = i.
WHILE i > 0
  IF a[i] = 10.
    PRINT A
  ELSE IF a[i] = 11
    PRINT B
  ELSE IF a[i] = 12.
    PRINT C
  ELSE IF a[i] = 13
    PRINT D
  ELSE IF a[i] = 14
    PRINT E
  ELSE IF a[i] = 15
    PRINT A
  ELSE
    PRINT a[i].
  Decrement i.
UNTIL i = 0

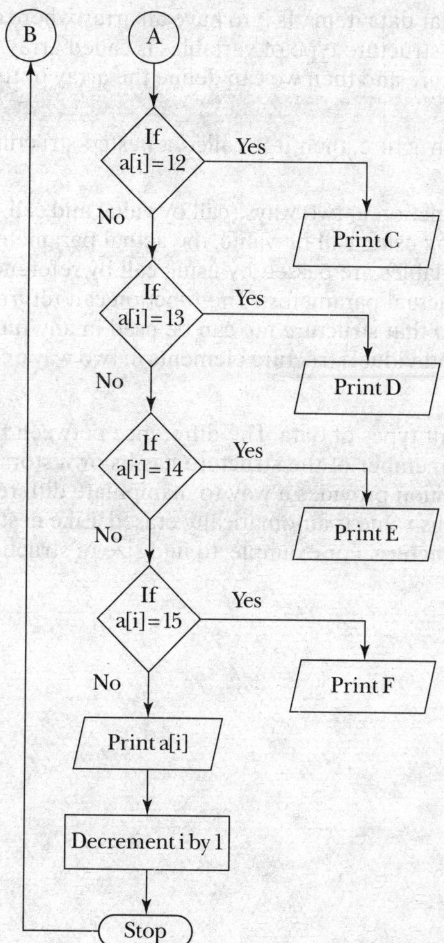

Programs using Structures and Unions

Structure is a collection of different types of data elements which are related together. The data items in a structure are called the members of the structure. In other words, we can say that the similar or different data types can be grouped to form a structure to represent the single entity. For example, suppose we want to represent complex number. We know that each complex number will have two components: Real and Imag. If both components may be of integer type then should we represent complex number as an array? The answer is No. This is because although complex number is a collection of two integer numbers (Real and Imag), these two integer numbers together make a single unit which is the complex number.

Dot operator: The structure variable cannot read or write the values in the single command. For example, if X is a structure variable,

```
scanf(%d,&X);
```

This statement produces error since a single statement cannot read the values for all members of X.

Each member of a structure is accessed by using three components: a variable name followed by a dot, and then the member name. Once the structure variable is defined, its members can be accessed by using dot operator. For example,

1. `bdate.month=11;`
2. `X.price=345.78;`
3. `X.pubyear=2008;`

In (1), structure variable `bdate` is followed by a dot and the field name or member name (month). Similarly, in (2) and (3), the structure variable name `X` is followed by dot, then the member name (`price` or `pubyear`).

Structures can be implemented in various ways:

1. **Array within structure:** Like the simple data type, an array can also be a member of a structure. When a structure consists of array elements, they are treated in the same way as normal arrays are treated. The array elements of a structure are also accessed by using the dot operator.

2. **Array of structures:** As we already know that an array is a collection of similar data items. Is it to have an array where all the elements are of type struct? The answer is YES. The collection of same structure type of variables is called array of structures. To declare an array of structure, we have to first define the structure and then we can define the array of that structure type.
3. **Nested structures:** When a structure is declared as a member of another structure, then it is called a nested structure. Structures can be nested to any depth.
4. **Function and structure:** The structure variables can also be passed to the function in two ways (call by value and call by reference) just like other variables. When the structure variable is passed by using call by value, the actual parameters are not changed if formal parameters are changed. When the structure variables are passed by using call by reference, then the changes made in the formal parameters are also reflected in the actual parameters. The function can return a structure also. The structures are generally defined as global declaration, so that structure tag can be used in any function. Apart from passing the whole structure variable, we can also pass the individual structure elements in two ways: call by value and call by reference.

A **union** is similar to structure in the sense that it is also a collection of different types of data. The difference between the two is that union stores values of different types in a single location and each member of the structure has its own storage location. In union, space is reserved for the largest data type only. Therefore, union provides a way to manipulate different kinds of data in a single area of storage. If a new assignment is made, the previous value is automatically erased. Like nested structures, we can have one **union within** another **union**, or a **union within** a **structure**. For example, to find size of structure and union, we have the following code:

```
union result
{
int marks;
char grade;
}
struct result1
{
char name[15];
int age;
union result perf;
}
```

Using the statements

```
printf("Size of union:%d\n",size of (data.perf);
printf("Size of structure:%\n",size of (data);
```

we get output as

```
Size of union = 2;
Size of structure = 19;
```

Eventhough int and char require 2 and 1 bytes, respectively, union reserves 2 bytes as int takes more space than char.

Program 17: Consider the following declaration and illustrate the application of size of operator to this structure.

```
struct
{
char name;
int num;
}student;
```

Solution

```
#include <stdio.h>
#include <stdlib.h>
#include <conio.h>
struct student
{
char name;
int num;
};
int main(int argc, char **argv)
{
struct student *stud; /*stud as pointer to stucture*/
printf(" \n Size of structure using sizeOf operator: %d",sizeof(student));
getch();
}
```

Output

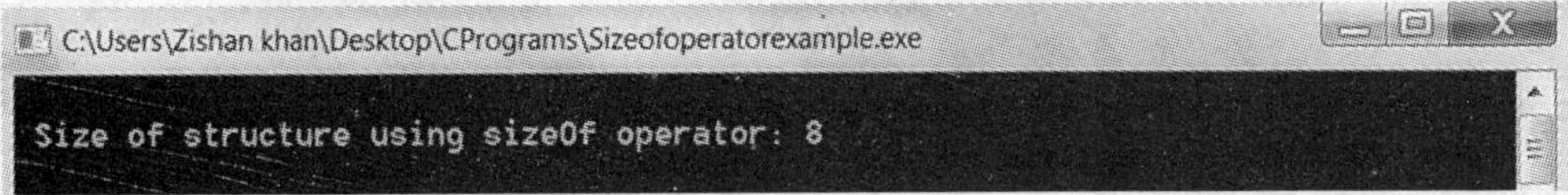

Explanation

In this program, stud is a pointer to the structure which holds the address of value of all members of the structure. The int has a 4 byte alignment requirement.
The char has a 1 byte alignment requirement but it also needs to have 3 padding bytes appended to them.
Thus, total byte alignment requirement = 4 + 1 + 3 = 8

Program 18: Write a program to display student records using union.

Solution

```
#include <stdio.h>
#include <conio.h>
void main()
{
clrscr();
union example
{
int rollno;
float percentage;
char name[10];
};
example X;
printf("Memory occupied X is:");
printf(sizeof(X));
printf("\n**Enter information** ");
printf("\n\nEnter roll no:");
scanf("%d",&X.rollno);
printf("\nEnter Name:");
gets(X.name);
printf("\nEnter percentage marks:");
scanf("%d",&X.percentage);
printf("\nThe result after execution **\n");
printf("\nThe roll no: %d",X.rollno);
printf("\n\nName:");
puts(X.name);
printf("\n\nThe percentage marks: %d",X.percentage);
printf("\n\nSize of X is still %d",sizeof(X));
getch();
}
```

Output

```
Memory occupied X is:10
**Enter information**
Enter roll no: 101
Enter Name: Himanshu
Enter percentage marks: 78.29
The result after execution **
The roll no:-27525
Name: Himanshu
The percentage marks: 78.290001
Size of X is still 10
```

Program 19: Write a program to accept records of 20 states using array of structures. The structures should contain name of the state and number of engineering colleges, medical colleges, management colleges, science colleges. Calculate and display the total colleges in each state and the state which is having the highest number of colleges.

Solution

```
#include <stdio.h>
#include <string.h>
```

```
#include <conio.h>
#include <ctype.h>
#include <stdlib.h>
typedef struct stateRecords{/*typedef does not create a new data type but gives new name
                         to existing data type*/
char nameOfState[20];
int numberOfEngineeringColleges;
int numberOfMedicalColleges;
int numberOfManagementColleges;
int numberOfScienceColleges;
int total;
}STATES;
void findHighestNumberOfColleges(STATES states[],int num)
{
int high;
char highestNumberOfColleges[20];
int i;
high=states[0].total;
for(i=1;i<=num;i++)
{
if(states[i].total>high)
{
high=states[i].total;
strcpy(highestNumberOfColleges,states[i].nameOfState);
}
}
printf("\n The highest number of colleges is in %s",highestNumberOfColleges);
}
void displayData(STATES states[],int num)
{
int i;
printf("\n Displaying all state records:");
printf("\n -----------------------------");
printf("\n Name \t \t Engg \t Med \t Mgmt \t Sci \t Total");
for(i=1;i<=num;i++)
{
printf("\n %s \t %d \t %d \t %d \t %d \t %d", states[i].nameOfState,states[i].
  numberOfEngineeringColleges,states[i].numberOfMedicalColleges,states[i].
  numberOfManagementColleges,states[i].numberOfScienceColleges,states[i].total);
}
printf("\n -----------------------------");
}
int main()
{
STATES*states;
int num,i;
printf("\n Enter number of states for which you wish to enter information:");
scanf("%d",&num);
states=(struct stateRecords *) calloc(num, sizeof(struct stateRecords));
if (states!=NULL)
{
for(i=1;i<=num;i++)
{
printf("\n Enter name of state %d:",i);
scanf(" %[^\n]s",&states[i].nameOfState);/*To input string with white spaces*/
printf("\n Enter number of Engineering colleges for state %d:",i);
scanf("%d",&states[i].numberOfEngineeringColleges);
printf("\n Enter number of Medical colleges for state %d:",i);
scanf("%d", &states[i].numberOfMedicalColleges);
```

```
printf("\n Enter number of Management colleges for state %d:",i);
scanf("%d", &states[i].numberOfManagementColleges);
printf("\n Enter number of Science colleges for state %d:",i);
scanf("%d",&states[i].numberOfScienceColleges);
states[i].total=states[i].numberOfEngineeringColleges+states[i].numberOfMedicalColleges+
  states[i].numberOfManagementColleges+states[i].numberOfScienceColleges;
}
displayData(states,num);
findHighestNumberOfColleges(states,num);
}
else
{
puts("Memory allocation failed.");
}
getch();
}
```

Output

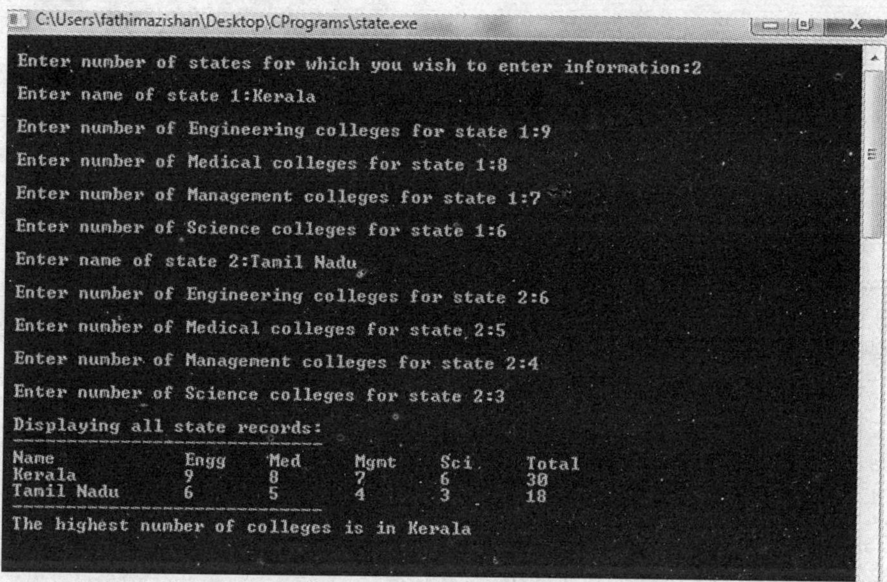

Program 20: Write a program to get students' details using structure.

Solution

```
#include <stdio.h>
#include <conio.h>
#include <string.h>
#include <stdlib.h>
struct student
{
int regno;
char name[15];
float marks[5];
float percentage;
};
void getData(int number, struct student stud[])
{
int i,j;
float total;
printf("\nEnter student data\n");
for(i=1;i<=number;i++)/*storing the data*/
{
printf("\nEnter registration number for student%d:",i);
scanf("%d",&stud[i].regno);
```

```
printf("\nEnter name of student%d:",i);
scanf("%s",&stud[i].name);
total=0;
for(j=1;j<=5;j++)
{
printf("\nEnter marks for subject%d:",j);
scanf("%f",&stud[i].marks[j]);
total=total+stud[i].marks[j];
}
stud[i].percentage=(total/500)*100;
}
}
void displayData(int number, struct student stud[])
{
int i,j;
printf("\n Regno\tName\tMark1\tMark2\tMark3\tMark4\tMark5\tPercentage");
for(i=1;i<=number;i++)
{
printf("\n ");
printf("%d\t",stud[i].regno);
printf("%s\t",stud[i].name);
for(j=1;j<=5;j++)
{
printf("%.2f\t",stud[i].marks[j]);
}
printf("%.2f\t",stud[i].percentage);
}
printf("\n---------------------------------------\n");
}
main() /* program which introduces keyboard input */
{
int number=5;
struct student stud[5];
printf("Keying in student data and then displaying\n");
printf("---------------------------------------\n");
getData(number,stud);
printf("Displaying data\n");
printf("---------------------------------------\n");
displayData(number,stud);
getch();
}
```

Output

```
C:\Users\fathimazishan\Desktop\CPrograms\FileHandling5.exe
Keying in student data and then displaying

Enter student data
Enter registration number for student1:5678
Enter name of student1:Mary
Enter marks for subject1:98
Enter marks for subject2:90
Enter marks for subject3:97
Enter marks for subject4:96
Enter marks for subject5:88
Enter registration number for student2:6789
Enter name of student2:Sam
Enter marks for subject1:65
Enter marks for subject2:78
Enter marks for subject3:89
Enter marks for subject4:87
Enter marks for subject5:86
```

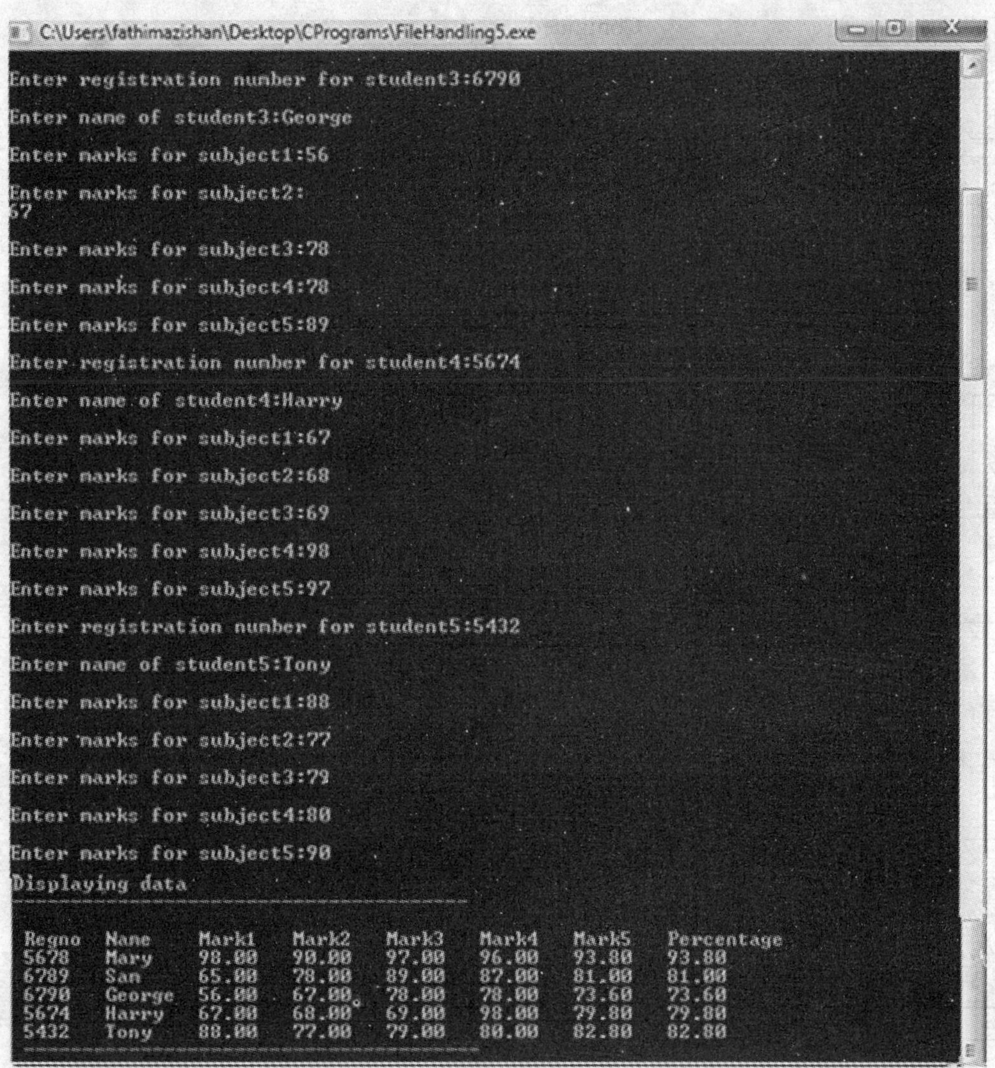

Flowchart

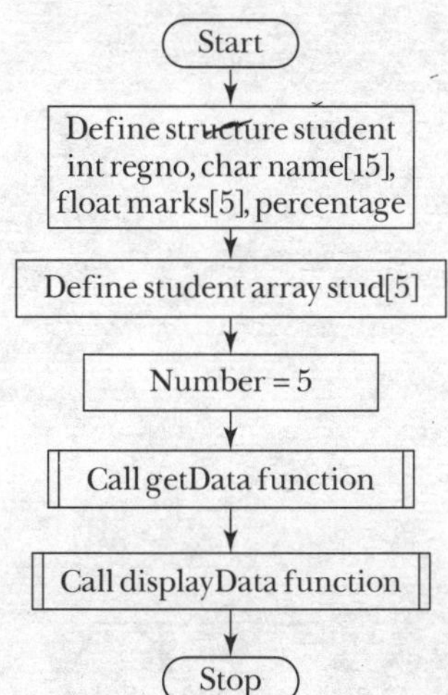

Pseudocode

```
START
DEFINE structure student with data regno, name[15],
marks[5], percentage
DEFINE student array stud[5]
SET number = 5
CALL getData function
CALL displayData function
STOP

getData START
PRINT "Enter student details"
FOR i = 1 to number
   READ stud[i].regno, stud[i].name
   SET total = 0
   FOR j = 1 to 5
      READ stud[i].marks[j]
      CALCULATE total = total + stud[i].marks[j]
      INCREMENT j by 1
```

(Continued)

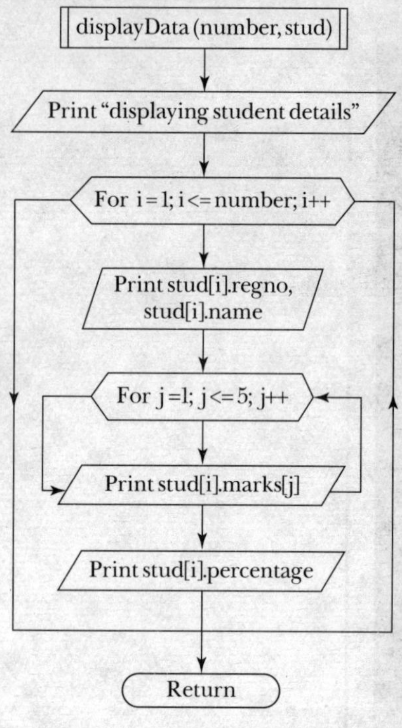

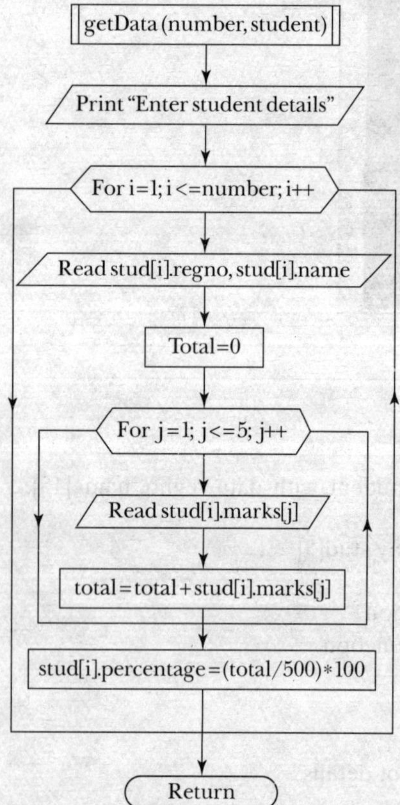

Continued

```
    UNTIL j <= 5
    CALCULATE stud[i].percentage = (total/500)*100
    INCREMENT i by 1
UNTIL i <= number
RETURN

displayData STARTS
PRINT "Displaying student details"
FOR i = 1 to number
    PRINT stud[i].regno, stud[i].name
    FOR j = 1 to 5
        PRINT stud[i].marks[j]
        INCREMENT j by 1
    UNTIL j <= 5
    PRINT stud[i].percentage
    INCREMENT i by 1
UNTIL i <= number
RETURN
```

Programs using Pointers

A variable which holds the address of the value is called **pointer**. In other words, we can say that pointer is a variable that can hold the address of other variables or address of a value. Therefore, using pointers we can access the memory locations and the data stored in those memory locations by indirect reference. Hence, pointers not only provide the access to the memory location, but also provide a method for dynamic memory allocation. They are the most useful and strongest feature of C. In fact, a pointer can point to any type of data item or a function.

Operators associated with pointers:

1. A pointer is also a variable, therefore, the declaration of a pointer variable is similar to that of a normal variable except for the addition of the unary `*` character. This symbol informs the compiler that the variable is a pointer variable. The `*` (asterisk) means "pointer to". For example, `int *ptr;`
2. "Address of operator" is a unary operator that returns the address of the variable following it. Since it is a unary operator, it requires only one operand and so it is represented by using the ampersand sign (`&`) followed by the variable name. For example, `ptr=&sample;`
3. "Indirection operator" is a unary operator that returns the contents stored at the memory location (address). It is also called "value at operator" or "dereference operator". This operator can be represented by a combination of `*` with a variable. For example, `ptr=&sample;`

Pointers can be implemented in the following ways:

1. **Pointers and arrays:** In C, arrays and pointers are closely related. In fact the versatility of pointers is established due to their ability to handle arrays. In C the array name acts as a pointer because the array name always refers to the address of first element of the array. So we can say that array name is a pointer which holds the address of its first element.
2. **Pointers and strings:** Pointers are very useful for the string manipulations as they make the manipulation of strings much easier. Pointers are used to perform various string operations such as string copy, string length, string concatenate, string compare, etc. In fact we can easily exchange the position of strings in the array using pointers.
3. **Pointers and functions:** Just like the normal arguments, functions can also have pointers as arguments. When we call a function we have to pass the address of the variable which can be stored in the corresponding pointer variables. In this mode of parameter passing, we pass the addresses to the function. It is similar to the call by reference in the sense that in this method also the changes in formal parameters are reflected in actual parameters.
   - **Function returning a pointer:** Functions can return any data type; they can also return a pointer variable.
   - **Pointer to a function:** A pointer to function is just like a normal pointer. It contains the address of the function, that is, the value of pointer to function is the address of the function name. Since the name itself is a pointer, therefore it is a constant pointer. A pointer to a function is declared as a pointer to the data type by the function, like `void`, `int`, `float`, etc. By using the pointer to function technique, we can pass the function as argument to another function.
4. **Pointer to void:** The pointer is a variable which can hold the address of some another variable of same type. In other words if `ptr` is an `int` pointer then it can hold the value of `int` type. So the address we put into the pointer must be the same type as the pointer. We cannot assign the address of a `float` variable to an `int` pointer. The `void` pointer is a special type of pointer which can point to any data type.
5. **Pointer to a structure/union:** Pointer to a structure/union is useful in accessing all the members of the structure/union using arrow (–>) operator.

Program 21: What is the value of b[0] in the following program code?

```
main()
{
int a[5]={1,3,6,7,0};
int *b;
b=&a[2];
}
```

Solution

```
#include <stdio.h>
#include <conio.h>
int main()
{
int a[5]={1,3,6,7,0};
int *b;
b=&a[2];/*b[0] will become equal to a[2] which is equal to 6*/
printf("\n Value of b[0]:");
printf("%d",b[0]);
getch();
}
```

Output

Program 22: Write a program to calculate the sum and average of n numbers.

Solution

```
#include <stdio.h>
#include <stdlib.h>
#include <conio.h>
int n;
int calculateSum(int *numbers)
{
int total=0,i;
for(i=0;i<n;i++)
{
total=total+numbers[i];
}
return total;
}
int main()
{
int i,total=0;
float average=0.0;
int *numbers;
printf("\n Enter n(sum and average of n numbers):");
scanf("%d",&n);
numbers=(int*) malloc(n*4);
printf("\n Enter %d numbers:", n);
printf("\n");
for(i=0;i<n;i++)
{
scanf("%d",&numbers[i]);
}
total=calculateSum(numbers);
printf("\n Sum of all n numbers: %d",total);
average=total/n;
printf("\n Average of all n numbers: %f",average);
getch();
}
```

Output

```
C:\Users\Zishan khan\Desktop\CPrograms\SumAndAverage.exe

Enter n(sum and average of n numbers):10

Enter 10 numbers:
13
65
36
21
89
43
27
19
32
55

Sum of all n numbers: 400
Average of all n numbers: 40.000000
```

Flowchart

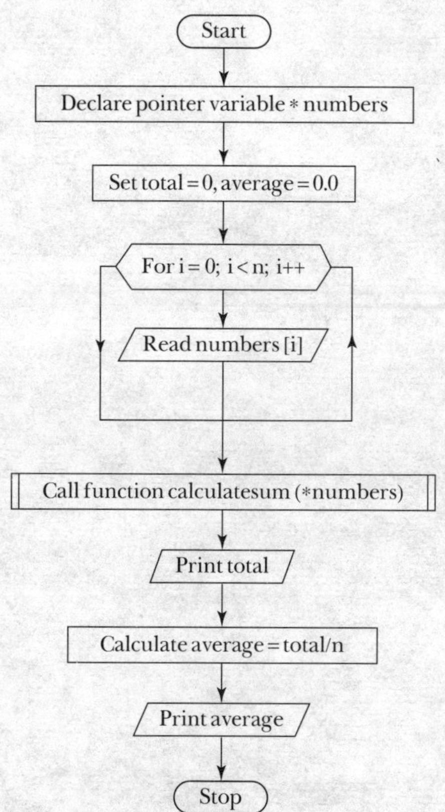

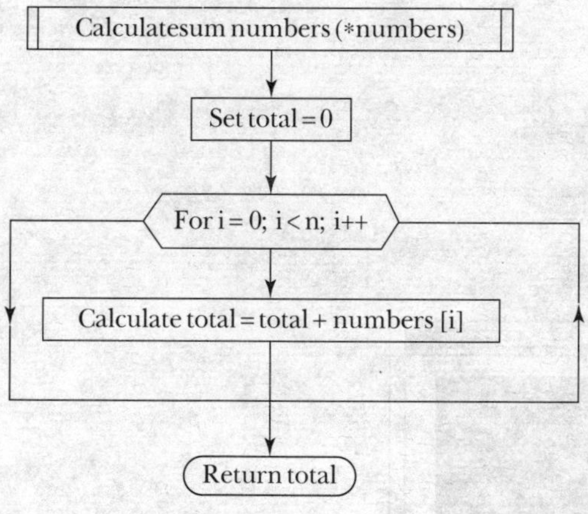

Pseudocode

START
DECLARE pointer variable *numbers
SET total = 0, average = 0.0
FOR i = 0 to n
  READ numbers[i]
  INCREMENT i by 1
UNTIL i < n
CALL function calculatesum(*numbers)
PRINT total
CALCULATE average = total/n
PRINT average
STOP

calculatesum STARTS
SET total = 0
FOR i = 0 to n
  CALCULATE total = total + numbers[i]
  INCREMENT i by 1
UNTIL i < n
RETURN total

Program 23: Write a program to concatenate two strings using pointers.

Solution

```
#include <stdio.h>
#include <stdlib.h>
#include <conio.h>
char* concatenateStrings(char *str1, char *str2)
{
int i=0;
while(str1[i])
i++;
```

```
int j=i;
while(str2[j])
j++;
char *str=(char*)malloc(j*sizeof(char));
i=0;
while(str1[i])
{
str[i]=str1[i];
i++;
}
j=0;
while(str2[j])
{
str[i+j]=str2[j];
j++;
}
str[i+j]='\0';
return str;
}
int main()
{
char *str1;
char *str2;
char *str3;
str1=(char *)malloc(100*sizeof(char));
str2=(char *)malloc(100*sizeof(char));
printf("Enter the first String\n");
scanf("%s",&str1);
printf("Enter the second String\n");
scanf("%s",&str2);
str3=concatenateStrings(str1,str2);
printf("the final string is : %s\n", str3);
getch();
}
```

Output

```
C:\Users\fathimazishan\Desktop\CPrograms\stringconcatenation.exe
Enter the first String
Love
Enter the second String
India
the final string is : LoveIndia
```

Programs involving File Handling

We have various input and output functions in C to read and display data, such as printf, scanf, etc. However, there are some limitations with these functions, such as

1. It is very difficult to handle large volume of data.
2. It is difficult to store the input data for future use.
3. It is difficult to store the output data for future use.
4. Some of the input data are in image form or in text form.
5. The data are stored into the main memory which has limited size.

To deal with such problems, there is a special kind of data structure called Files. A file is also called as an external data structure whereas other data structures we have discussed so far are called internal data structure. It handles the inputs and outputs to a program through disks. The file is a collection of records where each record may contain different fields. The records may be of same size or variable sizes. If the file contains all the records of the same size then it is said to be made up of a fixed length record. If file consists of records of different sizes then it is said to be made up of variable length records. The variable size of the records may be due the variable size of the field.

Basic Terminologies Associated with Files

The various terminologies used are as follows:

1. **Field:** It is the basic unit of the record which represents meaningful information about the record. This is characterized by the data type and size. For example, name, age, sex, roll number of any student.
2. **Record:** It is a collection of logically related fields (information) about any real-world entity. For example, student is a collection of logically related information such as name, age, sex, roll number, etc. Hence, any student may be defined by his/her name, age, sex and roll number.
3. **File:** A file is a collection of records. For example, a file of students of EEE branch or a file of all students in an institute.
4. **File organization:** It is concerned with the arrangement of records on the disks.
5. **Key field:** It is a field that contains unique value for each record, so the record in the file is uniquely identified by specifying the value of a particular field of the record.
6. **Index:** It is a pointer used to determine the location of the record in a file that satisfies some condition.

Basic Operations to the File

The efficiency of a file system depends on how efficiently these operations can be performed on the file.

1. **Creation:** First the file structure is created before feeding the data into the records. Creation of the file determines the name of the file; the position of the file where the I/O operation is performed; the file structure defined, whether it is a text file or binary file and the access method defined.
2. **Open:** This operation prepares the file for read and write operations.
3. **Retrieve or search:** This operation is performed to search for a record or a set of records having a particular value in a particular field or where the field value satisfies certain conditions.
4. **Insert:** This operation deals with the insertion of a new record or set of records at a specific location.
5. **Update:** The existing records of the file may be updated by changing the values of the fields or a new record may be inserted.
6. **Delete:** Any record or a set of records may be deleted from the file.

Various functions used for opening, closing, reading from and writing onto files are as follows. Out of these, the formatted functions are fscanf() and fprintf() and the rest are unformatted functions.

1. **fopen():** To open a file in read (r), write (w) or append (a) mode.
2. **fclose():** To close a file.
3. **getc():** To read a character from the file. For example, `c=getc(fp2);` where fp2 is the file pointer pointing to the file opened in reading mode. It returns EOF as soon as end of file is reached.
4. **putc():** To write a character onto the file. For example, `putc(c,fp1);`);where fp1 is the file pointer pointing to the file opened in writing mode. It returns EOF as soon as end of file is reached.
5. **getw():** To read an integer from the file. For example, `i=getw(fp2);`
6. **putw():** To write an integer onto the file. For example, `putw(i,fp1);`
7. **fgets():** To read a string from the file pointed by the file pointer and copy the string to a memory location referred by the array. For example, `fgets(text,50,fp);` where fp is the file pointer and 50 is the length of the string text.
8. **fputc():** To write a string to an opened file pointed by the file pointer. For example, `fputs(text, fp);` where fp is the file pointer and text is the string.
9. **fscanf():** To read a set of data values from the file. For example, `fscanf(f2,"%d %f",&i,&f);` where f2 is the file pointer pointing to the file opened in reading mode.
10. **fprintf():** To write a set of data values onto the file. For example, `fprintf(f1, "%d %f\n",i,f);` where f1 is the file pointer pointing to the file opened in reading mode.

Program 24: Write a program to copy the file into another file.

Solution

```
#include <stdio.h>
#include <conio.h>
int main()
{
FILE *p,*q;
char file1[20],file2[20];
char ch;
printf("\nEnter the source file name to be copied:");
gets(file1);
p=fopen(file1,"r");
if(p==NULL)
{
printf("cannot open %s",file1);
return 0;
}
else{
printf("\nEnter the destination file name:");
gets(file2);
q=fopen(file2,"w");
if(q==NULL)
{
printf("cannot open %s",file2);
return 0;
}
while((ch=getc(p))!=EOF)
putc(ch,q);
}
printf("\nCOMPLETED");
fclose(p);
fclose(q);
getch();
}
```

Output

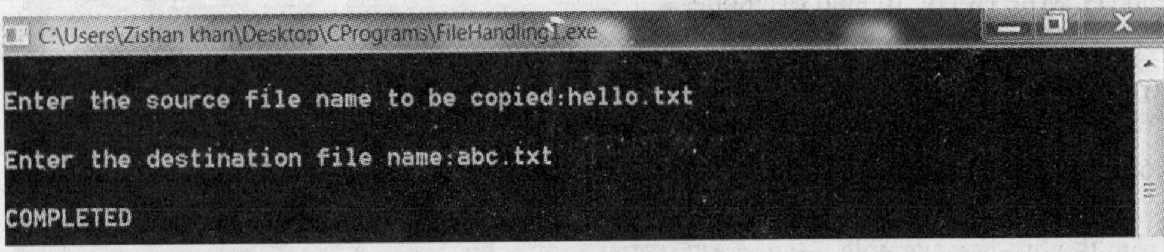

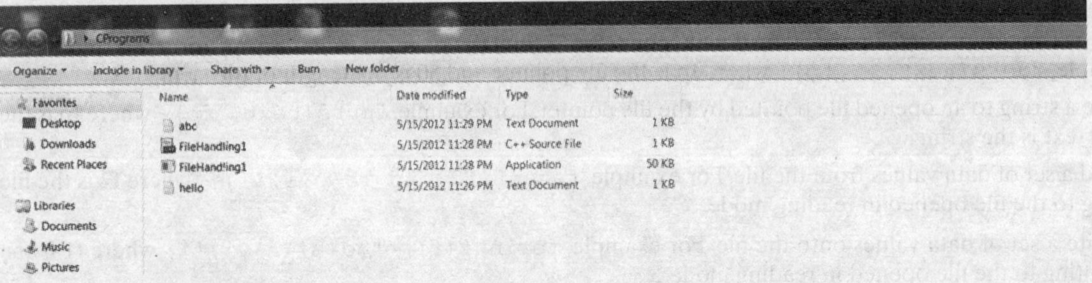

Flowchart

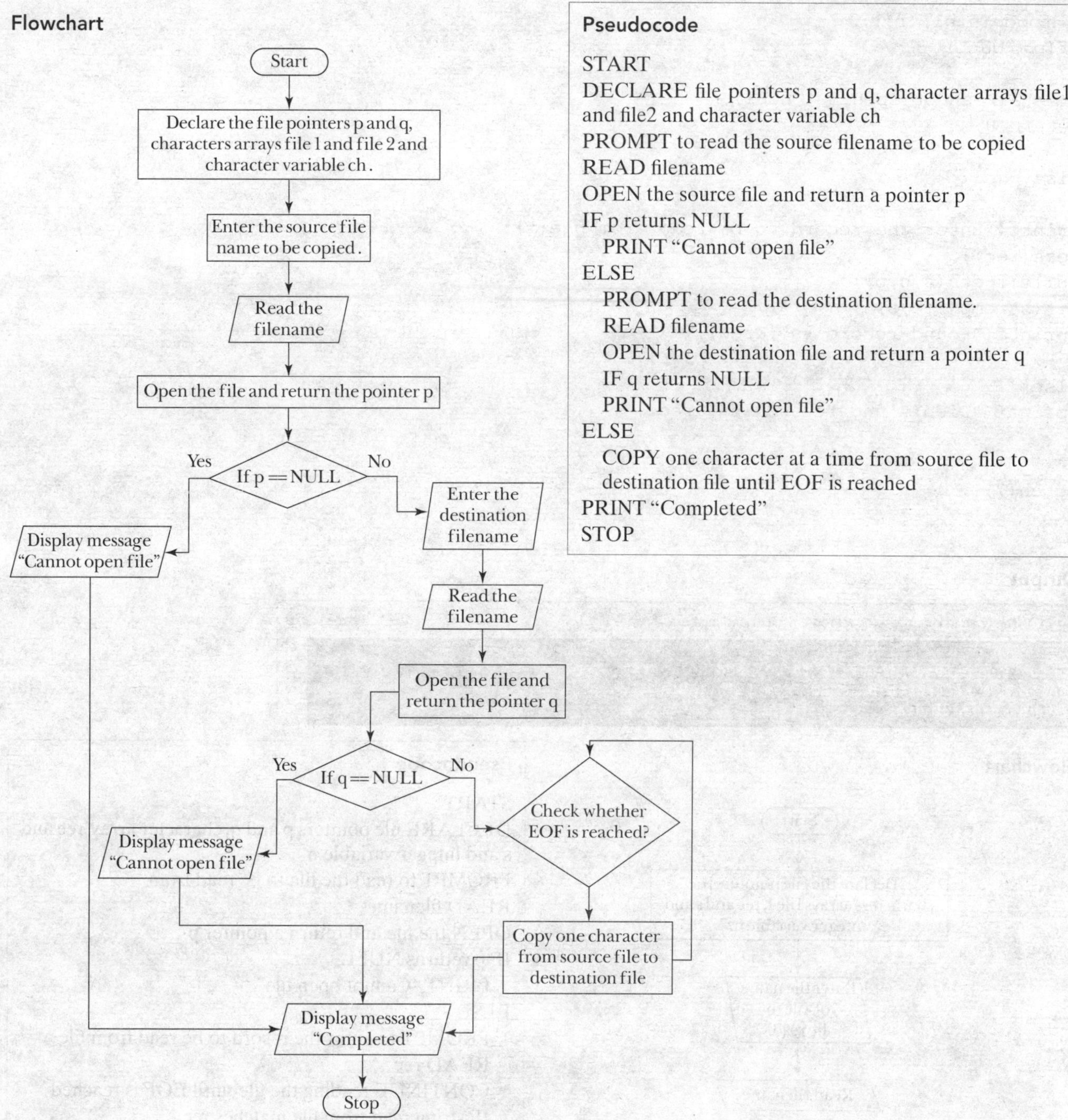

Pseudocode

START
DECLARE file pointers p and q, character arrays file1 and file2 and character variable ch
PROMPT to read the source filename to be copied
READ filename
OPEN the source file and return a pointer p
IF p returns NULL
  PRINT "Cannot open file"
ELSE
  PROMPT to read the destination filename.
  READ filename
  OPEN the destination file and return a pointer q
  IF q returns NULL
  PRINT "Cannot open file"
ELSE
  COPY one character at a time from source file to destination file until EOF is reached
PRINT "Completed"
STOP

Program 25: Write a program to read specific records from a file.

Solution

```
#include <stdio.h>
#include <conio.h>
#include <string.h>
int main(){
FILE *p;
char file1[20];
char rec[40];
char s[20];
int n;
printf("\nEnter the name of the file to be read:");
gets(file1);
```

```
p=fopen(file1,"r");
if(p==NULL)
{
printf("Cannot open %s",file1);
return 0;
}
else
{
printf("Enter the record to be read from file:");
gets(rec);
while(fgets(s,n,p))
{if(strcmp(rec,s) )
{printf("Found record %s",&rec);
}
else
{printf("Didn't find record %s",&rec);
}
}
getch();
}
}
```

Output

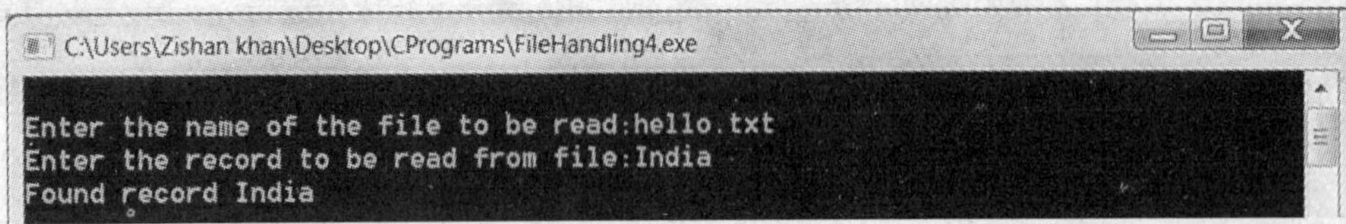

Flowchart

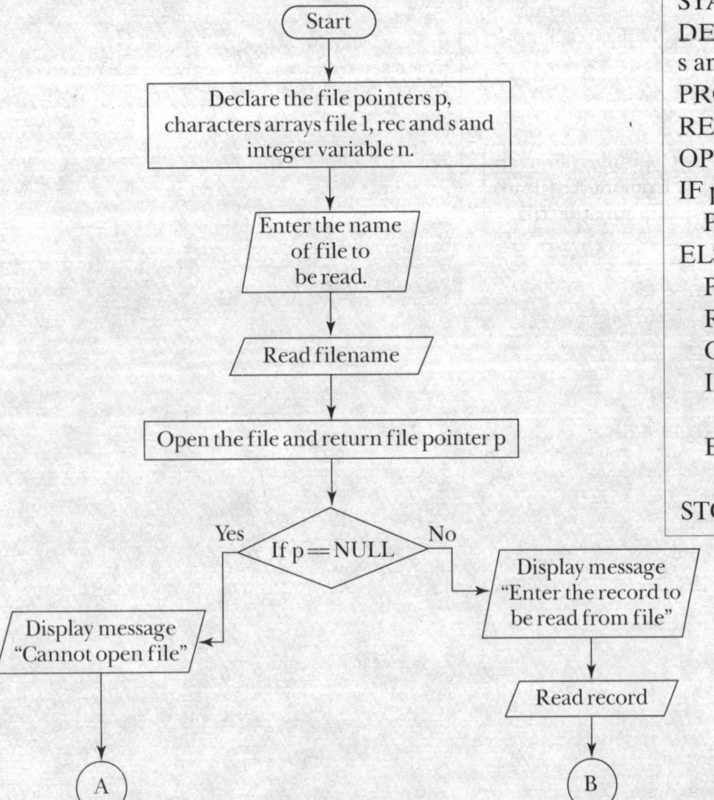

Pseudocode

START
DECLARE file pointers p and q, character array, rec and s and integer variable n
PROMPT to read the file to be read from
READ filename
OPEN the file and return a pointer p
IF p returns NULL
  PRINT "Cannot open file"
ELSE
  PROMPT to enter the record to be read from file
  READ rec
  CONTINUE reading the file until EOF is reached
  IF string read from file matches rec
    PRINT "Found record"
  ELSE
    PRINT "Record not found"
STOP

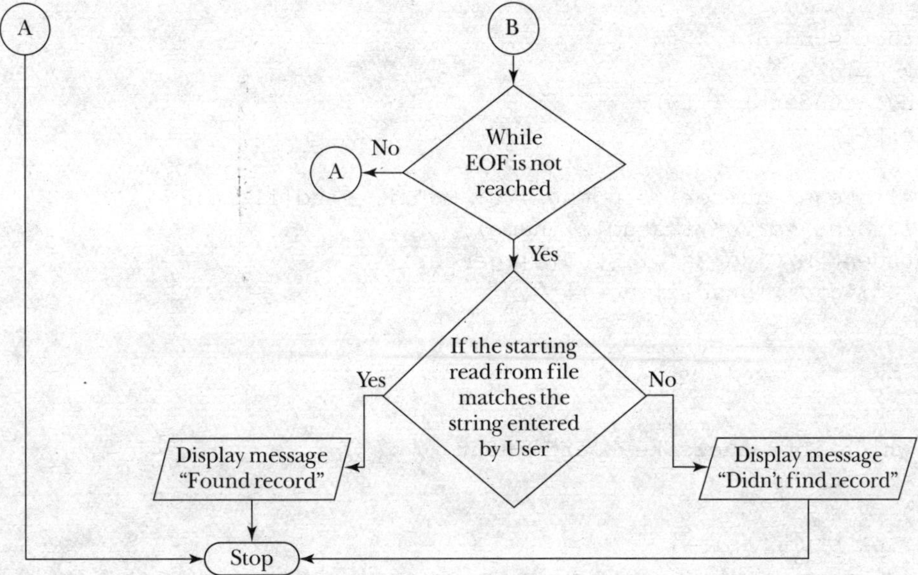

Program 26: Write a program to read and write students' information into the file using data members in a private access mode.

Solution

```
#include <stdio.h>
#include <conio.h>
#include <string.h>
#include <stdlib.h>
struct student
{
char id[6];
char name[11];
char gender[1];
int age;
};
void storeDataToFile(int number, struct student stud[10]);
void retrieveDataFromFile(int number, struct student stud[10]);

void storeDataToFile(int number, struct student stud[])
{
printf("\nEnter student data\n");
for(int i=1;i<=number;i++)
{
printf("\nID number (4 integer number) student %d:",i);
scanf("%s",&stud[i].id);
printf("\nFirst name student %d:",i);
scanf("%s",&stud[i].name);
printf("\nGender of student M/F %d:",i);
scanf("%s",&stud[i].gender);
printf("\nAge student %d:",i);
scanf("%d",&stud[i].age);
}
}
void retrieveDataFromFile(int number, struct student stud[])
{
FILE *fw,*fr;
if ((fw=fopen("abc.txt","a"))==NULL){
printf("File open for reading or writing failed\n");
}
else
```

```
{
fwrite(stud,sizeof(struct student),2,fw);
fseek(fw,0,SEEK_SET);
fread(stud,sizeof(struct student),2,fw);
for(int i=1;i<=number;i++)
{
printf("\nID number (4 integer number) student :%d: %s",i, stud[i].id);
printf("\nFirst name student %d:%s",i,stud[i].name);
printf("\nGender of student M/F %d:%s",i,stud[i].gender);
printf("\nAge student %d:%d",i, stud[i].age);
}
fclose(fw);
}
}
int main() /* program which introduces keyboard input */
{
int number;
printf("\nEnter number of students:");
scanf("%d",&number);
struct student stud[number];
printf("Keying in student data and then displaying\n");
printf("--------------------------------------\n");
storeDataToFile(number,stud);
printf("Displaying data\n");
printf("--------------------------------------\n");
retrieveDataFromFile(number,stud);
getch();
}
```

Output

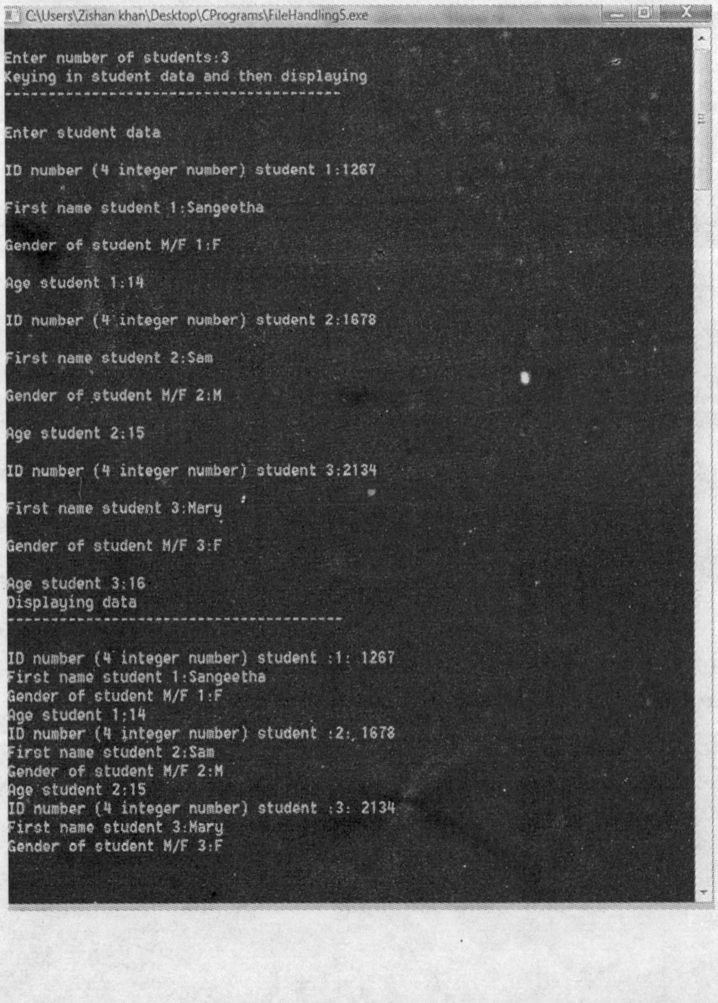

```
C:\Users\Zishan khan\Desktop\CPrograms\FileHandling5.exe

Enter number of students:3
Keying in student data and then displaying
--------------------------------------

Enter student data

ID number (4 integer number) student 1:1267

First name student 1:Sangeetha

Gender of student M/F 1:F

Age student 1:14

ID number (4 integer number) student 2:1678

First name student 2:Sam

Gender of student M/F 2:M

Age student 2:15

ID number (4 integer number) student 3:2134

First name student 3:Mary

Gender of student M/F 3:F

Age student 3:16
Displaying data
--------------------------------------

ID number (4 integer number) student :1: 1267
First name student 1:Sangeetha
Gender of student M/F 1:F
Age student 1:14
ID number (4 integer number) student :2: 1678
First name student 2:Sam
Gender of student M/F 2:M
Age student 2:15
ID number (4 integer number) student :3: 2134
First name student 3:Mary
Gender of student M/F 3:F
```

Flowchart

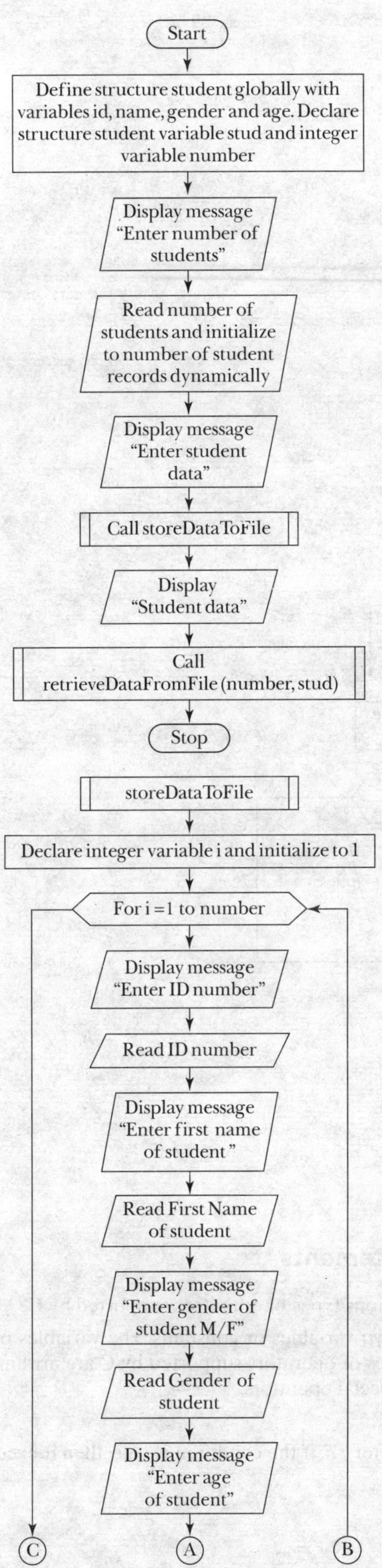

Pseudocode

```
START
DEFINE structure student globally with variables id, name, gender and age
DECLARE structure student variable stud
PROMPT to enter number of students
READ number
INITIALIZE to number of student records dynamically.
PRINT "Enter student data".
CALL storeDataToFile(number,stud)
PRINT "Display student data"
CALL retrieveDataFromFile(number,stud)
STOP
storeDataToFile STARTS
FOR i = 1 to number
   READ stud[i].id, stud[i].name, stud[i].gender,
   stud[i].age
   INCREMENT i by 1
UNTIL i <= number
RETURN
retrieveDataFromFile STARTS
DECLARE file pointers *fw,*fr
OPEN file to append entered data to file.
IF file open not successful
   PRINT "File open for reading and writing failed"
ELSE
   WRITE records to file from structure.
   READ records from file and store in structure array
   stud.
   FOR i = 1 to number
      PRINT Id number, First Name, Gender and Age of
      student
      INCREMENT i by 1
   UNTIL i <= number
   CLOSE file
RETURN
```

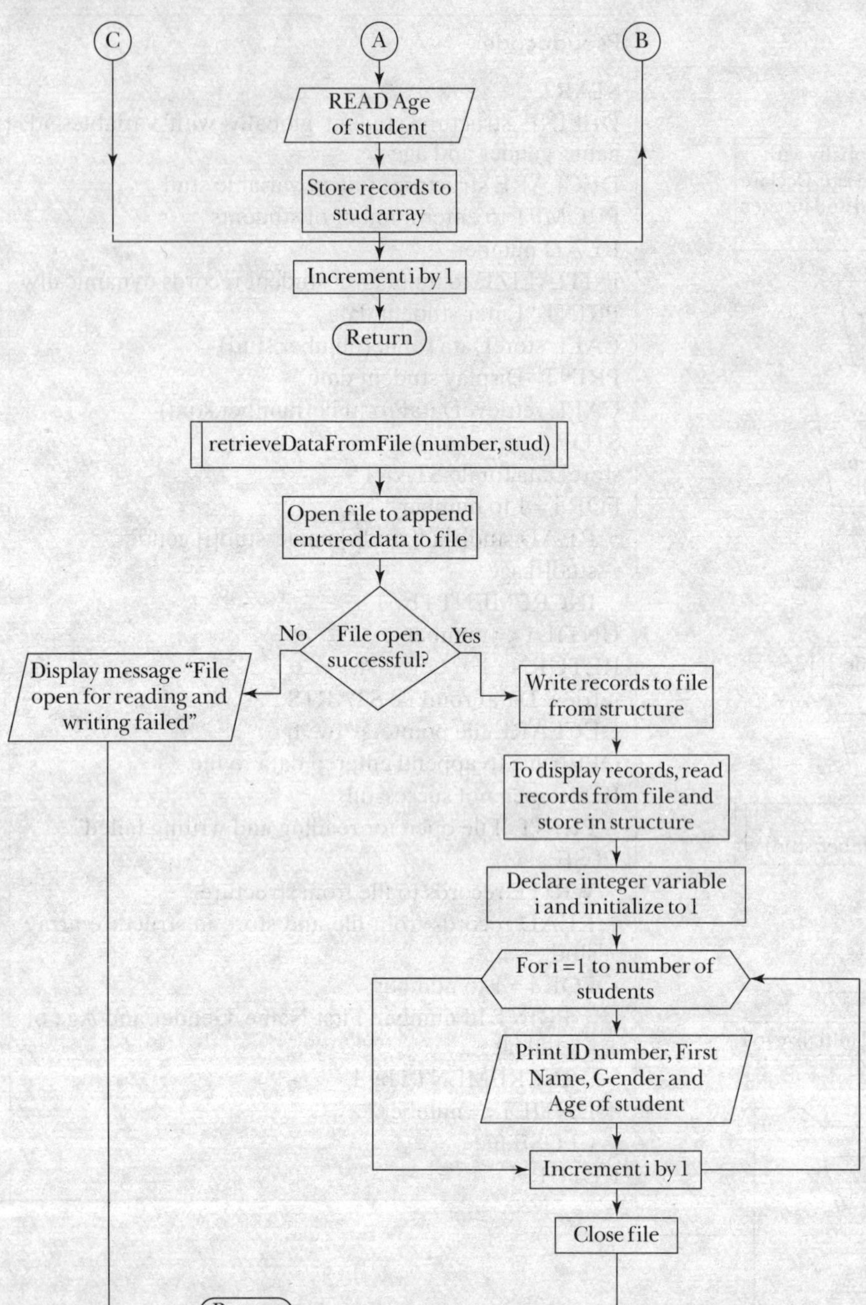

Viva Voce Questions

Simple Statements, Expressions and Control Statements

1. Differentiate between operator and operand. What are the various types of operators supported by C?

   Ans: Operator is a symbol such as +, –, etc. operating upon two variables or constants. The variables or constants on which operators act upon are called operands. The various types of operators supported by C are arithmetic operators, relational operators, logical operators, bitwise operators and special operators.

2. What is ternary operator?

   Ans: It is a conditional operator used to check the condition after "?"; if the condition is true, then it executes the statement after ":".

3. Differentiate between getchar() and scanf() functions for reading strings.

   Ans: Both functions are used to read one character at a time from the keyboard, however, in case of scanf, the input is formatted as specified by the format specifier.

4. What is the difference between while and do-while statements?

   Ans: In while statement, the condition is checked at the entry level. If it is true then body of the loop is executed. In do-while statement at least once the body of the loop is executed even if condition is not true because condition is evaluated at the exit level. The do-while loop is terminated by semicolon, whereas the while loop is not terminated by semicolon.

One-Dimensional and Two-Dimensional Arrays

1. What are the rules to declare an array?

   Ans: The array elements must be of the same type. The array can be declared as

   ```
   Storage_class Data_type array_name[size];
   ```

   where `Storage_class` can be extern, register, auto or static.

2. What is the purpose of subscript in array?

   Ans: Subscript refers to the particular element in the array. For example, `A[2]` means the third element of an array `A` because array index always starts from 0.

Functions

1. When is the function prototype not required?

   Ans: When the function is defined before the function call in the program, then function prototype is not required.

2. What is a `return` statement in function and how many return statements can be used in a function?

   Ans: Return statement is used to return the value from the function definition to the function call in the program. Only one return statement is executed in the function.

3. What is the difference between call by reference and call by pointers?

   Ans: In call by reference we pass the alias name or the reference and in call by pointers we pass the address of the variable. Therefore, in call by reference there are two names (original and alias) for the same variable but in call by pointer there is only one name for the variable. In both methods, the changes in the formal parameters are reflected in the actual parameters.

Recursive Functions

1. What is recursion?

   Ans: It is the ability of a function/procedure/algorithm to repeat itself until a certain condition is satisfied..

2. What is base condition? What conditions must be satisfied in case of recursive function?

   Ans: Recursive function repeatedly calls itself until a certain condition is met. This condition is called the *base condition*. The following conditions must be satisfied for using recursion:

   (a) There must be some base condition for which the function does not call itself.

   (b) Each time, the function calling should lead to the base condition

3. What are the different types of recursion?

   Ans: Recursion can be classified into two categories: Direct recursion, which occurs when the function calls itself directly, and indirect recursion, which occurs when the function calls another function that eventually calls the original function.

Iterative Problems using Functions

1. What is the difference between iteration and recursion?

   Ans: Iteration is generally used for repetitive computation in which each action is defined in terms of the previous result. It looks just like recursion, but this is not true. There are some differences between recursion and iterations as compiled in Table 1 in this exercise.

String Manipulations with String Functions

1. How is character array different from other types of arrays?

   Ans: Character array is a collection of characters that is always terminated by a null character. The character arrays may be single-dimensional or multidimensional arrays. The character arrays are also called strings. The null character is very important because it refers to the end of a string. So, we must declare the size of the character array one more than that of the actual number of characters we want to store.
2. Can a group of strings be stored in a two-dimensional array?

   Ans: Yes, we can store a collection of strings into two-dimensional arrays. The first dimension refers to the number of strings and the second dimension refers to the number of characters in each string.
3. What is the importance of null character in a string?

   Ans: Every string is terminated by the null character. So it is used as an end marker for a string.

Structures and Unions

1. Can you assign a structure variable to another? If yes, when?

   Ans: Yes, if both the variables are of the same structure type.
2. Can we pass a structure variable to a function? What are the ways to pass structure variable to a function?

   Ans: The structure variables can also be passed to the function in two ways (call by value and call by reference) just like other variables. When the structure variable is passed by using call by value, the actual parameters do not change even if the formal parameters are changed. When the structure variables are passed by using call by reference then the changes made in the formal parameter are also reflected in the actual parameter. The function, can return a structure also.
3. What are the differences between a structure and a union?

   Ans: A union is similar to a structure in the sense that it is also a collection of different types of data. However, the difference between the two is that, union stores values of different types at a single location whereas in a structure each member has its own storage location. In union space is reserved for the largest data type only. Therefore, union provides a way to manipulate different kinds of data in a single area of storage.

Pointers

1. What are the operations possible with pointer variables?

   Ans: Only addition and subtraction is possible with the pointer variable. We can perform other operations with the values.
2. How is an array and a pointer related?

   Ans: Array name always refers to the first element of the array and it holds the address of the first element so array name is also a pointer because pointer also holds the address.
3. What are the differences between array of pointers and pointer to pointer?

   Ans: The collection of pointers is called an array of pointers. In other words, an array of pointers represents a collection of addresses. Since each element of such an array is a pointer, hence it can hold the address of specified data type. The pointer to pointer is a pointer variable which holds address of another pointer. The pointer to a pointer is a form of multiple indirections and these indirections can be carried out to whatever extent desired.
4. Explain pointer to function.

   Ans: A pointer to function is just like a normal pointer. It contains the address of the function, that is, the value of pointer to function is the address of the function name. Since the name itself is a pointer, therefore it is a constant pointer. A pointer to a function is declared as a pointer to the data type by the function, such as `void`, `int`, `float`, etc.

File Handling

1. What is a file mode?

   Ans: The file mode specifies the purpose for which the file is opened. The file can be opened in various modes that describe how a file is to be used in the program; whether it is used for reading only (r), for writing only (w) or has to be appended (a).

2. What are formatted and unformatted file input/output functions?

   Ans: The file input/output functions are used to read and write characters/strings into files. The formatted functions are fscanf() and fprintf() and unformatted functions are getc(), putc(), getw(), putw(), fgets(), fputs().

3. How can output be displayed on the output device rather than file using fprint() function?

   Ans: To read the input from the input device and display the output on the output device rather than files, two standard keywords used are stdin and stdout. For example, `fprintf(stdout, "%f \n", f);`